Zombies Are Us

Contributions to Zombie Studies

White Zombie: Anatomy of a Horror Film. Gary D. Rhodes. 2001

The Zombie Movie Encyclopedia. Peter Dendle. 2001

*American Zombie Gothic: The Rise and Fall (and Rise)
of the Walking Dead in Popular Culture*. Kyle William Bishop. 2010

*Back from the Dead: Remakes of the Romero
Zombie Films as Markers of Their Times*. Kevin J. Wetmore, Jr. 2011

*Generation Zombie: Essays on the Living Dead
in Modern Culture*. Edited by Stephanie Boluk and Wylie Lenz. 2011

*Race, Oppression and the Zombie: Essays on Cross-Cultural Appropriations
of the Caribbean Tradition*. Edited by Christopher M. Moreman
and Cory James Rushton. 2011

Zombies Are Us: Essays on the Humanity of the Walking Dead.
Edited by Christopher M. Moreman and Cory James Rushton. 2011

The Zombie Movie Encyclopedia, Volume 2: 2000–2010. Peter Dendle. 2012

Great Zombies in History. Edited by Joe Sergi. 2013 (graphic novel)

Unraveling Resident Evil: *Essays on the Complex Universe
of the Games and Films*. Edited by Nadine Farghaly. 2014

"We're All Infected": Essays on AMC's The Walking Dead
and the Fate of the Human. Edited by Dawn Keetley. 2014

Zombies and Sexuality: Essays on Desire and the Walking Dead.
Edited by Shaka McGlotten and Steve Jones. 2014

Zombies Are Us

Essays on the Humanity of the Walking Dead

EDITED BY
CHRISTOPHER M. MOREMAN *AND*
CORY JAMES RUSHTON

CONTRIBUTIONS TO ZOMBIE STUDIES

McFarland & Company, Inc., Publishers
Jefferson, North Carolina

LIBRARY OF CONGRESS CATALOGUING-IN-PUBLICATION DATA

Zombies are us : essays on the humanity of the walking dead /
edited by Christopher M. Moreman and Cory James Rushton.
p.   cm.— (Contributions to Zombie Studies)
Includes bibliographical references and index.

ISBN 978-0-7864-5912-4 (softcover : acid free paper) ∞
ISBN 978-0-7864-8808-7 (ebook)

1. Zombies—Social Aspects.   2. Zombies—Psychological aspects.   3. Humanity.
4. Human Beings.   5. Zombies in literature.   I. Moreman, Christopher M., 1974–
II. Rushton, Cory.   III. Race, oppressiom and the zombie.   IV. Title: Essays on the
humanity of the walking dead.   V. Title: Humanity of the walking dead.
GR581.Z66   2011   398.21—dc23   2011031516

British Library cataloguing data are available

Front cover photograph by Dmytro Konstantynov;
design by David K. Landis for Shake It Loose Graphics

Printed in the United States of America

*McFarland & Company, Inc., Publishers
Box 611, Jefferson, North Carolina 28640
www.mcfarlandpub.com*

Table of Contents

III — *Zombies into the Future*

Acknowledgments

We would like to thank all of the contributors to this volume, for their patience and for their efforts and timeliness as we moved it forward. We'd also like to thank all of the people who submitted proposals to our initial call for papers (we received over 120 proposals), though we were able to choose only a fraction of them. We would also like to send a blanket thank you out to all of our colleagues who encouraged us in our interest in zombies, at our respective institutions as well as at conferences and other events. Theresa Duran deserves kudos for her excellent work on the index. Thanks are due the editor of *Studies in Religion/Sciences Religieuses* for permission to reprint Moreman's "A Modern Meditation on Death," appearing originally in volume 39 (2): 263–281 of the journal published here with substantial revisions. We must also give thanks to the good people at Piper's Pub in Antigonish for pouring the libations from which the seeds of this whole idea originally grew.

Introduction

They're Us:
Zombies, Humans/Humans, Zombies

"Today we discovered the importance of following the number one rule of zombie movies," reflects college student and zombie film aficionado Joss in the graphic novel *Zombies Calling*. "We never should've left the mall" (Hicks, 2007: 1). That the "mall" in this case is the dorm room she shares with two other students is immaterial: in the language of the zombie text, the mall is the place of relative safety during an outbreak of undead activity. This rule is matched by others: ordinary people can become extraordinary when they battle zombies, guns will become mysteriously and easily available when needed to fight zombies, and one member of the group will always sacrifice themselves in order to save the rest.

"The rules are unifying themes that run through all zombie movies," Joss explains to a skeptical friend, "kind of like Shakespeare and crossdressing" (Hicks, 2007: 3). Her friend wonders how Joss can compare zombie films to Shakespeare, with the latter playing his usual role of stand-in for the very idea of high literature — the assumption is that zombie films must suffer in comparison with the works of the Bard (or Dickens or Austen or whoever). While this introduction will not attempt a cannibalistic assault on the status of the Bard, it will note that the undead co-option of Austen already began with the phenomenally popular *Pride and Prejudice and Zombies* in 2009 (and an increasing number of other zombie/high literature mash-ups). Joss's invocation of the "rules" is not unique: the *Scream* (1996) series had plied the same metatextual waters a few years earlier, and *Zombieland* (2009) was organized around the central protagonist's acknowledgement that his new zombie-filled world would require adherence to new rules if he was to survive.

The standard take on those entries in the *Dead* series which follow *Dawn* is that they follow the law of diminishing returns. While each of the post–*Dawn* films (*Day, Land, Diary,* and *Survival*) will find its defenders — particularly the claustrophobic *Day,* with its stark anti-militaristic message — they are largely seen as evidence that lightning can't strike thrice, and neither could Romero. But Romero, to obnoxiously borrow a cliché, created

1

a monster. His shambling undead cannibal is less than fifty years old, and has developed a remarkable capacity to skip between and over genres which may be rooted in its ur-text, or *locus classicus*, *Night of the Living Dead*; here, the rules are first laid out:

> Zombies are the dead come back to life. Zombies feed on the living. Anyone bitten by a zombie becomes a zombie. The only way to kill a zombie is to shoot it in the head. All other zombie films obey these conventions [Adkins, 2007: 123, n. 2].

While widely accepted, the rules are not quite as universal as Adkins states, and each rule carries the need for interpretation. Zombies can always be produced through bites, but sometimes also through scratches and accidental ingestion of zombie flesh by a normal human; it is increasingly common (as in Romero's *Land of the Dead*, Robert Kirkman's *The Walking Dead*, and the French zombie vs. gangster film *La Horde*, 2009) for anyone to zombify who dies by any means (the last film mentioned, *La Horde*, gives a particularly confusing example when a man shot in the head comes back as a zombie, a creature the rules state is killed by shots to the head).

Zombies feed on the living, but sometimes that includes animals as well as humans; sometimes animals can become zombies, sometimes not. You can shoot a zombie in the head to destroy it, but other methods of decapitation work also; except, of course, when they don't. Sometimes, as in *28 Days Later*, the zombies aren't dead at all. Fan debates rage over how fast a zombie should be able to move.

In *Night*, a member of the media is heard blaming the zombie outbreak on a space probe returning from mysterious Venus. Many zombie texts take the "space radiation" theory seriously (most prominently *Fido*, 2006, which as a spoof of the 1950s is almost obligated to use space radiation as the origin for zombification), while others locate the catastrophe in a manmade virus or a military experiment gone wrong; these texts all make the zombie a matter of science fiction. But Romero has always been cagier, and his later films never mention Venus again (although *Shaun of the Dead*, 2004, does, amongst a host of competing explanations, most of which can be linked to other films). Instead, his characters are likelier to posit metaphysical explanations — hell is full, or God is angry that we're trying to find the secrets of his Creation. Even in *Day*, where we see scientists attempting to figure out what makes zombies tick, no real scientific explanation is offered. In Romero's latest, *Survival of the Dead*, a farmer on an isolated island has precisely the same success training a zombie as *Day*'s Dr. Logan does training Bub.

These conflicting explanations for the zombie plague are part of the answer to the genre's ability to proliferate and to generate generic "rules": the spiritual and scientific origins not only lead to two strands or perhaps sub-genres within the larger zombie genre, they also point to a more unexpected answer. John Russo's *Return of the Living Dead* includes a scene in which a character actually refers to the events of *Night of the Living Dead* as an isolated outbreak resulting from exposure to a chemical called "Trixie"; the motif of the Trixie outbreak could be used over and over again in different contexts, as it would be in the sequels to *Return* and in the *28 Days* series (both films and graphic novels). On the other hand, the vaguely spiritual explanation found in Romero's series (really a non-explanation or textual *aporia*) could be used in texts which weren't interested in explaining things at all. Romero and Russo, who worked on *Night* together, had decided to end their partnership: Romero would produce more serious sequels with titles that included the word "Dead," Russo would oversee a less political series associated with the phrase "Living Dead." The two series would sometimes be in direct competition, and both men were eventually involved with remakes of *Night* itself.

At the same time, and fundamental to the successes of the new genre, neither man owned the copyright to *Night*. A legal error meant that *Night* had been copyrighted under an earlier title (Gagne, 1987: 39): "Even today, *Night of the Living Dead* is available from many different distributors in innumerable VHS and DVD editions and downloads at various prices and in variable quality. That lack of copyright notice immediately placed the film in the public domain and cost the producers millions of dollars" (Pierce, 2007: 129). The loss of money, especially when the victim is as respected an individual as George Romero, is what's noticed most often; but more important in a wider sense is that this very lack of copyright created a situation in which anyone could use this new cannibalistic creature without the need to pay.

Another feature that lends itself to proliferation is geography: a universal apocalypse, by definition, takes place everywhere. While Matheson's *I Am Legend* (1954) could comfortably assert that the human protagonist is the last human on earth (if only to subsequently turn that assertion on its head), a multicultural and post-modern society took the basic outline — the world ends when humans become undead flesh-eaters — and suggested that if one "last man" could survive, paradoxically so could others. Romero himself established this, too, with his refusal to revisit living characters from film to film: the protagonists of *Night* were all dead, but *Dawn*'s Fran and Peter escape; some of the protagonists of *Day* seem to survive; and the heroes of *Land* were intended to appear again but to date have not done so.

It was only with *Survival* that Romero returned to a group of characters, a military group who appear briefly in the preceding entry, *Diary* (we are reluctant to include the "Machete Zombie" played by Tom Savini in *Land of the Dead* as a recurring character, though he is clearly modeled on one of the bikers who attack the mall in *Dawn*). The geographical focus changes in each film: Pennsylvania in *Night* and *Dawn*, Florida in *Day*, Pennsylvania again in *Land* and *Diary*, Maine in *Survival*. Later authors pick up on this in obvious ways, moving the action to London (*Shaun of the Dead* and the *28 Days* series); Tokyo (*Tokyo Zombie*); an unnamed city in France (*La Horde*); Atlanta (*The Walking Dead*); Milwaukee (the *Dawn* remake); a city modeled on Grand Rapids, Michigan (Paffenroth, *Dying to Live*, 191); Sydney, Australia (*Last of the Living*); and so on. Megan Sutherland reiterates the pattern in which Romero offers discontinuous visions of a single apocalypse, how the same central event affects different people and places: "In this sense, the opening scene at the bandstand [in *Land*] positions Romero's entire cycle of *Dead* films as the codification of a certain pattern of generic motions that now exist almost independently of motivation or circumstance" (Sutherland, 2007: 68).

If Sutherland is right — and it seems likely she is — it remains to be determined what kind of "motivation or circumstance" end up being important if we are not concerned with a single place or a single protagonist over time: freed of the need to establish what zombies are, how they operate, and what their existence prompts, the tradition of Romero's zombie apocalypse is increasingly supplemented and augmented by individual film-makers and writers wanting to explore what happens to *their* places when the end comes. Motivation and circumstance land in the local, albeit as a potentially endless series of permutations of the universal. In turn, this emphasis on the local makes us ask, as viewers, "What would we do if the dead rose up?"

Many zombie texts — perhaps most new ones, at this point — either hint at or overtly present an apocalypse, an end to humanity through zombification. This is not apocalypse in the ancient sense, a revelation of destiny being worked out. The zombie apocalypse is always accidental, unexplained, or somehow both. Above all, it is unexpected, with a key generic feature being the disruption of normal life. When Robin Wood asserts of the original Dawn that "the social order (regarded as in all Romero's films as obsolete and discredited) *can't* be restored" (Wood, 2003: 105 — original emphasis), he is pointing not to a consequence but to an essential feature of the genre. David Pagano agrees with Wood's assessment: "Therefore, beyond the general diegetic representations of massive and catastrophic sociocultural destruction, Romero's films invoke the particularly apocalyptic paradox that the world must end in order for there to be any future for the world" (Pagano, 2007: 71). Pagano notes that a kind of "qualified utopianism" (if such a thing is possible) obtains at the end of both *Day* and *Land*, but insists that Romero's films remain focused on movement rather than the achievement of any transcendental space usually associated with apocalypses, anything like the New Jerusalem of St. John's biblical revelation (Pagano: 71, 79).

There may be an unhelpful confusion of terms here. J. C. Davis' classification of ideal societies narratives into utopias (societies perfected by organization), arcadias (in which humans and nature live together in pastoral bliss, moderating their own desires), Cockaygne-societies in which desires are always satisfied by unending abundance, millenniums (in which a *deus ex machina* — or just a deus — solves all human problems and ushers in a perfect world, often an old arcadia restored), or perfect moral commonwealths (society exists as before, but each individual is personally perfected, revealing the essential strength of existing social norms) (Davis, 1981: 20–40). For Davis, utopias like that found in Thomas More's *Utopia* of 1518 are a particular kind of ideal society:

> Modern utopianism begins in the sixteenth century in a world of weak governments with limited aspirations .... Into this world of chaos, confusion, irregularity and incipient disorder the utopian injects images of a total and rational social order, of uniformity instead of diversity, or impersonal, neutrally functioning bureaucracy and of the comprehensive total state [Davis, 1981: 9].

This description looks far closer to the situation as it actually is at the end of *Land*: the zombie army marching into Fiddler's Green, named for a mythical paradise which first appears in song and story in the 1850s, is a uniform society in which ethnic and class diversity has been reduced to nearly meaningless differences of costume. Paffenroth notices the mythical allusion, but may be optimistic when he suggests that the remaining humans in Fiddler's Green will learn to live with the incoming zombies; but when one of the final lines is "We'll turn this place into what we always wanted it to be," anything is possible (Paffenroth, 2006: 131).

At the same time, in the core Romero texts and their most immediate followers, we do see something of apocalypse in its old sense, the revelation of truths and the birth of a new order. Paffenroth picks up on this when he suggests that, whether Romero intends this or not, his films are inherently moral, revealing the manner in which the cardinal virtues (love, kindness, cooperation) lead to survival — or, rather, that the lack of these virtues leads to death and, inevitably, to undeath. While many critics find it difficult to accept Paffenroth's reading of Romero's films, he has channeled that reading into a successful line of fiction (the "Dying to Live" series) in which a group of characters act virtuously and create a thriving community as a result, and a further project in which the medieval poet Dante has an encounter with the living dead which leads to his composition of the *Inferno*. What Paffenroth has done is to turn apocalypse into arcadia, a new kind of post-zombie pastoral. In this system, the community in Paffenroth's *Dying to Live* combines elements of the utopia and the perfect moral commonwealth, with its protagonists forced to learn virtue in the face of the undead hordes. In this, Paffenroth has brought Romero's vision to a (not the only one possible) logical conclusion; and he is not alone.

The on-going graphic novel *The Walking Dead*, written by Robert Kirkman, is an interesting case in point. With the avowed purpose of wanting to start where the usual zombie apocalypse movie ends — with a few survivors facing an uncertain future while on the road, a clear allusion to Romero's films — Kirkman's *Walking Dead* is advertised with a telling line: "In a world ruled by the dead, we are forced to finally start living."

Fourteen volumes in, Kirkman's series has become one of the best meditations on society popular culture has yet produced: what do we need to become in order to protect the virtuous and the innocent? By the time Kirkman's central protagonist, Rick Grimes, is seen stealing guns from a community that has accepted his band of fellow survivors (Kirkman, *Too Far Gone*, 20) or leads his core followers in a session of torture directed at a cannibal who has threatened them (Kirkman, *Fear the Hunters*, 109–21), it is clear that Kirkman's moral vision is significantly darker than Paffenroth's. "I do things," Rick confesses to his young son after the torture incident: "A lot of bad things, to help you and all the other people in our group" (Kirkman, *Too Far Gone*, 6). The community in which the group finds itself has also had to make hard choices, reminding us that the perfect moral community is difficult to achieve both externally and internally; the whole direction of the series, however, has taught us that before the zombie apocalypse, we didn't even know we had to make moral choices. To "start living" is to be forced to think.

In a similar vein, not all zombie texts bother to lament the world we have lost. A young character in Bobbie Metevier's "The Loneliest Man in the World" (in a collection edited by Paffenroth), someone whose post-apocalyptic community was once an impoverished neighborhood, reacts negatively when the re-formed government sends someone with promises to rebuild that lost world: "Do yourself a favor and get the fuck out. You know what this plague means to me? It means my moms [sic] don't have to work two jobs to keep food on the table. It means Mr. Leary ain't been bugging her for the rent" (Metevier, 2008: 172). With communal gardens on his home's roof and no need to go to school, who can blame him for refusing to mourn a world that did not serve his interests? What we are seeing in the birth of the post-zombie apocalypse sub-genre is a collapsing of the utopia/dystopia binary, with the persistent message being that to live is to struggle, and that we as humans need it to be that way.

The most compelling aspect of the zombie genre is that it is itself viral, somehow cannibalistic, that its ability to generate narrative and its growing propensity for a celebration of human engagement and effort allows it to colonize multiple other kinds of story. As a genre built fundamentally on disruption of a status quo, in a generic sense the zombie apocalypse can be worked into any other genre, like a cuckoo's egg: romantic comedy (*Shaun of the Dead*), cops and robber drama (*La Horde*), 1950s sitcom (*Fido*), air disaster narratives (*Flight of the Living Dead*), ad infinitum. Since the shock of the unbelievable can work to disrupt any narrative setting, and since that disruption is an essential component of the zombie genre, the zombie genre is perversely capable of being linked to all genres — it is infinitely adaptable. Once this became apparent, the production of zombie texts proliferated exponentially. It was literally a case of "just add zombies."

At this point, it may seem as though we have avoided much discussion of the "big" zombie texts outside of Romero's films (*28 Days Later* and its sequels [film and comic], Fulci's films, Russo's series) in favor of more obscure texts. In part, this is an attempt to get at the inner logic of the genre, past the alternately cursory or hyper-theoretical discussions which surround those pop culture artifacts lucky or unlucky enough to attract the academy's attention. That attention — usually skipping detailed contextual or intertextual work so that the text can be hammered into a theoretical framework as quickly as possible — can often obscure what the texts themselves are actually doing. So, if zombie texts are subject to their own generic constraints which contain, as part of those rules, a discussion about the human, we might see that more clearly in texts which are relatively under-examined.

The present volume brings together a range of perspectives on the zombie in terms of its relationship to humanity, or, more accurately in some cases, perspectives on humanity in terms of its inherent connection to the walking dead. The essays in Part I explore the ways that zombies and humans can become interchangeable. Philosophers Craig Derksen and Darren Hudson Hick explore those emotional qualities of the zombie that suggest, or at least trouble, notions of self-identity and human nature. They ask, for example, the extent to which the zombie of my neighbor and my neighbor are one and the same, a question which prefaces that wondering whether my neighbor and my self share anything in common. Identification with zombies is explored in Graham St John's investigation and interpretation of the ongoing raver sub-culture and its appropriation of zombie iconography as a source of self-identity.

Steve Jones moves even further to the fringes of zombie fandom, and deeper into the zombie/human relationship, in his enlightening gender-studies analysis of zombie-porn. The extent to which humans might identify with the zombie is terrifyingly explored by sociologist Suzanne Goodney Lea, who discusses not only the serial killer as in-human, but also the desires of some killers to ritually control their victims, thereby creating their own zombies. Legal scholars Sharon Sutherland and Sarah Swan move out of the individual context of the criminal mind to examine the ways zombification might infect the legal system itself.

Part II brings religious scholarship to bear upon the living dead, revealing the innately spiritual aspects of the zombie. Theologian Michael J. Gilmour begins by enumerating the appearance of zombie-like walking dead in the Bible, indicating a very early inspiration for the monster itself. James Reitter follows with a focused analysis of the blasphemous characteristics of the horror of Lucio Fulci. Keira McKenzie contributes the case for the zombie's acting as modern psychopomp, aiding the transition from the world of the living to that of the dead. Christopher M. Moreman follows this offering an argument for seeing the modern zombie as a type of meditation on death and mortality in the Buddhist sense.

The final Part III presents scholarship translating the zombie from Haitian folklore and the 1960s counter-culture into a clearly modern age. Videogame scholars Gareth Schott and Matthew J. Weise, for instance, offer two different perspectives on the zombie. Schott examines how videogames must alter themes of apocalyptic cinema in order to allow for the excitement of playing, and how young people react to these new forms of zombie horror as compared to themes present in zombie cinema. Weise, on the other hand, explores the ways in which important elements of the zombie myth are translated, or not, between film and videogame, which is not necessarily a uni-directional conversion.

Greg Pollock, tackling one of today's major global concerns, presents the zombie as allegorically allied with animalistic nature as he argues for the modern zombie's role in current ecological politics and fears of a global apocalypse. Finally, Sara Sutler-Cohen offers a view of the zombie's humanization as she wonders at the changing nature of zombies in some modern representations which allow for an evolution of the zombie, integrating them into society in various ways.

As a whole, this volume challenges the reader to read the zombie in its relationship to the human — the self or soul as the ultimate local — and vice versa. Humans, as *homo religiosus* (Eliade, 1968), have an innate drive to reach for meaning in and for life; as *homo narrans* (Myerhoff, 1980) they not only strive for meaning, but they long to communicate both what they find and how they get there. Zombies, as an abject reflection of our individual mortality, and harbingers of societal decay, force the viewer to consider the dark possibilities of a meaningless existence. They can paradoxically offer us a glimpse of worlds that might be better if we were forced to fight for our survival, for our joys, and for the right to define ourselves as we want to be. Or, at least, they force us to reconsider the nature of the meanings that we currently attach to self and society.

By examining the dark side that is the living dead we might come to recognize something of ourselves as the dying alive. We might even consider what it would be mean to drop the adjectives altogether, and simply live in the world. As someone says in Romero's *Dawn of the Dead*, as a few survivors watch hordes of zombies trying to claw their way into a shopping mall, "They're us, that's all."

PART I

The Zombie in Humanity

Your Zombie and You

Identity, Emotion, and the Undead

CRAIG DERKSEN and
DARREN HUDSON HICK

Philosophy often deals in what are called "thought experiments"—imagined scenarios that help us to illuminate and test our theories and intuitions—and philosophers have regularly found inspiration for thought experiments in film and literary fiction. Given the sheer volume of fiction devoted to them, then, it is perhaps surprising that zombies have so far been largely overlooked as a source of philosophical discussion.[1] It may be thought that zombies—being fanciful movie monsters—have little or nothing to teach us, and that such discussion could only be non-serious at best. As we hope to show here, however, zombies have a great deal to teach us—about our emotions, and about ourselves. In particular, we will use the possibility of zombies to explore the nature of fear—focusing on how the perceived nature of a threat can serve to alter the subjective character of one's fear. In the process, our discussion will explore central topics in metaphysics, epistemology, and the philosophy of mind, although a background in philosophy on the part of the reader is not expected. As well, examples will be drawn broadly from zombie fiction, though only a passing familiarity with the genre will be required of the reader.

Fear Itself

Before delving into the specifics of fearing zombies, let us first develop a schematic understanding of fear itself. There are a number of philosophical approaches to understanding the nature of fear.[2] For our purposes here, the most promising such school of thought is roughly called the "cognitivist" view of fear.[3] First set out by Robert M. Gordon in his paper, "Fear" (1980), and greatly developed by Wayne A. Davis in "The Varieties of Fear" (1987), the cognitivist approach to fear suggests that, at base, fear is propositional in nature. That is, all fears are fears that something is (or was, or may become) the case. Such fears involve certain cognitive and attitudinal states. First, Gordon notes, to be afraid that something, p, is (or was, or may become) the case requires caring about whether p or not-*p* (Gordon: 561). In a simple case, to say that I am afraid of my friend's Doberman is to say that I fear that the dog will harm me, and this requires my caring about whether or not I am harmed. This is an attitudinal condition — what Davis calls the *aversion* component (Davis, 1987: 289). Second, Gordon contends, fear of *p* requires uncertainty as to whether *p* will obtain (Gordon: 561). That is, if I am afraid of the dog harming me, then I neither know that it will, nor know that it will not do so. This is a cognitive condition — the *uncertainty* component.

As such, we might distinguish *propositional fear* (fearing *that*) with *experiential fear* (being in a *state* of fear). As Davis notes, the experience of fear is an "occurrent emotional state" involving certain involuntary kinds of physiological arousal — increased heart rate, increased respiration, perspiration, and so on. This is to say that experiential fear is a sort of *event* that happens to someone. Facing my friend's Doberman, something *happens to me*, and this is largely out of my control. Propositional fear, on the other hand, need not be occurrent, and may have no physiological effect whatsoever (Gordon: 561). For example, while I might accurately be described as being afraid of dogs, if I am not currently seeing or thinking about dogs, I will more than likely show no such symptoms of this fear. Propositional fear, as such, need not be associated with any particular event, but simply sits in the background.

Davis contends that, properly understood, one is in the state of *experiential fear* when one is in a state of such involuntary arousal — what we might call *physiological fear* (Davis, 1987: 287)[4] — and unhappiness as a direct result of one's occurrent *propositional fear* that something will be harmed — whether oneself, or someone or something else (Davis, 1987: 302).[5] So experiential fear arises from propositional fear — and specifically a propositional fear of some harm.[6] Propositional fear is, as such, an element of, or a necessary cause of, experiential fear.

To *propositional fear* and *experiential fear*, Davis (1987: 303–4) adds *reactive fear* (fear *of*). Certainly, one might be said to be afraid that some given dog might harm him, but one might also be said to be afraid *of* the dog. "He is afraid of the dog," Davies would say, expresses more than a propositional fear. It suggests that the subject *reacts* to the dog with fear. This might be expressed in an occurrent sense (he is experiencing such fear now) or in a dispositional sense (he is not currently experiencing such fear, but he often does). He is afraid *of* the dog only if he is fearful that something will be harmed specifically *by* the dog. We might call this perceived object associated with one's fears the *locus* of the fear — what one's fears are directed towards — to be distinguished from the perceived harmful outcome. And these should likewise be distinguished from the *cause* of one's fears. That is, while the dog can be said to be both the cause and object or locus of the fear, we might imagine another case in which a pill swallowed by someone causes that individual to experience some unwarranted fear. The fear may even lack any clear object (such that the subject is afraid of *something*, but nothing specific). What he is likely *not* afraid of, however, is the pill itself, or the chemical changes in his brain. This is the cause, but not the object of the fear.

As fear of *p* (some state of affairs) requires the desire that not-*p*, such fears have a tendency to motivate "vulnerability avoidance." That is, fearing that a dog will harm me will typically motivate me to avoid the dog's jaws. If I am forward-looking enough, it will also typically motivate me to avoid being in any situation in which the dog has any *opportunity* to harm me.[7]

The loci of one's fears may be many and varied. One might be afraid of dogs, certainly, but one might also fear open spaces, cell phones, Mondays, and, of course, zombies. In an effort to universalize the cognitivist account, Davis has built into his view the notion that, at base, all fears are fears of being harmed — that is, that the propositional component, p, is essentially always the same. If I am afraid that p, it seems on Davis' account, I am afraid of some harm. However, in so universalizing his account, it seems Davis has sanitized away something critical to the nature of fearing something: not all fears *feel* the same.

To begin, fears can vary quantitatively. It might be said that I am a *little* afraid of spiders, substantially *more* afraid of dogs, and *very* afraid of sharks. This is a matter of degree, and would seem to result from some combination of the perceived likelihood and degree of harm. If I live in and rarely leave the desert, it might be strange to say that I am "very" afraid of sharks, as I am extremely unlikely to encounter any. On the other hand, it might be *because* I am very afraid of sharks that I choose to live in and rarely leave the desert. It would make sense that if I am only a *little* afraid of spiders and *more* afraid of dogs, then (1) the *amount* of physiological arousal I experience in encountering one is likely to be higher than that in experiencing the other; and (2) the lengths to which I am willing to go to avoid encountering the locus of my fear are likely to be correspondingly greater in one case than the other. In addition to this sliding scale of the *degree* to which I am afraid, however, it seems that even where the perceived likelihood and degree of harm are at least roughly constant, differences in the *locus* of one's fear can color the experience in important ways. These are differences in the *quality* of one's fears.

Imagine that you are on vacation, and are bobbing in the ocean surf. Despite the beautiful day and pleasant surroundings, certain fears might arise in you. It might occur to you, for instance, that you know little about these waters, and that for all you know, they might be teeming with sharks. On the other hand, it might occur to you that you didn't study the tide tables, and there could come along at any moment some powerful rip current that could sweep you out into the open sea. As such, you might develop an occurrent fear of sharks, and you might develop an occurrent fear of open space. In each case, the imagined harm and its likelihood (for all you know) might be roughly equivalent, but in each case, the fear itself is going to *feel* different. It may be that fears feel different because the imagined scenarios in which each harm occurs are themselves likely to feel different, though this does not seem to fully capture the difference. Rather, the fear seems to — for want of a better word — carry a *flavor* associated with its locus. The fear of being torn apart by unseen sharp teeth in the water is simply going to be a different kind of subjective experience than the sickening dread of being swept away into all that openness, and if a cognitivist approach seeks to capture the nature of fear, it seems that reducing the propositional fear simply to a fear of being harmed loses something in the process. I am not simply afraid of being harmed: I am afraid of being torn up by hundreds of unseen teeth, or of being set adrift in the vastness of the ocean. The *locus* of one's fear, and not merely the perceived harm, informs one's propositional fears, and this in turn informs the resulting physiological arousal. This is to say that the locus of one's fear is an irreducible element of the *content* of that fear, and not simply what the fear is directed towards.

Zombies and Emotion

THE HORDE

Whether in films, comics, novels, or video games, perhaps the most ubiquitous scene in zombie fiction is that of some lone individual or small, isolated group of survivors encountering a gathering multitude of the undead — the zombie *horde*. As regards emotional responses, the horde is a relatively simple case, so let us begin here. If these works have taught us nothing else, it is that facing a zombie horde is not altogether unlike facing a swarm of bees, or for that matter an advancing lava flow (if we are talking about slow-moving zombies) or a tidal wave (if we are talking about fast-moving ones). The zombie horde is like a force of nature — a persistent and unified threat — and scenes of zombie hordes tend to play out much like disaster movies. At best, the zombie horde seems to act with a very basic sort of hive mentality. Perhaps more accurately, the horde seems to act according to what biologists call a "taxis" — an innate behavioral response causing an organism to move towards or away from some particular stimulus. Although most commonly found amongst simple microorganisms, taxes are found among some higher organisms as well. Cockroaches, for example, are negatively phototactic — moving away from light sources — while moths are positively phototactic — being drawn to the light. In most cases, rather than displaying any individual, higher-order thinking, the horde seems to swarm according to a basic innate directive. However, unlike moths, zombies are drawn to living human flesh, specifically with the instinct to eat it. This is true of paradigm cases, as in George A. Romero's "Dead" films and associated remakes, Robert Kirkman's *The Walking Dead* comic-book and television series, Max Brooks' *World War Z*, the British television series, *Dead Set*, and others. In the *Return of the Living Dead* films, the dead are drawn specifically to brains.

With the unified horde as the locus of our fear, the propositional fear amounts to something like, "I am afraid of being torn apart, devoured, or otherwise mortally harmed by the zombie horde." The horde represents a unified threat, and escape requires moving around, beyond, or through the horde. Depending on the sort of zombies composing the horde, the occurent experiential fear may be more or less pronounced. If the horde is composed of slow-moving and meandering corpses, the subjectively experienced fear may seem relatively muted, especially when compared with the more pronounced and panicked fear sure to be experienced in facing a horde of fast-moving and rampaging ghouls. Although the imagined harm is equivalent in each case, the likelihood of that harm obtaining is almost certainly greater in the latter case than the former. As a result, the difference here would seem to be more a matter of degree than of kind. However, the slow-moving horde may also present a threat that seems patient, incessant, and simply tireless. Where the threat of the fast-moving horde is *immediate*, the threat of the slow-moving horde is *persistent*. Although mindless, the slow-moving horde simply continues to grow with each passing minute, and so too does the associated fear.

THE AGENT

It seems overly generous to attribute "wants" or "desires" to the zombie horde — or at least if we want to say that the horde or any of its composite zombies *desires* to eat our flesh, we mean it in the same way as saying the moth *desires* to get to the light. And even if we do want to go so far, the horde doesn't seem to choose *whether* or *how* to act on this desire — it simply acts. On occasion, however, an individual zombie may present a new problem: apparent rational agency.

The fourth installment of George A. Romero's "Dead" series, *Land of the Dead* (2005), is essentially *about* rational agency. The dead have overwhelmed the planet, driving survivors to live in secluded, fenced enclaves, and for want of a better word, the zombies are *evolving*— they are learning to learn. Having developed a rudimentary language, the dead are organized by the reanimated "Big Daddy," who trades his gas pump for an automatic rifle, and leads his fellow zombies in an assault on the city ruled by Kaufman. When Kaufman betrays his henchman Cholo, Cholo seeks revenge, planning his own attack on Kaufman and the city. Although Cholo is bitten and turned into a zombie in the process, his goal essentially remains the same. When the city falls to the dead, Big Daddy and Cholo both come for Kaufman. Kaufman and the other survivors have learned to live in precarious proximity to the walking dead, perhaps dropping their guard in the process. But if you are Kaufman, what makes Big Daddy or Cholo especially frightening isn't just that he wants you dead — it's that he seems to have thought it through. He seems to be executing a *plan*.

Standardly in philosophy, rational agency is described as the capacity for a thing to make and act according to reasoned choices.[8] Such an agent does not simply respond to stimuli according to innate biological imperatives, but rather *decides* which desires to act on, and how. The agent acts on *reasons*. Insofar as it is acting rationally, the agent seeks optimal ends and optimal means to those ends. Now, there is ongoing debate as to whether *anything* qualifies as an agent of the sort we are considering — indeed, it is not altogether certain if agency is even *possible*.[9] Our worry here, however, is not whether something *has* agency, but whether it *appears* to. A flesh-eating abomination that is drawn to you like a moth to a flame would be a formidable threat; one that could decide how best to get the job done would be another kind of threat entirely. Non-agent zombies represent a relatively simple threat, even when massed as a horde. The agent zombie is anything but simple, and the threat is complex. When the threat is complex, so too is associated fear arising from it.[10]

Where an agency-free zombie seems at best drawn to you as a stimulus, an agent zombie could follow you, lie in wait for you, organize others to surround you, or even (if it is clever enough) set traps for you. A threat that can reason — can strategize — offers any number of possible harm scenarios. And as the cognitivist account of fear is grounded in an uncertainty component, it seems reasonable to posit that the more uncertain the threat, the more pronounced the fear. Put another way, there is more than one propositional fear associated with the same locus: that the agent zombie is following you, that the agent zombie is lying in wait for you, that the agent zombie has laid traps for you — whatever your imagination can dream up. As the propositional fears are compounded, the experiential fear will be not only enhanced, but also fragmented among its many propositions — a sort of pronounced paranoid fear.[11]

This issue of agency and the emotional affect thereof is closely tied with the psychological concept of the "uncanny" first proposed by Ernst Jentsch in "The Psychology of the Uncanny" (1906/1995).[12] Experience of the uncanny involves an inability on the part of the observer to properly categorize some object or event because it is ambiguous — appearing both familiar and unfamiliar at the same time. As such, the uncanny can bring about in its observer an acute uncomfortable feeling. On our analysis, such a feeling is not itself an aspect of the experienced fear, but is in addition to it, and would be directed at the same locus. The experience of the uncanny, Jentsch notes, can be particularly strong in cases where there is "doubt as to whether an apparently living being really is animate and, conversely, doubt as to whether a lifeless object may not in fact be animate" (Jentsch: 11). This is, of course, precisely the issue with zombies, and in fiction is used to particular effect. Jentsch notes that, "[i]n storytelling, one of the most reliable artistic devices for producing uncanny effects easily is to leave the reader in uncertainty as to whether he has a human person or rather an automaton before him in the case of a particular character" (Jentsch: 13). The question of agency rests on whether the creature at hand, while animated, is like a machine, simply operating on innate biological instincts, or whether it is something more. Sometimes the agency of a zombie is unclear; at other times it seems utterly apparent. In *The Return of the Living Dead* (1985), the undead voice their desires — unlike paradigm zombies, they want to eat *brains*, and they are more than willing to discuss the matter. (One zombie tells the protagonists that the undead eat brains to curb "the pain of being dead"). More to the point, they seek out strategic means to satisfy this desire. Having helped to devour a pair of EMTs, one zombie uses the ambulance's CB radio: "Send ... more ... paramedics." When the paramedics arrive, they are ambushed.

Settling the issue of agency explains one sort of reaction to the zombie. The zombie is dead and *yet* animate thus producing the doubt necessary for the uncanny response. However, this gives rise to a further problem: the problem of *horror*. Where the uncanny rests on *ambiguity* in categorization, horror rests on *incongruity* in categorization. And where Jentsch discusses the subjective experience of the uncanny in terms of discomfort, the experience of horror tends to be described as akin to disgust. Rarely is the term "zombie" actually used in zombie fiction — and this may be for good reason. The word is never used, for example, in *Night of the Living Dead* (1968), and is used only once in *The Return of the Living Dead*. In *Shaun of the Dead* (2004), a clearly distraught Shaun tells Ed not to use "the zed word." To call something a "zombie" is to admit the kind of thing that it is.

In *Purity and Danger* (1966), anthropologist Mary Douglas theorizes that something that crosses certain culturally-entrenched boundaries of classification is seen as "impure." The East African Nuer people, she notes, treat infants born with deformities as baby hippos mistakenly born to humans, and "return" them to the river (Douglas: 39). In north Congo (now Zaire), Douglas claims the Lele people avoid flying squirrels because they are unable to classify them as animals or birds (Douglas: 168). When something resists classification — because it seems to belong in more than one category but comfortably in none — Douglas argues we see it as impure, as an abomination. Building on both the psychology of the uncanny and on Douglas' study, Noël Carroll argues that our reactions of disgust and fear to the elements of horror may be based on a similar principle. With zombies, the categories at hand are those of the living and the dead. (The same would be true of vampires, ghosts, the mummy, and other "undead" creatures). While deceased, zombies certainly don't *act* that way. Carroll notes,

[M]onster X's being categorically interstitial causes a sense of impurity in us without our awareness of what causes that sense. [Monsters] are unnatural relative to a culture's conceptual scheme of nature. They do not fit the scheme; they violate it. Thus, they are not only physically threatening; they are cognitively threatening. They are threats to common knowledge [Carroll, 1987: 56].

As with the uncanny, while the emotional effect of horror is perhaps conceptually distinct from that of fear, the locus remains the same. And Carroll seems to indicate that the horrific can itself give rise to fear. He notes that the lead character in Romero's *Night of the Living Dead*, Barbra, "when surrounded by zombies, screams and clutches herself in such a way as to avoid contact with the contaminated flesh" (Carroll, 1987: 53). There is, first, the propositional fear of being devoured, and second, the distinct propositional fear of being contaminated.[13] While the locus of the fear remains the same, the experience of that fear may be qualitatively different. The matter becomes only more pronounced — and complicated — when that locus is the reanimated corpse of one's loved one.

The Person

Fear of being devoured by the walking dead is one thing; fear of being contaminated is another entirely. But perhaps more horrifying still is the prospect of having to kill (or, in our case, *re*-kill) someone close to you. In the 1990 remake of *Night of the Living Dead*, the character of Tom recounts a story in which he and his cousin are attacked by his uncle's zombie, and Tom's cousin has killed himself:

I know he's dead. He shot himself. I mean, Uncle Rege coming after him and all, y'know. I run down here and got the shotgun, but what could I do, y'know? I couldn't imagine shooting Uncle Rege. I couldn't imagine doing a thing like that.

Instead of shooting his uncle, Tom seeks refuge in the cellar. Stories like this are a staple of zombie fiction,[14] and those of us familiar with the genre would tend to think that such sentimentality betrays a naïve misunderstanding of the nature of zombies — Uncle Rege is dead, and whatever has come back isn't him. However, this isn't so clearly the case. The inclination to see one's reanimated loved ones *as* one's loved ones may indeed be justified, and thus so too the fear of killing them.

In the literature of philosophy, the matter would seem to rest critically on issues of personal identity. The central question of personal identity is: what is it that makes you the same person today that you were yesterday, or a year or a decade ago? After all, if you aren't the same person that you were yesterday — if the two of you are *distinct* persons — it seems we can't reasonably hold you responsible for *that* person's acts. And if you won't be the same person tomorrow that you are today, there seems little reason to look forward to tomorrow, because someone else is going to be experiencing it — not you. Traditionally, proposals to what makes you the same person today that you were yesterday fall into two camps: theories of bodily continuity and theories of psychological continuity (see Martin and Barresi, 2003).

Proponents of the bodily-continuity perspective contend that you are the same person today that you were yesterday because you are a continuation of the same body (see Williams, 1970). Granted, the body changes a little, day by day, as you shed skin and hair, develop wrinkles, and the like, but this does not mean it is not relevantly the same body. You might put a new coat of paint on your house, or fix the plumbing under the sink, but we still want to say in a meaningful way that it is the same house — and so too with your body. The body can survive such small-scale changes, and insofar as you are identifiable with your body, so too can you. If this view is correct, then the matter applies as equally to Uncle Rege as it does to you — never mind that somewhere in the interim, he died. That is, because the creature before you is a continuation of same body as Uncle Rege, that creature *is* Uncle Rege — fully and completely — and in killing the creature, you *are* killing (or re-killing) Uncle Rege. Granted, it may come down to you or him, but the agonizing prospect of being responsible for killing one's uncle is certainly an understandable basis for fear, and one incurring a propositional and experiential fear distinct from that of the simple fear for one's life.

However, most would balk at the notion that simply having the same body as some being at some different time — whether regarding the living or the undead — is sufficient (or even necessary) for being the same person,[15] and philosophers tend to adhere more commonly to psychological continuity views of personal identity. Drawing predominantly on the work of John Locke (1694), psychological-continuity proponents contend that what makes you the same person that you were yesterday (or a week, year, or decade ago) is that you maintain the right sort of psychological relationship with that individual. On Locke's view, you are the same person that you were a week ago because you participate in the same stream of consciousness. In particular, you maintain an unbroken chain of memories with that individual. While you might not remember being a toddler, there is *somebody* who remembers being that toddler, and someone who remembers being *that* person, and so on, up to you.

The central problem for applying the standard psychological-continuity view to the standard zombie case is that it seems impossible that the zombie *could* be the same person as Uncle Rege. Putting aside issues of non-undead zombies — as in the "infected" in *28 Days Later* (2002) and *28 Weeks Later* (2007), the "phone crazies" in Stephen King's *Cell* (2006), and cases of Haitian Vodou (Voodoo) zombies — the problem is that, at some point, Ungle Rege *died*— that is, he *ceased to have psychology*.[16] With brain-death, there is simply no mind to be psychologically continuous *with*. It is like cutting a piece of string in half— once cut, you now have two pieces of string, not one long, continuous one. And similarly, once lost, psychological continuity seems irrecoverable. On this view, undead Rege simply isn't (indeed, can't be) the same person as Uncle Rege. Although perhaps alleviating the fear that one might be forced to kill Uncle Rege, such relief is sure to be replaced with the emotional horror of facing a thing both like and unlike the man you once knew and loved.

Conceivably, one could eliminate these problems by maintaining a strict Cartesian distinction between mind and body, such that the mind is capable of existing without *any* body. On such a view, it seems either *always* possible that the zombie is Uncle Rege (because no amount of harm to the body — including death — is going to have any effect on the mind), or seems utterly *impossible* that it is Uncle Rege, because on such a view none of us *are* our bodies, or are even connected to them in any substantial fashion. Then, of course, any problem for zombies is just as much a problem for the rest of us.

Isn't it odd, though, that aside from trying to eat your flesh, the Rege-zombie some-times *acts* an awful lot like Uncle Rege? Zombie fiction is replete with the undead acting in at least superficially human ways. In Romero's *Dawn of the Dead* (1978), a small group of survivors seek shelter in a shopping mall, and are surprised to find that the dead, too, have amassed there. One survivor, Francine, asks, "What are they doing? Why do they come here?" Her companion Stephen replies, "Some kind of instinct ... memory of what they used to do. This was an important place in their lives." The matter is further explored especially in *Land of the Dead*, in which zombies superficially resume their earlier lives as gas attendants, musicians, and the like. If the psychological-continuity account is correct, however, it wasn't *their* lives that the mall was important to, for the zombie is not the same person as his living counterpart. And going to the mall isn't what *he* used to do — it's what someone *else* used to do; someone with whom the zombie merely shares a body. Moreover, on this account, the zombies' memories are not real memories at all. For something to qualify as a real memory of yours, it must be a recounting of an event that actually happened to you. Insofar as your zombie isn't you, it has no real memory of *being* you. Rather, at best, it would seem to have a *false* memory.

Philosopher Derek Parfit (1971) takes a different stance on the issue of personal identity. Indeed, Parfit suggests rejecting the term "personal identity" altogether, and instead talking about "survival." Parfit contends that many of the problems that arise in theories of personal identity do so because the notion is too rigid. For instance, while in one sense, we might say you *are* the same person as 3-year-old you, in another sense you are utterly unlike this person: you have none of the same memories, probably a radically different personality, and none of the same cells in your body. Parfit's view suggests it stretches coherence to talk about personal identity here. Instead, he would say, the toddler has *survived* as you — at least to a substantial degree. And the same might hold true for zombie-you. Given the difference between identity and survival, Parfit suggests we replace talk of memories with talk of *q*-memories, being apparent memories that one has for the right reasons — specifically causal reasons. Roughly, if you have a memory-belief of an experience that happened to *somebody*, and that belief is based on that experience in the right causal way, then it is a legitimate *q*-memory, even if, strictly speaking, the person to whom the remembered experience occurred wasn't you. If, by some causal mechanism, zombification allows for *q*-memories to cross the death-divide, then your zombie would *q*-remember your experiences.[17] Parfit suggests that survival comes in degrees: the greater the number of *q*-connections (including *q*-memories, *q*-desires, *q*-intentions, etc.), the greater the degree of survival. Has Uncle Rege "survived" zombification — at least to a reasonable degree? From your outside perspective, determining this would seem to depend on what evidence is available. The greater the similarities, the greater the weight of evidence, and seemingly the greater the reason to fear that in killing the zombie, you are killing Uncle Rege. Inter-estingly, as Parfit's view potentially makes biological death a non-issue for determining survival, on this account precisely the same factors for survival or non-survival are at play in such non-undead zombies as those in *28 Days Later*.

Problematically, however, a complete *lack* of evidence does not seem to support the belief that Uncle Rege *hasn't* "survived" zombification. Let us consider a different sort of zombie movie: Wes Craven's *The Serpent and the Rainbow* (1988). In this film, while investigating the pharmacological basis for Haitian Vodou (Voodoo) zombification, Dr. Dennis Alan is himself "killed" and revived as a zombie. Although not a true death, the film portrays zombification as the effect of a "zombie powder" whose active ingredient, tetrodotoxin, produces a near-death state reducing the body's vital signs to imperceptible levels. While in this physical state, however, Alan remains fully conscious, even through his burial.[18] This extreme form of locked-in syndrome raises an unsettling prospect: even without any outward signs, there may still be a fully active mind inside what appears to be a dead body. And, allowing for cases of "true" zombification, why not also allow for the possibility of a fully-active mind locked into the shell of a reanimated corpse? In other words, how are you to know, when facing the reanimated corpse of your Uncle Rege, that Uncle Rege isn't still *in there*? In such a case, while it might be problematic to say that the zombie "is" Uncle Rege, it nevertheless *contains* Uncle Rege, and in permanently killing the zombie, you are surely doing the same to your loved one. With this prospect in mind, it seems that one might always hold a reasonable basis for the fear that in killing the zombie, you are killing Uncle Rege.

Your Zombie and You

A flip-side to the case of Uncle Rege raises a relevant and important sort of fear not yet dealt with in this essay: the fear of *becoming* a zombie. Whether coming about as the result of being bitten by one of the undead, or simply from dying during the zombie apocalypse, the fear of being resurrected as the walking dead is a familiar one in zombie fiction. In Romero's films and associate remakes, the rules of death have simply ceased to apply, and anyone who dies (unless suitably brain injured) will return as the walking dead. In many other films, such as *Planet Terror* (2007), only those bitten by zombies will become zombies, a trope similar to classical treatments of vampires and werewolves. Other cases are less "infectious"— for example, in *I Was a Teenage Zombie* (1987), bodies are only zombified after being dumped in toxic water. In Romero's *Dawn of the Dead*, the character of Roger lies dying, and says to Peter, "I don't want to be walking around ... like *that*." Roger tells Peter that he is going to try to *not* come back, asking Peter to shoot him if he does. This fear, common throughout zombie fiction, seems to be a fear of becoming something else — something *wrong*. Essentially, it is a fear of becoming the object of horror.

Some philosophers would argue that the fear of becoming a flesh-eating automaton is altogether irrational — even in the face of a horde of flesh-eating automatons. The problem is this: if *you* cease to exist at death, then anything that happens at or after your death cannot harm you. Indeed, death itself cannot serve as a reasonable locus of fear. As Epicurus famously writes, "[S]o long as we exist, death is not with us; but when death comes, then we do not exist. It does not then concern either the living or the dead, since for the former it is not, and the latter are no more."[19] Having died, you aren't becoming *anything*, for *you* will have ceased to exist. As we have seen, however, the notion of zombies serves to complicate this issue.

On a strict view of psychological continuity, it seems accurate to say one cannot *become* the walking dead, for whatever it is that will occupy your body will not be you.

On a Parfit-styled view, however, it may be that you could "survive" zombification, even though you have died in the interim. The matter would seem to rest on the issue of "recovery"—on whether there are enough causal links connecting your psychology to that of the zombie. If the zombie *is* merely an automaton, drawn instinctively to eat living human flesh, it would be difficult to say you have survived to any degree—this isn't you; it is only your body. However, were the zombie to recover to some degree your memories, personality traits, and the like, it seems more and more apt to say that you have survived. In Frank Herbert's "Dune" series, the character of Duncan Idaho, an ambassador and warrior, is felled by a fatal head injury. However, in *Dune Messiah*, Idaho's corpse is resurrected as a "ghola" named Hayt.[20] And while having a personality of his own, Hayt is wiped of Idaho's memories and controlled through hypnosis, not entirely unlike classical Vodou zombies. Eventually, however, Hayt shrugs off his controllers and manages to fully recover Idaho's memories and personality. Idaho has essentially fully recovered from zombification.

The prospect of fully recovering from zombification does not seem a reasonable basis for fear—if anything, it seems a reasonable basis for *hope*, the optimistic inverse of fear. Likewise, the fear of your deceased body being resurrected seems an unreasonable basis for fear, provided the resulting zombie is simply an instinctive machine with no psychological connection to you, for in such a case, it seems improper to say that *you* have survived. What *does* seem a reasonable basis for fear, however, is anything in between—that is, any survival falling short of full and complete survival. Whether you are "locked in" the zombie, a passive observer without any control over the body, or whether you retain some but not all of your memories and personality, it seems you have survived to at least *some* degree, and so *you* are being harmed. You have become the locus of your own fears. Worse still, you have become the object of horror—a thing categorically both like *and* unlike you, a horror you cannot escape.

Brains?

Do you have reason to fear the zombie apocalypse? That would seem to depend, first, upon your belief in the likelihood of such an event, and, second, on whether or not you are averse to it happening. However, the point of this essay has not been to convince you to begin stockpiling water and weapons. Rather, we have employed the undead because they have—perhaps more than any other sort of being—a great potential to teach us about fear and fear-like states. As an extended thought experiment, our responses to zombies provide a structured approach for thinking about emotion that highlights certain key points, namely changes in character and feel of emotion based on perceived differences in the nature of the object. The apparent nature of the zombie as living or dead, autonomous or automatic, person or animal or object, or even as specific individual, changes the very nature of our fear.

Zombies represent a surprisingly complex class of cases, and perceived differences in zombies serve nicely to illustrate the complexities of human emotion—even such an apparently basic emotion as fear. Perhaps you aren't afraid of zombies—say, because you utterly disbelieve in the possibility of encountering them. Fair enough; some people aren't afraid of spiders, sharks, or mad dogs either. However, we needn't thus abandon what we have learned here. If we make the reasonable move and apply these insights to emotions and their objects in general, we now have a reasonable and useful structure to frame our investigation. The *feel* of one's emotions is dependent upon the beliefs one has about the objects of one's emotions. Even minute differences in how an object of fear is perceived can drastically change the qualitative character of the emotion. In this manner, our beliefs about objects can teach us about our emotions, our emotions can teach us about our beliefs about objects, and the relationship between the two can teach us much about how our tasty brains work.

NOTES

1. Here, we discount (as being zombies in name only) David Chalmers' (1996) "philosophical zombies"—beings who look and act just like us, but who lack inner conscious experience or "qualia."

2. Most commonly, the fear of fictional creatures will arise in philosophy in terms of what is called the "paradox of fiction"—that in dealing with fiction we seem to inexplicably develop strong emotional reactions to fictional characters and events, things we know do not exist, and yet we seem perfectly rational in doing so. Although we will not deal with this problem directly, we will be sensitive to concerns arising from various proposed solutions to the paradox.

3. Other approaches include "functionalist" views (see Kraut, 1986; Millikan, 1989) and "evolutionary" views (see Matthen, 1998).

4. Kendall Walton (1978: 6) has famously called such an involuntary physiological state (considered apart from any propositional fear) "quasi-fear."

5. Davis distinguishes experiential *fear*, as such, from experiential *anxiety*, which he contends involves the same relationship between propositional fear and involuntary arousal, but without any necessary condition of unhappiness.

6. Gordon contends that non-human animals may experience a *state of fear* (what we would call *physiological fear*) without an underlying *propositional fear*, as they may undergo a fight-or-flight response, which would seem to at least in some cases arise from physiological arousal, but seem to lack the appropriate linguistic faculties and propositional attitudes inherent to propositional fear. (See Gordon: 565).

7. This discussion of fears having a *tendency* to motivate vulnerability avoidance is from Davis (1987: 294–298). Gordon (566–569) argues that fear is not fear *unless* it brings about such avoidance. As Davis makes a strong case that at best there *tends* to be such vulnerability avoidance, we refer to his approach rather than Gordon's.

8. *Rational* agency should be distinguished from *moral* agency, being a capacity (and responsibility) for acting according to moral reasons.

9. Most obviously, the notion of agency seems to conflict with the notion that we are subject to the same universal and necessary laws of the universe as anything else, a theory known as "determinism." For perspectives on this clash, see Watson (1982).

10. Whether in a single film or a series of films, the notion of zombie agency tends to be introduced rather late, with the complexity of the issue giving new life to the associated fear, in the same way that "Big Daddy" gives new reasons for fear among the survivors in *Land of the Dead*.

11. An alternative on zombie agency in fiction is that while themselves unthinking, zombies are like puppets controlled by a zombie master who himself has agency. From this, precisely the same problems arise. See, for example, the 1932 Bela Lugosi film *White Zombie*, the Inferi of *Harry Potter and the Half-Blood Prince* (2009), Piers Anthony's "Xanth" series of novels, and the comic-book series *Tales of the Zombie*.

12. Jentsch is followed in his study of the uncanny by Freud (1919/2003), who takes the matter in a different direction from that of our present concern. The visceral affect of the uncanny is further explored by roboticist Masahiro Mori (1970), though again in a direction transverse to our own.

13. Contamination in this sense might be simply akin to, say, touching uncooked meat, but it may also represent the fear of being *turned into* a zombie. More on this below.

14. In Kirkman's comic-book series, *The Walking Dead* (issue #11), farmer Hershel Greene corrals captured zombies—including that of his own son—in his barn, in the hopes that they may be "cured." In *Shaun of the Dead*, the title character very nearly gets himself shot trying to keep someone else from shooting his mother's corpse. In Stephen King's novel *Pet Sematary* (1983) and its film adaptation (1989), Dr. Louis

Creed buries his recently-killed toddler, Gage, in a Mi'kmaq burial ground known to resurrect the dead, hoping to bring back his son.

15. Here, philosophers tend to rely on imagined examples of "body swapping"—putting the mind of one person into the body of another, and vice versa—contending that "personhood" intuitively follows the mind and not the body. See, for example, Perry (1978).

16. *The Return of the Living Dead* series mark a potential deviation from the norm as, for example, the characters of Freddy and Frank apparently manage to die without any loss of stream of consciousness. They may very well have died midway through speaking a sentence, or they may have died off-screen—on this matter, the film is ambiguous.

17. In the comic-book series *Tales of the Zombie*, told uniquely in the second person, the eponymous character regains the memories of Simon Garth.

18. Craven's film is based very loosely on the non-fiction book of the same title by Wade Davis (1985). Davis's theories regarding Vodou zombification are further explored in *Passage of Darkness: The Ethnobiology of the Haitian Zombie* (1988). The scientific controversy surrounding Davis' theories is explored in Booth (1988).

19. Epicurus, 31, in Oates (1957). Fear of death should notably not be confused with a fear of *dying*, being something else entirely. For an excellent outline and defense of this position, see Green (1982).

20. Throughout the "Dune" series, gholas are ordinarily treated as clones of the deceased. As such, it would be difficult to classify them as zombies. In the case of Idaho, however, it is originally *his* corpse that is resurrected as Hayt.

Rave from the Grave

Dark Trance and the Return of the Dead

GRAHAM ST JOHN*

Amid the aural assault you catch a line from Donne's *Holy Sonnet 10*: "Die not, poor Death, nor yet canst thou kill me." Behind the chilling caterwauls, a petrified girl whispers "Are we still alive?" The former line is used in Xenomorph's (1998) anthemic "Necroid Millenium," and the latter DarKDescendent's "The Invasion" (*Brazilian V.A.Mpires*, 2008), sonic bookends to a decade in "darkpsy," a genre of psychedelic trance (psytrance) music that has arisen in popularity internationally. Also known as "horror trance" or "night trance," performed by DJs before crowds of enthusiasts during the darker hours at psytrance events around the globe, darkpsy revels in the gothic liminality of the zombie, and other monstrous icons. Part of a larger ethnographic and documentary project on psytrance (St John, 2012), this essay investigates dark trance (and zombie raves), documenting how the zombie illustrates a desire for social re-animation among youth in the contemporary world.

Lifted from horror cinema and computer game fiction, apparent in vocal samples, label sensibilities, fashion, and body modifications, and evident in post–apocalyptic aesthetics, the living dead caricature is manifest. Simultaneously dead and alive, with protagonists seeking transit from death to life, the zombie is a liminal figure ready made for the dance party. After all, a tagline for *Return of the Living Dead* exclaimed that the dead were "back from the grave and ready to party." The dance floor has become a critical topos for the zombie since it signifies the desire to return from deteriorating lifeworld conditions, to be revived from the isolation, even social "death," of modern life. It is on the psytrance dance floor that the zombie holds such purchase for it offers a symbolic assemblage emblematic of the altered states of mind and flesh sought and achieved there, an iconic repertoire for the dispossession of routine selfhood. Moreover, it is a device appropriated in the collective performance of re-enchantment from a spiritless and disembodied lifeworld. As the living dead archetype articulates self-dissolution, the zombie has become allegorical of the desire for social revitalization. Yet, the zombie possesses a deep ambivalence that renders

*A huge thanks to Eric Haanstad for his astute commentary on an earlier draft. Thanks also to Rachel Scott for her corrections.

24

this monster an ideal icon for *ecstatic entrancement*. Thus I begin with a discussion of the zombie as a historically ambivalent signifier for ecstatic dance.

Ravenous Crowds, Ecstatic Trance and Demon Jockeys

Rave to the Grave, the fifth and most recent film in the *Return of the Living Dead* franchise, made its debut on the SciFi Channel in October 2005. This teen zombie shlocker directed by Ellory Elkayem offers little relief from the risible deluge that followed the original film in the series. The tale eventually unfolds on a present day Halloween rave, where hundreds of young American party-goers have dropped "Z" capsules, a recreational drug made from the fictional nerve agent "trioxin."[1] With the avaricious student chemist responsible for converting the trioxin into "Z" played by the film's only black actor (Cory Hardrict), it thus offers traces of the mendacious black man, if not the ill-willed "voodoo" priest evident in early zombie cinema. There are no prizes for guessing that the product of this black alchemy transforms white kids into the living dead. Drooling heavily, hallucinating, costumed ravers (some of whom are in "zombie" costume, while others are badly portrayed as "dead head" hippie types) are ultimately motivated to munch on the brains of fellow party-goers, whose demise precedes their reanimation in living death. Vocalizing an uncanny resemblance to anti-rave campaigners, having tried some "Z," Jeremy (the DJ) reports that it "takes you to the height of ecstasy and to the brink of death." If we replace "Z" with "E" ("Ecstasy" or MDMA), its obvious synonym, the comment might have passed from the lips of any number of moral crusaders who've waged tirelessly to ensure that MDMA remains a Schedule One controlled substance in the U.S.—indeed ensuring the passing of legislation that was apparently Reducing America's Vulnerability to Ecstasy (i.e. the so called "RAVE Act").[2] Having said that, if this was a cautionary tale it was produced in the style of a bawdy frat flick, sans Rodney Dangerfield. In one scene, a Z'd-up kid takes a bite out of some cheerleader hiney, a departure from the established motivation: "brains."[3] With the carnage unfolding on the Halloween dance floor, as zombie ravers are driven to wanton acts of savagery, and as the "rave" becomes the context for ravenous excess and less-than-human conduct of the kind that may have occupied the wildest fantasies of anti-rave crusaders (self-)appointed to the task of defending innocence and virtue, the film is set for its apocalyptic finale. A helicopter with "United States of America Police" painted on its side, launches a missile and obliterates the rave. Mission accomplished. While many who have suffered this film will have likely welcomed *any* conclusion, it was an unsettling ending nevertheless, offering Z-grade fatalism to well over a decade of anti-rave and anti–Ecstasy hysteria that, in the Midwest at least, had begun on October 11, 1992. That was the night of the notorious raid on Grave Rave, a Milwaukee Halloween warehouse party where, according to Mireille Silcott (1999: 111), 1,000 ravers were arrested and thrown into jail for the night "on drugs, and in fancy dress."

A bizarre conflation of fact and fantasy emerges. *Rave to the Grave* was released in the same year Utah county Sheriff Tracey deployed all means at his disposal to oversee a massive raid on a rave south of Salt Lake City called "Versus II."[4] The paramilitary operation mounted against a rave with a Biblical reference in one of the most religiously conservative regions of the U.S. involved 90 officers in Kevlar body armor who were equipped with MP5 assault rifles, tear gas, Taser guns, and K9 units. Footage of the white heat-signatures of dance floor revelers illuminated against a night-black background shot from a police helicopter using thermal imaging photography was later used by various news networks, where ravers were thereby portrayed in a fashion that, at that time, was typically reserved for "terrorists"—i.e. those remotely viewed as ghoulish apparitions, often moments before their obliteration via smart bomb. Through this process of public dehumanization, where a field of young people dancing to techno music are transformed into a shambling spectral massive, the party might well be mistaken for a field of zombies. (Mis)representing ravers in this fashion, the footage exposes a phenomenon that has long caused anxiety in the West: the ecstatic trance dancer, and especially collective ecstatic entrancement. I am being very deliberate with this phrase, which does not simply refer to the state of *ecstasy*—associated with the Greek *ekstasis*, which means "to stand outside of oneself," including one's gendered identity (see Gilbert and Pearson, 1999: 104–05; Hemment, 1996: 23), and which implies the retention of self-autonomy, conscious design, or even the body's own prediscursive awarenesss (Landau, 2004)—but an *entranced* state, which implies the relinquishment of individual will and autonomy to an external power, higher energy, or extraordinary life force. The history of electronic dance music (EDM) scenes illustrates commerce between these tendencies which fuel new socio-sensual spaces, cultures, and dance movements. For James Landau (113), the ecstatic condition of the unbound raving body is a "desubjectified cognitive state that can best be understood as a corporeal style of being, i.e. a nonreflective awareness autonomous in its 'freedom' from ideology, language and culture." As we know, "Ecstasy" is the common name for MDMA, the principal club dance drug, desirable and maligned by varying stakeholders. An entactogen facilitating the dissolution of one's personal boundaries, MDMA enables individuals to transcend their separate selves in the company of strangers and friends, potentiating the euphoria of group mindlessness, and yet, subject to constant use and abuse, the same drug (often depleted of MDMA and cut with methamphetamines) may inaugurate personal crises, often associated with the depletion of serotonin. At the same time, a common motivation is to "surrender" one's will to the DJ, his/her (though usually his) affecting rhythm, and the *vibe* predominating. Here one may be said to "spend" one's extraordinary "energy," often assisted by a battery of psychoactives, including LSD and other "psychedelics" like mescaline or psilocybin containing mushrooms, substances which are more commonly designated "entheogens" (along with, for instance, DMT) and are thus ostensibly responsible for *engendering the divine within*.[5] Within psytrance scenes, extraterrestrial aliens and interdimensional allies have been recognized to direct visions, motivate journeys, and enable hallucinations, such as the "machine elves" made popular by Terence McKenna (1993). A combination of these ecstatic and entheogenic states has triggered labels for those so-affected, including "munted," "e-tard," "wasted," "spaced," "tripper," and indeed, "zombie," a not unexpected designation since the latter is a figure both ecstatic (out of one's self) and entranced (animated by an external power).

The zombie is the perfect symbol of ecstatic entrancement, ripe for adoption, for instance, by the Mutoid Waste Co. band who, in mid–1980s London, were the driving force of the post-apocalyptic anarcho–punk rock and proto-rave "zombie beat" warehouse parties held in the squatted Coach Shed behind King's Cross Railway Station on Battle-bridge Road. There, and in other punk and techno/punk crossover scenes, the living dead appealed as a twisted parody, a clown-like caricature of apathy and conformity, yet at the same time a means to become awakened from the hypnagogia of the present. Since George Romero's classic *Night of the Living Dead* and Jorge Grau's *Living Dead at Manchester Morgue* (1974), zombies typically *demonstrate*[6] a loss of faith in social, religious, and political institutions, and have become appealing to those seeking anti-authoritarian symbols, where this figure is equal measure godless goth, heir to a nihilistic wasteland, and libratory anarchist. This monstrous ambiguity lies at the center of the zombie's appeal, notably within the "zombie raves" of the last ten years (especially in the U.S.) where the archetype elicits *unruly-yet-driven* crowd conditions.

The unrestricted movement of the (collective) body in dance has been hazardous to social order throughout history. The undisciplined psychical and physical conditions of ecstatic dance have long concerned fundamentalists and officials who have railed against unruly dance through edicts, confessional codes and moral panics since Plato through Puritan and Protestant reformers (Wagner, 1997). The intoxicated and unsupervised crowd gathering at sites of social pleasure (festivals and dances) has raised particularly acute anxieties around which there have been proscriptions and prohibitions, even brutal repression (Ehrenreich, 2006). Post–1950s *dance cultures*—youth and music cultures for whom ecstatic trance is a principal activity—have been the subject of considerable anxiety. This is the case with ecstatic crowd states associated with jazz and rock and roll, but it is EDM cultures that have evidently caused greatest concern. While pre-rave stimulant based and queer dance cultures, from mod (around 1964–66) to Northern Soul (early 1970s, Wigan and Blackpool), disco (1970s New York and Chicago) and punk (1970s) (see Shapiro, 1999: 20), would raise heat from conservative elements, given its explosive popularity and global scope rave would constitute an especially troublesome field of folk devilry. While acid house posed a threat to Middle England's "rural idyll" in the late 1980s (see Hill, 2002; Sibley, 1997), a more insidious threat became manifest in those combining acid house techno with mobility. While there had been anarchists, crusties and travellers before, raving travellers and sonic squatters would be the loudest and most menacing of freaks. Andrew Hill (2003: 226) observes that the mobility of participants in the early acid house orbital-rave scene rendered them especially threatening to Conservatives for whom the existence of massives trespassing across their rural constituencies proved intolerable. This was illustrated by the fate of the Peace Convoy, the mobile community traveling the seasonal UK free festival circuit who were violently ambushed and decommissioned by police in the 1985 "battle of the beanfield" (Worthington, 2005); and in the response to the explosion of free open-air dance parties operated by Spiral Tribe and other anarchist sound systems who, following the impromptu festival on Castlemorton Common in 1992, were arrested and charged with "conspiracy to cause a public nuisance," sparking one of the longest and most expensive public trials in UK history (see St John 2009a: ch 2). Where sensational stories of "crusty" mobs appeared in *The Sun* and *The Daily Mail* in the early 1990s, the common allusion to "mob" was, as Hill (drawing on Tilly, 1995: 153) observed, not only an abbreviation of "mobility" but an evocation of the *mobile vulgus* evident in the "great unwashed" traversing the English countryside in the 1980s and 1990s. The *mobile vulgus* has a long and lasting legacy, and according to Hill, the anxieties "that surrounded the mobility of participants in Acid House presents an updating of long-running fears that can be traced back to the emergence of modernity and the wandering of the figure of 'the vagabond.' Fears of the vagabond were exacerbated by the unpredictability of this figure's movements, that rendered them harder to monitor and control" (2003: 227). Anxieties over noisy moving vulgarities reach back much further, however.

In seeking explanation for a slate of laws accommodated within the UK's 1994 Criminal Justice Act, especially those defining and incriminating post-rave dance music and party-going outside permitted and surveiled precincts, Jeremy Gilbert (1997) finds some parallels in the time of Plato, who sought the banning of the Bacchanals, disdained as "bestial gatherings." Commenting on the traditional Western abhorrence for the mob outlined by John S. McClellend (1989), Gilbert indicates that the response by authorities signifies the "fear of the unreasoning crowd" whose unstable mobility sees it "[o]scillating unpredictably between unity and plurality" (8). A crowd that is *both* unreasoning (compulsive) and purposed (compelled) is the beast that must be slain: corralled, tagged, shot in the head. Given that raving, a word harkening back to early 1950s and 1960s traditional jazz scenes in the UK where it evoked apprehension (McKay, 1996: 103), potentiates a condition which is "precisely neither a purposeless mass nor a unified collective entity with a definite purpose" (Gilbert: 9), this "group organism" in Douglas Rushkoff's (2004: xiv) terms, would be subject to ordinance and surgical interventions resembling efforts to contain the explosive carnival, which has historically threatened to break its cultural levees and swamp the everyday, becoming a rampaging "carnival without closure" (Presdee, 2000: 52). A critical part of the problem for authorities is that the unlicensed organic dance carnival possesses indeterminate spatial and temporal parameters. With undefined conditions of mind and body, combined with uncertain physical and temporal boundaries, states resort to sometimes brutal efforts to vanquish the raving demon.

Response to the carnivalesque mob is reminiscent, perhaps even nourished, by the mythology of Dionysus, particularly as conveyed in *The Bacchae*. Indeed, in efforts to make sense of the local reaction to a psytrance party she co-organized in Chianti, Italy, in 2008, Chiara Baldini (2010) finds Euripides' Fifth Century B.C.E. story highly resonant. In *The Bacchae*, the cult of Dionysus holds a mesmerizing affect on the citizens of Thebes, particularly women, some of whom, driven into a savage frenzy, hunt down and tear apart the body of King Pentheus. This cultic response, Baldini argues, holds mythic correlation with the figure of the DJ, who, in Chianti, were foreigners, Goa freaks, techno-hippies, widely travelled (typically male) freak-ambassadors, who, with charismatic dreadlocks, exotic tattoos, strange piercings, and effeminate appearances, were "perfect representatives of the foreign god, the god who arrives, the god of dancing, clamour, nocturnal feasts, some of the most common epithets of Dionysus" (Baldini: 176). Often perceived as a lone agent animating the dance floor massive (despite the reality that a network of musicians, producers, technicians, designers, performers, stage managers, and of course the dancers themselves, are involved), the DJ is an ambiguous figure who may hold a *rapturous* or *rupturing* impact, becoming the target of desire and enmity. As Baldini observed, the manager of the park where the Chianti party occurred, and other locals, held the abject "hippies," especially the DJs, with contempt, a prejudice fueling their curiosity.

The cult of Dionysus, as portrayed in *The Bacchae*, is more generally a mythical embodiment of the ambivalence associated with ecstatic trance, offering a caution to the threat posed to social order. Cautions are sometimes not nearly enough, as when disturbed revolutionaries take it upon themselves to crash the party. Pizza deliveryman, Kyle Huff, performed this task in Seattle on March 26, 2006. After attending an all-age zombie-themed rave called Better Off Undead, and having spray-painted "NOW" on the pavement outside, Huff walked into an after party with a 12-gauge pistol-grip shotgun, a handgun, and several bandoliers, shooting dead six people before fatally turning a gun on himself. The Capital Hill massacre was apparently motivated by Huff's twisted hatred for the lifestyle of "hippy" ravers, as conveyed in a note he allegedly wrote to his twin brother. Whatever Huff's apocalypse "NOW" was designed to achieve, the incident fueled hysterics regarding the socially rupturing conditions of rave, with the *Seattle Times*, for example, calling for a "thorough review" of all-age raves (Feit and Savage, 2006).[7]

Fortunately, such extreme responses are rare. But, the anxieties that Baldini faced in Italy are redolent within transnational psytrance. Israel, where psytrance is a popular music, is exemplary. Following centuries of dormancy, notes Assaf Sagiv (2000), the Bacchanalia "returned with an intensity unknown since the end of the classical period [...] the ancient fertility cults which the zealous followers of the Hebrew God sought to extirpate three thousand years ago have come to life again in the land of Israel." While this 1990s "culture of ecstasy" generated a moral panic among Zionists for whom growing youth transnationalism (Meadan, 2001) had cast a Dionysian shadow across the Holy Land, aggressive policing tactics have been adopted throughout Europe in efforts to contain the raving trance menace. In 2003, for example, the third annual Samothraki Festival (attracting 10,000 people, including thousands of foreign "freaks"[8]) held on the northern Aegean island by that name was broken up by Greek police. This was noteworthy, not least since that event, in the region associated with the cult of Dionysus, was terminated by authorities in the year prior to the Athens Olympic Games, the institutionalized exultation of altered states of human consciousness in its most legitimate, individualized, and productive form: competitive sport. Conflated with "hedonism," the "Dionysian" has grown to signify an unindividuated mass, a collective figure without objective other than that of reckless consumption, the drive to excess. But at the same time, a desirable experience that, if bottled, could be shifted for a tidy sum. The Dionysian holds an ambivalence that is apparently only matched by the figure of the zombie, or more accurately, the "zombie apocalypse," where the Dionysian may be said to have been reborn in the contemporary.

In recent history, in media panics and public commentary, moral champions have fulminated in response to transgressive dance moves and movements, trance cults and cultures, while others have invoked the allegory of the zombie to characterize antagonists as braindead massives in possession of base appetites, ravenous consumers, soulless as much as mindless, all body without functioning organs. Within fundamentalist Christian circles, and certainly if we are to follow the author of the now defunct website www.truthaboutraves.com who performed a disturbing, if not darkly humorous, Increase Mather impression, the raver is possessed by the devil himself. More generally, a loss of faith is considered to precipitate a fall into the godless path of the non-believer, who walks, nay shambles, into temptation. In other sermons, the unconscious are transfigured by commodities, the fetishizing of things under capital. They are thus animated by possessive materialism, as notably conveyed in Romero's 1978 shopocalypse, *Dawn of the Dead*. And if it's not possessions that are performing the work of possession, it is a kind of "false consciousness" that entrances, for instance, the wretched "hippie" who, dispossessed of establishment values, rational faculties and even his/her humanity, is hypnotized by cult leaders or activated by drugs into zombified violence such as that characterizing "The Family" in *The Omega Man* (1971) and the psychotic acid-taking anti-hippies of *Blue Sunshine* (1977). Derogation falls on raver-tourists forming massives zoned-out in rituals of "disappearance" from the lifeworld, blissfully anaesthetized from meaning yet all the while animated, if only by forlorn efforts to simulate hippies (Melechi, 1993; Rietveld, 1993). Simon Reynolds (1997: 86–7) became especially damning of the "loved up" rave scene. "Suddenly," he railed,

> the clubs are full of dead souls, zombie-eyed and prematurely haggard. Instead of togetherness, sullen moats of personal space reappear; smiley faces give way to sour expressions, bitter because they've caned it so hard that the buzz can't be recovered. For some, any old oblivion will do; they become connoisseurs of poisons, mix 'n' matching toxins to approximate the old high.

And special criticism is reserved for UK hardcore of late 1992 when "happy rave tunes gave way to 'dark side' jungle. Stripping away the squeaky voices and melodramatic strings ... DJ/producers created minimalist drum & bass, the voodoo sound of compulsion for compulsion's sake."

Zombiedom here follows Reynold's pharmacological raveology: the turn from collective meaning and identification into individualized excesses. Still, it's a more sympathetic reading of popular dance forms than, say, Adorno. For the latter, the "jitterbug" exemplified the zombified masses of the 1930s and 1940s swept from individuality into the mental slavery of standardized mass consumerism, where choice is a charade. Indictments cross into the aesthetics of dance music movements too, whose torchbearers have been known, for instance, to lay charges against a soulless "robotic" music whose dancehalls are haunted by human automaton. In the 1970s habitués of disco were often taken to be mindless zombies by proponents of various other musics, from punk to funk. Among the former were London punk rock act Disco Zombies, and among the latter George Clinton, though his attack on "metronomic" disco also harbored contempt for an unreproductive (gay) dance music (see Shapiro, 2005: 111). Inheriting DJ techniques and a dance sensibility that had evolved in the New York disco underground, the "freak" trance dance scene in Goa, India, has also attracted critique of interest to us. By the late 1990s, after the rise and fall of "Goa trance" as a marketed label and the escalation of rave tourism to the region, Arun Saldanha was prompted to deploy the language of the zombie in his ethnography of Goa trance parties (in Goa). In a Deleuzian race materialist approach, Saldanha identifies "the zombie-like density of white bodies" on Anjuna's "zombie beach" (2007: 191), with the implication that, seeking distance from domestic tourists, Goa freaks become an individually undifferentiated white mob of varying nationalities. In this perspective, reinforced in Saldanha's dialogue with freak interlocutors — where the latter pass for little more than vapid spooks and the interviewer a social scientist of the zombie — we are introduced to the exclusive world of the "pathologically viscous" (ibid.: 89) mob, who are collectively animated by the goal of becoming wasted, consuming their own minds, seeking and obtaining the luxurious. Voracious drug monsters with no life outside the excesses of the present.

Dark Trance: The Carnival of the Dispossessed

Dark trance is a genre of psytrance, an electronic dance music culture emerging from "Goa trance" that mutated into a transnational movement with a multitude of regional scenes (see St John, 2010a). Where Goa trance offered the distinct possibility of self-transcendence achieved through virtual outer-space travel and the concomitant cosmic contact with an other (alien) self, the comparatively sinister "darkpsy" is nevertheless cloaked in a playful Dark Romantic sensibility. While the psychedelic gnosis remains evident, by stark contrast to other genres emerging in the psychedelic electronic continuum, such as "progressive psychedelic" (or "morning" trance), dark or "night" trance is shaped by a distinctly gothic "sonic fiction" (Eshun, 1998). Optimized for the nocturnal conditions of psytrance parties and festivals that have flourished globally and which host a range of psychedelic electronic genres, darkpsy possesses fast, sometimes punishing, bpm (beats per minute) starting at around 150 and pushing up over 170, typically employing vocal samples and scores from horror cinema produced on tracks which, when performed by DJs in conjunction with the efforts of VJs, lighting technicians, décor artists and stage designers, effect dancescapes infused with suspense during those hours of the sun's absence. But, while the effect is to orchestrate a socio-sonic nightmare, the "horror" is rarely absolute since the nightscape is patterned by elements consistent with the carnivalesque: outrageous symbolic recombinations, asymmetrical humor, high merriment. The night-trancescape often holds shlock-horror exploitation aesthetics along the lines of the *House of 1000 Corpses* (2003) mixed with *Hostel II* (2007) and *Scooby-Doo on Zombie Island* (1998). We might even suggest that the dance topos is dark-ludic in character, where the "horror" is as abstruse as the zombie itself, a figure as terrifying as it is comical, sinister albeit dead-ordinary, holding an uncanny familiarity yet strangely unknowable.

Having said this, darkpsy antagonists are committed to reproducing an atmosphere that is certifiably gothic by comparison to "morning trance" and "progressive trance." This is the landscape of the dark carnival which has transited from the festal aesthetic ruled by the sun. Darkpsy emerged as a recognized and marketed genre coinciding with the post–Iraq invasion period, in which German, Russian, and Brazilian artists have dominated. Among the first wave of darkpsy, the Manic Dragon Records compilation series, *Multiple Personalities*, raised a standard around themes that were to become prevalent in the genre: schizoid behavior, psychosis, dark influences. The series name is a clever reference to the two artists who would typically collaborate on each album track. The first album of that series was mastered by German dark trance pacesetter Mark Petrick (aka Xenomorph), who in fact performs opposite himself on the release. "Schzoid Transpersonal Progressions" by Xenomorph vs Xenomorph (*Multiple Personalities*, 2005) conjures cruel winds that howl over a quickening heartbeat. Sonic experiments in the dark side reach back some distance within psychedelic electronica, at least to the alien ambience of Juno Reactor who encounter the realm beyond in the haunting hour length odyssey "Lu.ci-ana" (*Luciana*, 1994). But it was Petrick who had drawn the circle and imported the dark occult into the psychedelic trance continuum. With a post-apocalyptic sensibility, his is a sonic screed on a world gone mad, as captured on the now classic "Abominations" (*Cassandra's Nightmare*, 1998), which stepped off the precipice with a reading from the work of "Sutter Cane" in John Carpenter's 1995 film *In the Mouth of Madness*, and a harrowing line from *Exorcist III* (1990): "God is not with us now, there is only the darkness here, and your death."[9] In 2003, Petrick released the Hermetic Kabbalah inspired *Qlippoth* on his own Gnostic Records. Speckled like an old B&W film suffering from magnetic tape deterioration, the opening track "Sepulchre" uses lines from Roman Polanski's *The Fearless Vampire Killers* (1967) and the Italian gothic horror film *Black Sunday* (aka *The Mask of the Demon*) (1960), from which the 17th-century condemned witch Princess Asa Vajda (played by Barbara Steele) announces: "it is I who repudiates you and in the name of Satan I place a curse upon you. Go ahead, tie me down to the stake."

Within dark trance, losing one's mind is the zeitgeist projected in an interactive theater. In the lead up to this, across a range of EDMs, from techno and breakbeat, and harder and faster bass styles on the "speedcore" or "terrorcore" continuum, the 1990s saw an accelerating complexity in form, with frenetic and fractured bass lines hurtling dancers into disorienting frenzies, twisting bodies amid the breaks, destabilizing minds in a cacophony of muffled TV news-bites and radio broadcasts, with countless spokespersons issuing a white noise of unintelligible communications. This development might have been expressed in X-Dream's sample from Allie Light's documentary *Dialogues with Mad Women* (1994) where the experience is reported to be like having "several radio stations inside your head" (on the title track from *Radio*, 1998), but this was before the arrival of a distinct 21st-century horror trance with its dedication to experimenting with new music software and cinematic vocal samples, film scores and game sound tracks to affect the sensation of a fractured self. The frisson was worked, for instance, by Australian Adam Walter (aka Scatterbrain), whose proto-dark trance album *Infernal Angel* (2003) hosts the brooding "Possessed" in which Professor Pacoli from *The Fifth Element* (1997) is heard to announce that "when the three planets are in eclipse, the black hole like a door is opened. Evil comes spreading terror and chaos." The mood is then upstaged by Darth Vader who drops the heavy wood: "If you only knew the power of the dark side." After becoming committed to the mental asylum in "Scattergram" (which exploits samples from *One Flew Over the Cuckoo's Nest*, 1975), by the album's end listeners have been made intimate with the dark side. More generally, artists have sought to exploit a nightscape vulnerability where dance floor occupants are suspended inside the grindhouse story lines of slasher thrillers. Chainsaws are common, as sonic surf-riders flee from the serrated leads, are pounded into submission, carved into segments. A sense of hopelessness pervades this aesthetic, and within the dread caterwauls Demonizz (on "Aknofobia," *Contagion Vol. 1*, 2008) bursts out with "do I look like someone who cares what God thinks?" Amid the godless ambience, a little girl breathes: "My mommy always said there were no monsters. No real ones. But there are, aren't there?" To which Ellen Ripley (from the 1986 film *Aliens*) responds: "Yes, there are" (Chi-A.D. "Monsters," *Neighbourhood*, 1999). A decade later, inside escalating War on Terror bpm and adrenalin kickdrums, a pandemic has taken hold, fast predators lurk, and a boy whispers: "They come for me when it's dark" ("Inferno" by Principles of Flight, *Ministry of Chaos* compiled by Mindcore, Yabai, 2008). Encounters with the diabolical provoke fear-filled inquiries: "What was that?" (on Gorump Peyya vs Acid Goblins' "Brain Hack," *Multiple Personalities 3*, Manic Dragon, 2008); or more pointedly "What the fuck is that?" (Mindcore's title track on *Ministry of Chaos*, Yabai, 2008). Questions keep mounting as, with the assistance of muffled screams and soundscapes of unspeakable suffering lifted from horror cinema and survivor games, DJs replicate a host of demons, invoke curses, call in mass abductions, and orchestrate broad-spectrum uncertainty. Walking among and menacing human-kind, the monstrous are liminal figures whose anomalous characteristics render them attractive to dark trance DJs and enthusiasts thrilled by the atmosphere of the sonic creepshow. Amid growing threat-levels and accelerated beats, dark carnival goers tour the edges of in/human nature, sightseeing their own monstrous potential, where "they" might in fact be *us*, and "it" *you*.

Dark trance carries a sonic fiction that, as a variation on the pursuit of transcendence within psytrance, amplifies and projects the shadows of the mind. But rather than depicting an insane, mad, or even "dark," figure, the typical zombie is bereft of subjectivity, is a shambling corpse — indeed our own shambling corpse. While Frankenstein and his contemporaries show up here (to demonstrate the tragic potential of science and technology) there is arguably no more unsettling "they" or "it" than the zombie, for this is a tragic figure emblematic of our mortal fate, ultimately triggering insecurities associated with annihilation of cognizance in a godless universe. According to Jamie Russell (2006: 8), the zombie is a symbol of humankind's most primitive anxiety: the fear of death. Expanding on this theme, Sarah Juliet Lauro and Karen Embry (2008: 89–90) argue that it signifies the terror associated with our inevitable loss of consciousness. This lumbering specter holds a mirror to the "inanimate end to which we each are destined." The zombie's own craving for "brains," the seat of cognizance, signifies the undignified struggle for immortality in a world emptied of spirit. Thus, Multi Evil's "Brains Only" (*Double Trouble*, No Comment Records, 2008) samples the notorious dialogue between embalmer Ernie Kaltenbrunner and a live corpse in *Return of the Living Dead*:

ERNIE KALTENBRUNNER: Why do you eat people?
ZOMBIE: Not people. Brains.
KALTENBRUNNER: Why?
ZOMBIE: The PAIN!
KALTENBRUNNER: What about the pain?
ZOMBIE: The pain of being DEAD!

I suppose it could be argued that this dialogue speaks to the voracious appetite belonging to a distinctly American nihilism, concentrated alongside other greedy and groping monsters eagerly consumed (Latham, 2002), or to the deadening effect of labor under capitalism (Newitz, 2006). Yet here, the intention is rather mute, an echo of the fact that the monster's own voice is rarely heard. But while this poses a challenge to digital poachers, zombie cinema remains a rich resource of sonic data lifted and remixed in the psychedelic theatre of the festal trance dance floor where habitués are exposed to "white label" sounds — that is, tracks that have not yet been released, but which offer creative reworkings of existing material to diverse audiences with varying experience and expectations. Those who will have recognized the origins of the lines sampled by Exaile on "Let Loose" (2004) may have smirked in recognition as Johnny mocks his sister at the beginning of *Night of the Living Dead*: "They're coming to get you, Barbra[...]. They're coming for you! [...] Look, there comes one of them now!" While most will have been blind to their exposure to classic zombie dialogue, they couldn't have avoided the fact that many more of "them" were on their way. Trancers will likely have been more familiar with the lines from the 2004 remake of *Dawn of the Dead* reproduced by Ananda Shake on "Caution" (2005), including: "Are these people alive or dead?" Dropping victims into the dance-zone of a first person screamer, "Zombies" by Russian darkpsy producer Dezkizzio doesn't offer much resolution to the inquiry, the title of the Various Artists album on which it was released only contributing to the perplexity: *Don't Forget About It to Remember* (2009). Icons of a noctambulistic fantasy gained appeal among participants in an EDM culture seeking to forget their troubled lives, which perhaps evinces the popularity of Hollywood's *Resident Evil* game/film franchise among Israeli psytrance producers including Dynamo, Space Monkey and Psytekk.

As these examples demonstrate, the zombie would become the perfect icon for the night carnival of rave, and more specifically trance. Espousing a view Stallybrass and White (1986) will have found curious, "[t]rampling over our cherished certain certainties," according to Russell "the zombie is, above all else, a symbol of our ordered universe turned upside down as death becomes life and life becomes death" (8). What precisely is the nature of trance within this carnivalesque environ? As psytrance events involve extraordinary behavior across a spectrum of spectacular self-presentations and altered states of consciousness, its self-identifiable "trance" is rather more complex than common historical and analogical reference to West African derived "possession trance" implies (see St John, 2009b; 2012). Enthusiasts who dance across a spectrum of behavior may be seen to seek *dispossession from* a troubled and dispiriting lifeworld. This is a complex transitional world. While some seek forgetfulness, perhaps even an apocalypse of subjectivity, others are unusually compelled to alter their personal and social circumstances (see St John, 2010b). Passing into (ego) death and yet animated, the zombie is a transitional figure par excellence, offering a performative repertoire of symbols and gestures. Indeed it is a folk trope exhumed and fashioned as a parodic axiom for the unpredictable yet potentially transcendent condition of the dance floor. Being simultaneously dead and alive, anaesthetized and mobilized, is the source of its semiotic excesses, which likely accounts for the zombie's continuing success and explosive reappearance across cultural, media and dancescapes, from "fleshmobs" (a variation of "flashmobs," also called "zombie walks" or "zombie crawls"),[10] to zombie themed darkpsy events, such as the tribute to Lucio Fulci and George Romero, "Dance with the Zombies," held on 31 October, 2009 (Halloween/Samhain) in Basel, Switzerland by Hotzenplotz. That event featured a solid lineup of darkpsy artists including Italian, Dark Whisper, and screened films such as Fulci's *City of the Living Dead* (1980) and *Zombie Flesh Eaters* (aka *Zombie*, 1979), Romero's *Night of the Living Dead* and *Dawn of the Dead*, and Dario Argento's *Suspiria* (1977). All artists performed in zombie drag fashioned by a make-up artist (likely Gino De Rossi) who worked on Fulci's films.

Zombie Apocalypse: Staying Alive, Dead

Darkpsy's embrace of a post-apocalyptic ecstasy, manifest in diverse cinematic depictions of the living dead and other post-human states, signals an attraction to renewal. Trance enthusiasts are implicated in a seasonal festal culture, and are thus heir, if sometimes remote, to intercalary events in which death/rebirth is historically ritualized, and in which vitality is made integral to celebrations of death. It is possible that open-air psytrance festivals condense this cycle in the course of a day or a week, with, for instance, the diurnal activities of the typical summer psytrance celebration punctuated by a noctivagous carnivalesque where the fete grows a Halloween-like ambience after dark, and before sunrise. Indeed, mortality is integral to fall seasonal celebrations, exemplified by Halloween which is rooted in the Celtic harvest festival of Samhain which marked the end of summer when the dead — ghosts, demons, fairies, etc. — walked among the living (Rogers, 2003). But Halloween has become a complex festival in North America and elsewhere. While imitation of the dead and otherworldly beings in contemporary forms of "mumming" (masking and costumes) continues, October 31 magnifies a brazen tricksterism, a youthful vitality, defiant in the face of death. This defiance echoes a hipster individualism deeply rooted in the American imaginary (Leland, 2004), and holding an even deeper legacy in European Romantic traditions, which came to a head in the 1960s when the revitalizing function of seasonal celebrations was appropriated in the interests of alternative cultural demands, often characterized as a "return" or "transition" (to compassion, to the senses, the body, nature). It was the "hippie" or "freak" who inhabited the grounds of this "transition," a liminal figure performing the transit between social formations, living between worlds, perhaps even remaining there as a career liminary. In the freedom from a life perceived as soulless and impassive, stifled by ordinance, dictated by religious dogma and mediated by news cartels, an experiential authenticity has long motivated dissidents such as hippies, the Beats and their rootless predecessors in bohemian enclaves and in Romantic, traveler and pagan traditions over the last two centuries. Motivated by the drive to radical immanence, improvisation, and sensuality, the pursuit of a culture counter to that predominating lays claim to the possibility of the Self's unmediated encounter with the Other. While we can postulate that this state of alterity is experientially diverse, and that it involves shared altered states of consciousness assisted by a range of psychoactive substances from cannabis and charas, to ketamine and methamphetamines, MDMA, LSD and DMT, darkpsy contextualizes an especially gothic psychedelicism heir to this tradition.

Unlike the restless spirit who seeks passage to the afterlife, committed to make transit back to life, the zombie is a figure ready-made for this revitalizing freakscape. Perhaps this is what Ady Connor (aka Scorb) had in mind with tracks titled "Rave from the Grave (Squid Inc. rmx v2)" (*Further Ambivalent Tendencies*, 2005), and later "Rave to the Grave" (*Snowlightz*, 2008). It is no coincidence that the dance party/festival has become prime real estate for the zombie caricature since this space offers habitués the opportunity to become enervated from the doleful matrix of unfulfilling labor, of dead-end careers and relationships, an open-air zone often situated in forest, desert, beachfront or bushland where one might awaken from one's *screenage* detachment from nature's elements and cycles. It is, furthermore, a desire to be enervated from states of social isolation, a circumstance involving alternative states of embodiment enabled by the furious pace of the night and in the swarm organism of the party where the individual body exceeds its own limits. And yet curiously, as noted already, the swarm possesses a collective intelligence, a hive-mind we know as the "vibe." The vibe approximates that which Victor Turner deemed "existential communitas." A Latin term borrowed from Paul Goodman meaning "a relatively undifferentiated community, or even communion of equal individuals" (Turner, 1969: 96), "communitas" is characterized by a speechless synchronistic social conflagration which "presses always to universality and ever-greater unity" (Turner, 1973: 202). The zombie is strikingly resonant with this theme especially in its post–1950s incarnation as a swarm of the afflicted bent on increasing their own numbers, as in *Zombies of Mora Tau* (1957), or dedicated to self-replication within the post–apocalyptic scenario of the *Invasion of the Body Snatchers* (1956)—the cinematic advent of the zombie communitas, or *zommunitas*. While cinematic zombies do not typically share a momentous interactive synchronicity, as do those experiencing the communitas of religious pilgrimage, and while participation in the trance-rave is typically anathema to the acts of barbarism associated with the zombie, the ravenous zombie ultimately seeks boundaries that are "ideally coterminous with those of the human species" (Turner, 1969: 131). Perhaps Elias Canetti's (1962) "crowds," especially those animated by the desire for "increase," are even more apt here given the pathos endemic to their character.

But for the trancer, the zombie demonstrates social revitalization. And so here the zombie is never simply pathological, a harbinger of doom, nor signaling humankind's fall from grace, but a figure whose exhumation and reanimation allegorizes a revival, howsoever temporarily, from the listless isolation and social entombment of the present. The vampire could hardly be axiomatic here since that monster is singular, aristocratic, individual, and thus not the embodiment of the crowd, the great unwashed. The zombie is rarely elevated as is Dracula, but is to be gazed upon as one would a mirror, a window upon ourselves in our most othered (i.e. dead) condition. While this vehicle of transcendence from isolated rationality may be post-apocalyptic, we learn much about the mode of "apocalypse" assumed from the "splatstick" screenplay of popular "zom com" films like *Return of the Living Dead*, Peter Jackson's *Braindead* (1992), and *Shaun of the Dead*. These films made concerted efforts to rupture mortal boundaries as the dead crash the party, storm the orgy and swarm the pub. In Jackson's film, the freaky antagonists were back from the dead, and having taken their stimulants, became the life of the after (death) party. As Russell writes, these films:

> confront the abject with a buoyant sense of playfulness. Certainly there is horror and disgust in their visions of body trauma and secretions, but its playfully neutered[...]. Indeed these movies are at their best when highlighting the way in which this Otherness suggests an absurd universe that may be godless but appears to have its own internal comic logic. Physical existence is tinged with comic ignominy [158].

This mortifying luddism has crept into electrosonic fiction. With tongue firmly in cheek, the following marketing detail evokes B-grade zombie cinema. In a variation of the plot in *Return of the Living Dead* (and in Steve Miner's 2008 *Day of the Dead* remake), the digi-pak gatefold on *Attack of the Living Trance Zombies* compiled by DJ Pantiestheclown (2008) offers a causal explanation for zombie trancers in a botched weapons experiment,

> years ago some of the worlds top scientists and psychologists tried to create the ultimate mind control device. The intended result was to be a powerful weaponized sound wave capable of

incapacitating millions. According to recently de-classified documents, that experiment went terribly wrong. The test subjects were dancers at an open air festival in rural North Carolina. The results were unspeakable. Many of the dancers became so entranced they became zombies. Neither alive nor dead, incapable of anything except movement to the sound, these undead trancers craved only the frequencies which created them. Even the scientists themselves were unable to resist the overwhelming sound waves. Almost all records and traces of this experiment were erased. The sounds were thought to be destroyed until several months ago outbreaks started occurring all over the world. Apparently the wavelengths were uncovered and restored by an eccentric sound manipulator known as pantiestheclown with some help from friends across the world. These frequencies are very dangerous and should be handled with caution. There are no known survivors from exposure to this pandemic. Be advised, LISTEN AT YOUR OWN RISK, and prepare yourself for THE ATTACK OF THE LIVING TRANCE ZOMBIES!!!!*

This narrative clearly associates trancers with the zombie trope. It also speaks to the effect of optimized sound production and performance effecting altered states, a theme evident in zombie cinema since the "ultrasonic" reanimating machine in Jesús Franco's *The Brides of Dr. Jekyll* (1964). Involving an incapacitating "sound wave," the cause is contextually appropriate for entrancement, and the DJ assumes the role of wicked alchemist. In other productions, legendary live sound alchemists, Eat Static, held their own views care of Ed Wood's 1959 cult classic and popular candidate for worst film ever made, *Plan 9 from Outer Space*, which features a race of extraterrestrial beings in flying saucers reanimating the dead who are motivated to inflict world-wide chaos. The cover of Eat Static's *Alien Artifacts* (2004) features self-exhuming dead apparently responding to the signals of an overhead flying saucer, and the cover of *De-Classified* (2007) features a Soviet fighter tailed by a flaming flying saucer, with *Plan 9* quotes splattered across its eclectic soundscapes.

The embrace of increasingly complex cinematic zombie motifs and motives within psytrance amplifies the monster's inherent ambiguity. Traditionally "a potent symbol of the apocalypse," the zombie expressed fears of being abducted into eternal slavery, becoming a living dead workforce, anxieties that gave life to the zombie in its homeland of post-revolutionary Haiti, enervating its initial popularity in the U.S. in the 1930s (i.e. during the Great Depression) and its "economic zombification" of the American populace. It then became an expression of further anxieties throughout the 20th-century including domestic and racial tension, Cold War paranoia about Communist brainwashing, post–1960s political disenfranchisement, and AIDS era body horror (Russell: 8). These trends do not, however, account for the efflorescence of the zombie as an allegory for revitalization in the present. The zombie is no longer simply a doom-laden nihilist, but is coded with subjectivity, even a possible symbol of hope. Recently, there has been an argument, a "manifesto" no less, claiming the zombie as a "paradox that disrupts the entire system," a "slave rebellion" and not simply a "slave." Invoking the "negative dialectic" of Marcuse, and signaling the death of the individual necessary for a posthuman (post-capitalist) future already lived in the present, here the zombie harbors greater value for what it is not than what it is (Lauro and Embry: 94, 96). I make no such claims here since, for one thing, literary and cinematic mutations have seen the trope depart dramatically from de-subjectified states. In Romero's oeuvre especially, zombie subjectivity has evolved significantly, even becoming politically engaged and morally empathetic in *Land of the Dead*. As Russell (189) observes, in that

Reprinted with permission from Nicolo Pastor of Psyber Tribe Records, San Francisco. Compiled by Nathan Powers.

film the enigmatic black character "Big Daddy" is like "a zombified Black Panther, a civil rights revolutionary who leads this living dead underclass on a riot against the Establishment." While one might even posit that the ragtag ghoul army in that film signifies terrorist "blow back" on the administration of Bush II, the return of the globally oppressed, here I want to simply state that the caricature, in its varying guises, offers a narrative and performative repertoire, one that appears to evoke a more millenarian than apocalyptic symbol.

But the precise condition of this subjectivity remains a moot point, a symptom of the icon's ambiguity. In efforts to establish distinction from those considered bereft of cultural cache, the language of the zombie emerges to maintain what Sarah Thornton (1996) identified as "subcultural capital." "Progressive" sensibilities are formed against the rabble of unlearned proles of "full on" and "dark" trance, whose mob-like *karahana* (which in Israel refers to the condition of "going crazy" in the context of a trance party) reinforces the sophistication and intelligence of detractors. Yet, at the same time the zombie trope is wielded by those for whom it is an appealing marker of identity. This appears to be the case, for example, with the annual "Zombie Butt Touch" party in Philadelphia, PA initiated by Keith Tritton in 2007. Featuring a diverse lineup of DJs though predominantly psytrance, the third annual event on April 4, 2009, named Dance of the Dead, was promoted as "a fully zombified extravaganza featuring professional zombie makeup artists." Here, the zombie trope is adopted within an inclusive, eclectic and open ethos which differentiates rave/trance from more exclusive or paranoid scenes (i.e. where you may find a limited range of music styles). And thus here we encounter the zombie-as-everyman, the very article of unpretentiousness, embracing rather than afraid of the "other," a grotesque figure sprouting from the petri-dish of Bakhtin's (1968) carnival, a figure whose organic decaying form, funky shuffle and death-like liveliness is axiomatic of a common humanity, a "down to earth" persona. The performance of the "zombie" trope within psytrance may then articulate the desire for freedom from distinctions, an inclusivity, it might be pointed out, which contributed to the tragedy of Seattle's Capital Hill massacre, where the killer — unknown to others at the "zombie rave" — was invited to an after-party where he took several lives, including his own.

But this hardly prevents efforts to belong to the night, where inhabitants of the dark carnival discharge their personal resources, unwinding and exceeding their selves in synesthetic tapestries. Dousing and arousing their sensoriums with a variety of chemical compounds, animated by frantic polyphonic bass-lines, engulfed in theatrical haze, pierced by laser light, a loose foot in front, an arm dangling here, and a head swiveling there, enthusiasts of the interactive creep-show shamble into the night. By 5:00 A.M., throwing their bones under a raging storm of electronic voodoo in the shadows of subsonic speaker cabinets stacked high, nasal fluids have dried in rivulets on ghoulish faces. Dwelling for hours in the direct line of siege breaking decibels, they have been exposed to a sonic maelstrom, and are committed to a collective exertion which Emile Durkheim might have deemed "effervescent." In festivals of longer duration, where sweat, hair and effluvia have been stomped into the dance floor over several days and nights, a *collective putrescence* is a more accurate description. But where decadence and waste prevail, the signs are that habitués are not afraid of truly living, having discharged, indeed shared, their "accursed share" in Georges Bataille's (1988) terms. Far from a realm in which patrons become tragically dispossessed of their lives, these are experimental laboratories in which life is consumed and shared at its fullest, and in which limits (of the body and mind) are continually tested and exceeded.

Conclusion

The zombie is the chief icon adopted in this ongoing experiment. While it may lack in brains, the zombie is a profound device through which to think. This indeed indexes the role of monsters of which the zombie is the most perplexing exemplar. This essay has discussed dark trance in an effort to further our understanding of the role of this anomalous figure in modern life. Simultaneously dead *and* alive, the zombie is an ambivalent symbol burdened with an excess of meaning. Dance movements characterized by ecstatic entrancement have been contexts for the variable adoption of this figure and its fleshy and semiotic excesses. Moral, cultural and intellectual authorities have invoked the zombie to characterize dance cultures as vulgar, spiritless and braindead massives, evoking fears of the mob, apprehension of states of collective abandonment, mindless consumption, racial discrimination and apathy. For protagonists, however, we find an unequivocal appropriation of, and identification with the gothic liminality of the zombie, an archetypal icon of dispossession, by signaling the simultaneous rupturing of rational selfhood, and performance of collective animation. From zombie raves to dark trance, the living-dead caricature is allegorical for the desire to transcend states of disembodied isolation and loneliness, its popularity burlesquing the desire for social revitalization.

NOTES

1. In the *Return* films, "trioxin" is experimented with by a bumbling U.S. military whose objective of raising a zombie army, the "voodoo" superweapon, is contiguous with a cinematic trope since *The Revolt of the Zombies* (1936).

2. The British film *The Scotland Yard Mystery* (1934) was possibly the first film depicting the death-like trance effects of a drug (and likely echoing rising social anxieties about alcohol or marijuana use).

3. Though, it should be stated that these rules had already been "broken" in earlier sequels with, for instance, the zombie temptress Julie of *Return of the Living Dead III* (1993) getting razor sharp on her fellatio victim Mogo—arguably eating the "small brain." See also Rushton, forthcoming.

4. It is largely due to the amateur film shot by Jeff Coombs, which was immediately uploaded to the Internet, that people around the U.S. and the world were alerted to the gravity of this incident.

5. An "entheogen" has been designated as a substance which evokes the divine within (see Roberts, 2001). DMT (*N*,*N*-Dimethyltryptamine) is a tryptamine naturally-occurring in many plants worldwide and is created in small amounts by the human body during metabolism.

6. Rooted in the Latin *monstrō*, meaning to demonstrate or display (see Gelder, 2000: 81), a "monster" possesses a "pedagogic intention," its grotesque form and recombinant symbolism throwing into relief core elements, rules and tenets to a population of viewers and believers (see Turner, 1967: 105–6).

7. Though such calls failed since the shootings did not transpire at the rave in question, which was a secure event in compliance with local regulations.

8. The term "freak" here refers to those who have adopted a countercultural lifestyle since the 1960s in mutation from common and dominant modes of cultural conformity.

9. Reminiscent of the implicit nihilism of estranged sugar plantation owner Paul Holland in Jacques Tourneur's 1943 classic *I Walked with a Zombie*: "There's no beauty here, only death and decay.... Everything good dies here, even the stars."

10. A notable event occurred on October 29, 2006, when 894 people in zombie-drag gathered at Monroeville Mall in Pittsburg (the set of the original *Dawn of the Dead*). See http://www.crawlofthedead.com. Events now include the annual Zombie Parade (since August, 2001) in Sacramento, California, and the World Zombie Day food drive charity.

Porn of the Dead

Necrophilia, Feminism, and Gendering the Undead

STEVE JONES

Zombie porn straddles the boundary between discourses — of philosophic concerns regarding zombies as non-conscious animated entities, of misogyny and non-consent associated with necrophilia (MacCormack, 2008: 123), and of feminist concerns regarding pornographic representations. The phenomenon problematizes all of these fields of thought, and it is this very complexity that draws my interest, raising the following questions (among others): how do we gender the zombie, and to what ends? Does an animated body (which may or may not be capable of conscious thought) hold any claim to aspects of identity such as gender, even if those zombies are sexually engaged with individuals that do claim such faculties? Can a zombie be sexually violated, and can we utilize terms such as "misogyny" when dealing with the partially formed zombie-subject? What are the implications raised by combining the graphic depiction of sex with horror motifs?

I will begin by situating the current study in relation to these points, focusing on the central binary division of male from female, and discourses that seek to animalize, subordinate, and de-humanize women. Historically, women have been framed as a locus of both disease, and of impending social disaster — I draw attention to these discourses to make the case that the traditionally "blank" zombie can be read as female, written out of male fear of feminism and women's increased social empowerment. I then relate this to a brief history of zombie cinema, concentrating specifically on changes in zombiedom occurring after the mid–1980s, when the zombie became a figure increasingly invested with identity (pointing to gender as a key facet connoting subjectivity). I will then move on to outline a brief history of zombie sex-cinema before addressing my case study, *Porn of the Dead* (2006). In hardcore zombie pornography, the bodies are explicitly sexed, and so it is no longer a case of reading gender into a "blank" figure, but instead investigating how the zombie motif is used in relation to normative gender ideologies that correlate male with masculinity and female with femininity. Where the first half of the essay is attentive to the zombie as metaphorically symbolizing a (patriarchal) fear of feminist politics, my reading of *Porn of the Dead* is concerned with what impact the graphic portrayal of zombie sex has on our model of undead subjectivity and the politics of gendered bodies. *Porn of the*

Dead is a film that depicts violent heterosexual intercourse, and this leads me to consider how we might scrutinize these images for what they reveal about contemporary gender politics — particularly whether we have moved on from the subordinating discourses outlined in the first section of the essay concerning women and disease, social disruption, sexual difference and animalism. Furthermore, the excessiveness of the zombie (in its refusal of the fundamental alive/dead binary) is probed in terms of its radical potential, and whether it can lead us to reassess ideological boundaries, or if it ultimately reconstitutes normative hegemony.

The Zombie as Gendered Metaphor

Historically, the zombie has been a monster tied into identity politics; racial concerns were seemingly unavoidable given the zombies' Haitian origins (Russell: 9–16), a topic later revisited via the lynching motifs of *Night of the Living Dead* (1968).[1] It is also no surprise that critical perspectives on the zombie have followed the trajectory set out by Romero's follow-up *Dawn of the Dead*, a key example of an expressly political Horror film that investigates the negative effect of capitalism upon the self.[2] Communal issues are inherent to the zombie-lineage because, "[l]ike humans, zombies aren't social isolates"— an observation that highlights the uncanny nature of these doppelgangers; "there is always something 'nearly me' about the monster" (Webb and Byrnand, 2008: 84). It is thus clear that the zombie is apposite to represent facets of our own social identities that require cultural "processing" in order to work through the horror they represent.

Zombies appear to aptly allegorize the position of the subject under ideology due to their dual nature as unconscious and instinctual beings, which also embody active potential — zombies at once unwittingly follow the established order, and yet threaten to overthrow and defamiliarize "normal" relations to that system. While my own reading will not dwell on psychoanalysis, Webb and Byrnand's suggestion that the zombie "gestures towards who and what we might be: someone with the capacity to reject the symbolic order," clearly embodies such a revolutionary ethic, probing the relationships between "physiological requirement" and how "desire is mediated by culture" (Webb and Brynand: 87–8). Such potential is the result of the zombies' presence as body evacuated of selfhood. Thus, another key branch of zombie studies (epitomized by the work of Kirk, 2005; Heil, 2003; Dennett, 1995; and Locke, 1976) is concerned with what zombies reveal about human consciousness.[3]

I am not concerned with ontological, post-colonial or Marxist readings directly, instead I aim to locate the current study somewhere in-between; the issue of Otherness, especially when tied into body-politics, is exacerbated in *Porn of the Dead* via the zombies' attainment of a specific identity marker — gender. The body is a "socially inscribed surface" (Horner and Keane, 2000: 2), a crucial battleground that may be "potentially subversive" (Currie and Raoul, 1992: 2). The gendering of zombies is a matter that has received little scholarly attention, but one that (I hope this study will prove) offers important insights into the cultural climate that spawned representations of gendered zombies (illustrations of which I will come to in due course).

Before I turn to specific examples, let us apply the gender reading to the zombie in general terms. The zombie has been traditionally formulated as asexual, offering no clearly gendered traits. However, we should consider that the zombie is typically soft-bodied, and largely passive, invading and attacking based on opportunism rather than intent and pre-meditation (of which they are incapable). It is also a creature that is wrought in binary opposition to the present humans, who are active (who plan in order to facilitate their survival), who tend to carry weapons and tools (thus evincing their evolutionary "superiority," and perhaps even possession of the phallus if one is psychoanalytically inclined), and who are repulsed by the irrationality and potential threat to civil order that the zombies embody. In this reading, in accordance with dominant ideological norms, the zombie is a creature that may be gendered female, and the binary opposite (human) gendered male.

This follows the claims that "adult women were generally seen as: 'more submissive, less independent ... more easily influenced... [and] less objective'" than men (Boverman et al. cited in Ussher, 1989: 73). While I do not wish to suggest that such ideological precepts are accurate (in fact my intention is to debunk such assumptions), it is interesting to consider what the political "message" of the zombie narrative is in such a light. It is the group might of the zombie (coded female) that threatens to overturn the ordinances of human (coded male) dominance, leading to the apocalypse; the zombie may then embody patriarchal fear of increasing female liberation, suffrage, and the rise of feminism. In such a reading, taken from the perspective of the patriarchal order (the humans with which we identify, as opposed to the inarticulate zombies), it is the violent potential of the Other that overpowers the accepted system, inevitably dominating via an unstoppable reproductive regime. This interpretation overturns MacCormack's assertion that "zombie films frequently disregard gender for viscera"; that "the focus on gore necessarily challenges reading gender through the flesh, because when the flesh is destroyed or reorganized these aspects become arbitrary" (MacCormack: 104) — here, the reorganization of the flesh embodies a specifically socio-political reordering, gore linking the violence of social injustice to the substance of the body.

Such readings have been overlooked by the academy, but seem distinctly appropriate given the history of discourses that have demonized and disempowered women. The zombie is a creature that is like, yet Other to, their human counterparts, and this similarity/difference is akin to the sexed binary; both sides (male/female, or human/undead) belong to the same genus, "our closeness" being indicated by the fact that "viruses (mostly) travel between like species" (Webb and Byrnand: 84). The scientific approach may allow us a point of entry into the social inequality argument, because "[t]he separation of mind and body as the basis for 'objective' knowledge led to additional masculine/feminine dualities: reason or unreason, universals or particulars, subjective or objective, doing or being, culture or nature, order or disorder" (Currie and Raoul: 3); tropes which are readily applicable to the binary of human/undead that I have already outlined.

Science has historically attempted to define non-genital physical difference between males and females that signify their biological differences (see Schiebinger, 2000: 25), and this has been interpreted by feminist scholars as an attempt to "reflect natural rather than social processes, and to justify gender inequality" (Currie and Raoul: 1). Moreover, this is coupled with a cultural imbalance that insists that "apparently 'neutral' presentations of the 'human' body" have "functioned as a veiled representation and projection of a masculine which takes itself as the unquestioned norm" (Grosz, 1994: 188). "The neutral body" then, according to Grosz, is "filled in by the male body and men's pleasures" (ibid.: 155–6). This bias has been so readily accepted ("proven" by the discourses of "objective" science) that "unfair assessments" of women's "abilities and potential" came to be "embodied in law" (Currie and Raoul: 8), making the gendered body a site of political contention. Bronfen equally avers that the body is the pivotal point where "physical materiality and its visual or narrative representation" interface, being inextricable from "aesthetic as well as diverse scientific discourses ... involving the distinction between masculinity and femininity, but also ... where to draw the line between the living and the dead" (Bronfen, 2000: 112).

Let us return to the elements of femininity that have been ideologically vilified, and that are central to our reading of the generic zombie as female. Barbara Creed observes that "[t]he feminine imagination is seen as essentially non-violent, peaceful, unaggressive. This is the very argument that patriarchal ideology has used for the past 2000 years to control women" (1993: 156). As Creed goes on to explore (an argument to which I will return specifically in relation to *Porn of the Dead*), women have also been represented in opposition to this stereotype — as violent and uncontrolled. The zombie embodies both tropes at once, being both simultaneously passive and aggressive. In fact, zombie lore is gendered, and this is based on the same ideological subordination that Creed describes; Marsella proclaims that according to Haitian beliefs, "females are more likely than males to have the 'possession' experience" (Marsella, 2008: 229), and this seems to be directly related to Sydie's observation that women are stereotyped as "naturally more impressionable, and more ready to receive the influence of a disembodied spirit," being "feebler both in mind and body" (Sydie, 1987: 5).

The central bias at hand is "[t]he mind/body dualism" that situates "males [as] the guardians of culture and things of the mind," while "associat[ing] females with the frailties and contingencies of the mortal body" (Schiebinger: 1). It is perhaps apposite then that the monstrous female is represented as an animated, degenerated corpse because women have been historically "conceptualized as being ruled by their ... unstable and inherently weak" bodies (Ussher: 1). The suggestion that "autonomy ... is synonymous in western culture with maturity, independence, and full subjecthood, but for males only" (Raoul, 1992: 267) is the norm, renders that dualism of existence (segregation between mind and body in the constitution of selfhood) a gendered division. Feminists have fought for recognition that this binary is evidence of patriarchal bias. My contention is that the representation of the zombie as "[t]he same, yet not identical ... 'people without minds' ... both us and not us" (Webb and Byrnand: 85) reveals the same bias (that normalizes "us" as male, in the same way that the inert body is assumed to be male) — being uncannily similar to assertions that "women are essentially irrational, rooted in a determinate bodyliness, unable to maintain a proper distance between subject and object, and not fully agents of their own will" (Shildrick, 2002: 36). Shildrick continues to make explicit this connection between gender bias, the impossible split inherent to female positioning, and an aura of menace; "[m]onsters ... [l]ike women ... refuse to stay in place: they change shape, they combine elements which should remain separate" (ibid.: 29). Female sexuality has been rendered a dual point of desire and horror in such theorization, and this will be of central importance to my reading of the sexual zombie in *Porn of the Dead*. As Ussher avers, "One of the ways in which this contradiction operates is in the categorization of women within the Madonna/whore framework, which describes the pure, virginal, 'good' woman ... unspoiled by sex or sin: her counterpart, the whore, is consumed by desires of the flesh" (Ussher: 14). Again, it is apposite that the ambiguous figure of the zombie is the cipher for this split; "as an asexual creature, woman is moral ... as an incipiently sexual creature, woman is always a sexual resource ... this move, which entails separating female feeling from consciousness ... suggests how amenable the figure of woman was to representational manipulation" (Poovey, 1990: 36). The instinct to feast then, may be replaced with another "animalistic" urge — to copulate — that may equally signal the threat to ideological hegemony that supposedly arises from women becoming "uncontrolled."

The zombie's perpetuation of disease is indicative of such a fear being inextricable from unregulated reproductive capacity, thus connoting that female sexuality is a social ill. Creed observes that "horror involves a representation of and reconciliation with, the maternal body" that aims to "eject the abject and redraw the boundaries between human and non-human" (Creed: 14), yet here reproduction involves a characterization of the reproductive body that is partially destructive, complicating the lines between life and death, the abject corpse and the human. As Creed notes, Margaret Miles stipulated that the "image of woman" is "quintessentially grotesque" because of her "associations with ... sex and birth" (Creed: 43). However, when Creed discusses the potential pleasures of Horror as akin to "returning to that time when the mother-child relationship was marked by an untrammeled pleasure in 'playing' with the body and its wastes" (13), she does not account for the literalization of the reproduction motif found in explicit (rather than metaphoric) zombie sexuality; that births and aborts simultaneously, that produces and yet renders the subject as waste, that propagates and signals an end, that is sexual and profoundly rewrites maternity. Because of its excess (usurping the "quintessentially grotesque" status of women by combining a form of sex and birth which has no nine month incubation delay), the sexual female zombie is so excessive as to be seditious. This becomes all the more pertinent in light of Shildrick's assertion that "the pregnant female body itself is always a trope of immense power in that it speaks to an inherent capacity to problematise the boundaries of self and other" (Shildrick: 31).

Of course, before we stray too far from the ideological center, we ought to also note that Aristotle claimed that in reproduction "the body is from the female, it is the soul that is from the male" (cited in Currie and Raoul: 2). Thus, in accordance with the normative mind = male/body = female dichotomy outlined above, it makes ideologically normative "sense" that this female form of reproduction (without semen) should produce soulless young. Moreover, this destructive form of duplication only appears to recreate the undead mother's image, bolstering the fear that "the womb" is "the matrix of all problems," and that "women's sexuality is dangerous and threatening" (Ussher: 3 and 15). We return then to the zombie as a figure that designates revolt, threatening the patriarchal order — the reproductive motif thus acts as a metaphor for increased power, infecting the populous, overturning the world order of the "majority" with disease and chaos.[4] As Sceats delineates, "if a woman is infected with desire, she ... ceases to be [a] passive recipient of kiss and penetration and becomes instead active and penetrative herself.... [G]ive a woman a taste of the vampiric/erotic, and she will become depraved and may even run riot, infecting the whole of society" (Sceats, 2001: 114–5).

In my reading of the zombie, the fear embodied is that because they lack rational control (in the eyes of dominant ideology), if women are permitted power and freedom, they will become unstoppable. The correlation of female sexuality with disorder requiring restriction here is nothing new — science's patriarchal bias has been implicated in the historic oppression of female freedom; "[a]s nineteenth-century women became increasingly vocal about their discontent their doctors began to" apply diagnoses of "hysteria and neurasthenia ... to every woman who spoke of women's rights or who attempted an independent act" (Ussher: 138; see also Schiebinger: 26). Primarily, the fear is one of "infecting" the human characters in the zombie narrative, and this exposes "male fear of female sexuality" (Sceats: 114), more generally.[5]

Thus, the zombie is horrific according to a patriarchal stance, and the narratives ask us to conspire with such a position, reading the zombies as a monster. As Creed would have it, "the monstrous is produced at the border which separates those who take up their proper gender positions from those who do not" (11) — a division that Shildrick utilizes for its revolutionary potential; "[t]he issue is not so much that monsters threaten to overrun the boundaries of the proper, as that they promise to dissolve them" (Shildrick: 11). The very presence/existence of the monster, Shildrick argues, is enough to disturb the expected normative binaries, even if only by offering an alternative that does not fit the system where norm is measured against Other (Shildrick: 75).

The possibility of social change is made all the more plausible by these manifestations of ideological fear, despite their attempts to define female empowerment as hostile and ugly. After all, "the Undead corpse is the nemesis, but also the *product*, of a repressive civilization" (Clark, 2006: 199, my emphasis), and the fear embodied in a model of increasing power demonstrates the potential of unity against forces that seek to enforce subordination. The first stages of change are discourse-based, that is stemming from feminism itself. This reading of the zombie acts as a logical extension of feminist interventions that "reinserted the body into history, bringing to light issues that had previously been considered too vulgar, trivial or risqué to merit serious scholarly attention" (Scheibinger: 1), including the "bodilyness" of women, and its associated inferiority to the rational concerns of "male" discourse. Indeed, the take-over is such that Horner and Keane suggest that "[i]n feminist literary and cultural criticism, 'the body' crops up with such regularity that the overprivileged 'mind' seems to have had its day" (Horner and Keane: 1).

All of this overturns Grant's assertion that "Romero's undead demand the suspension of normal (bourgeois) values, particularly those of patriarchy" (Grant, 1996: 211). However, the problem that I am yet to address is the investment of agency in the "blank" zombie — that the zombies' very balance between conscious/alive and unconscious/dead states may be read in terms of political motivation, that the zombie may be decoded as gendered, and relevant to concerns of disempowerment. This comes to the fore when we investigate what happened to the zombie after the mid–1980s.

The Return of the Thinking Dead:
Identity, Sexuality and the Zombie

The issue of feminism was explicitly raised by Savini's remake of *Night of the Living Dead* (1990). Even if the zombie continued to be asexual, Barbara, who remained catatonic for the majority of the running time in the original film, became the sole survivor, her rationality implicitly critiquing the fruitless destructive bickering of her male counterparts. In Grant's reading of the reinvention of Barbara, he insists that Romero's oeuvre signals the zombie as male; "*Dawn* self-consciously uses the zombie as a conceit for macho masculinism and conspicuous capitalist consumption" (Grant, 1996: 202). However, his later citing of Johnston is revealing—she states "here is only the male and the non-male: in order to be accepted into the male universe, the woman must become a man ... [s]he is a traumatic presence which must be negated" (Johnston, cited in Grant, 1996: 207). In this case, it is apparent that both Fran in the original *Dawn of the Dead* and Barbara in the remake of *Night of the Living Dead* are not necessarily counterpoised to the men they inhabit spaces with, but are phallusized (both coming to occupy active, gun-toting positions). In the case of *Day of the Dead* (1985), Sarah begins the narrative as a leader, attempting to maintain her position as active weapon wielder, despite Rhodes' attempts to impose patriarchal dominance. In all three cases, it is the female protagonist's violent agency that marks them as human—a category implicitly gendered male in juxtaposition to the monstrous Other (the zombie) that is as catatonic as the original *Night*'s Barbra, again aligning ideological femininity with the zombie.

So far we have discussed the zombie in abstract terms—what the monster embodies in the general sense as a metaphor for gender bias. However, this does not account for the ways in which the zombie has shifted in meaning in the cinematic landscape. As stated at the outset, the zombie began as occupying a racialized Other position—as a Haitian slave figure, the kind of mindless or hypnotized zombie found in *White Zombie* and *I Walked with a Zombie*. Other "zombies" of the period, those found in the Universal monster pictures (*The Mummy* [1932], *Dracula* [1931], *Frankenstein* [1931]), were rather more invested with identity and conscious motivation—especially seeking partners of the opposite sex, which is a key drive for all of these monsters (even if Frankenstein's creation had to wait until 1935 to encounter the *Bride of Frankenstein*).[6] When the zombie resurfaced (in its most influential form) in 1968 with *Night of the Living Dead*, it became an expressly political or metaphoric beast. This trend continued throughout the 1970s and early 1980s via vehicles such as Romero's sequels *Dawn* and *Day of the Dead* as well as returning to its Haitian roots via Lucio Fulci's unofficial Italian sequels to *Dawn of the Dead*, the *Zombi* films (1979 and 1988), *Zombie Holocaust* (1980), and the explicitly racialized "third-world" zombies of *Zombie Creeping Flesh* (1980).

However, it is *Return of the Living Dead* that saw the advent of a new breed of zombie. Romero may have reinvented the zombie in the 1960s and set the evolutionary wheels in motion, but it is O'Bannon's post-modern reinvestigation of the monster that signaled a shift in what the zombie signifies. *Day of the Dead*'s Bub may have begun to show signs of conscious (rather than simply robotic) behaviors, but it was *Return*'s version of zombiehood that portended zombie-subjectivity; here, those infected (Frank and Freddy) bemoan the onset of rigor-mortis, a zombie torso asserts that it "hurts" to be dead, and the zombies request "more paramedics" in gambits that reveal complex strategic ability. Here then, the zombie becomes a far more complex creature, and their manifestations of subjectivity make the zombie less irrational (or simply "pure motorized instinct" as proclaimed by the doctor of *Dawn*), and more akin to their supposed binary — the human.

What followed was the literalization of gender into zombie identity, overturning McCormack's assertion that "[z]ombies are bodies, nothing more," having "[n]o race, no gender, no sexuality" (MacCormack: 104). The previously asexual walking flesh — blank bodies that I have read in relation to femininity — became inextricable from defined gendered roles (both masculine and feminine), manifesting as the "ladies' man" Bud the Chud (of *C.H.U.D. 2* [1989]), the "ladies who lunch" found in *Flesh Eating Mothers* (1988), and the eroticized self-harming Goth, Julie in *Return of the Living Dead 3*. By 1992, audiences were treated to the sexually active (and reproducing) priest and nurse of *Braindead*. It is perhaps worth noting that all of the above examples fall into the cate[-]gory of Horror-Comedy, as does the teen sex-comedy, *Night of the Living Dorks* (2004), in which the central protagonist Philip loses his genitals during his quest for intercourse with Uschi (having to then staple them back on). The same can be said of the heavy-handed satire, *Zombie Strippers* (2008), in which the strippers become the ultimate meat-objects (and better dancers) when they are infected by the zombie-virus. They are juxtaposed with the mindless patrons of the club who continue to "consume," declaring the women to be "beautiful" despite (or because of?) their degeneration. Arguably, these examples indicate the horrific potential of such a manifestation, requiring carnivalesque humor to dispel or excuse the disruptive, repulsive potential of the gendered zombie.

While on first glance these narratives may appear to conform to Castronovo's suggestion that the presence of the "eviscerated subject, starved of history and culture, provokes questions about the desirability of political emancipation" (Castronovo, 2000: 141), I argue that the point is to delineate the need for social metamorphosis — even if the narratives are unable to offer a solution, they can inform us of the basis on which change is necessary. Contrary to Briefel's assumption that the "gendering of ... pain felt by monsters [in Horror film] and the sadistic acts they subsequently commit provides an unfortunately reassuring stability," it is the gendering of monstrosity that may cause us to question (rather than submit to) the "safe parameter around the spectators' alleged masochism in choosing to sit through a horror film" (Briefel, 2005: 25). Even if we dismiss cinema's potential to signal ideological dissatisfaction on the basis of the "knowability" of texts belonging to genres (i.e. that in Horror we expect to be horrified, and can pass over any real-life potential for change on the basis that the film's depiction of alternative belongs to the fantasy and its modes of representation), the case may be very different when we combine the gratifications of Horror with the sexual pleasures offered by zombie pornography.

Before we move on to investigate the implications raised by specific examples of recent zombie sex, it is important to note that the zombie had been juxtaposed with sexual activity prior to *Porn of the Dead*. As Russell delineates, Amando de Ossorio's Spanish Blind Dead films (*Tombs of the Blind Dead* [1971], *Return of the Evil Dead* [1973], *The Ghost Galleon* [1974], and *Night of the Seagulls* [1975]) "build up a thematic link between the zombies and the sex-obsessed narratives in which they appear ... repeatedly foreground[ing] the issue of sexuality" (Russell: 88), while D'Amato's *Erotic Nights of the Living Dead* (1980) "plays like a dated porno flick cut with bouts of zombie violence" (Russell: 134), refusing to allow the zombies to participate in intercourse. Although some have referred to the monster of D'Amato's follow-up *Porno Holocaust* (1981) as a sexually active zombie (see Bishop, 2010: 185; Russell: 135) it is not made clear that the being in question is undead *per se* in the film itself. That aside, Russell's research pegs *Erotic Orgasm* (1982) as the first zombie porn film, although it is notable that the other examples of legitimate zombie porn he lists (rather than films that juxtapose sex and zombies) are made after *Return of the Living Dead*'s post-modern revival; these include *The Revenge of the Living Dead Girls* (1987), *Night of the Living Babes* (1987), *Gore Whore* (1994), *At Twilight Come the Flesh Eaters* (1998), and *Zombie Ninja Gangbangers* (1998) (Russell: 135). Other more recent entries include *The Necro Files* and its sequel (1997 and 2003), *Repenetrator* (2004), *Otto; or Up with Dead People* (2008), and my central case study *Porn of the Dead*. In these pornographic examples, the zombie is unambiguously sexed, and this is a key marker of the zombie's entry into subjectivity.

Fucking Horrible: Consent, Predation, and Disease in Zombie Porn

My aim is to explore the problems outlined above in relation to *Porn of the Dead* and its fantasies; how the sexualization of the undead complicates the zombie identity (especially in terms of consent), how gender binaries are revealed and negotiated in this space, and whether the representations of sex on offer are only to be read as misogynistic, as this may not be a term readily applicable to the zombie, and may be problematized by the excessiveness of the text's fantasies. Pornography, being concerned with fantasy, neglects some of the more problematic aspects of the sexualized zombie, or at least turns them into a positive. One may immediately be struck by the use of necrophilia as a motif, especially since "necrophilia is one of the few sexual taboos that remain in the secular, post-modern Western world" (Downing, 2003: 157). The intent is probably to shock, and market differentiation has no doubt acted to increase the sales of the product, despite the controversy inherent to such a release.

The fantasy that zombies are animated corpses in part negates the necrophilic taboo, which is based upon the principles of defilement and consent. As Dudley observes, "[t]he offense of necrophilia is that it attempts ... to convert a subject that has become an object back into a subject again" (1999: 289)—here the connotations of the sexualized object make the split more complex, as it revolves around a fantasy of the object's coming into being. The inarticulate undead person is situated somewhere between points of discourse — they are neither human nor non-human. They are unable to consent (or to withhold their permission) without an understanding of human socio-sexual politics, or retention of an identity that ties into that schema. Bourke avers that "some types of people are deemed to be unable to consent to sexual intercourse in the first place.... Slaves, for instance, were simply not human enough for the concept of 'consent' to be relevant.... They were inherently rapable" (Bourke, 207: 76),[7] and this summates the quandary raised by fantasy which treads a line between necrophilic fetishization of the corpse, enjoyment of a lack of consent or of power exploitation, and perhaps even desire for the assent of the person/body being fucked. In the non-porn film *The Stink of Flesh* (2005), Nathan keeps a female zombie (hereafter, fembie) captive in a shed to "look at" her, and eventually rapes her, only to be later killed by her in retaliation. In such cases, it is clear that the zombie has some form of subjectivity—she is not only animated, she is aware of her body, feels pain, and is able to protest against her situation. Fundamentally, it is worth noting that both human and zombie understand that the animated corpse is a she, and this is not because of her genitals per se, but his investment in and labeling of her gender. In *The Stink of Flesh*, her protests are articulated by Nathan's memory of murdering the woman in the first instance, her struggles (verbal and physical) against his advances, and the chaining of her body to prevent her from harming him and to keep her in stasis. Nathan then understands he is raping her, and is aware that this is why she kills him at the finale.

Porn of the Dead works in a slightly different way because while some of the zombies retaliate, biting their human sexual partners is an extension of the sexual moment rather than an attempt to avenge themselves on the humans. This is indicative of the fantasy of porn; as Williams observes "rape, considered as a violent sexual crime that coerces its victims, is an impossibility" in porn's "separated utopia" (Williams, 1989: 164). Indeed, the zombies tend to make the same kind of consensual noises that the humans do—Sierra Sinn clearly says "oh yeah" during the first half of her scene, then appears to have been told that zombies cannot speak, as she spends the second half making remarkably similar sounding affirmative growls that are not quite words. Just as the human males (hereafter, hu-men) are clearly not disgusted or fearful enough to inhibit their arousal, the male undead display their consent and gendered responses to the situation via their erections. Again, Williams' vision of the porn utopia, where participants are ever-ready for sex (in this case, whether they are living or dead), rings true. This negates the physiological problem faced by the undead Dan of the non-pornographic film *Shatterdead* (1994), who complains that he "can't get hard without blood," and where the gun strap-on Susan fashions for him has to suffice. *Shatterdead* is a film that centralizes the physical and philosophical problems faced by the conscious undead that can remember, emote, articulate, and be aware of their physical degeneration, but cannot die. *Porn of the Dead* does not dwell on such concerns, although their disavowal speaks volumes about the film's bodily fantasies. I will return to the issue of consent, as this problem is exacerbated by the gendered binaries of the text, which first require detailed exploration. *Porn of the Dead* is complicated by gendered difference in its scenes—three scenes feature fembies with hu-men, while the remaining two involve human females with male zombies (hereafter, manbies). As I have already outlined, a crucial trope of gendered binaries includes attempts to designate male and female bodies as physically divergent. These center on considerations of sexual organs (and genital horror), reproduction, and disease. Throughout my delineation of these tropes, I will aim to highlight how *Porn of the Dead* problematizes male as well as female bodies.

I have already highlighted how discourses have historically framed female bodies as monstrous, or metaphorically aligned with the zombie—let us now consider how women's genitals have been vilified in particular. Barbara Creed's treatise on the Monstrous Feminine is one of the central academic texts to explore the implications of the female body in Horror film. In keeping with the zombie-as-female reading I have already established, Creed envisages a negotiation of male fear of the female body that visualizes female genitalia in forms such as the razor-teethed cannibalistic mouth — the *vagina dentata* that seeks to castrate (Creed: 105–21; see also Clark: 203; Grosz, 1995: 293). This psychoanalytic trope is invested in framing the female body as problematic for men, but castration serves a more complex function given the zombie motif and the pornographic context in which it is presented in *Porn of the Dead*.

Creed suggests that typically male castration/death is framed differently to the female rape (as it is associated with pleasure/eroticized), to reveal "the film's ideological purpose — to represent woman as monstrous because she castrates" (Creed: 130). However, in *Porn of the Dead*, the fembie is already (sexually) monstrous, and the hu-men are equally horrific, being aggressive towards the fembies seemingly because they lack the ability to protest their exploitation (other than through post-coital penile mastication). However, by including the film's only castration in its opening scene, what is accentuated is that the males are lacking inasmuch as porn frames men as fundamentally constituted by their penis,[8] ever-ready to aggressively exploit women, be they alive or otherwise, who are depicted in their entirety. The men of pornography are intent only on fucking, and are thus portrayed as even more one-dimensional than the zombies (who are only partially formed subjects). They also lack the ability to facilitate their own subjectivity because that is all they are present for — this especially evinced in the film's opening castration, whereby the male performer's semi-presence as erection is removed, demonstrating our mistake in reading the fembie as the less formed half of the coupling here.

Moreover, the film is bookended with a similar motif: the final scene features a fembie biting off the hu-man performer's finger (as an echo of the opening castration), and disemboweling him after his climax (which, just as the castration, serves to undermine male desire for sex by evincing its futility in the face of zombies' continued existence). That the male performer persists with intercourse after losing his finger (in fact it spurs him on) underlines that the hu-man desire (supposedly rational and superior in ideological terms) is wilfully impetuous and short-lived. While it may be argued that the aggressive fembie resembles the black widow spider or "the well-known inclination of the female mantis to devour the male in the act of coitus" (Grosz: 282) in her animalistic response to sex (thus again evoking subordinating discourses that surround female sexuality), it is hardly sufficient to declare that only the female is framed as animalistic predator here. The male performer (zombie or human) is equally found guilty, and is reminiscent of Callois' description of "male sexual drive" as "automatic" — even when "headless" the male mantis "doggedly persists in its automatic sexual movements" (cited in Grosz: 283), much like the pumping porn male who impulsively persists despite their partner's resurrection from the dead, or the threat of physical injury. Thus, Dirty Harry's screams of "no, anything but that" quickly turn into "yeah" as Sierra Sinn exposes his penis — his erection is instantaneous and uninhibited by her monstrousness, usurping her outward hideousness.

The lines of predator and victim are ambiguously wrought here, reversing the typical coercion trope that we see elsewhere in the film; Trina Michael's fearful screams at the presence of the zombies quickly turn into the same automated affirmative statements that preceded it in her human-human sexual interaction. Again, even if it is just signaled by porn's "separated utopia" (as William's suggests), some subjects (as Bourke asserts) are inherently "unrapable" — though this goes for the male performers as much as the females here. Yet this is not to suggest that "[w]hen a man is raped, he too is raped as a woman" (de Lauretis, 1987: 152), because his role is otherwise defined according to an expressly stereotyped porno-logic; male pleasure is central to the assignations. Greer's reading of the male body as invested with "aggressive, conquistadorial power, reducing all heterosexual contact to a sadomasochistic pattern" (cited in Currie and Raoul, 1992: 18) then is valid, but the "power" is rendered fragile. The lines of sadism and masochism in the coupling are interchangeable (both parties being violent or submissive at different junctures), and the zombie is the ultimate conquering victor.

The tenets of power, dominance, and agency are tied into an ideo-logic of blaming that Poovey discusses in relation to prostitution; "syphilis turns prostitution into a crime; in making the sublimely unselfish woman a carrier of disease, it transforms female susceptibility into active agent of death" (Poovey: 36). Disease may act as an extension of the societal/moral corruption posed by women according to this model. Here, the fembies are largely passive to male lust, yet they are "blamed" for their physical manifestation of disease. They are capable of embodying this form of agency only because they are partially conscious. Grosz stipulates that "[i]t is not the case that men's bodily fluids are regarded as polluting and contaminating for women in the same way or to the same extent as women's are for men" (Grosz: 196–7). However, what we have so far neglected is that in the gender balance of *Porn of the Dead*, the zombies are not only feminized; male fluids are equally responsible for the spread of contagion, just as male desires are implicitly as blameworthy as female sexuality. Both are rendered monstrous, whether human or otherwise, and it is the explicit sexualization of the zombie that calls us to question this.

What we may note is that sexual difference is key — be it human-zombie or male-female. This echoes Douglas' claim "that in certain cultures each of the sexes can pose a threat to the other, a threat that is located in the polluting powers of the other's body fluids," something that Grosz goes on to suggest "may prove a particularly significant site for an analysis of sexual difference in the era where sexuality has become reinvested with notions of contagion and death, of danger and purity, as a consequence of the AIDS crisis" (Grosz: 193). Via its use of castration/disembowelment in conjunction with popshots, *Porn of the Dead* maintains an "abjection toward bodily waste, which reaches its extreme in the horror of the corpse; and abjection toward the signs of sexual difference" (Grosz: 193). Yet, in doing so it aligns semen — which usually connotes pleasure in pornography (Williams, 1989: 101) — with disease. Semen is thus abject, rejected from the body, answering Grosz's claim that "[t]here are virtually no phenomenological accounts of men's body fluids ... the come shot functions primarily as a mode of metaphorization of the invisible and graphically unrepresentable mysteries of the vagina and women's interior" (Grosz: 198). Here, because at key moments (that book-end the narrative) the comeshot is juxtaposed with the exposure of male interiors (thus making the male body a site of horror), semen acts in as an extension of the same motif, exposing the "unrepresentable mysteries" of the unexplored male body. This is crucial if we are to avoid the trap that Schiebinger identifies; that "[b]y leaving male bodies unscrutinized, feminists have tended to reinforce the notion of the male as the unmarked sex, the human standard of perfection from which the female can only deviate" (Schiebinger: 14).

A binary is maintained that is bodily — be it alive/dead or male/female because there are no scenes based around human-human or same-sex interactions. Both sexes are portrayed as unclean and abject, yet this balance is concerned with infection across binary divisions. This is made clear because the film contains no zombie-zombie sex, only human-zombie couplings. The spread of disease is accentuated by the make-up that smudges off the zombie participant and onto the human during each sex scene. In preserving a figure with full conscious capacity (if we can assign such status to the humans here), one participant retains agency. The blame for spreading disease is shared by men and women in the film, only because there is an equilibrium of male and female humans in the narrative. Strangely though, because of their status as a more fully formed subject, the human participant is arguably more responsible for their own infection than the zombie is.

So far I have predominantly focused on the hu-man/fembie scenes of *Porn of the Dead*, yet the film is notable for the balance it strikes; two of the film's five scenes involve manbies with human females, and it is here that the sex-difference becomes crucial. The manbies may be ugly and one dimensional, but they are (make-up aside) virtually indistinguishable from the hu-men performers, where there is a marked distinction between the growling fembies, and the highly vocal female human performers. This divergence is most notable in the contrasts between Sierra Sinn's zombie (that, as aforementioned, has to stifle routine groans of "oh yeah"), Ruby's virtually silent corpse-like zombie, and the endless labored dialogue of humans Trina Michaels and Hillary Scott ("that's a big fucking zombie cock in my fucking pussy"). Another series of disparities are evident in comparing Trina's manbie counterparts who say "oh yeah baby" and "suck my cock" quite openly, in the same manner that Dirty Harry does in the first scene (whose sophisticated dialogue includes such timeless gems as "come here you fucking crazy fucking whore zombie fucking bitch"), where Rob Rotten's human mortician role blurs the line further; being virtually silent, his disinterested pumping makes him more robotic than his fembie lover.

If there is a confusion inherent to the zombie-human matrix then, because of its insistence on heterosexed couplings, it is played out along gendered lines. The human and zombie males blur roles—some humans being zombie-like, some zombies being too human—while the women are markedly different in their articulations of zombiedom and humanity, even if they are equally exploited and subordinated. That said, both the human and zombie versions of femininity are as animalistic and ugly as each other here, just as the human and zombie males are undifferentiated in their mechanical routine of thrusting. While the human women are more expressive, what they do articulate is an assent to aggression (such as Trina's "feed me" referring to three loads of zombie-semen), or a determination to frame their bodies in abject terms (exemplified by Hillary's lengthy discussion of her "ass juices").

Perhaps this should be read as passing comment on women's complicity in their own subordination and the rise of what Levy terms as "Female Chauvinist Pigs" (Levy, 2005)—while I will return to the misogynist implications of *Porn of the Dead* shortly, it is sufficient to note for the point in hand that the human females here self-suffer to a remarkable degree. Hillary Scott audibly choking herself on the male performer's member and being soaked in her own saliva (while common in recent porn) is made exceptional by its situation amongst the Horror tropes of the film. The exaggeratedly light, soft-focus version of her masturbation (and the "innocence" connoted by her pig-tails) in the preceding moments are transformed into a contrasting nightmare (literally, one from which she awakens after the pop-shot) that is dark, and originally began (as seen in the title-sequence) with a contrasting crucifix masturbation, the red lighting even obscuring what juices are meant to be blood and which are vaginal moisture. The challenge to hegemony arises in the complexities of how atrocity functions — monstrousness is embodied both in the zombies (of either sex), and the tacit deal struck by performers in the "porniverse" that pleasure is everything, even death. *Porn of the Dead* then, rather than hiding its mistreatment of women, makes a point of it (to whatever ends), and in doing so, demands that we pay attention to its negotiation of sexual inequality. Where Sceats observes that the "nongenital" penetration of the vampire lends itself to "ambiguity" — "[t]hey can be of either sex and any sexual orientation ... they confuse the roles of victim and predator" (Sceats: 107) — in zombie porn, the identification of gendered identity is manifested exactly as genital penetration. There is no confusion of sexual orientation here, and despite the fembies' attacks on the hu-men, the tone is biased towards male domination.

This reading of *Porn of the Dead* contradicts Downing's contention that "[t]he strategy of setting necrophilia up as an 'identity' allows for the dominant hegemonic categories of gender and hetero- or homo-sexuality temporarily to take a back seat" (Downing: 166), because despite the deviance insinuated through necrophilic overtones, the film still functions according to a hetero-sexed binary and appears to maintain, rather than challenge, normative ideologies. Alternatively, we may wish to interpret adherence to heterosexuality as somewhat more confrontational, insinuating that zombies enter into the identity system in a recognisable way, inasmuch as they discriminate between sexes, conforming to a human mode of sexual identity (here, heterosexuality) rather than a new sexuality (which is "beyond" a hetero/homo/bisexual axis) that one may expect to arise from living/undead interactions. According to its own logic, that system is exposed as brutal and perverse, inequality being literalized by the violent sex enacted by decomposing beings of both sexes. Gender is of evident importance to the film, not only because of its genital focus, but because there are no same-sex couplings — it is thus presumed that the sex of the zombie and human matters to the participants and the viewer (no matter how repulsive the couplings might be).

Utilizing standard pornographic tropes makes those places where the formula deviates even more jarring. Those standards that are adhered to *Porn of the Dead* include genital close-ups, the habit of framing the women as speaking to and looking at the camera (an implicitly male viewer) during the sex act, and a routine of standard sexual behaviors that typify the current genre trends (oral sex, doggystyle, missionary, reverse cowgirl, anal, facial comeshot). Even the extreme porn trends for skull-fucking, ass-to-mouth insertion, and cock gagging are persistently worked into the habitual intercourse. Yet despite these, the film makes use of many jarring techniques that are unusual in hardcore pornography. Visually, the standard over-lighting (see Poyner, 2006: 27; Willemen, 1992: 179) that typifies porn's desire to "show" is replaced with grimy darkness, smoke, and red/blue lighting — the overlighting of Hillary Scott's masturbation scene only accentuates this. Her clean bedroom equally draws attention to the barren, vandalized padded cell of the final scene, or the filth of the pit in the first scene (the newspaper lining the pit that sticks to the performers' legs embellishes this). The aural landscape is constituted by a stark juxtaposition of death metal music and diegetic sound that are panned hard left and right, augmenting each other. The "natural" sound includes the thunder effects (a standard Horror trope), fly noises (adding to the sense of dirt and rotting, again in contrast to Hillary Scott's masturbation scene which is accompanied by the twittering of bird song), the animalistic grunting and screaming of the performers, and ludicrous dialogue ("Yeah that's a good zombie ... suck that fucking cock, fucking zombie"). Visual effects are also employed such as stuttered motion (achieved by altering the shutter-speed), slow motion (accompanied by decelerated sound, again magnifying the animalism of the performer's grunts), and a grainy filter added in post-production (making the film appear to be bleached/over-exposed and damaged, including regular pubic hairs chasing across the frame). Most obviously these audio-visual effects are combined with literal juxtapositions of sex with bloodshed and non-reanimated cadavers (in scene three). As may be apparent, the film does its utmost to counter its routine porno-tropes with jarring alternatives to the norm.

If more proof of this agenda were needed, the central third scene begins as an explicit attack on the norms of porn which it opposes. The scene begins with a disinterested crew filming Trina Michaels copulating with an unidentified (human) male performer, one watching crew member picking his nose with boredom. Prior to the interruption of the zombies, Rotten finds time to explicitly (and not particularly subtly) critique the porn industry's self-imposed limitations, the director of the faux-shoot telling the performer to "grab those titties ... not too hard!" Moreover, the faux-director's swearing is bleeped out (a trait only utilized in this scene), and this is made all the more conspicuous by the mis-bleeping of some words — hence it plays out "**** her doggiestyle, yeah fuck her doggi-est***," implying that censorship is both erroneously and arbitrarily imposed. In addition, in the scene that follows (featuring director Rob Rotten as the hu-man performer), he audibly directs Ruby (his co-star). Regardless of whether this is intentional or accidental, its inclusion adds to the disruption of normalized standards occurring here.

The conventional elements conflict with these defamiliarized elements that act as an extension of the film's desire to be two things simultaneously — both porn and horror (much in the same way other binaries (male/female, alive/dead) are established and equally problematized). It is perhaps testament to the success of this balance that the film was not favorably received, being dubbed as "so grungy and nasty to be a total turn off" by *DVD World*'s reviewer (2006: 83) and "one big unappealing mess" by Zach Parsons (2006).[9] In part, this may arise from a realization that by exposing the routines of porn, the film is attacking its unquestioning, zombie-like consumers — befitting Marianne Valverde's fear that porn may consumers into "selfish, disengaged, univocal individuals" (cited in Currie and Raoul: 195). Regardless of how aggressive and offensive the representations are, the argument that the film is solely misogynistic or of no interest on this basis overlooks the complexities of its modes of representation, and what this may reveal about gender politics.

Reserection: Misogyny, the Viewer and the Limits of Equality

At this stage it is worth qualifying that I am whole-heartedly among those who found *Porn of the Dead*'s treatment of women to be offensive. The persistence of cock-gagging in all scenes (especially where coupled with strangulation), spitting (particularly a manbie spitting into Trina Michael's mouth), dual oral (coupled with the dialogue "slap me with those cocks"), fish-hooking, come gargling, and hair pulling are activities I find to be particularly deplorable. I am, however, less than convinced that the film should be read simply as a misogynistic statement that purely takes pleasure in this hatred on the basis of how much displeasure is inherent to the combined Horror-porn form, and the relish with which the filmmakers combine the two. I am also aware that I am writing as a heterosexual male, and that all of the films I have considered here are male authored. I am less interested in justifying Rob Rotten's cultural politics than I am in investigating the complexities raised by this text — there is every reason that we should read the film as a critique of current pornography that presents some of the vilest imagery of male pornographic pleasure in a continuum with the Horror it so interchangeably evokes. As Russell contends of the Blind Dead films, the "catalogue of sexual abuse is not necessarily simply misogynist" — it "plays an integral role in the[ir] ... thematics" (Russell: 89). *Porn of the Dead* is difficult to stomach, and its propensity to move is the source of its power; the potential of that power requires exploration rather than avoidance, however grueling it is to witness. The point of zombie porn may be to awaken us from passivity, or thinking that we are living in a state of gender equality. As Castronovo declares "[n]ecrophilic scenarios arise when the formal principles of freedom are compromised by material histories that attenuate and embed political subjectivity" (Castronovo: 129). For this reason, it is important that offensive behaviors are so brazenly flaunted, as the evocation of such representations fundamentally signals that everything is not okay.

Before we delve into misogyny, it is worth considering what the appeals of Horror-based zombie pornography might be. It may be inferred that the appeal of the zombie is that the male viewer can fill the partially blank space left by the creature — either the manbie that they may wish to be, or the fembie in which they may invest their desire. Integral to the fantasy here is the nature of the zombie as passive aggressor, in combination with sexual stereotypes (those that unite female sexual animalism/voraciousness and vulnerability, in conjunction with stereotypes of male sexual aggression). The attractions of such an amalgamation may be explained by Sceat's observation that "transposition of women into penetrators and men into passive recipients is a reversal that not only casts women into a rapacious role, but explicitly emphasizes the pleasures of passivity for men" (Sceats: 188). Thus, the over-assertion of male dominance in the narrative may connote its opposite — a desire for passivity on the part of the (presumed) male viewer, which is in keeping with the nature of pornography as a medium that requires the viewer's distance from the onscreen fantasy. Alternatively, we may wish to consider that the male-female dichotomy is set-up in a typed fashion to expose the problem of that very duality (especially since the zombie highlights and exacerbates such tropes). The fantasy (whether intended as radical or not) hinges on sexual difference, and we should not overlook that while the zombie may offer a potential liberation for women (in becoming free to explore and perform aspects of aggression and sexual freedom typically denied from femininity, via the fantasy-space of the monster), the males (alive or dead) continually re-inscribe a traditional gendered system via overt sexual aggression. Here then, the zombie porn model seems to epitomize Dworkin's fear that "the female body" is a "terrain upon which hostility towards the female sex is re-enacted by men" (Currie and Raoul: 18).

Part of the problem is that the fantasy evoked is necrophilic, a desire typically associated with sadism — that is "sexual pleasure from inflicting physical or mental pain on others" (Berest, 1970: 210). Solomon suggests that necrophilia is among the sadistic perversions that are "excessive" in their "expression of ... domination, perhaps mixed with hatred, fear, and other negative attitudes" (Solomon, 1974: 344). Part of the sadism here involves the political oppression of women, which is manifested as the necrophilic desire to reduce the subject to object. This is connoted in MacCormack's discussion of the outlawing of necrophilia, which asks that we "invest the cadaver with volition, thus in necrophilia the corpse is a victim of rape against its 'will'" (MacCormack: 119). The zombie is a figure that resists such objectification (thus partially overturning the desire to oppress here) because of their inherent sexual identity — they cannot be simply reduced to the status of animal "whose consent or lack of it cannot exist" (Levy, 1980: 195). The misogyny of the activities depicted in *Porn of the Dead* may then not necessarily rely on sadistic investment in the pain of the female, but in a negation of their ability to feel pleasure or pain — the fembies being interchangeable from the human females in this respect. Just like the zombies who return to the mall in *Dawn of the Dead*, these are animated bodies simply going through the motions (though the males in the film, as I have already delineated, may also be accused of automation in the same sense).

Despite his focus on Jacobean theater, Dudley's reading of the necrophilic motif proves enlightening here, especially in relation to the potential gender-politics at play and the overturning of the "natural order." As Dudley states, "necrophilia is often destructive, misogynist, obsessive, totalitarian. It is also nostalgic" — it is thus a trope associated with ideological oppression, and a resistance to (political) change; "necrophilia is the displaced, uncanny desire to dig up the past and make it live again — to recover a trace of the lost other in order to fill the cultural and institutional gaps created by new ideologies" (Dudley: 291). Part of the fear evoked is also implicitly that the past, while revered and longed for, is just that — past, not present. Thus, what is evoked is a fear for the end of the patriarchal order. If this is implicated as part of the male pleasure here, it is linked with the notion of "playing at" the overturning of patriarchal hegemony, which finds a parallel in the utilization of the animated dead. This is a complex balance, especially since its enactment involves dominance over and submission to female power. It also entails coming to terms with, rather than an "attempt to distance themselves from, the very kind of corporeality — uncontrollable, excessive, expansive, disruptive, irrational — that [men] have attributed to women" (Grosz: 200).

The zombie metaphor seems apposite for a revolutionary reading. As Clark identifies, "[t]here's no going back for the survivors of the zombie plague; their only option is to disregard the previous system and move on in an effort to pioneer an alternative social order" (Clark: 206), a view shared by Webb and Byrnand — "there is no (evident) way out. Your only option, when faced with the zombie menace, is to kill or be killed. Either way you're screwed, because you are dead, or you have become what you fear" (Webb and Byrnand: 91).[10] Given that zombies are presented as ugly/unknowable to the current order, and that the dominant regime is typified by violent responses towards women (enforced through aggressive sexual acts), there is little to suggest that we would choose to be part of such a system — and this reveals the lack of freedom we have in conforming to such ideologies.

The zombie cannot be read as a purely revolutionary icon, as we may argue that its pre-linguistic nature may instead signal its regressive status, thus rendering the zombie immediately inferior to "civil masculinity" and the full autonomy of the conscious subject. Another consideration worth making is what occurs if there are no survivors to herald the new order — the zombies are the new way, again making them an object of fear for those who depend on the established order to constitute their identity (that is, all of us). Here, the zombie make-up may be an ideological red-herring. The sexed zombie at first appears to offer us a potential point of fracture, however fantastic; the zombie narrative begins with conscious, non-rational beings who escape discourse because they designate a space "outside the symbolic order" (Webb and Byrnand: 97, n. 1). Yet, there is no way of escaping the ideological, and this is arguably why *Porn of the Dead* does not shy from the normative aspects of gendered identity. As the make-up smudges between performers during these sex scenes the true monster is revealed — and most terrifying of all, it is within us all; those aspects that require both men and women to behave in ways that subordinate women.

However, it is the complexity of the zombie-presence that threatens patriarchal hegemony in combination with the narrative's modes of representation that offer us a less restrictive outlook. Because the couplings are human/zombie, inequality is stressed, especially as living females seem to be inferior even to the undead males. The fembies are the amplified enactment of femininity as positioned by subordinating patriarchal discourses; in centralizing genitalia (and thus sexed difference), the film uses the physical to distract from the real point (which is behavioral). MacCormack notes that because it is in part an "onanistic practice," necrophilia "confus[es] subject and object" (MacCormack: 118) (and perhaps this is the implication raised by utilizing the motif in pornography). The confusion here is not one of investing an object (cadaver) with a subject (part of the fantasist's self), but a slippage between poles of the gender binary — the discourses that separate men as being "of the mind" and women "of the body," together forming a whole; the androgyn that is the apex of desire envisaged in Plato's *Symposium* (Raoul: 267). The attempted over-exertion of normative sexual tropes equally heralds that the system is in jeopardy — gender slippage is manifested via the undead's life/death convergence and the explicit balance of male and female zombies. This is a pantomime of gender difference, enacted as monstrous intercourse. The zombie-human interactions are excessively normative. While the formal disruption indicates that we are to find the couplings strange and horrific, the behaviors enacted are uncannily in keeping with ideologies that seek to retain masculine power, and so it is that dominance that is ultimately critiqued.

Read in such a political light, zombie porn counters hegemonic discourses that declare us to have "stable bodies with complementary sexual organs" and that "only a few body parts are allowed to be invested with sexual significance and then pronounced complementary" (Lindenmeyer, 1999: 51). Pornography's inherent eroticization of genitals may be thus read as an appropriate mode by which to critique a fascination with sexual difference — after all, the usual stark lighting that exposes and prioritizes genitalia is debunked in *Porn of the Dead*. Sexual difference is fundamentally excessive to the zombie-being (the nature of zombiedom is of being without identity), and zombie-desire inherently hinges on a devaluation of genital difference. As Clark observes, "[t]he Undead refuse any sort of curfew on their erotic pleasure; they want it bad, and they want it all the time. They will bite any flesh ... this reactivates the entire body as an erogenous zone and takes the focus away from civilized genital contact" (Clark, 2006: 202). Indeed, the film ends with Nikki Jett's zombie enacting just that — an investment in the bowels as her erotic goal. So the zombie, being eternally hungry, is perfectly suited to the utopia of porn, where the participants refuse to curb their bodily urges, but here the subjects repudiate adherence to restrictive foci on specific areas of bodily pleasure or disgust. "The desire found in and for these [zombie] bodies," as MacCormack argues, "goes beyond any recognizable sexual structure" (103), even disrupting the expected formal motifs of hardcore pornography.

In this sense, the fabric of the body is resurrected, becoming a new political cipher — and the extremity of the depictions is in keeping with this agenda. As Bronfen delineates, "[r]eclaiming the body as a site of self-empowerment" involves "staging an enjoyment of excess, self-consciously enacting a liberation from the constraint of final, totalizing and authoritarian categories" (Bronfen, 2000: 120). Bronfen also observes that "images of the body" are crucial in such power moves, because they "function as the medium for formulating and perpetrating cultural prescriptions and forbidding," becoming "the site at which a given culture can repeatedly renegotiate its privileged collective self-representation as well as its hegemonic values" (Bronfen, 2000: 112). Thus pornography, as a genre concerned with explicitly exposing, scrutinizing, and perhaps even shaping the body (Schiebinger: 2), again proves its appropriateness in this respect. However, the final threat to imposed ideological order arises from another aspect of *Porn of the Dead*'s adherence to porn-norms. While Webb and Byrnand contend that the zombie-narrative closes when "something is reconciled; the horror is put back into the closet, out of sight — until the next relapse" (Webb and Byrnand: 89), *Porn of the Dead* rejects narrative trajectory, having no closure, offering no explanation for the plague or any explicit connection between the scenes. Because there is no narrative drive, there is no change — even if we witness the repercussions of immanent shifts. That is to say, we see the dead coming back to life, but not directly as a result of zombie attack. This suggests that it is beyond the film's ability to articulate change within its own span because its disconnected moments refuse to assign agency — thus cause and effect cannot be gendered. The problem/cause is not identified, and so there can be no "hope" for reclamation of the old human order. Zombies are present, they are everywhere, and no-one can do anything to stop it. If we are to read this as a feminist call-to-action, it is also worth noting that the humans here are unfazed by the presence of the monsters. They may perceive the zombies as monstrous and may be harmed by them, but in their current state, the zombies are unaware of the power they hold, behaving as humans do, and so may be understood as a warning against complacency.

Conclusion: The Radical Potentials of Excess

To summarize the complex problem we are faced with, let us return to the issue of necrophilia; "necrophilics view the corpse as a safe object that offers neither resistance nor opposition, eliminates all risks of rejection and retaliation, and enhances their sense of being alive because the dread of annihilation is projected onto the corpse" (Dujovne, 2004: 635). So at once it is the case that necrophilic fantasy is seemingly sadistic; that males (and

Dujovne explicitly refers to necrophilics as male, and the corpses as female) are willing to entirely negate female subjectivity. But hidden therein lie the seeds of destruction — an admittance of "potential annihilation." We then have to consider that the corpse is animated — while inarticulate, the zombie is able to demonstrate resistance, and so the danger of overthrow becomes more apparent (given that the framing scenes of *Porn of the Dead* end in the destruction of male sexuality, it is implicit that usurpation is a certainty). But we also need to account for the presence of manbies in a heterosexualized space, and the fact that this is, above all, a fantasy — thus it may be a case of "playing at" danger with the knowledge that the status quo will remain. If one side is exaggerated (the radical potential of overthrow of the normative sexual system, embodied by the zombies), so is the other (male sexuality becomes monstrous, too aggressive).

While MacCormack suggests that "masculinity is already so culturally transparent that it does not bear on identity" (MacCormack: 130), here the representation of masculinity is so excessive (even beyond the grave) that it draws more attention to itself than femininity does. The necrophilic taboo allows a critical space in which male desire becomes unwieldy, abnormal and defamiliarized even to the male viewer. After all, critical dissatisfaction with the film suggests that Freud was mistaken in his insistence that "[t]he sexual instinct overrides resistances such as "shame, disgust, horror or pain" with the result that the object of sexual desire is raised to the status of the sacred" (Freud, 1957: 152) — not least since the bodies here are degraded rather than valued. Because of its status as pornography, and the insistence of performers looking into the camera, the viewer is implicated in the deviance of the necrophilic mode; "necrophilia ... calls to mind the marginal and the extreme. It points to the guilty or the sick few, and allows the rest of culture to escape to the moral high ground, where it may continue to indulge its duplicitous fantasies" (Downing: 168).[11] The film's refusal to allow us to distance ourselves from aberrance suggests that we must come to terms with the ideological binaries that the film seeks to destabilize — our disgust then, should issue us into recognizing our own complicity in the same ideological systems that seek to justify social biases.

The situation is thus more difficult than Downing's assertion credits: "[t]hat [necrophilia] should operate as a silent coda for the male possession of the female is inherent in the logic of disavowal subtending such strategies" (Downing: 168). In *Porn of the Dead*, it is important to note that the human females do not instigate sex with corpses as the humen do — Hillary Scott is awoken by oral sex, and Trina Michaels is pounced upon. No matter how willingly they go along with it, this is a far cry from the male desire for the corpse as seen in the final two scenes. The first three scenes thus frame the assignations as a kind of reverse necrophilia, where the corpse desires the human. Either way, when the human is the instigator, it is explicitly rendered as a male fantasy, and the imagery of degradation (if it is to be read as erotic) is concerned with female submission to male desire. Thus necrophilia is framed (both in *Porn of the Dead*, and in Downing's view) as a male fantasy (an imbalance in itself), but one that is framed as psychologically abnormal — therefore missing the point that it places salient images of "'normative" sexual relationships/inequalities under scrutiny. This is because "[s]exual difference entails the existence of a sexual ethics, an ethics of the ongoing negotiations between beings whose differences, whose alterities, are left intact but with whom some kind of exchange is nonetheless possible" (Grosz: 192). The "exchange" in question must occur between fantasy and political reality, life and death, as well as male and female here. While Clark notes that "Eros is the instinct that brought humans together and created civilization in the first place ... reproduction and the continuation of the species are only incidental by-products of the overwhelming urge to obtain total physical bodily pleasure from other humans" (Clark: 201), it is worth remarking that while the fantasy of porn seems to centralize male pleasure, that indulgence is correlated with horrific aggression in *Porn of the Dead*. Moreover, the fembie bite (and it is only the females that we see biting in both *Porn of the Dead* and *Repenetrator*), divests the hu-men of their central ideological status as phallic controller, directly disturbing male bodily boundaries, and evincing the blurred line between the binary separation by evoking female aggression over male pleasure (manifested via the preceding popshot). This is the true climax, as women exceed the male capacity to subdue them, and it is unclear (given its status as the new "money-shot" in this Horror-porn climate) if this is a moment of terror or pleasure.

Briefel argues that "the female monstrous body is completely knowable ... once the female body bleeds, it will breed a very predictable form of horror ... compound[ing] our identification with the female monster — her changes and pain become our own" (Briefel: 24). But perhaps in *Porn of the Dead* the results are not so predictable. Firstly, there is no change — there are static positions due to a lack of narratorial direction. We must then also question if the pain does "become our own" in an identificatory sense, or if it becomes ours to own, as we (whomsoever that may be) are expected to gain pleasure (or horror) from it. The very slippage between porn and Horror is what makes the response unpredictable. Finally, it is worth noting that the "female monstrous body" to which Briefel refers is confused with the non-monstrous (standard porn-body) of the human females here, and potentially even with the manbie-bodies, depending on which binary we favor (be it male/female, or alive/undead). That the human female bodies are made monstrous in ways that differ from the degeneration of the fembie bodies, and that the hu-man bodies are made vulnerable (made to bleed) here, complicates the matter further. My argument is that it may be easy to discount or disavow *Porn of the Dead* with accusations of misogyny, but we may wish to see what political commentary its excesses offer, rather than being distracted by its over-exerted fantasies.

NOTES

1. For an example of reading the zombie in relation to post-colonial politics, see Castronovo (2000: 113–148).

2. See Webb and Byrnand (2008) for a reading of the zombie in relation to "neoliberal economics ... globalization," and "capitalist production" (85).

3. See also Beisecker, forthcoming.

4. The capitalism reading may become more palatable in this sense, as it relates desire to unalloyed greed.

5. See Sceats (2001) for a dissection of the vampire (another undead creature) in relation to gender, and in terms of infection of male sexuality.

6. For more on gender in zombie films of the 1930s and 1940s, see Dendle, 2007: 48.

7. By way of a useful comparison, Braidotti (2004: 92, 95–7 and 107–10) discusses the nature "technophilic anthropomorphism" and the automaton as erotic object.

8. While I am unconvinced by the reading, Clark's assertion that the "swaying ... engorged" bodies of

zombies are like penises (Clark, 2006: 203) makes for an interesting point of comparison to the porno-landscape and its male performers that are like one-dimensional permanent erections.

9. See also reviews by Devon Bertsch (2008) and Robert Cettl (2008) that complain of the same problems.

10. While the authors are concerned with economics, it is worth considering what happens when "screwed" is literalized in the zombie porn narrative.

11. Other authors concurring that necrophilia is a deviant activity include Gutierrez and Giner-Sorolla, 2007: 854–5; Canter and Wentink, 2004: 491; and Balint, cited in Levy, 1980: 191–2.

Modern Zombie Makers

*Enacting the Ancient Impulse to
Control and Possess Another*

Suzanne Goodney Lea

The zombie is an intriguing concept that transcends both time and place. Stories of zombie-like creatures have been told for centuries, across the entire globe (Curran, 2009). The idea that the dead might return from their graves on certain nights of the year, or that one might create and have mastery over a creature that can traverse the boundary between the living and the dead, continues to engage. For most of us, that curiosity is explored at movie theaters or in books, with ghost stories told around a fire, or via the lore or legend associated with the Halloween season. Sometimes, though, intrigue can become obsession.

For a few very unique individuals, the zombie concept engages a much more primal dimension of their identities. Not having been fully socialized themselves, these individuals find deep appeal within the idea that they might have a completely obedient sexual "partner." An abusive and/or neglectful childhood has rendered these modern zombie-makers incapable of negotiating the complexity of human interaction. Instead, they seek to dominate would-be interaction partners, as if to ensure that social exchanges abide by some predetermined pattern or script.

Most of us take for granted the fact that we have learned the rules of our society, i.e., how to relate to our fellow humans. We fret when we make the most minor *faux pas*, and most of us know how to act within most of the social situations we encounter. We all struggle at times with what to say or how to respond to others, for instance at a funeral for a young child, which is a very uncommon event. However, most of us know how far to stand from acquaintances or colleagues when talking with them, how to ask an attractive potential sex partner out for a date, or when to leave a party lest we overstay our welcome. And while most of us have met the occasional person that seems to struggle with the most basic social interactions, such as the person that walks up to a group at a party and says something that is either a non-sequitor or completely inappropriate, the vast majority of us do manage to simply "pick up" the complex and nuanced norms that govern social decorum via interaction with our parents, siblings, peers, and other significant others.

Many of the people who do not assimilate this complex matrix of interactional skills live frustrated and isolated lives. Other than a few socialization initiatives delivered to individuals who are clinically-diagnosed as having severe interactional challenges, there is little effort made to provide this kind of socialization to those people who can function in a rudimentary way but who did not fully acquire the knowledge and skills required to negotiate the subtleties of social interaction. In part, since most of us learn these skills passively via interacting and watching interaction, there is a limited understanding of how to teach such skills. In effect, then, most of the people who do not acquire these skills passively become unable to navigate the social exchanges required to attain a decent job or a romantic partner. The result is a profoundly isolated individual who may simulate unattained interaction via fantasy. Notably, advances in internet technology such as games like *Second Life* may provide an outlet in which isolated people can find interaction without the demands of on-the-spot, in-person exchanges with "forceful, demanding others" (Chapman, 1972: 183). Few such isolates become violent or aggressive, but some do — usually in an effort to acquire sexual interaction partners that they cannot manage to woo and/or maintain using more traditional interactional tools.

This essay will explore two specific cases of such marginalized individuals: Jeffrey Dahmer and Dennis Nilsen. In both cases, these men committed multiple murders with the goal of having a sex "partner" who would completely abide by the killer's wishes and have no volition of their own. Though separated by an ocean (Dahmer lived in Milwaukee, WI, and Nilsen lived in London, England), the two men's patterns of finding, killing, and subsequently symbolically engaging with their victims' remains were strikingly similar. Dahmer explicitly engaged the zombie concept to construct his would-be "partner," and while Nilsen was less explicit in appropriating the zombie motif, his motivation for killing was quite similar. The questions explored here include why these men aspired to possess completely compliant partners, how they enacted their wishes on a psychological level, and where their efforts fit within the broader zombie lore.

Zombie Lore

Historically and across various cultures, zombies have been conceptualized in several ways. The most common zombie motif is that of a dead person brought back to life, based usually upon religious lore such as that which has animated the tradition of Halloween. For centuries, October 31 has marked All Soul's, or All Hallow's, Eve. In many cultures, this is viewed as a night when the barrier separating the worlds of the dead and living is opened so that the dead might again roam the earth and come to visit their still-living loved ones (Campbell, 2005). Such beliefs probably derived from the era before modern medicine, when doctors and shamans had no clear means of discerning when and if someone was dead. The funeral "wake" likely extends from this time and was literally conceived, initially, as a period when loved ones would sit with the newly deceased person and make sure they did not wake up (Tebb, Vollum, and Howden, 1905). Sometimes they did. Such concern existed about burying someone alive that some 19th-century cemeteries would bury a tube extending from a "safety casket" up into the cemetery above so that a dead person who woke up could both breath and ring a bell to let the night watchman know they were still alive (Bondeson, 2002). Until the end of the 19th-century, there existed a real concern that someone might be buried alive and this possibility may have inspired both the Dracula and zombie lore (Bishop, 2010).

An alternative zombie motif is that of a doctor ("witch doctor," mad scientist, etc.) rendering a living person half-dead, a motif popularly associated with Haiti. The most famous version of this concept was exemplified in Wes Craven's film, *The Serpent and the Rainbow*, in which a doctor with magical powers injected people with a mixture that slowed their vital signs so that they seemed dead. Another version of this tale probably lent Francois "Papa Doc" Duvalier much of his political power: he was said to be a voodoo priest and a powerful witch doctor who could make his enemies into zombies, over whom he would have supreme control (Campbell: 42). Papa Doc kept a human skull on his desk to symbolize this power and to remind others' of his abilities (ibid.: 45). According to Haitian legend, a field hand named Ti Joseph is said to have turned nine men into zombies, only to have them working for him in the fields so that he could collect the wages of ten people for his one-person work day (Davis, 1988: 72). Haitians largely, then, posit the zombie concept as a cautionary tale. One fears becoming a zombie, or zombification (Davis, 1988: 74–75; Bishop, 2010: 54–55). Embalming is uncommon for the poor in Haiti, and so families will sit at a grave for as long as 36 hours, will cut open a body before burial, or will inject poison into the deceased's heart so as to prevent their becoming a zombie (Bishop, 2010: 55). One might guess that the conditions hastened by the recent earthquake, such as the necessity of mass graves, may have inadvertently played on one of Haitians' worst fears.

This second zombie model arguably informs the framework by which Dahmer and Nilsen conceptualized their desires to find and control a sexual "partner." This motif appropriates the concept of the enslaved, rather than infected, zombie (Bishop, 2010: 54). The zombified individual is not dead, but neither is he or she fully alive. The zombie lacks volition, and its owner seeks either to use it as Ti Joseph did — either for labor, vengeance, or as a completely controllable lover. Dahmer, in particular, was drawn into the occult and, specifically, zombie lore, creating a small shrine in his apartment where he put the collected skulls of his victims (Ressler, 1997; Masters, 1993). Drawings found in his apartment after his arrest illustrated his plans to expand upon this shrine (Ressler, 1997). Dahmer also engaged in cannibalism and displayed decapitated heads and sex organs in his apartment as a means, he said, of trying to connect with or retain qualities of his victims (Dahmer, 1994). Both Dahmer and Nilsen sought to create a lover that was completely compliant (Dahmer; Masters, 1986).

Analee Newitz, in her exploration of capitalist monsters, suggests that "alienation is what it feels like to be someone else's commodity, to be subject to a boss who 'owns' you for a certain amount of time" (Newitz: 51). To become a zombie, in effect, means that one would be owned, potentially, thoroughly and forever. Unlike reanimated undead, represented by the Frankenstein tale, the zombie retains no will, or sentience, of its own. To be a zombie-maker is to fully consume another — and to create something that is decidedly unique in a mass-produced age.

Theoretical Background

Sociologists understand personal identity formation as a product of social interaction. As conceived by Cooley (1902), an individual develops a sense of self via the reflection provided by interaction with the other, a concept he terms the "looking-glass self." A normal individual will develop a number of selves, held together by a central self-concept that, if healthy, integrates and manages these various identities. Each of these selves will be most easily and frequently conjured via interaction with the others or the situation that facilitated its development. According to Sheldon Stryker's version of "Identity Theory," the various roles, or identities, that we take on in our lives are oriented into a salience hierarchy (Stryker, 1968), which certainly changes based upon the "institutional context or period of one's life" (McCall and Simmons, 1966: 77). One's twenties are often turbulent precisely because they lack the consistent role structure that, say, the thirties or forties typically provide (spouse, parent, professional, etc.). Moreover, a consistent, day-to-day salience hierarchy could be at least temporarily changed by, for instance, a trip back home, which is likely why the holidays are so stressful a time for many of us. Returning to another period of one's life can upset the salience hierarchy to which one has become accustomed.

Reflecting upon the idea that selves generate from interaction, one might pause to consider what might happen to the identity development and structure of someone who either lacked significant interaction or rejected such interaction because they felt they harbored what Erving Goffman (1963: 41) terms a "discreditable stigma," or an aspect of the self that one perceives would drive others away if they were to discover it. Such individuals might be termed "self-selected isolates" and could be said to be rejecting the "looking glass" (Cooley, 1902) of social interaction. Goffman's discussion of a discreditable stigma (41–2) suggests that someone with such a stigma (1) perceives himself as deviant in a way that is not obvious to others, (2) fears that, if anyone knew of the deviance, the results would be socially disastrous, and thus (3) keeps this part of him- or herself carefully hidden. This implies that someone could hold a conception of himself outside, at least, of any immediately accessible direct social interaction. I would term this "unshareable" sense of self a "negative identity."

Such an identity cannot become "recentered" (Britt and Heise, 1992: 344) or neutralized (Sykes and Matza, 1957) via differential association (Sutherland and Cressey, 1974), or interaction with select individuals who can facilitate the reframing of an identity most people might see as negative, such as "thief" or "gangster," into an identity that might be positively viewed among a select subgroup of individuals.[1] Such processes allow, for instance, that a "badass" (Katz, 1988) might be viewed negatively by "outsiders" but, within his or her peer group, might find positive aspects in a commitment to this role. An avoidance of interaction with what Chapman (1972: 183) terms "forceful, demanding others" allows an individual to explore discreditable roles without having to take into account the normalizing effects which such others provide.

The psychological literature typically describes "sociopaths" or "psychopaths" as lacking a conscience — i.e. they know the rules but do not internalize them or live by them (Hare, 1993). Neil MacKinnon (1994) suggests, however, that anyone who has mastered language possesses a generalized other, and that the knowledge of social norms and mores and such are embedded in the affective dimension inherent to language. Hence, we might conclude that self-selected isolates *do* possess this cultural knowledge by virtue of sharing our language. However, self-selected isolates seem to understand that part of who they are is at great odds with these cultural norms. Thus, they may be compelled to want to escape this "generalized other." Avoiding social interaction might allow them to escape the constant engagement of these cultural norms, which is innately a part of verbally interacting with others. It may be that these individuals come to see themselves as so deviant, so "bad," that they have difficulty maintaining an active generalized other. By living within our society and sharing our language, however, they incorporate the generalized attitudes into their self-processes so that they can largely abide by the societal rules. Finding these social expectations to be untenable, they attempt to banish this generalized other by retreating into a fantasy realm of their own creation, wherein they are the ultimate conscience. Georg Simmel (1950: 118–19) surmises: "Isolation, insofar as it is important to the individual, refers by no means only to the absence of society." On the contrary, the idea involves the somehow imagined, but then rejected, existence of society. It may be, then, that sociopaths know the social rules but, because they hold such a negative core conception of themselves, "reject the existence of society" (Hare, 1993: 81) by trying to deaden the regulating impact of the generalized other.

In some cases, this view of self as "bad" emerges early in the life course. In most cases, there will have been some uniquely disturbing developmental issue(s), which might include either severe abuse and/or long-term or frequent isolation due to illness or injury not handled with the necessary sensitivity or due to intentional punishment. These are *catastrophic* childhoods. The critique is often leveled that many people have difficult childhoods but "turn out fine." Here, though, we are considering individuals who have experienced extremely abusive childhoods. For children who are severely abused or neglected, peer relations also become challenging. These young people do not fully learn how to function within their society. For most of us, this is something we learn from our upbringings, from parents and siblings. If peer-rejection occurs early in the life course, this seems to further retard the process of incorporating social roles. There has been very little exploration of the effect isolation might have upon the self-processes of an individual. Researchers who do ethnographic research on schoolchildren find that there are some children who are consistently rejected by their peers and thus become pervasively isolated (Eder, et al., 1995), even from a very early age (Corsaro, 1985). Corsaro (121) suggests that, "through interaction with peers, children learn that they can regulate social bonds on the basis of criteria that emerge from their personal needs and social contextual demands." If a child does not experience sufficient such interaction as they develop, it would be likely that they would not learn how to manage social interaction in an appropriate way and would thus be likely to have increased difficulty fulfilling many of their personal needs. This is evidenced by interviews with "social isolates," as documented by Thomas and Heise (1995: 436). We are social creatures who generally do need interaction. As sexual needs become more compelling with the onset of puberty, the lack of social alacrity causes special problems for isolated teens who do not know how to manage the interaction that would allow them to experience sexual fulfillment with another individual (Keppel, 1997).

Perceiving no opportunities for social interaction and even a danger in pursuing it for fear of having a discreditable stigma discovered, this sort of individual might turn inward. What used to be called play will be termed fantasy by outsiders because one is supposed to outgrow play, replacing it with real roles and their resultant responsibilities. Fantasy "occurs as internal communication manipulating symbols developed in and reflecting the social process," to appropriate the earlier quote from George H. Mead (1934: 128). Most social isolates interact with some aspects of society. Even the "Unabomber," Ted Kaczynski, regularly visited the library and read extensively from its periodicals and recently-arrived books. Additionally, mass media allows that we can all easily appropriate from the broader culture. Jeffrey Dahmer, "the Milwaukee cannibal," for instance, fashioned himself as the emperor from the *Star Wars* series (Ressler, 1997). This became a mainstay of his fantasy play, and I suspect that it was no coincidence that the emperor in that series was a minimally-defined character, except to be characterized as very bad and extremely powerful. The emperor role would likely have confirmed Dahmer's sense of himself as bad but would also have facilitated the exploration of power. As the character was so under-developed in the first *Star Wars* trilogy, it provided a good basic framework for fantasy play, wherein ambiguity in the incorporated concept is desirable as one fashions the incorporation based upon his or her own needs.

As suggested earlier, peer rejection would seem to impede the usual flowering of identities, which occurs in early adulthood. Isolates remain within a fantasy-dominated, "safe" realm wherein they feel in-control and able to be "their self." There are thus no forceful, demanding others to potentially discredit them. As a negative identity is not social, it could become a repository for an array of negative self-feelings that one might have about him/herself. Such an identity would not likely diversify in the same way that social roles do because it is not based upon varying interaction. One may appropriate different scripts, perhaps playing the emperor one day and Satan the next, but all of these scripts would be incorporated into a generalized identity of "badness" for there could be no unshareable identity that would be perceived as a good identity — powerful, yes, but not good. It is also possible to view this situation as a split self-concept with one side being positively-oriented and supporting positive, interactive roles and the other warehousing a set of negative roles. Under this second conceptualization, the negative roles that might be fashioned via adaptation from the mainstream culture would be viewed not as different scripts but as distinct identities. This second conceptualization echoes George McCall and Jerry Simmon's (1950: 77) discussion of a clustering of selves which might be "compartmentalized" or "disassociated" from others at a particular time and perhaps even over time.

I suspect that most of us do have a dual self-concept. In the vast majority of us, however, we have developed a sufficient number of social roles so as to be socially integrated, committed, and thus controlled (Hirschi, 1969). Still, after a bad day at work, we might, as we try to get to sleep, imagine ourselves to be "bad boy" Dennis Rodman, telling our bosses what they can do with that holiday-weekend project. We might also have one or more sexually "deviant" roles via which we explore sexual fantasies and roles. Sexual roles, because we have created such a Puritanical society, seem especially prone to being secreted. Some people will, for instance, go through their entire lives hiding the fact they are gay or bisexual, fearing "discovery" (Weinberg, et al., 1994). Early on, they will hear various denouncements of men being attracted to other men, as was the case in Jeffrey Dahmer's upbringing (Ressler, 1997). They might be accused of being a "fag" or otherwise slandered growing up. Until or unless they meet an individual or group that views being attracted to the same sex as a positive thing, they will not be "recentered" and might forever live in fear and secrecy.

In the case of some closeted gay men's management of a secret self, Laud Humphreys (1970) illustrates how they might explore their sexuality while remaining anonymous. He discovered an extensively ritualized social sphere wherein no one actually "knew" the individuals with whom they were having sex. Nearly all participants consistently maintained what would be called a "situational self" as they "realized" their secreted sexuality. In fact, it seems that fantasy play typically demands some kind of ritualization to facilitate the repression of the "generalized other," or the social rules. We are usually compelled by the generalized other to acknowledge and respect the autonomy of others, but this sense must be suppressed if we seek to dominate and control another person. Importantly, fantasy is non-verbal (Forisha, 1979), which seems notable if MacKinnon (1994) is correct in suggesting that the conscience is embedded within language. Social researchers know little about people's fantasy worlds, but it does seem that some people will use music (Masters, 1986) and/or alcohol or drugs (Jeffrey Dahmer's confessions to the Milwaukee, WI, and Bath, OH, police departments; Masters, 1993) to facilitate it.

Dahmer and Nilsen: Modern Zombie Makers?

Many people who examine the details of a case such as that of a serial killer like Jeffrey Dahmer's would likely conclude that Dahmer was a compulsive, psychologically disturbed, macabre man. Dahmer killed seventeen men over the course of nearly fifteen years, most of them at his apartment in Milwaukee, Wisconsin. Dennis Nilsen, who grew up in Scotland, killed at least fifteen men over the course of just five years while living and working in London, England. I would like to make an alternative case here, however, by considering the details of Dahmer's case, and to a lesser extent Nilsen's case, through the lens of zombie mythology. I have many more details regarding Dahmer's actions and reasoning than I do Nilsen's, and Dahmer much more explicitly incorporates zombie lore into his fantasy world. Nonetheless, Nilsen resonates similar motivations, experiences, and conceptual understandings as those articulated by Dahmer, and so I include details from Nilsen's case here as well. Both men are very unusual in that they enacted an intense and violent fantasy world upon real others. In both cases, these men needed to suppress their inclination to see these other men as real, living other people. To enter their fantasy realm, in which each was master, both men used alcohol and drugs to quiet their generalized other. Nilsen articulates this well in Masters' (1986: 113) account of Nilsen's crimes: "I must have put half a glass of Bacardi in the glass. I put the earphones on, sat down, and listened to the whole sequence of records. He was dead. I kept on drinking. With the music and the drinking, I could get away from what was around me. In the morning, the record player was still going around." Their victims ceased to exist as real people with their own experiences, hopes, and demands and instead became extras in a very private drama by which both

Dahmer and Nilsen hoped to possess — and in Dahmer's case even consume — an idealized other. This was the lover we all wish for: the one that will do just as we want them to do, always and without questions, and that will never leave us.

Reflecting back to the theoretical model I outline above, the first thing that is clear from Dahmer's confession to police is the extent to which he was motivated by isolation and a deep desire for companionship mixed with a complete inability to accommodate the demands that another person inevitably makes — including the most basic one which is that they may leave when they want (Dahmer, 1994; Masters, 1993; Ressler, 1997). Several times within his confessions (State of Wisconsin, 1991), he says, "that's basically it, I just didn't want him to leave." Investigators note that "they [the victims] would tell him they had to leave by a certain time and he wanted them to stay (ibid.: 42)," a sentiment confirmed by both Brian Masters' biography of Dahmer (1993) and by FBI agent Robert Ressler's interviews with him (1997). At the most basic level, his drive could be summarized as, "I wanted to keep him." Dahmer (State of Wisconsin, 1991: 22) states that:

> he received physical pleasure from being with the victims when they were alive and would have preferred that the victims remained alive; however, he states that it was better to have them with him dead than to have them leave. He states that when he felt when [sic] they were to leave, that is when he would decide to kill them.

Strong feelings about being left alone developed after his mother and brother left in the midst of the very hostile divorce of his parents and then, weeks later, his father, not realizing that his estranged wife had moved out, also abandoned Jeffrey at the end of high school. Left alone in the family home with no food or money, "he began hating to sleep alone at night." This early experience was reactivated years later, just months before Dahmer was arrested after his killings escalated:

> He also states that he was fired from his job on July 7, 1991, and he had known the week prior that he was going to get fired and he feels this is the reason why the killings escalated because he was alone at night and did not want to be alone. He had no company and felt that these individuals would keep him company [State of Wisconsin, 1991: 25].

Dahmer's own father confirms Dahmer's account in *A Father's Story* (Dahmer, 1994).

This issue of control is central to Dahmer's motivation and is also the impulse that connects him to the zombie lore. The zombie has always symbolized the ultimate power and control over another person that becomes less a person than one's personal slave. No longer can this individual assert their own will; they must do as you please. In cultures that embrace the idea that a very powerful person can turn other people into zombies, this resonates with a primal fear: that you will be somehow alive but no longer you and totally under the will of another more powerful being. When he was cutting up his victims, Dahmer says that "he also had the feeling that the victims could not leave him anymore because he had complete control over them" (State of Wisconsin, 1991: 124). And while Dahmer describes himself as being "basically a loner" most of his life (ibid.: 38), he also states that "he likes to be alone, and he especially likes to be alone when he kills people and cuts them up because it makes him feel more secure and more dominant" (ibid.: 157). And while he admits exploring the occult and other dark media as a means to understanding and engaging his unshareable self, he notes (ibid.: 157) that ideas to cut people up or kill them "were his own and that they were uniquely his own. He felt power in the fact that they were his own private thoughts and that while he was doing this he felt it was his own private world that belonged to no one else: he states he was always a loner, he took pleasure in the fact of knowing that he had a private world of his own that no one else knew about."

Dahmer talks about drawing people into this world by way of a "potion" (ibid.: 77): "he would have the sleeping pill broken down into a powder form in the bottom of either a glass or a cup and when he would prepare the drink for the individual, using either coffee or rum and coke, he would use the glass or cup that contained the powdered sleeping pill substance. He stated this would dissolve readily and the victim was unable to determine that anything was in his drink." Dahmer and Nilsen both also detail how they would effectively drug themselves as well, in preparation for the "interaction" they were about to have. Both men effectively describe putting themselves into a state of trance. As noted above, Nilsen did so by drinking heavily, sometimes using drugs, and also using music to engage his fantasy world (Masters, 1986). It is likely that inducing this state of trance sub-dues the generalized other that regulates us to social norms, which do not include homicide. Dahmer says that he "had at least a twelve pack" before he killed his first victim (State of Wisconsin, 1991: 143). According to police files, Dahmer also indicates, "that he didn't drink everyday but when he planned to get someone he would start drinking after he planned and then he was usually drunk when he killed them" (ibid.: 143). He related that he even drank when he was cutting up the bodies, saying that "it helped to make it easier when he was doing this" (ibid.: 143).

Once the victim was dead, which was often a very quick and utilitarian effort effected only to keep the victim from leaving, the focus for Dahmer, especially, was to make the most adored victims part of himself. Both Dahmer and Nilsen dismembered their victims, but in Nilsen's case, this was put off as long as possible (Masters, 1986). Nilsen would store the victim's body in the apartment and take it out each evening after work to spend time with it. He would wash the body in the tub, sit next to it for an evening of television, and lie next to it in bed at night.

In effect, it seemed like Nilsen felt as if he might be doing his victims a favor. Of one, he says:

> I gently undressed him and carried him naked into the bathroom. I washed him carefully all over in the bath and sitting his limp body on the edge. I toweled him dry. I laid him on my bed and put talc on him to make him look cleaner. I just sat there and watched. He looked really beautiful like one of those Michelangelo sculptures. It seemed that for the first time in his life he was really feeling and looking the best he ever did in his whole life. I wanted to touch and stroke him, but did not. I placed two mirrors around the bed, one at the end and one at the side. I lay naked beside him but only looked at the two bodies in the mirror. I just law there and a great peace came over me. I felt that this was it, the meaning of life, death, everything. No fear, no pain, no guilt. I could only caress and fondle the image in the mirror. I never looked at him. No sex, just a feeling of oneness. I had an erection but felt he was far too perfect and beautiful for the pathetic ritual of commonplace sex [Masters, 1986: 124–45].

Nilsen dismembered the bodies of his victims only once the decomposition had become too severe and simply to hide the evidence; truly he was "killing for company," as Masters (1986) suggests in the titling of his biography of Nilsen.

In Dahmer's case, the dismemberment was in part a matter of concealing his crime, but it was much more ritualistic. Both Nilsen and Dahmer would take Polariods by which to remember their victims (Masters, 1986; Masters, 1993). Dahmer's Polaroids, in which he posed his victims' bodies, were particularly macabre, though the effort to pose and, as Nilsen expounds above, visually appreciate their victims' bodies makes one think that both men were attempting to create some sort of artistry. Dahmer also took power in possessing parts of their bodies, going even so far as to actually consume some particularly meaningful parts. Investigators note that Dahmer "states that he feels that by eating parts of the victim, this is one way of keeping them with him even longer and making his victims part of himself" (State of Wisconsin, 1991: 22). Police records also report that that Dahmer "would cut off the penis and body parts, and put them in formaldehyde to preserve them and then look at them and masturbate for gratification" (ibid.: 22). Dahmer notes that he only kept body parts of the men that were especially attractive to him: "when he did keep more items of these individuals, it was because he liked them more or they appealed to him more" (ibid.: 138). Or, he "did not keep any of the body parts because the man wasn't his type." He remarks (ibid.: 15) that "he would masterbate [sic] in front of the body parts and skulls he had collected because it brought back memories of the victim."

Towards the end of his years of killing, Dahmer actually did try to make a zombie by getting a would-be victim very drugged and then attempting a rudimentary lobotomy by drilling a hole into the victim's frontal cortex (Masters, 1993; Ressler, 1997). The idea was to create someone that would be alive but would neither leave nor make any demands upon Dahmer. This endeavor brought Dahmer under police scrutiny when Dahmer left this would-be zombie alone, after the victim had passed out. This victim, who had a drill-hole through his frontal cortex, actually awoke and escaped the apartment. He was intercepted by neighbors, who called authorities to report that there was a disoriented, naked boy in the apartment's parking lot (Prudhomme and Cronin, 1991). The victim was Asian, just fifteen at the time, and was speaking in his native Cambodian. Dahmer, who had left for the bar and had been gone for a couple of hours, returned to find neighbors and police directing their attention at him. Assessing the scene, Dahmer, as reported in his confession to police and corroborated by Prudhomme and Cronin (1991), decided to spin a tale that would diffuse the situation:

> He related that due to the fact that he was able to convince all these people, in positions of authority, his parents and neighbors who questioned him regarding his activities, it gave him a feeling that he could get away with his crimes. He felt that he had the ability to make people see a phase [sic—*face*] of him that only he wished them to see and that this encouraged him to continue with his crimes, feeling that he would never be caught [State of Wisconsin, 1991: 157].

Dahmer put his arm around the boy (who Dahmer perceived to be a young man), said a few things to the police to indicate that this was a lover's quarrel, and led the boy back into his apartment, where he would be killed minutes later. Police did not want to be involved in a gay lovers' spat, nor did they want to be in this poor, largely black neighborhood. The police did not notice that the boy was bleeding from the brain (they later said that it was dark and that brain blood, which is a deep, dark red, is very hard to see in the dark), and they did not ask to see identification (Prudhomme and Cronin, 1991).

Dahmer was especially fixated on skulls. In all, he kept eleven skulls, four torsos (which he was trying to dissolve in a giant drum), two hearts, various other inner organs, and one full skeleton. In the case of one victim, he removed the entire skin, noting that the face "was just like a mask" (State of Wisconsin, 1991: 158) in that "the entire skull portion of the skin came off in one complete piece and while it was off it actually looked somewhat like a mask you can buy at a party store" (ibid). He even bought makeup to use in "hiding marks or discolored skin" on the genitals he kept "because he wanted it more of a flesh color" (ibid.: 84). In many cases, he bleached and painted skulls, saying that "he wanted to keep the skull of his victims, because to him the skull represented the true essence of his victims" (ibid.: 132). In fact, he created an altar of skulls, and police found plans for expanding that altar when they searched Dahmer's apartment (Ressler, 1997).

The Long, Dark Impulse to Control and Possess

For both Dahmer and Nilsen, social interaction presented unbearable challenges. Most of us are frustrated by the prospect of trying to get our way with others: our parents and siblings, initially, and later our peers, our first and future lovers, our boss, and eventually our own children. These struggles animate much of our social interaction. How many hours are spent ruminating over how to get our spouse to see things our way or to work around a boss's dysfunctional leadership style without angering or belittling him or her? Most people manage to figure out strategies for negotiating these struggles, but some notably do not: the young, especially, are at risk of a violent expression of their frustration to get a lover to stay. In Dahmer's case, especially, the deep compulsion to keep people to which he was drawn clearly drove his violent trajectory.

At the heart of the idea that one might make a zombie of another person lies the idea — the wish, really — that we might somehow have complete power over someone that still functions as a person. They could work for us, kill for us, or love us. They seem alive but they have no volition. In fact, though, it is the "forceful, demanding" character of the other (Chapman, 1972: 183) that makes interaction engaging and enriching but also quite terrifying. We seek acknowledgement, acceptance, and love from others, and these are things that can only be truly given if they are given freely. A bully like "Papa Doc" can intimidate others into "giving" these things, but the ability to really see a person in all their complexity and to then love them generates from a place of joyful abandon. Young children are innately able to do this, and they can sometimes overwhelm a cynical, guarded adult with their unbridled affection. A dictator and his lackeys, an insecure lover, or a controlling boss: all of these can get other people to act as if they admire or respect them, but all are also driven to be more and more aggressive or manipulative in their quest to force this behavior. At the end of the day, though, what many claim to want is *genuine* affection and acceptance, something that can only come from someone that has the freedom to give it. Of course, it may well be that, despite people's claims, many do not actually seek this. One can point to many relationships that willingly construct power in different ways: master-slave liaisons within BDSM communities, for instance. Within those relationships, the submissive partner willingly gives their will — often in all aspects — over to the dominant partner. There are also entire societies — Russia, as an example — that seem to thrive on an autocratic model that seems decidedly persistent.

In the case of both Dahmer and Nilsen, the inability to navigate social interaction drove them into a very isolated and private world wherein they had power and control over others. In their fantasy worlds, everyone stayed and loved them forever. Eventually, they gained such confidence in themselves from this imagined affection that they attempted to draw in real others, finding that they inevitably wanted to leave. The answer for both Dahmer and Nilsen was to make the other person stay, but this was ultimately not satisfying. The ultimate goal of someone who *wanted* to stay remained forever elusive, driving the compulsion that much harder.

To most of us standing on the outside, this can all seem very macabre and disturbed. Are these men not simply mentally ill? One could certainly make that argument, but it also seems possible to imagine other possibilities. Romantic euphemisms are animated by the idea of "consuming" the other. Obviously, few take this literally, as Dahmer did, but we need not go back so very long ago to find that the Celts placed the remains of deceased famed personalities in a small waterway so that others could drink of the water, which they believed carried the "essence" of the deceased individual (Campbell, 2005).

Another interpretation of Dahmer's consumption of these others is offered by Newitz (2006) and her exploration of capitalist monsters. Arguing that there are racial, gender, and class-based narratives by which to interpret such anomalies, one realizes that Dahmer could be viewed as engaging any and all of these lenses. Dahmer's victims were nearly entirely non-white and impoverished. Dahmer claims that he had no racial motivations, that he was just looking for the most attractive men. For just $50 offered to compensate them for letting Dahmer take their pictures, however, most victims went willingly with him. What ensued was a complete domination of these victims. While Newitz argues that Dahmer was a complete failure economically, given his upper middle-class background, she would contend that he defined his expertise in terms of his ability to gain mastery over another person and to, ultimately, completely possess them. Dahmer's Polaroid pictures of his crimes depict him posing corpses as he systematically dismembered them. This was what he did well, but really his interest seemed to be more in the possessing than in the mastery of task. Still, one cannot help but think that Dahmer also appreciated his ability to create something truly special in a mass-produced age. This can be inferred based upon Dahmer's father's recounting of how Dahmer carried the head of one victim with him to work in a bowling bag (Dahmer, 1994). He simply put the bag in his locker, but there seemed to be a thrill in having something so unusual. Perhaps he felt as though this made him some true standout, in contrast to the mundane bore he might otherwise seem to be.

Nilsen's back-story bears some commonalities to Dahmer's. A run-of-the-mill bureaucrat who was competent but shy and who stood out not at all, Nilsen effected his crimes with the efficiency one might expect of a bureaucrat (Masters, 1986). For Nilsen, the goal was not so much to possess, or consume, his victims. In his case, he was seeking companions and, perhaps, a creation — an object — that was all his own, which is a concept that resonates with Annalee Newitz's (2006: 45) suggestion that serial murder might be viewed as a sort of art defined by stylish imitation but with the goal of creating something that is nonetheless uniquely personal. In an age of mass produced goods, Nilsen was able to create something that could not be had at any price: a complacent companion all his own. A person once fully animated now just a shell after Nilsen secretly stole its spirit. Now, this former person exists simply to serve Nilsen until decay necessitates disposal of the beautiful shell. Nilsen, too, took Polaroids as souvenirs of his unique experiences. Both men recount posing their victims post-mortem so as to appreciate their visual beauty, suggesting that they were attempting to, in a way, create truly unique art in a mass market culture, which echoes Newitz (2006: 182–183) who suggests that part of what motivates mass killers is the desire to create something unique in a mass market society.

For both Nilsen and Dahmer, there is an isolation and a banality to the modern existence. Desperate for friends and social connection but unable to relinquish control, each, in his own way, turned to an effort to create a companion of their own. Rather than reanimate the undead, each stole the life and will of a living person, forcing them into their own personal fantasy realm. These victims became servants to the will of these men. In the hours prior to their deaths, the victims were at their mercy. In a rare case, the would-be victim was so personable as to "ruin" the fantasy (Masters, 1986; Ressler, 1997). Those were the ones that got away. The others lived on in the private worlds of these men, as literal — in a few cases, for Dahmer — or figurative zombies: dead or semi-dead beings intended to fulfill the needs of their masters.

Conclusions

The concept of the forceful, demanding other as a core component of social interaction, which orientates the basis for social development and adjustment within a sociological framework, can prove quite illuminating when considering some people's behavior in the face of what is at once a global society that generates more of a sense of anomie and isolation than perhaps any ever has while still somehow promising that one might forge an exceedingly intimate connection with a significant other. Without a forceful, demanding other acting upon us, it may be far too easy for the human animal to rationalize negative, hurtful behavior. At the end of the day, our id may desire to have a zombie all our own: a person who will love us unconditionally and do our bidding.

We love to watch when a famous person is exposed as a fraud — a conservative minister is outed as a closeted gay man who uses drugs, for instance. Perhaps, though, part of the reason that we like to watch and cheer for that person's demise is that not a few of us are hoping no one is noticing what we might be doing while we think no one is watching us. Not so far behind all of our posturing of civility lie ancient urges to possess and control those people that we deeply love and could love that much more if only they would do as we say.

We regard Dahmer and Nilsen as modern monsters, and we observe their creations with an intent horror. While most of us would likely never go to the pathological extremes to which these men went to create an "ideal" partner, most of us can probably appreciate their motivation. The lover that will never leave seems ideal, except that the zombified other is like a mirror: they do as we say and say what we want. Most of us realize that, ultimately, this mimicry is not authentic, and therefore unsatisfactory. For Dahmer and Nilsen, however, it is seemingly enough.

NOTES

1. I base this "positive"—"negative" classification of identities on the work of Timothy Owens and Suzanne Goodney (2000), wherein they conceptualizes self-esteem in similarly dichotomous terms, proposing that an individual may incorporate both kinds of esteem within their schema of self-perception while still maintaining an overall view of him or herself as either (a) generally good and likeable or (b) bad and unlikable. I suggest here that the esteem that a given role might have for a person is dependent upon whether or not s/he can find interactive support for that role.

"Corporate Zombies" and the Perils of "Zombie Litigation"

The Walking Dead in American Judicial Writing

SHARON SUTHERLAND and SARAH SWAN*

In 1968, with the release of George Romero's *Night of the Living Dead*, the zombie infiltrated Western popular culture with a vengeance. Since then, the zombie has continued to haunt the popular imagination. Scholars have examined how screenwriters and directors have used the zombie to symbolize a wide range of fears — from the overt fear of possession and mind control, through fears of atomic radiation, to such modern concerns as mindless consumerism, meaningless existence and the social and individual impacts of drugs and mental illness. Current scholarship looks to the newest iterations of zombies in videogames and online gaming worlds, a testament to the flexibility of the zombie metaphor: the zombie fills the need of gamers in these environments just as they have served to represent the fears of previous generations. In all its iterations, the zombie has proven an adaptable metaphoric device. As Marc Leverette (2008) notes, "it may ... be the symbolic emptiness that gives them their power; people can fill them with whatever fear they want" (203). In this essay, we consider the zombie metaphor in a particular context, that of American judicial decisions. As legal scholars, we are interested in extending the examination of zombies into the previously unexplored realm of case law — a staid and traditional environment in which the zombie as metaphoric device has also, perhaps surprisingly, proliferated over the past decade. We consider the myriad of metaphoric purposes the zombie serves in legal decisions.

Perhaps not surprisingly, our examination into zombie references in American judicial decisions revealed many non-metaphoric references as well. There are cases alleging copyright infringement of *Dawn of the Dead*, judicial discussions of the phenomenon of "zombie computers" (a term derived in another sphere and imported into case law), and a number of "DUI" offenses committed following consumption of a "zombie." While our focus is not on these types of references, the sheer volume of zombie references in general demon-

*The authors gratefully acknowledge the research assistance provided by former law student and zombie aficionado Timothy Luk.

76

strates the prevalence of zombies in North American culture, and the permeation of popular culture into judicial awareness such that we do not necessarily need to conclude that the judges who utilize zombie metaphors have all watched *Dawn of the Dead* or played *Resident Evil*. Zombies seep into our collective consciousness through many means: for many judges, it may be hearing defendant after defendant claiming an inability to form the requisite *mens rea* for a crime because an excess of drugs has brought about a zombie-like state, or it might be a lengthy explanation of the similarities of Romero's zombies to the zombies of a new videogame where a judge is asked to decide if the one is too close an imitation of the other. Certainly, judges who draw on zombie metaphors in writing their reasons for judgment, believe that the reference will be clear and will communicate a readily understood meaning to litigants and to the legal community.

The exploration of American case law as a text for zombie references illuminates aspects of both the case law, and of the zombie metaphor. Firstly, the fact that we identified over 200 instances of the metaphoric use of zombies in case law since 1956 (when the first metaphoric reference we found occurred) demonstrates the degree of cultural saturation of the image. Judges write for the understanding of two audiences: the litigants whose cases they decide, and the lawyers and judges who may rely upon their written reasons in the analysis and argument of future cases. For both of these audiences, clarity of expression is essential. Whereas a novelist might choose to employ an unusual and challenging metaphor that requires her reader to contemplate meaning(s), a judge is tasked with ensuring that her judgment is readily accessible. The pattern of use of zombie metaphors in legal writing follows behind the growth of popular culture's use of zombies, becoming relatively common (and arguably more complex) only when judges assume a general understanding of the image and the characteristics attached to that image. Whereas Dendle (2001) refers to the period between 1968 and 1983 as the "golden age of zombie movies" (7) and 1983 has been cited as the year zombies "hit the mainstream" in popular culture (McIntosh, 2008: 11), the golden age of judicial zombie metaphors does not begin until approximately 1993, and it is still going strong. What might be termed cultural saturation sufficient for the judiciary to assume common understanding of zombie traits occurs about 10 years after the popular culture literacy.

Secondly, the zombie metaphor in judicial decisions connects to the work of scholars in the field of Law and Literature. In his *Poethics and Other Strategies of Law and Literature*, Richard Weisberg (1992) picks up and expands the earlier arguments of Benjamin Cardozo that judicial opinions stand or fall on their language, including the "appropriateness of the fit — the fluidity harmony — between the word used and the aspiration to justice that every legal pronouncement should embody" (7). Whether or not one follows this line of reasoning to its conclusion that the form of the legal argument cannot be separated from its substance, it is clear that the form of the judgment is important. Well-crafted judgments are cited over and over by advocates and judges for their clear statement of legal principle. The best statements of principle become more and more embedded in case law and form the basis for future legal reasoning. When a phrase such as "evil zombie" captures the content of a legal argument so succinctly and appropriately that future advocates can argue for the application of the "evil zombie rule," this popular culture figure becomes embedded in our understanding of the law. In all likelihood, the metaphor will significantly outlast the specific references that gave rise to it, and it will accrete new meanings as it is used relative to future understandings of the zombie. Rhetorical studies have explored in detail how metaphors expand meaning: when applied to case law as a text which evolves through the repetition and refinement of metaphors (amongst other forms of language), the potential for expanded meanings is considerable.

Additionally, this study collects zombie metaphors that are, perhaps, unfamiliar and less accessible to many. Through it, we are able to share some colorful writing about zombies with those interested in the topic more broadly. In speaking of metaphor generally, Knowles and Moon write that "where we have a choice, we choose metaphors in order to communicate what we think or how we feel about something; to explain what a particular thing is like; to convey a meaning in a more interesting or creative way; or to do all of these" (Knowles and Moon, 2005: 3). We have already noted that judges choose their language in order to communicate and explain; there can be little doubt that they also choose zombie metaphors in order to create interesting and creative images. It is worth examining some of these purely colorful metaphors in light of the importance of the texts in which they are contained. And, finally, as Nina Auerbach (1997) has written (about vampires, but we believe the same applies to zombies), our monsters blend into and reflect the cultures they inhabit (6). Here, then, are some themes emerging from the legal culture which these particular zombies inhabit. We have divided our discussion below into the aspects of the zombie captured by metaphors: the inability to think or function, mind control of individuals and legal persons, and unkillability or the tendency to rise from the dead. We end with a discussion of the use of zombie references in some cases for purposes of color and impact.

"To Be a Confirmed Drug Addict Is to Be One of the Walking Dead" (Robinson v. California)

From its origin in Vodoun magic and religion, the zombie has had a close association with drugs. While mystical practices supposedly caused a death-like state from which practitioners could revive the sufferers, Vodoun zombification has been described as "the result of pharmacology, the careful administration of powerful neurotoxins" (Bishop, 2006: 197).[1] Other studies of the history of the zombie have noted that this pre–Romero zombie figure was the dominant zombie image before 1968 (McIntosh: 4–5). It is not surprising then, that the sole zombie reference from the 1960s would adopt this image of the zombie and associate it closely with drug use. In the 1962 case *Robinson v. California*, Mr. Justice Stewart delivers a vivid, and presumably edifying, description of the drug addict as one of the walking dead, drawing a picture of the gruesome physical resemblance between the addict and a zombie in great detail:

> The teeth have rotted out; the appetite is lost and the stomach and intestines don't function properly. The gall bladder becomes inflamed; eyes and skin turn a bilious yellow. In some cases membranes of the nose turn a flaming red; the partition separating the nostrils is eaten away — breathing is difficult.... Good traits of character disappear and bad ones merge. Sex organs become affected. Veins collapse and livid purplish scars remain. Boils and abscesses plague the skin; gnawing pain racks the body. Nerves snap; vicious twitching develops. Imaginary and

fantastic fears blight the mind and sometimes complete insanity results.... Such is the torment of being a drug addict; such is the plague of being one of the walking dead [627].

In this particular instance, the connection of the drug addict with zombie serves to greatly increase the effect of the description of the addict. Having already identified the description with the "living dead," the judge creates a mental picture that draws on the reader's assumed knowledge of zombies — presumably from pre–Romero films. The effect is intensified by the image of rotting flesh. One imagines that the Court wished to convey a strong message about the horrors of drug addiction in adopting this metaphor.

The connections between drugs and zombies continue through the case law of later years, and become only too common as defendants in any number of cases seek to excuse their actions as taking place in a state of zombification due to drug or alcohol abuse. The array of drugs which arguably render one a zombie are greatly expanded by the case law from the usual puffer fish toxin identified with Vodoun zombification. Criminal cases, usually in exploring the defendant's mental state at the time of an offense, discuss the potentially zombifying effects of crack (*U.S. v. Farley*), a combination of Valium with alcohol (*Watkins v. U.S.*), a daily consumption of one and a half pints of vodka plus beer (*Eberle v. City of Newton*), heroin (*Nunez v. State*), cocaine (*U.S. v. Kramer*), pain medication (*Holland v. Apfel*), anti-psychotic drugs (*Langley v. Barnhart*), medication for "nerves" (*Callahan v. Campbell*), and OxyContin (*Bodie v. Purdue Pharma Co.*).

Similarly, it is not unusual for extreme emotion, mental health issues or abuse to be cited as causes of zombie-like affect. In these instances, the phrase is usually employed to indicate a lack of emotion rather than mindlessness and loss of requisite volition as in the case of drug use, although we learn from *U.S. v. Kramer* for example, that one can be "so ill" during a plea that one could be a zombie and not know "in depth" what was happening. These types of references do not only originate with the judiciary; they often appear in cases where judges are discussing the merits of pleas that a party was "like a zombie" at some relevant time, rather than introducing the image as part of the decision.

"[Just] Signed Contract After Contract ... Like Zombies" (McDonald v. Ritchie)

The fear of mind control and possession of the physical body has been an aspect of zombies since their earliest images. This feature of the zombie has found fertile ground amongst the judiciary who have applied the image of the zombie in a number of settings in which an individual or individuals have given up power over their own decision-making relying instead on some controlling person to make all choices for them. For example, a plaintiff in a class action lawsuit might give up his own decision-making role and choose to remain ignorant of the issues and rely upon the advice of counsel, thus becoming a "zombie-like tool" for the plaintiffs' class action lawyers.

Similarly,

Many elderly persons report they fear the loss of independence more than they fear dying or even abuse.... One elderly person for whom a guardian had been appointed observed: "I cannot tell you how much worse my mental condition is since I have been a 'thing' of the court's without life — my life is over. I would prefer death to living as a guardianship zombie the rest of my life" [*In re Conservatorship of Groves* FN 17].

Despite this elderly ward's sense of zombification under guardianship, the California Court of Appeal has denied the court's capacity for mind control.

Of course a party can always refuse to comply with an order of court if he is prepared to face the consequences. No court has the power to compel a person, zombie-like, to perform acts he refuses to perform [*Ritchey v. Continental Ins. Co.* 5].

These images of powerlessness and mind control serve the purpose of emphasizing the extreme degree of helplessness either experienced or claimed. The image can also be used to express utter disbelief with the notion of such helplessness, as in the following comment on what the judge clearly viewed as self-serving testimony:

We are expected to believe that when their friend, Dick McDonald told them about a possible oil investment, very wealthy and successful people blindly became zombies and began to invest in serial investments, considering only Richard McDonald's recommendation. We are led to believe that these people did no independent investigation, asked no questions, and just signed contract after contract to invest in oil wells like zombies [*McDonald v. Ritchie* para. 12].

While the judge in *McDonald* did not believe that educated and successful people would sign contracts without any thought of their own interests, there are many circumstances in which a special relationship between parties might be seen to give rise to undue influence. In at least one instance, the court has used the zombie image to clarify the degree of influence required for a legal finding of undue influence: it need not, it seems, amount to zombification.

The danger of a confidential relationship is not confined, as appellant claims, to situations in which the pastor turns his parishioner into a zombie or automaton. Rather the law recognizes the danger of undue influence in the pastor/parishioner relationship because of the trust instilled [*The Bible Speaks v. Dovydenas* 760].

Applying "The Evil Zombie Rule" (In re Hedged-Investments Associates)

The mind control aspect of the Haitian zombie has also found a notably receptive home in insolvency law where its use has been extended beyond control of individuals to control of corporations, partnerships and other forms of legal personhood. Since 1995, it has been possible to refer to "zombie" corporations when speaking of dummy corporations controlled by a principal or parent corporation entirely for its own purposes. The "leading case"[2] on what has come to be known as the "evil zombie rule" and the source of that colorful phrase is the 1995 Illinois Court of Appeal case, *Scholes v. Lehmann.*

Scholes is a complicated case in which the receiver for corporations owned by the principal in a collapsed Ponzi scheme brought actions in fraudulent conveyance against the principal's ex-wife, her new spouse, and an investor and a number of charities all of whom had received benefits from the Ponzi scheme through the corporations to the detriment of the other investors. In making his point that the corporations had been under the inappropriate control of the principal, Chief Judge Posner wrote:

> The appointment of the receiver removed the wrongdoer from the scene. The corporations were no more Douglas's evil zombies. Freed from his spell they became entitled to the return of the moneys — for the benefit not of Douglas but of innocent investors — that Douglas had made the corporations divert to unauthorized purposes.

The *Scholes* case has been cited for its "evil zombie rule" in more than thirty cases since it was decided. So common are the references, that by 1996, lawyers making submissions to the courts could ask the judge to "apply the 'evil zombie' rule announced in *Scholes*" to the case at bar (*In re Hedged–Investments Associates*).

One wonders if the language and vividness of the image isn't a reason why the case has become a leading one. Certainly numerous other cases have dealt with the issue of dummy corporations under the control of a single person and subject to inappropriate use, but the expression of the rule which has been embedded in case law is Chief Judge Posner's "evil zombie." Clearly the image captures the sense of the issue under consideration, and perhaps also captures the imagination of the lawyers and judges interpreting it. The image of absolute mind control attached to zombies is now thoroughly ensconced in American insolvency law, and will be safely preserved there as more modern zombie images evolve.

"This Would Turn This Case into an Unstoppable Zombie, Yielding Only to the Lethal Force of Dispositive Court Action" (In re Merck and Co., Inc.)

From approximately the time that zombies "are considered truly to have hit the mainstream in 1983, when they appeared, along with Michael Jackson, in his music video 'Thriller'" (McIntosh: 11), the legal community has been struggling with a growing awareness that legal processes were not keeping pace with changes in society. Academics, judges and reflective practitioners have all echoed the same concerns that the legal system has become too ponderous to adequately serve its purposes. Critiques focus on a wide variety of causes and contributing factors, but there is general agreement that court processes are frequently too slow given the legal aphorism that justice delayed is justice denied. Certainly this plodding nature, reminiscent of plodding zombies, might be read into some of the growing number of zombie metaphors which address specific cases that are drawn out endlessly by continuing motions and applications and appeals, etc. The aspect of zombies most clearly drawn upon by judges in speaking of long and drawn out litigation is their unkillable nature, and their ability to rise from the dead. For example, in the thrice resurrected case of *Langer v. Presbyterian* the judge notes: "Since this conduct occurred, three final judgments have been entered, the last of which one hopes is final, and yet, the 'zombie' litigation over this conduct continues" (3). The Court in *Iberoamerican Electronics, S.R.L. v. Moore Business Forms, Inc.* fears a similar result for multiple cases should parties be permitted to attach harsh conditions to orders regarding jurisdiction when dealing with foreign parties:

Requiring defendants to waive any foreign procedural bars of the new forum could entice plaintiffs to file suit in Florida.... In the fashion of zombies rising from the Florida soil, dead suits would be resurrected to return and walk their homeland courts [296].

In other circumstances, government has given rise to statutory zombies — changing statutes such that old arguments are resurrected.

This laid the issue to rest for 30 years, but in 1988 it sprang back to life like some kind of statutory zombie when the Legislature inexplicably deleted the phrase "which has approached," from section 21801, subdivision (a). This essentially ... breathed life into the argument ... [*People v. Marsh* 769–770].

We further see the zombie precedent rise from the grave where courts have relied upon an old case in reaching a conclusion that ignores more recent statutory changes:

The cases thus present a tale of zombie precedent. A rule definitively extinguished by statutory amendment in 1989 continues to prowl, repeatedly reanimated by mistaken citation and dicta [*Crowell v. Knowles* 931].

In all of these instances, the court relies upon a general understanding of zombies' nature to emphasize the perceived folly or flaw in the system. Impact and enhanced meaning is achieved by drawing on the image of the undead.

While many such references repeat the pattern of identifying the undying litigation, statute, etc. with zombies, it would be remiss to neglect to quote from the particularly colorful dissenting opinion of Doggett, J., of the Supreme Court of Texas in a judgment dealing with an "arcane" rule of law (*Stewart Title Guar. Co. v. Sterling*, 12–13).

Visiting the graveyard of abandoned legal precedents, the court today mystically revives the corpse of *Bradshaw v. Baylor University*... and the one recovery rule it embodied. We had previously pronounced *Bradshaw* dead in determining that "[t]he reasoning behind the one recovery rule no longer applies." ... and concluding that "to the extent it conflicts with this opinion, we overrule *Bradshaw v Baylor University*.... Now this court has awakened yet another dead tort principle to roam the land, terrorizing victims. As in *The Night of the Living Dead*, an unthinking zombie is raised to prey on the living. When this court has resurrected enough of these monsters, the landscape of tort law will be bleak indeed, and let the victims beware. The one recovery rule of *Bradshaw* is dead, and because I prefer to let the dead rest in peace, I dissent.
... To most members of the Bar and all members of the public the subject matter of today's writing is truly arcane. However, the process by which this court arrived at its decision — a process involving disregard for its own recent precedent, a statute, and the majority view in order to change the ground rules of litigation — should be of concern to all. This is not the last dead tort principle that this court is eager to resuscitate. Like the movies, this opinion will have its sequels. Unlike the movies, the havoc the court effects on our traditional tort law will cause direct harm to the lives of thousands of ordinary Texans.

The Highly Colorful

Justice Doggett leaves us in little doubt that judges sometimes use zombie metaphors purely for effect, whether to enliven their own day while drafting a dense and challenging judgment, to attack the logic of the majority when writing in dissent, or to make the point that the issues themselves are so frivolous that they should be dealt with in a frivolous manner. We see a clear example of the latter in the dissenting judgment of Ortega, J., in the California Appeal Court decision in *Rezec v. Sony Pictures*. Justice Ortega, J., writes in a clearly sarcastic vein:

> This is the most frivolous case with which I have *ever* had to deal. Imagine the great contribution this case will make to our quality of life and to justice in America. Why, it may eventually protect us all from war, pestilence, famine and death. A new day will dawn from which time no one will ever again be fooled by a promotion touting a movie as the greatest artistic accomplishment of the ages. From that day on, all persons will be able to absolutely rely on the truth and accuracy of movie ads. No longer will people be seen lurching like mindless zombies toward the movie theater, compelled by a puff piece. What a noble and overwhelming undertaking [145].

Illinois Bankruptcy Judge Hollis, no doubt familiar with years of "evil zombie rule" insolvency cases, builds on that image and brings in more modern zombies' need for new blood, while adding a vampiric twist.

> ... GM/GMAC raised CTC from the grave into which its long-standing insolvency and the $3.5 million conversion had put it, and pushed their new zombie back into the world of commerce with a 100,000 jolt in the form of the Penske Obligation. But like all zombies, CTC needed new blood, which it found in the form of goods and services from its vendors and employees. However, the zombie was bested by its vampire controller, GM/GMAC, which sucked that new blood right back out, and CTC eventually was placed involuntarily in its Chapter 7 tomb [*In re Chicago Truck Center, Inc.* 277–278].

The inclusion of a need for blood in this picture of a zombie is an interesting one inasmuch as Chief Judge Posner's evil zombies spoke strictly to mind control and did not import any drives from the zombie corporations themselves. New zombie images continue to develop in popular culture, however, and these new images may well add to the understanding of existing metaphors.

How thoroughly conversant the population, and the judiciary, has become with zombies and zombie metaphor can be seen by contrasting the first instance of judicial comment on the term "zombie"—a 1956 comment that refers with apparent distaste to a colloquial expression for clearly void letters of patent as "vulgarly dubbed 'zombies'"—with the highly informed discussion by Ortega, J., in *People v. Long* where the judge expresses concern that the defendant's argument that he was in a zombie state would require the jury "to delve into 'zombie' behaviour and state of mind" to determine whether the defendant was "a slow, lurching, drooling, flesh-eating zombie as depicted in the original 'Night of the Living Dead,' or a fleet-of-foot, screaming, flesh-eating zombie that wreaked havoc in the most recent 'Dawn of the Dead.'" Having established his *bona fides* as a Romero fan, the judge goes on to speculate:

> Would either type pick up a gun in the first place or (if one did) know how to hold the gun and pull the trigger? Probably not. Would a zombie be able to drive off in a car? Undoubtedly not. Would a zombie have shot his wife in the neck as opposed to savagely gnawing on her neck? Certainly not. In any event, these questions are best left to great philosophers, but not to a jury trying to determine whether the defendant deliberately shot his wife in the neck" [*People v. Long*, 1].

The Final Frontier

While it may be an acceptable strategy to make the arguments that a criminal defendant was in a zombie state, corporations are zombies, adult guardianship renders one a zombie of the court, and court cases themselves can become unstoppable zombies, there remains one area of legal process where it is entirely improper to suggest zombification: one must not suggest that the decision-makers themselves are zombies. A Florida state prosecutor with a flair for colorful, and hopefully hyperbolic, language learned this as he was chastized by the District Court of Appeal for suggesting that a ground for appeal should be that the jurors at trial were "lobotomized zombies" (*Klepak v. State*). The Court found those comments "improper" and expressed concern that allowing such a ground for appeal could make future jurors reluctant to serve or acquit, presumably for fear of later being attacked as lobotomized zombies.

In *U.S. ex rel Harris v. Wilson*, the judge also expressed a concern to protect jurors from zombification. In that case, the concern was that jurors, prevented from having even the most casual conversations for fear of being interrogated on the nuances of those conversations would be forced to walk the halls like zombies, effectively shutting down the administration of justice.

Conclusion

The image of the zombie in American case law reveals much about the zombie metaphor itself, and the legal processes in which it becomes entangled. The metaphor of the zombie illustrates the horrific effects of drug addiction and some mental illness, expresses a fear of losing control and being overpowered by the court in the context of guardianships, demonstrates a particular type of power in corporate structures, describes litigation which is unfettered and unstoppable, and generally adds color to case law. Its mere presence in judicial writing indicates its prominence in popular culture, and its frequency suggests the metaphor vividly encapsulates various characteristics of people, society, and power dynamics which cannot otherwise be artfully expressed. Its usefulness as a metaphor for these disparate states and situations makes it likely that the zombie will indeed continue to live on, and to embody many of the fears and concerns connected to the cases considered.

NOTES

1. While scholars debate the accuracy of this assertion, it is relevant to our argument not that this statement be factually correct, but only that this theory of Vodoun zombificiation was widely disseminated and likely understood to be factual by many members of the public in the 1960s, including the judiciary.

2. A "leading case" is the most important case on a particular point of law. Lawyers and judges rely upon it, and the framing of legal principles within it, in analysis and argument of cases. Here, the case is the first statement of the "evil zombie rule."

PART II

Zombies in the Sacred

The Living Word Among the Living Dead
Hunting for Zombies in the Pages of the Bible

Michael J. Gilmour

"Why do you look for *the living* among the *dead*? He is not here, but has risen."
— Luke 24:5[1] (italics added)

In addition to a convenient sequence of terms so suitable for a essay on zombies and the Bible, this fitting question gets to the nub of our fascination with the living dead. Stories about spirits and specters may abound, even in biblical literature,[2] but somehow such immaterial forms of existence feel remote. We cannot touch a soul or a ghost. We can touch bodies though, and the idea of corporeal life in a graveyard intrigues because of its proximity and urgency; bodies die and decay all around us and we know ours will do the same in time. A morbid curiosity — *What if...?* — is irresistible. This question also fascinates because the angels posing it and the women they address are standing *inside a tomb* at the time (Luke 24:2–4).

Zombie fans remind me of these women who wander into the habitation of the dead. Like them, they too visit scary places when they consume the carnage-strewn films and literature of the genre. What is more, they also bring a deep curiosity about possible infringements of the laws of nature. What would happen if the dead were to rise from their graves? What would it look like? To follow through on this awkward analogy, if zombie stories are a modern-day counterpart to the spooky tomb, and if audiences resemble the women standing in it, then the ghoulish purveyors of macabre stories about the living dead must be angels. Those messengers of God in the ancient gospel story knew what (or better, who) the women were looking for and they offered a response to their unspoken queries. *Yes, the corpse you saw placed in a tomb got up and walked away.* Modern-day storytellers do the same through their arts, entertaining while they creatively explore mysteries surrounding death, burial, and decay. What would happen if rotting corpses could move? What would it look like? The answers filmmakers and writers in the zombie genre put forward are quite different from that offered by the angels, to be sure, but they are answers just the same.

87

The Living Dead and Religion

I anticipate a few incredulous readers, surprised by a proposed link between the Bible and zombies. Of course, general connections between religion and these stories will surprise no one. Many zombie stories make overt and sustained connections between the living dead and religion by introducing storylines associated with Haitian Vodou beliefs and rituals, a hybrid of West African and Caribbean traditional practices, and Roman Catholicism.[3] There are many examples of this. In Victor Halperin's classic (in the genre) 1932 film *White Zombie* starring Bela Lugosi, a resident of Haiti warns visitors of "zombies, the living dead, corpses taken from their graves and made to work in sugar mills and the fields at night." In this movie, drugs and Vodou ritual produce what one character describes as a "lethargic coma" giving the appearance of death. Once buried, the "dead" emerge from their tombs, without memory (though curiously, the story's zombie protagonist retains the ability to play piano!). Another clear example is the Wes Craven film *The Serpent and the Rainbow*, based on the book of the same name by Wade Davis. In the novel, Davis refers to the transformation of one Clairvius Narcisse into a zombi (his spelling), the result of a sorcerer's spell and exploitation of the victim's greatest fears. As Davis puts it, "To the Haitian peasants Narcisse really did die, and what was magically taken from the ground was no longer a human being"; "[Narcisse] and his family claim he was the victim of a voodoo cult and that immediately following his burial he was taken from his grave as a zombi" (Davis, 1985: 163, 17). Though he ultimately takes his own films in a different direction, George A. Romero acknowledges this tradition in *Dawn of the Dead* (1978; similarly in the 2004 remake) when Peter mentions words spoken by his grandfather, a Vodou priest from Trinidad: "When there's no more room in hell, the dead will walk the Earth." A version of this idea appears also in the novel *Pride and Prejudice and Zombies*, in which Mrs. Bennet refers to the good Lord's decision to "shut the gates of Hell and doom the dead to walk among us" (Austen and Grahame-Smith, 2009: 10).

In many other zombie stories — especially those in the post–*Night of the Living Dead* (1968) era — this Caribbean connection is largely absent or at least muted and a variety of non-supernatural causes account for the disaster. In *Dead and Deader* (2006), a beetle's bite is responsible, whereas the Apache Geronimo's "secret medicine known as the White Man's Curse" is to blame in *Undead or Alive* (2007).[4] Other explanations include radiation from space (*Night of the Living Dead*, 1968); an ambiguous disease or virus (*Dawn of the Dead*, 1978 and 2004); a Sumatran Rat-Monkey's bite (*Braindead*, 1992); hypnosis (*King of the Zombies*, 1941); Nazi greed (*Dead Snow*, 2009); biological weapons (*Resident Evil*, 2002; *Day of the Dead*, 2008); and the bite of an ape infected with "rage" (*28 Days Later*, 2002).

Vague spiritual explanations distinct from Vodou myth exist too, as is the case with the plague (a significant term in biblical writings) of "unmentionables" in *Pride and Prejudice and Zombies*, in which characters refer to the living dead as "Satan's servants." Charlotte Lucas, for one, is "Condemned to serve Satan!" after "Hell's dark business had been carried out" (i.e., after a zombie bit her) (Austen and Grahame-Smith: 67 and 99). The 1936 film *Revolt of the Zombies* also introduces an undefined religious dimension to its storyline (references to "the zombie ceremony"; an "old religious custom"; etc.). The Cambodian priest

Tsiang insists his "gods say he must create zombie soldiers."[5] Though the cause behind each zombie threat tends to be ambiguous, Kim Paffenroth reminds us, with reference to Romero's films in particular, that plausibility is not the point: "the story that each movie offers is to look at one very small band of survivors in their struggle to survive, not to find explanations" (Paffenroth, 2006: 2, 3).

Even though Vodou zombie stories and their secular counterparts differ from one another in significant ways, both adapt ideas vaguely familiar to horror fans from biblical narratives. Linda Hutcheon suggests audiences find pleasure in adaptations of earlier texts because they combine "the conservative comfort of familiarity" with "the unpredictable pleasure in difference — for both creator and audience" (Hutcheon, 2006: 173). The very notion of bodies rising from their graves (think resurrection here) and the consumption of flesh and blood (think Eucharist here) is at least superficially part of our cultural capital because of the Bible. Whether we read it or not, the macabre tales about the living dead mingle "the comfort of ritual ... with the piquancy of surprise" (Hutcheon: 4). Perhaps this explains why we love zombie stories so much ... that and all the blood and gore.

Zombie Fans and Bible Readers

"The sea gave up the dead that were in it."
— John the Seer (Rev. 20: 13)

"Known adaptations obviously function similarly to genres: they set up audience expectations [...] through a set of norms that guide our encounter with the adapting work we are experiencing. [...] What is intriguing is that, afterward, we often come to see the prior adapted work very differently as we compare it to the result of the adapter's creative and interpretive act."
— Linda Hutcheon (121; see also xiii, xiv).

True to Hutcheon's claim, I can no longer read John the Seer's creepy statement without thinking of George A. Romero's *Land of the Dead* (2005). Those ancient words invariably conjure up slow-moving corpses walking out of the surf each time I read them. This also brings to mind Max Brooks' novel *World War Z*. Here it is the story about the boy — patient zero — returning from a swim with a bite mark on his foot, and his description of zombie hoards roaming the world's oceans that I remember: "They say there are still somewhere between twenty and thirty million of them, still washing up on beaches, or getting snagged in fisherman's nets. You can't work an offshore oil rig or repair a transatlantic cable without running into a swarm" (Brooks, 2006: 8, 299).[6] This is not an isolated experience. As I devour zombie fiction and film this habit of associating carnage and Canon persists. Why is that? The resemblances I perceive between the Bible and zombie fiction may be no more than coincidence, and we must always be cautious of fabricating literary parentage where none exists. I suspect my reaction to the sea giving up the dead falls into this category; there is no particular reason to suspect Romero or Brooks of "citing" Revelation in these scenes so I am likely imposing a connection where none actually exists.

Other similarities between the living dead and the living word suggest more than audience-generated associations, most obviously the fact that both emphasize the reality of bodily reanimation. What is more, that other quintessential element of zombie terror, the consumption of human flesh, parallels words spoken by Jesus of Nazareth in the Gospels:

> I tell you, unless you eat the flesh of the Son of Man and drink his blood, you have no life in you. Those who eat my flesh and drink my blood have eternal life ... for my flesh is true food and my blood is true drink. Those who eat my flesh and drink my blood abide in me, and I in them [John 6: 48, 51, 53, 54, 55–56].

The ritualized consumption of the body of Christ has ancient roots, reaching back to Jesus' call to remember his body and blood in the bread and wine: "Take, eat; this is my body.... Drink from [the cup] ... this is my blood" (Matt. 26: 26–28). Stripped of all its rich symbolism and reduced to wooden prose, the Eucharist language of consumption appears horrific. To my mind, repeated emphasis on such fundamental narrative elements — resurrection and bodily consumption — involves far more than an arbitrary, idiosyncratic connection made by individual readers/viewers.

Contemporary stories about the living dead constantly recycle terms and themes found in the prophets though to be sure, the ancestry of modern zombies is long and varied. One survivor in Brooks' novel (2006: 33) astutely observes similarities between the plague-ridden menace and the Jewish legend of the Golem and Mary Shelley's *Frankenstein; or The Modern Prometheus* (1818). Kim Paffenroth examines George Romero's nightmarish films in light of Dante Alighieri's (1265–1321) *The Divine Comedy*, concluding, "that much of the imagery of zombie movies is borrowed, consciously or unconsciously," from the *Inferno* (Paffenroth: 22). Bob Curran's (2009: 19 & *passim*) work on the zombie family tree reaches back to include the mythologies of the ancient Babylonians, Egyptians, and Greeks in his list of "similar tales" about those either brought back from the grave or returning on their own terms. Marina Warner (2002: ch. 3) discusses the writings of Lafcadio Hearn and Jean Rhys, among others, in her treatment of literary contributions to the form. The Jewish and Christian canonical writings fit comfortably in such an inventory of influence. Monsters wander all through the pages of the Bible and the ancient stories and mythologies lying behind its narratives — Leviathan, Satan, the Beast from the Sea, and many others of their ilk (see Beal, 2002) — so it is no wonder modern day masters of horror pick up on its language and stories, especially given the Bible's massive influence on the Western imagination. In the case of zombie stories in particular, we find the ideas of the prophets emerging from those ancient writings as so many corpses from freshly dug graves.[7]

Recognizing the Canon in All That Carnage

Another awkward analogy. Survivors often recognize a particular zombie in a shuffling mob of revenants. They might identify this loved one or acquaintance because there is enough continuity in appearance between that creature's first existence and their second. The clothes are usually dirty and bloodstained, there may be physical wounds and even missing limbs, but the living can still name their assailants. As a crowd of ghouls breaks through defenses at the farmhouse in *Night of the Living Dead* (1968), Barbra knows it is her brother dragging her toward certain death ("Johnny, no!"). The uninfected do not always realize an acquaintance is a zombie at first, an error in judgment usually made only once. Lewis suspects nothing of the sweet neighborhood girl Vivian just before she bites his throat in the opening sequence of the *Dawn of the Dead* remake (2004). Zombies' actions also reflect certain continuities between their life and their living death. We see this in the gas attendant zombie in *The Land of the Dead*; he wears his work overalls with nametag throughout the film, just as he did in life, and even pumps the gas he later ignites to kill Kaufman. Johnny appears to track Barbra to the farmhouse, hunting for *her* in particular. Vivian seems to go to Lewis and Ana's house intentionally just because *they* are her neighbor-friends. They look and act the same, they look and act differently.

This combination of recurrence and difference between first life and second "life" provides a useful analogy to consider the reanimation of the Bible in zombie fantasies. Just as there is some resemblance between one's pre-infected and infected state, so too the similitude of certain storylines between the Bible and zombie genre is hard to miss (e.g., resurrection and the consumption of flesh and blood). On other occasions, we are not so sure about continuities between a zombie and that creature's former life. The infected look and act differently than they did prior to a bite. Their disfigurations are so extreme and their behavior so unexpected that even their nearest and dearest recognize them only with difficulty. So too with biblical influences on the genre; it is a long way from the cultures and writings of the ancient world to the modern cinema, so we may have trouble spotting the holy books in the midst of a zombie attack because the distortions resulting from adaptation are so extreme as to overwhelm almost completely any residual traces.

Still, the book of life has much to say about death and contributes in various ways to modern stories exploring its mysteries. Corpses, burial, resurrections, bodily decay, pain and torment, enduring and unwanted existence, all of these subjects fascinate the biblical writers whose compositions in turn have such a massive presence among cultural artifacts of the Western world, including stories about the living dead. Even in our increasingly post–Christian cultural context, the Bible's contributions remain a persistent artistic force. Where do we find those tenuous links between the living word and the living dead? I offer but a few examples, subjects present in the prophets and reanimated in zombie film and fiction in all their bloody glory.

Separating the Living and the Dead

Almost every zombie film involves a division of space and eventual crossing of boundaries. The uninfected take refuge *inside* some kind of fortress, whether a farmhouse, or shopping mall, or tavern, or military bunker, while the shambling infected are *outside*, gradually breeching whatever defenses those in peril construct. The outsiders ultimately enter the stronghold en masse through collapsing structures, until the firing of the last bullets and the inevitable demise of (at least) the most unlikeable defendants. (If any survive, they tend to be good-hearted, or have some other redeeming qualities.) Without such violation of space — the dead mingling with the living, the infected with the uninfected — there is no story.

Every zombie film cashes in on the astonishment of characters seeing dead people move again, which is breech of space. Reanimation goes against everything we know to be normal and right. It defies science, experience, and cultural taboos because the dead are not supposed to inhabit the realm of the living. So too for the ancients. The question asked in Luke 24: 5 ("Why do you look for *the living* among the *dead*?") is a reasonable one given the emphasis placed on keeping the living and the dead apart in the ancient Jewish and early Christian writings. For instance, the priests of ancient Israel were not to touch dead bodies except for one's "nearest kin" (Lev. 21: 2), and those called Nazirites who make special vows to God were not to go near any corpse at all, including "father or mother, brother or sister" (Num. 6: 2, 6–7). When in a strange land Abraham buys property specifically, he says two times, so that he can arrange to bury his wife "out of my sight" (Gen. 23: 4, 8). Moses instructs the relatives of the dead Nadab and Abihu to carry their bodies "to a place outside the camp" (Lev. 10: 4). Quick burial is also a concern, usually occurring the day of death, as we see in the New Testament stories about the bodies of Jesus (Matt. 27: 57–61; Mark 15: 42–47; Luke 23: 50–56; John 19: 38–42), Ananias, and Sapphira (Acts 5: 1–11).

Fear about the exposure of one's body after death also reflects this deeply felt urgency to keep the living and the dead separate. Improper care of one's corpse was a terrifying prospect, so it is no wonder it features in prophetic warnings of divine wrath: "Your corpses shall be food for every bird of the air and animal of the earth, and there shall be no one to frighten them away" (Deut. 28: 25–26; cf. 2 Sam. 21: 10; Ps. 79: 1–2; Isa. 34: 2–3; Jer. 7: 33).[8] Qoheleth insists that even though a man lives a long life and has many children, if he "has no burial [...] a stillborn child is better off than he" (Eccles. 6: 3). The indignity of non-burial presumably accounts for the honor bestowed on the poor man Lazarus in Jesus' parable; the rich man in the story receives proper burial but Lazarus "was carried away by the angels to be with Abraham" (Luke 16: 22) because in his case, there was no one to care for his remains.

Persistent Life, Elusive Death

> People will seek death but will not find it; they will long to die, but death will flee from them.
> — John the Seer (Rev. 9: 6).

For many, the fate of their corpse is not an immediate concern. Physical death eludes a surprising number of people in the Christian Bible, and this is not always a welcome thing. We often hear biblical laments about persistent life/elusive death from those who suffer. Job, for one, complains that he did not die at birth (3: 11), adding that he loathes his life and would not live forever if he had his way (7: 16). He wonders about the fate of those in misery who continue to live, asking why they wait in vain for death to come. He is himself among those "who rejoice exceedingly, and are glad when they find the grave" (3: 20–22). Others would choose death over life out of principled anger against God, like the prophet Jonah who prays for death instead of life (4: 3; cf. 4: 8).

The prospect of an elusive death, as every zombie fan knows well, terrorizes the living.

The nightmare takes a slightly different form in each story but all share a familiar dread that includes the following elements: those who should be dead are not; zombies hunt the living; a bite from these hunters will result in the victim's continued existence, their own reanimation, allowing the cycle to continue indefinitely. This prospect of unwanted "life" after death so frightens people they often arrange for someone to destroy their brains when or before it happens. The "stricken" Charlotte Lucas in *Pride and Prejudice and Zombies* agrees to marry the tedious and obsequious minister Mr. Collins because she wants "a husband who will see to [her] proper Christian beheading and burial" (Austen and Grahame-Smith: 99).[9] On other occasions, survivors take the initiative to destroy an infected friend or relative in the interest of self-preservation. When Sarah Bowman runs over her infected mother in *Day of the Dead* (2008), she needs to remind her distraught brother Trevor, "it wasn't her." In *28 Days Later*, Salina explains the situation clearly:

> Look, if someone gets infected you got between 10 and 20 seconds to kill them. It might be your brother or your sister or your oldest friend. It makes no difference. And just so you know where you stand, if it happens to you, I'll do it in a heartbeat.

This is no small task for most survivors left with such a grim assignment, as Shaun well knows: "I don't think I got it in me to shoot my flat mate, my mom, and my girlfriend all in the same evening" (*Shaun of the Dead*, 2004).

Resurrections and Burial Rituals

> "Shoot em in the head, they seem to go down permanently when you shoot em in the head. Then you gotta burn em."
> — advice given in a television interview while a pyre glows in the background (*Dawn of the Dead*, 2004)

Unwanted persistent life is a recurring image in biblical literature and so too is language referring to the impermanence of bodily death. The dead do not stay dead. The expectant psalmist is confident he will not "see decay" (Ps. 16: 10 New International Version; cf. Acts 2: 27; 13: 35). We read of the physical resurrections of specific individuals (e.g., 1 Kings 17: 17–24; Luke 8: 49–56; maybe Acts 20: 7–12) and expected mass revivals (e.g., 1 Thess. 4: 16–17). The gospel writer Matthew includes a curious detail about one of the strange phenomena occurring when Jesus died:

> The tombs also were opened, and many bodies of the saints who had fallen asleep were raised. After [Jesus'] resurrection they came out of the tombs and entered the holy city and appeared to many [Matt. 27: 52–53].

Some of these accounts of un-dying involve reference to un-burying, as in the last citation. Mary and Martha's brother Lazarus walks out of his tomb when "they took away the stone" (John 11: 41).[10] On Easter morning, mourners find "the stone, which was very large, had already been rolled back" (Mark 16: 4). A second century writer describes further the events preceding Jesus' emergence from the tomb: "That stone which had been laid against the entrance to the sepulchre started of itself to roll and gave way to the side, and the sepulchre was opened" (*Gospel of Peter* 9.35).[11] Zombie stories also refer to the un-burying of corpses, as in the cemetery scenes in *Return of the Living Dead*, and the account of Arthur Fiske who "struggled from the grave" in a Laurell K. Hamilton short story: "The flowers shuddered. The mound heaved upward.... A hand clawed free, ghostly pale" (2008: 208). In *Pride and Prejudice and Zombies*, characters express concern when the warmer weather arrives because "when the ground again softens" the "unmentionables" are able to leave their graves (Austen and Grahame-Smith: 167; see also Brooks, 2006: 191).

Circumstances often force survivors to forgo the usual rituals associated with mourning and burial. "They must be destroyed as quickly as possible," according to a report in *Land of the Dead*, "there's no time for funeral arrangements." This usually generates a great deal of anxiety like that known to the women arriving at Jesus' tomb on Easter morning. With spices in hand "so that they might go and anoint him" according to custom, they are concerned about potential hindrances. They mention explicitly the large stone blocking the entrance to the tomb (Mark 16: 1–3) but presumably the Roman soldiers guarding the entrance way intimidated them as well (see Matt. 27: 65–66). Because of the plague that causes reanimation, loved ones in zombie apocalypses must burn or dispose of cadavers in ways that are more efficient, as in *28 Weeks Later* (2007) where we see authorities throwing body bags on large fires and military personnel moving through the streets with flamethrowers to eradicate the infected.[12]

Some biblical resurrection stories are obviously symbolic. Ezekiel receives a vision promising the restoration of Israel (37: 11). Seeing a valley full of bones, the Lord instructs him to speak to them, saying, "O dry bones ... I will cause breath to enter you, and you shall live. I will lay sinews on you, and will cause flesh to come upon you, and cover you with skin, and put breath in you, and you shall live" (37: 4–6). Sure enough, as Ezekiel does this, "there was a noise, a rattling" as bones come together, sinew and skin appears, and the breath of life returns. The dry bones "lived, and stood on their feet, a vast multitude" (37: 7–10). The fact that the prophet uses metaphoric language here, whereas zombie stories describe literal resurrections, is not relevant. The point is that the Bible presents visions of the truly dead coming to life and walking the earth once again, thus providing artists with an imaginative and conceptual space in which to construct their own versions of resurrection.

Decay and the Damned

> "Don't gag if one of the Dead brushes up against you, pressing its maggot-infested face up close against your own. Remember: Zombies don't react to things like that. Zombies *are* things like that."
> — Adam-Troy Castro, "Dead Like Me" (2008: 371— italics original).

The Bible is rather gory. When biblical poets depict the carnage of God's judgments, we find some casualties who could easily stumble out of their stories into a George A. Romero film without any sense of anachronism: "their flesh shall rot while they are still on their feet; their eyes shall rot in their sockets, and their tongues shall rot in their mouths" (Zech. 14: 12).[13] Other accounts of the damned are as horrifying as Zechariah's vision of zombies.

One particularly gruesome text describes the enduring nature of postmortem bodily existence in *gehenna*, a place where the "worm never dies" (Mark 9: 48; alluding here to Isa. 66: 24). *Gehenna* (here symbolically representing "hell," and usually translated so, as in Mark 9: 44, 45, 47) refers to the Valley of Hinnom located to the south and southwest of Jerusalem, a place associated with violence and idolatry, including child sacrifice, in earlier texts (e.g., 2 Chron. 28: 3; 33: 6; Jer. 7: 31; 19: 4–6; 32: 35). Following the reign of Israel's righteous King Josiah (see 2 Kings 23: 10–14), it became Jerusalem's garbage heap, a place "pervaded by maggots and the stench of decay, where fire smoldered day and night" (Boring, 2006: 284). Jesus refers to this burning garbage in Mark 9: 48, a place where residents of the city would leave the rotting corpses of humans and animals to the worms that do not die, to maggots. Jesus' statement indicates that the bodies of the damned will rot in *gehenna*/hell — maggot ridden — in perpetuity.

One difference between Ezekiel's vision of bones, mentioned above, and more modern reconstitution stories is the state of decay. "The dead smelled," as Susan Palwick puts it, "and they were visibly decayed, depending on the gap between when they had died and when they had been revived. They shed fingers and noses. They left behind pieces of themselves as mementos" (2008: 139). Survivors refer to zombies as "stenches" in *Land of the Dead*. Zombie movies and stories are normally concerned with the *recently* departed who are returning to life, not those whose state of decomposition is so far along as those in Ezekiel's valley of death.[14] Other biblical resurrections emphasize this fact too, that it is the *recently* dead who come to life. It is an early and deeply rooted belief of Christian tradition that Jesus' resurrection occurred after three days in a tomb (see e.g., 1 Cor. 15:4). Jesus raises his friend Lazarus from the dead and the story includes the detail that he had "been in the tomb four days" (John 11:17). This is time enough for decomposition to begin but not enough to reduce the corpse to bones, something anticipated by the man's sister. When Jesus calls for the removal of the stone covering the entrance to the tomb, she warns "Lord, already there is a stench because he has been dead four days" (11: 39). Contemporary stories about resurrections also refer to the smell of rotting flesh, as in *Pride and Prejudice and Zombies* when the feisty Elizabeth Bennet catches "the scent of death" when unmentionables draw near (Austen and Grahame-Smith: 57; see also 172). One survivor in *World War Z* likens the smell of a zombie to "the beach, like rotten kelp and salt water" (Brooks, 2006: 67).

Anything beyond a few days would make recognition of the now-stirring corpses impossible. As noted, resurrected individuals in biblical and modern stories tend to emphasize continuity between first life and second "life"— biblical survivors recognize Jesus and Lazarus, and movie and literary survivors often identify revenant friends and relatives. Some decomposition but not complete decomposition ... a makeup artist's dream!

Even closer in description to the living dead is the fate of Antiochus IV Epiphanes, ruler of Syria, whose physical body rots away zombie-like while he still lives and breathes. The cause is divine, as the God of Israel strikes this enemy of the Jews with "an incurable and invisible blow" (2 Macc. 9: 5–10). This writer's *Schadenfreude* is hard to miss. The account of Antiochus' lengthy and ghastly death emphasizes physical decay, and deserves repeating in this context (confident as I am that no one reading about zombies will find it terribly troubling):

... he was seized with a pain in his bowels, for which there was no relief, and with sharp internal tortures — and that very justly, for he had tortured the bowels of others with many and
strange inflictions [...] he fell out of his chariot as it was rushing along, and the fall was so hard
as to torture every limb of his body [...] the ungodly man's body swarmed with worms, and
while he was still living in anguish and pain, his flesh rotted away, and because of the stench
the whole army felt revulsion at his decay. Because of his intolerable stench no one was able to
carry the man who a little while before had thought that he could touch the stars of heaven [2
Macc. 9: 5–6, 7, 9–10].

Physical decay is a staple of zombie films, which often feature the ghastly pallor of a corpse
complete with various grim injuries. Yet despite the gory pattern of violent, lingering death
in sacred Scripture, we should note the far greater terror from the perspective of these
ancient theologians is spiritual in kind.[15]

Returning to the Garden

Finally, I note the tendency in some movies to include (or include and then proceed
to crush!) notes of optimism invoking Eden. The creation story opens with a scene of
chaos out of which God brings order, separating land from water and light from darkness.
Following the fall of the first humans, chaos returns until the re-creation of the world suggested by the flood narrative when God once again separates land from water. Other biblical
writers also envision a return to paradise at dark moments in the biblical record, including
the New Testament apocalypse that ends the biblical story right where it begins. Genesis
opens with a scene of primordial chaos with the earth described as a "formless void" with
"darkness covering the face of the deep" but in Revelation, "the first heaven and the first
earth has passed away, and the sea was no more" (Gen. 1: 2; Rev. 21: 1). Chaos is gone and
Eden returns: "On either side of the river is the tree of life with its twelve kinds of fruit"
(Rev. 22: 2; cf. Gen. 2: 9). Zombie stories depict the disintegration of modern societies,
often alluding to contemporary disasters like the AIDS epidemic, environmental crisis,
and terrorism, and yet many of these stories include gestures toward a return to garden
innocence just as we find in the Bible.

A recording coming from a military outpost promising "salvation" draws survivors to
the compound in Danny Boyle's *28 Days Later*. Jim, Salina, and Hannah quickly discover
the soldiers are mad, given to an *Apocalypse Now*–like violence and inhumanity. At one
point, Major Henry West ominously tells Jim that, "Secondary to protection, [the military's]
real job is to rebuild, start again." Jim realizes the implications of this statement, that the
soldiers will make Salina and Hannah into sex slaves in an effort to start repopulating the
human race. There is a counterpart to this dystopian vision of Eden at the very end of the
movie where the three survivors are safe and comfortably settled in the domestic space of
a quaint cottage, located in a beautifully pastoral landscape as planes pass by promising
rescue.[16] The developing romance between Jim and Salina, happy in the cultivated lands
around the cottage is a clear echo of Adam and Eve in the garden, as opposed to their
postlapsarian toils in the harsh world east of Eden.[17] The sequel *28 Weeks Later* develops
these themes, depicting a failed attempt to restore Eden. After the spread of the disastrous

infection in the first film, the sequel documents efforts to repopulate the United Kingdom, beginning with a secure section of London. Survivors return to their homeland, to what the director's commentary refers to as "a new world" and a "garden of Eden." Naturally, mayhem ensues and the infection spreads as the movie unfolds. Unlike *28 Days Later*, however, there is little reason for optimism at the end of this film. Rather than beginning with chaos and ending in Eden, as in the first film, this one reverses the structure, beginning with an attempted return to the garden but closing with evidence the infection is spreading through continental Europe.

The film *28 Weeks Later* resembles others that lack hope, or at least leave some uncertainty about whether conditions will improve. In the remake of *Dawn of the Dead*, following an ending promising a new start on a zombie-free island, there is ambiguity and cynicism reintroduced as the credits roll. At this point, the survivors on the boat making their way to "Eden" begin filming their journey but soon, as we watch the homemade video, zombies appear and attack, presumably leaving no survivors. The same idea occurs in *Day of the Dead* (2008). As the survivors drive out of the urban setting of the disaster into a soothing rural landscape — again, with an Adam and Eve in the characters Trevor Bowman and his girlfriend Nina — a zombie head jumps up into view scaring viewers just before the credits begin. Eden is not so safe after all.

Horrifying Conclusions

The Bible deserves attention from those tracing the imaginative landscape out of which the living dead emerge. Zombie fantasies captivate because they explore the interstices between life and death, and biblical literature does the same, belying the notion that death is the end. The premise of my argument is a simple one. The Bible's enormous influence on Western art forms implies contribution to the twisted (I mean this affectionately) imaginations of writers and filmmakers working in the zombie genre, however oblique. Speculations about the seemingly porous borderlines separating life and death are not unique to the Jewish and Christian Scriptures but as we think about Western art forms, their contributions are inestimable. Northrop Frye (1981: xviii–xix) asks why the Bible, "this huge, sprawling, tactless book sit[s] there inscrutably in the middle of our cultural heritage like the 'great Boyg' or sphinx in *Peer Gynt*, frustrating all our efforts to walk around it?" Also commenting on its massive cultural contributions, Robert Alter (2000: 17–18) suggests reasons why the canon holds such appeal for creative writers.

> The Bible in part seizes the imagination of the modern writer because of his acute consciousness of it as a body of founding texts, marking out one of the primary possibilities of representing the human condition and the nature of historical experience for all the eras of Western culture that have followed antiquity.

This inescapable influence holds true for the macabre tales about the living dead. I am not suggesting contemporary writers and filmmakers deliberately mimic or echo biblical texts in all instances but rather that their cultural inheritance, broadly speaking, owes much to its representations of the human experience, including references to and stories about postmortem existence.

I began by comparing the women at Jesus' empty tomb to zombie fans, and I close the same way. When they entered the tomb, these women knew two things. First, that Jesus was physically dead. They watched his execution (Luke 23: 49) and saw his body placed in the tomb (Luke 23: 55). Their preparations of "spices and ointments" to anoint that body (Luke 23: 56; 24: 1) further indicates their assurance of his corporeal death. Second, they knew Jesus spoke of bodily reanimation on a number of occasions before his death (e.g., Luke 9: 22). They might not have believed it (they were looking for a corpse in that tomb, after all) but the idea was there. One suspects they must have entertained some *What if?* scenarios, no matter how incredulous they were. Zombie fans live with a similar dissonance. They *know* bodily resurrections do not occur — they too have witnessed deaths and burials — but they cannot resist flirting with the *What if?* of the imagination.

NOTES

1. Unless otherwise noted, I cite the New Revised Standard Version of the Bible. Because I am concerned with the Bible's influence on works of the imagination and not interpretation, I focus on common surface-level readings of its stories, not the nuanced analyses of biblical scholarship.

Some quibble about nomenclature, insisting the terms "undead" and "living dead" are properly reserved for vampires, not zombies, which are "walking dead" (see Jones, 2010: 1). Most storytellers lack such precision. A. E. Moorat (2009: 109), for one, treats the terms revenants, zombies, and undead as synonyms, and to my mind, George A. Romero's *Night of the Living Dead* forever links his titular term to zombies, not vampires.

2. E.g., the Israelite King Saul summons a medium to "Bring up Samuel [from death] for me" (1 Sam. 28: 11), something that clearly annoys the ghostlike prophet who appears, asking, "Why have you disturbed me by bringing me up?" (28: 15).

3. I am grossly oversimplifying here, as a reading of Bob Curran (2009), chap. 3, makes clear. For a story involving references to the Loa, spirit figures associated with Vodou, see Jasper Bark (2009: 173, 177–78, 183–84, etc.).

4. For another zombie story linked to Native American history, specifically the Battle of Little Bighorn and Custer's Last Stand, see Sherman Alexie (2008: 68–77).

5. These "robot soldiers" must be reanimated corpses because in one scene they do not "die" when shot. This film also includes zombies of a different sort. Armand Louque learns how to control the minds of living people by placing his "right hand so [on the forehead], the symbol of the third eye of Siva."

As a point of interest, General Mazovia hints at a motive for producing zombies other than forming an army. Suspecting Louque knows the secret of zombies he says to him, "Dr. Faustus with his alchemy and the help of his satanic majesty discovered the secret of renewed youth. Just what is the secret you found?" The reference to Faustus suggests reanimation is a way to cheat oblivion, to hold on to life and perpetual youth. The brevity of life is a recurring theme in the Bible as well (e.g., Ps. 103:14–16; Isa. 40:6–8). By emphasizing postmortem spiritual existence, the short span of a natural life is no longer a terror to the faithful, according to the Scriptures. Indeed, the physical body is something one does *not* preserve at all costs in the context of these writings (e.g., references to willing martyrdom, as in Dan. 3:14–18; Mark 8:34).

6. For other underwater zombie scenes, see Rick Hautala's "Ghost Trap" (2010), and the famous zombie/shark battle in Lucio Fulci's, *Zombi 2* (1979).

7. Explicit references to the Bible (most often the New Testament) occur in various zombie stories, as in the words of the preacher in the film *Undead or Alive* (2007) who cries out "Judgment Day!" He alludes to Rev. 6: 1–8 when he adds, "the four horsemen ride, the dead they walk among us." Many other religious references are more general in nature, as in the language of a television anchor in *Shaun of the Dead* who announces, "religious groups are calling it Judgment Day," without further elaboration.

8. In the Greco-Roman world, the poor organized burial clubs as a way of safeguarding against exposure after death, and ensuring a minimum of remembrance (see Ferguson, 1993: 132–33, 228). For discussion about Jewish burial norms in late antiquity, see Evans (2003: esp. chap. 1). Proper burial and exposure of the dead is a concern expressed in other ancient writings outside the biblical tradition, such as in Sophocles' *Antigone* from the fifth century B.C.E.

9. Cholo in *Land of the Dead* is an exception. He chooses to find out how the other half lives, as he puts it.

10. The biblical story about Jesus raising his friend from the grave is the inspiration behind John Connolly's zombie story "Lazarus" (2010: 1–8). There is a twist in this short story, as one might expect. Instead of a resurrection to full life, this Lazarus is a mere shell of his former living self. "His sisters [...] wanted their brother back," Connolly writes, "but all that they loved of him died in the tomb. They wanted fine wine, but all they received was an empty flask" (7).

11. Taken from Schneemelcher (1991: 224).

12. There is at least one exception in these stories. In Andrew Currie's *Fido* (2006), special funerals are available that address concerns about reanimation. Morticians solve the problem by detaching the head, and burying it separately from the rest of the body.

13. Humans are not the only victims of this horrible plague Zechariah describes; it falls also on "the horses, the mules, the camels, the donkeys, and whatever animals may be in those camps" (14: 15). Animal victims are not always included in zombie films, though there are exceptions, such as a pet dog in *Undead or Alive*. Stephen King's *Pet Sematary* (1983) and Mary Lambert's film adaptation (1989) feature animals returned from the grave. On the subject of animals and zombies, see also Paffenroth (6).

14. One exception is David Wellington's *Monster Island: A Zombie Novel* (2006). In one scene, we read about liberated mummies in the Egyptian wing of the Metropolitan Museum of Art in New York: "An inside-out graveyard where the dead were put on display for schoolchildren." One "truly ancient mummy who was little more than rags and bones was trying to pry open a massive sarcophagus with his splayed fingers" (140).

15. The human body is short lived — as the psalmist puts it, lasting "seventy years, or perhaps eighty, if we are strong" (90: 10) — but the human soul, theologically, is eternal. For this reason, the language of spiritual death is far more pervasive in the Jewish and Christian Scriptures than attention to physical death.

16. There is an emphasis on the value of family in the film, particularly the relationship between Hannah and Frank, who does not survive. Salina remarks at the contentment this father-daughter relationship provides. At another point in the film, Frank refers to a group of uninfected horses running free as a "family."

17. In the alternate ending included with the DVD, Jim does not survive.

Religion, Blasphemy, and Tradition in the Films of Lucio Fulci

JAMES REITTER

The zombie is arguably the most popular monster figure of the last 30 years of horror cinema. After the pioneer film *Night of the Living Dead* (1968), the zombie has been the subject of, or critical component to hundreds of films. We see zombies everywhere, from video games and cartoons to advertisements in big business. The subject has even invaded recent science, as fire ants that are impregnated with fly larvae exhibit "zombie-like" behavior before their heads fall off (Moore, 2009). Although Romero is the undisputed godfather of zombie cinema, his Italian counterpart Lucio Fulci is worthy of critical recognition for his unique portrayal of the undead in films such as *Zombie* (1979), *City of the Living Dead* (1980), and *The Beyond* (1981).

More than simply a schlock gore hound in the tradition of Herschell Gordon Lewis,[1] Fulci offers viewers more than what they bargained for. While many modern gore films are so exaggerated that they become laughable (and even exploit this idea — see Peter Jackson's *Braindead* aka *Dead Alive* (1992) as the best example) gore can play another role in horror cinema. As Morris Dickstein (1984) states in "The Aesthetics of Fright," "Films with a great deal of gore in them play to our voyeurism in another way. They shatter taboos, perhaps the last taboos we still have now that every sort of sex can be freely shown" (67). In particular, Fulci asks his viewers to question the meaning of being alive (and dead) itself— the last taboo — through his images. Jonathan Penner, Steven Schneider, and Paul Duncan (2008) explain that "[The zombie films of Fulci, Romero, and the various adaptations of the book *I Am Legend*] are violent in the extreme — violating bodies, tearing people apart as they tear apart all sense of normalcy. Nothing is sacred, as there obviously is no God.... They ask us to face ourselves at our worst — not just metaphorically as decaying, undead cannibals, but literally as a society decaying and cannibalizing itself" (109). However, where Romero asks us to look at our society in terms of racial prejudice, materialism, military paranoia, and socio-economics through his zombies, Fulci uses no such metaphor. His zombies are not meant to represent any crisis or conflict in our society; they prey on what is primitive and fundamental in all of us. Despite religious commentary that appears to be intrinsic to Fulci's zombies (reanimation due to opening the gates of hell in *City* and *The Beyond*), they shed all religious associations once reanimated and become empty shells of death. In fact, I argue that all allegory, symbolism, and metaphor are dropped once the dead become undead in Fulci's zombie films (with the notable exception of Father Thomas in *City*). It can be argued that the undead in *Zombie* are a result of the blending of Catholic and Haitian theology, but aside from a casual reference by the character, Dr. Menard, as only one of several theories as to why the dead are walking, these reanimated, predatory corpses are entirely free of religious affiliations. As Stephen Thrower (1999) notes, "Fulci's zombies — far more revolting and putrescent than Romero's — exuded a foreboding reek of Death beyond the cerebral allegory of the American hit [*Dawn of the Dead* (1978)]" (15). He is more concerned with the image itself, rather that any metaphorical or allegorical implications. Once the dead become undead, the previous foundations of religion become merely tangential and social commentary never factors into the context of his films. Fulci's zombies aren't intended to represent any external religious, political, or social anxieties.[2] It is my contention that the zombies themselves are at once an aesthetic assault to illicit pleasurable disgust[3] and a primal assault on our notions of not only what it means to be human, but how we negotiate and rationalize life and death.

Released in 1979 in an effort to capitalize on the success of George Romero's *Dawn of the Dead*, Lucio Fulci's *Zombie* (aka *Zombi 2, Zombie Flesh Eaters*) set new standards for the zombie in cinema — and the amounts of gore and shock it could produce. *Zombie* was originally marketed as an Italian continuation of Romero's sequel and bashed as vastly inferior by critics such as David Sanjek (2000), but such dismissive associations have changed over time and *Zombie* has come into its own as an industry benchmark of sorts.

Perhaps the most significant difference between the two films is the portrayal of the zombies themselves. This is due to Fulci himself, who had insisted on a different conceptual vision of the zombie, special effects artist Gionnetto De Rossi, and an incredibly meager budget of less than $500,000 (Thrower: 16). While Romero's zombies are pale with a noticeably bluish hue (*Dawn*), Fulci's living dead in *Zombie* are dusty and bleached — possibly a result of rotting in the sandy earth of the fictional Caribbean island of Matul as opposed to the urban/suburban dwellings of Pittsburgh. The contrasting portrayals of aesthetics provide a fundamental foundation for each film: the invasion of the familiar by the familiar-but-changed (Romero), and the invasion of the unfamiliar into the familiar (Fulci). Although explanations are left intentionally ambiguous, Romero's undead are the result of either inter-stellar radiation/nuclear contamination (mentioned briefly in *Night*) or an overflow of Hell (*Dawn* and *Day of the Dead* in 1986). The zombie plague comes from modern civilization itself and originates out of human concepts — an irony that Romero successfully incorporates in each chapter of his undead films (although some of his films do not fully disclose the cause of zombies). Fulci's *Zombie* calls back to a pre-industrial time, relying on the Haitian/Third World origins of the zombie as a product of paganism and witchcraft. As Fulci states in an interview from *Fangoria* magazine, "I wanted to recapture the moody atmosphere of witchcraft and paganism that must have been prevalent when Europeans first settled in the Caribbean during the 1700s. That's when the concept of zombies — human slaves brought back from the dead — first became popularly known to western civilization" (qtd. in Thrower: 19). Indeed, Fulci's undead recall the slave class. They are clothed in little more than loose, tattered tunics. Critics such as Stephen Thrower and Jamie Russell do well to argue the religious implications of Fulci's living dead in *Zombie* by labeling it as "a perverse reflection of Italian Catholicism" in relation to the body as a sacred subject that becomes mutilated, but the film does not necessarily emphasize such agendas (Russell, 2006: 130). While Fulci does offer some explanation as to the origins of the zombie — a blending of "Catholicism from Spanish conquistadors" and "African tribal rites" — these theories are tangential at best. Fulci's horror descends to a more fundamental and visceral plateau than political, religious, racial, or socio-economic analogy. While such philosophies and ambitions do make us human, Fulci attacks something more basic in all of us, and is more threatening because of it. His attack is not merely on the loss of a soul, but on the loss of cognition and reason itself. These "beings" are far more threatening than the consequence of damnation, a murderer, or a predatory animal. They are shells of life and are driven to devour it. Fulci does away with any explicit (or even implied) motive.

If Fulci was not attempting any type of symbolic meaning through his zombies, then the image becomes the focal point. As Sanjek explains, Fulci's films "not only deny us any protection or distance from their effects but endorse a kind of obscene literalism, defying their audiences to dismiss the undeniable gruesomeness of their imagery" (322). There are three main images/sequences that established and affirmed the film's place in horror history. Ask most horror film fans about Fulci and the scene that makes audiences squirm the most is the infamous eye gouging of the good Dr. Menard's (Richard Johnson) wife (Olga Karlatos). Second, for sheer audacity and inventiveness, nothing can top Fulci's underwater battle between a zombie and a shark. This sequence is so memorable and unique that it has become a favorite subject of independent t-shirts at horror conventions and film festivals. Finally, the third image is the rising conquistador zombie with an eye socket full of writhing worms. The aesthetic design of this zombie was so revolting that it was chosen as the face of the film. Lobby posters showcase the headshot of this zombie with the accompanying (and unforgettable) tag: "WE ARE GOING TO EAT YOU!"

The outrageous eye-gouging sequence begins just over forty minutes into the movie as we see Mrs. Menard showering, hoping to cleanse herself of this nightmare. Having already voiced her disapproval of her husband's "methods" and "research," Mrs. Menard positions herself as Dr. Menard's foil: she will turn him in to authorities once they head back to civilization. Of course, both of them know they will never return. After she towels and dresses (in little more than a sheet), we see her image through a window as the zombie might. At this point we are voyeurs, watching this woman in an intimate, vulnerable state. A few minutes later, Mrs. Menard realizes there is a threat. Provoked by noises, she attempts to close the door to her room. At the 44.00 minute mark, the fingers of the zombie slip in between the door and the frame. Here is where Fulci's direction is at its zenith: the struggle to close the door takes an astounding 46 seconds, wrenching every bit of suspense possible. After finally securing the door and blocking it with a dresser, Mrs. Menard rests against it, but the zombie persists. The door starts to splinter and the zombie reaches through to grab a hold of Mrs. Menard's hair — as she is facing it. As the zombie slowly pulls Mrs. Menard closer, it becomes apparent that a large splinter caused by the splitting door will penetrate her right eyeball. In his study of the films of Lucio Fulci, Thrower provides symbolic analysis of this sequence. Thrower presents various interpretations, all based on the penetration and destruction of the eye/"I." In addition to the obvious gender readings of the sequence where the woman gets penetrated through the eye/"I" by an assumed male zombie via the wooden splinter, Thrower theorizes that "if the Holy Father is watching everything I do, let him see this moment where I penetrate [and destroy] the observing 'I'" (28). This attack on voyeurism that simultaneously prevents the victim from seeing and forces the audience to watch has become a trademark of Fulci and provides support for his debatable status as an auteur. Such destruction of the eye as victim/audience is also explained in relation to Mario Bava's *Black Sunday* and Dario Argento's *Terror at the Opera* (Hunt, 2000: 325).

What makes this sequence stand alone is the duration of it, and the fact that Fulci does not cut away at the moment of penetration. In fact, he lingers on it: "Herein lies part of Fulci's unique, capricious charm. He obviously delights in rattling the cages of the movie-going petit bourgeois by dwelling longingly and lovingly on the most atrocious splatter scenes, even to the extent of making most of the audience feel like real perverts for watching along" (Balun, 1997: 58–9). In total, the sequence lasts a mere 40 seconds, but any observer will agree that the experience (and impression) lasts much longer. One reason for this is that the actual impalement is not merely into the eye, but well into the skull, as the splinter is a full ten inches in length (Balun: 30). Philip Brophy (2000: 281) describes the contemporary horror film as a blending of the "Hitchcock debt" (sophistication that "tells") and the "[Herschell Gordon] Lewis debt" (exploitation and gore that "shows"). Fulci not only shows the gore that is often only implied in horror film but revels in it. He languishes in the discomfort he creates, and refuses to let the audience escape from it.

The second sequence that viewers recall is certainly one of the most bizarre and unique zombie attacks in the pantheon of cinematic undead. After the film begins with a particularly gruesome attack from a bloated zombie on a sailboat in the Harlem River, New York City, the next zombie encounter — almost thirty minutes into the movie — is unforgettable. As topless scuba diver Susan (Auretta Gay) explores the Caribbean waters, she is pursued by a bull shark. Curiously, the shark swims just above her as she "hides" among the coral and plant growth. Just as the threat passes, a zombie attacks her from out of her very hiding place, allowing for no sanctuary. After a brief struggle, she manages to escape the underwater zombie. In an unprecedented (and still unequaled) twist, the zombie turns its attention to the circling shark. The zombie even loses half an arm to the shark and sinks back to the depths of the island waters.

The most visually reprehensible zombie in all of Fulci's films is the conquistador rising from the earth to bite Susan's neck. As with every memorable sequence, Fulci takes his time to show the emergence of the zombie — complete with an eye socket full of wriggling worms. Aside from the horrible reanimation of this living death, there is an unidentifiable horror,[3] a cold, remorseless brutality driving this corpse that surpasses any religious or scientific threat and directly challenges human life and its history. Similar to Amando de Ossario's zombies of the *Blind Dead*,[5] this reanimated corpse is ancient, dating back approximately half a century. Decayed but not disintegrated, it not only represents an assault on who we have become, but also who we once were. In essence, it is attacking our very existence, past, present, and future. This zombie figure, more than any other, represents death — not as something inevitable, but suddenly pursuant and predatory. Although it is still slow moving (as opposed to the recent rash of fully animated if not superhuman zombies as seen in the 2004 remake of *Dawn of the Dead* and the zombie-like infected of *28*

Days Later in 2002 and *28 Weeks Later* in 2007), this zombie is far more sinister than earlier undead creations. In *Zombie*, viewers and critics are not threatened by the allegory presented. Instead, we are horrified by the image itself but find pleasure in the revulsion as well.

Fulci released a rather curious entry into the catalog of zombie films with *City of the Living Dead* (aka *Gates of Hell*) in 1980. This effort, a non-linear nightmare that is initiated by a priest's suicide hanging which unlocks the gates of hell, features two types of zombies: the hallucinatory recently dead and the more traditional long dead reanimations. Both are aesthetic departures from his previous efforts seen in *Zombie*. In fact, *City* has less to do with the unrelenting death of zombies than seemingly random apocalyptic events. For at least three quarters of the movie, Fulci's undead are a cross between monstrous temporal beings and zombies. They are certainly dead (and brought back to life), but they do not feed on humans. These zombies are entirely disinterested in human flesh; two of the killings are by way of removal of the skull and brain from the back. There is no biting here, let alone consuming. This is rather curious given the obvious and purposeful religious overtones (more or less only inferred in *Zombie*). If the body is sacred, Fulci mutilates it beyond any practical or symbolic use. There is no consumption — only purposeless destruction. This "waste" of the body thwarts Judeo-Christian motives that either revere the body as a holy object or, in the sacrament of Holy Communion, consume it as a path to salvation. Indeed, the spark that ignites this chain of events is the hanging of Father Thomas (Fabrizio Jovine) in a Dunwich cemetery and a decrepit corpse briefly emerges from the shallow earth. This initial corpse appears to be a blending of the ancient conquistador undead from *Zombie* with the blue hue associated with Romero's portrayal; audiences are on familiar ground: symbolic allegory and "traditional" zombies.[6] However, this comfort does not last long.

In a rather unique sequence for a "zombie" film, Mary Woodhouse (Katherine Mac-Coll) apparently dies from her vision of Father Thomas' suicide and is subsequently buried. After her casket is placed in the earth (half covered by laborers until their shift is over), we realize that she was only catatonic from the shock of her dream and is now trapped inside the coffin (this is to be fully exploited with Wes Craven's *The Serpent and the Rainbow* [1988]). A reporter on the case hears Mary's screams emanating from inside the coffin placed in the earth and proceeds to use a pick axe to bust open the secured lid as Mary awaits helplessly inside. The strikes from the axe narrowly miss her head and she is removed successfully. Fulci is playing with the audience by exploiting the familiar conventions of horror films. Critics such as Michael Grant (2004) and Isabel Cristina Pinedo (2004) have called attention to the application of such purposeful manipulation in regard to narrative (this is particularly true for both *City* and *The Beyond*), and as we will see, Fulci's subversive design can even be attributed to the portrayal of zombies themselves.

After a bizarre shift in narrative that introduces viewers to Bob (Giovanni Lombardo Radice) via an encounter with an inflatable sex doll and the decomposing body of an infant, the second zombie we see is the reanimated corpse of Father Thomas. Similar to *Zombie*, the appearance of the undead is marked by an auditory clue: in the Caribbean, it was the beating of drums; in Georgia, it is a type of supernatural growling. A social (and sexual) deviant, Bob hides out from the pursuit of vigilante neighbors in a neighborhood garage. He is befriended by Emily (Antonella Interlenghi), but they are interrupted by the growl and subsequent Romero-like appearance of Father Thomas, who smothers Emily with a handful of worms and muck. Due to the noticeable absence of the expected zombie bite, Emily's condition becomes quite curious and uncertain. Did she die? Was she just scared or marred? The entire segment bathes in ambiguity, and that is the intent. Fulci subverts all of the assumptions he foregrounded earlier. By establishing the monster as a conventional zombie in the beginning of the film, we are surprised and confused by the actions of the reanimated Father Thomas. The Father Thomas zombie comes and goes with jump cuts at entirely unpredictable intervals. There is no familiar biting—only a vague and undefined smothering. Bob has no idea what to make of it all, and neither do we. In contrast to *Zombie*, Fulci focuses his horror on the unknown in *City*, but he still manages to keep the gore intact. The image is revolting, the attack is unprovoked, and the meaning remains ambiguous. Fulci, through his portrayal of zombies and temporal shifts in narrative, forces us into uncertainty.[7]

Father Thomas continues his haunting ways in a prelude to what will be the first of three image sequences that define the movie (similar to *Zombie*). Once again, Fulci takes us into the realm of the familiar as we see a young couple taking advantage of their time alone in a parked car. The audience fully understands that *something* will happen, but is in no way prepared for what Fulci has in store. As the petting increases, Rose (Daniela Doria) attempts to slow the advances of Tommy (Michele Soavi of *Cemetery Man* (1994) aka *Dellamorte Dellamore*). Father Thomas appears and simply gazes at Rose, who suddenly begins to bleed from her eyes. This is a clear and explicit example of Carol Clover's theory about the gaze in horror films: "horror movies are obsessively interested in the thought that the simple act of staring can terrify, maim, or kill its object" (1995: 192). Rose has seen something not only blasphemous, but horrific. She is frozen in the moment, trapped by the potent gaze of the damned Father. What was once a means of control in classic horror films such as *Dracula* (1931) and *White Zombie* (1932) has now become fatal. Jamie Russell (2006) extrapolates Fulci's habitual attack on the eyes to an attack on traditional narrative expectations of an audience. "The eyeball horror is always closely linked to [...] [an] attack on narrative, as our cinematic gaze is ruptured by Fulci's refusal to adhere to conventional storytelling. Violence against the eye becomes a metaphor for the loss of meaning that the zombie apocalypses of these films embody" (Russell, 2006: 140). However, the scene does not end there. After Rose's eyes overflow with blood, she begins to foam at the mouth, all the while remaining completely frozen under the gaze. The bubbling white foam quickly turns red, and Rose soon vomits all of her internal organs in a gruesome stream. Fulci gives us another iconic gore sequence that goes well beyond the power of suggestion so revered by classic horror critics such as Carlos Clarens (Hunt, 2000: 326). Fulci again shows us everything, far more than what we want to see. Tommy's death by way of removing the brain via a fist through the skull is a mere afterthought of the carnage that preceded it.

The goal becomes quite clear: destroy Father Thomas before the gates of Hell can open on All Saints Day. However, the supernatural priest isn't the only one who haunts the living. Emily, the first victim, randomly appears in front of her younger brother John-John (Luca Pasiner). What is significant here is the condition of Emily. In direct opposition to the undead from the beginning of the film, this zombie is wet and oozing with all sorts of viscous, slimy drippings. As Thrower describes, "The zombies, when they appear, are psychedelic and disheveled, messy Jackson Pollack–faced entities possessed of both ghostly and ghoulish skills" (164). Stephen Prince correlates this "slime aesthetic" from John Carpenter's remake of *The Thing* (1982) to Jean-Paul Sartre's essay, *Being and Nothingness*, and states "that slimy and sticky substances, because of their ambiguous nature, are fundamentally perceived as defiling and malignant" and as "the men face dripping, twisted asymmetrical thing [...] they confront the shadow side of their human order" (2004: 125, 126). Prince's analysis can easily be attributed to Fulci's temporal zombies in *City*. In fact, due to the disappearance and reappearance of these zombies at unpredictable intervals, I would argue that Fulci's zombies in *City* would be more appropriate examples of defiled and malignant shadows of the human order. Such a shift in zombie aesthetics was fully exploited in later films such as *Return of the Living Dead* and *Near Dark* (1987). Emily is not a musty, decrepit ghoul that is awakened after years of inactivity. She is recently deceased, but is much worse for wear than her death would indicate. She has gone through a transformation that renders her flesh raw and infected. There are no missing body parts. She does not shuffle helplessly. Instead, she is virtually motionless. Like Father Thomas, her power is in her gaze, but she is also grotesque — an abomination far more revolting than the blue-hued priest.

After a series of bewildering appearances and gaps in conventional narrative, Fulci delivers his second shocker. The town scapegoat Bob — now blamed for Emily's death as well as some trouble in a local bar — has run out of luck. Following a series of tormenting visions, Bob finds refuge in a neighborhood garage. He is soon discovered by the resident daughter, and the two share a forbidden joint. Unfortunately, the girl's father comes in and disrupts the party. Bob is quickly on the wrong end of a worktable drill, and Fulci doesn't waste the opportunity. Mr. Ross slowly forces Bob's head into the running drill, and the shaft penetrates his entire skull, emerging at the other end (reminiscent of the lengthy "splinter scene" from *Zombie* both in terms of penetration and the excruciatingly slow approach of the drill towards the temple). Again, the actual death by drill isn't so remarkable. It is the way that Fulci directs the action on screen. Fulci takes his time and shows us everything. Horror cinema often bails at the last moment, inferring the awful action. Fulci does the opposite. He lingers on the carnage, forcing us to watch due to the duration of the scene. We cannot simply shut our eyes and recover.

This theory also holds true for the "maggot scene" that generated intense reaction from viewers, and actors alike. In yet another random sequence, the remaining characters (Mary) newspaper reporter Peter Bell (Christopher George), the psychiatrist hero Gerry (Carlo De Mejo), and his incest-obsessed patient Sandra (Janet Agren) are swarmed by live maggots that come bursting through a window blown out by a storm. Over twenty pounds of maggots were used in the scene, and Fulci even glued some onto the actors' faces (Dendle, 2001: 73). When the maggots finally stop blowing into the room, the audience is just as paralyzed as the characters are; Fulci doesn't let either one off the hook. We see the maggots crawling on everything — they literally cover the floor in movement. They blanket a ringing telephone, creating a barrier between the supernatural situation the characters are trapped in and the outside world. Finally, they swarm on the characters themselves, invading clothes and tangling in hair. The audience is revolted, but is also having fun.

The zombies return with Emily's attack on Sandra. Like before, she randomly appears (with the accompanying sound effect) and smashes through the back of Sandra's skull, much the same way that Father Thomas disposed of Tommy earlier. She shows no interest in consuming Sandra. It is a purposeless, incoherent attack. John-John almost falls victim to the same fate, but he is rescued by Gerry. In a curious reversal of Father Thomas' power over Rose, Gerry prevents the attack by gazing and willing Emily away. However, this newfound ability does not last long as a neighborhood bar is overrun with temporal, oozing zombies.

As the loose plot lurches forward, Mary and Gerry locate the source of these events and enter into the mausoleum of Father Thomas. As Mary and Gerry submerge into the underground depths of the burial chamber, Fulci shifts his directorial vision that recalls the zombie iconography of *Plague of the Zombies* (1966). The mausoleum becomes a dark labyrinth of stone passages, filled with ancient skeletons and blue lighting. We are on familiar ground once again, returning to the zombie from the beginning of the movie. It seems that the Dunwich zombies are "traditional" while the ones encountered in Georgia are more ethereal (and "fresh"). This contrast may well be perceived as a veiled attack on Catholic sensibilities and limitations as being old and decrepit themselves — an issue that Fulci himself admits to taking on throughout his career, especially in films like *Beatrice Cenci* (1969) and in 1990's *Demonia* (Curci and Gingold, 1995: 64; Thrower: 165). Although they are still a derivation of Catholic blasphemy, the ethereal zombies in Georgia have very little to do with rising from the dead and are much more dangerous than the dusty undead from the cemetery. We never see them "re-animate." Instead, they simply appear, manifest in a physical form for their attack, and then disappear. These zombies are not mere apparitions, but physical manifestations that appear as temporal and spatial "breaks" that disrupt our world.

Father Thomas finally appears to both Mary and Gerry and the final confrontation takes place as the decrepit zombies close in. The assaultive gaze of the zombie priest makes Mary's eyes bleed and viewers prepare for another extravaganza of gore. However, as Father Thomas and Mary are locked in a hypnotic stare, Gerry takes advantage and disembowels Father Thomas with the shaft of a massive wooden cross. He quickly bursts into flames, as does the surrounding zombie horde. These zombies are not defeated by the traditional gunshot to the head, but are instead destroyed by flame. The gates of Hell are closed with the destruction of the sacrilegious priest, and all zombies are consumed by spontaneous combustion (this result is unattainable in *Zombie* as there is no single cause for the rampage and the undead are never destroyed, although the survivors do manage to escape only to find New York overrun). Contrary to this relief, Fulci is not quite done with his manipulation of audience expectations. In one of his more memorable "head scratchers," Mary and Gerry successfully emerge from the mausoleum. John-John starts running toward them in celebration. The two adults appear to be relieved, but as the child approaches, their expression changes from relief to shock and horror. The screen then fragments, as if a window is broken, and the credits roll. Despite the "victory" of Father Thomas' destruction, the illusion of normalcy for both the characters and the audience is shattered. The audience never sees the horror that Mary and Gerry see (a subversion of the film's visual approach where we see everything).

Lucio Fulci presents viewers with yet another type of zombie in his smorgasbord of supernatural horror and disgust, *The Beyond*.[8] The film begins with a flashback (shot in sepia) to 1927 in Louisiana, where a band of vigilantes believe a painter named Schweik (Antoine Saint John) has cursed both the hotel where he currently resides and the town. Sentencing him as a warlock, they proceed to execute him in three stages: whipping with a chain (a reference to the influential *Don't Torture a Duckling* from 1974), being nailed to a stone wall with railroad ties, and finally splashed with flesh-eating acid. The setting then jumps to modern day New Orleans, at the same hotel. Liza (Katherine MacColl, continuing her lead status) has inherited it, and is renovating to reopen. Viewers barely get a chance to reorient themselves before a worker falls from a two-story scaffolding after seeing a mysterious woman with milky white eyes from inside a window. As panic ensues, Dr. McCabe (David Warbeck) enters and takes the fallen man to a nearby hospital.

Supernatural events quickly snowball as Schweik's apocalyptic painting is discovered and the bell for his room suddenly rings. Soon, a plumber arrives and begins work down in the flooded basement of the hotel. As plumber Joe inspects a deteriorating wall, a hand bursts forth from the other side. In a moment of Fulci brilliance, a finger of the attacking hand penetrates into the right eye socket of Joe and pushes his eyeball out, forcing onto the audience the violating image as the monster removes the victim's ability to see. Where Fulci penetrated Mrs. Menard's eyeball in the famous splinter scene of *Zombie*, he now ejects the eyeball of Joe. Fulci employs the same inversion later in the film as Martha (Veronica Lazar)—an old caretaker of the hotel—gets forced onto one of the protruding railroad ties left from Schwiek's execution by the plumber, who is now a zombie. He grabs her by the face and pushes her back onto the extending tie. The tie head penetrates the back of Martha's skull and emerges through the eye socket, thereby ejecting the eye. While neither episode matches the excruciating scene from *Zombie*, the Fulci's inversion of *Zombie*'s eyeball penetration to eyeball expulsion as cause of death is rewarding. Martha is killed by the zombie plumber in the same way that he is killed by the zombie Schweik. One can even argue that there is a complete sequence of eye horror in these three films: In *Zombie*, Fulci penetrates the eye; in *City*, the eyes deteriorate while inside the skull via bleeding; *The Beyond* exploits the expulsion of eyes. The director is stripping the visual control away from the audience. Elaborating on Russell's analysis discussed earlier, Fulci also removes our ability to make logical sense of what we are seeing on the screen, even more so than what he experienced in *City*. Critic Michael Grant (2004) further develops this concept, arguing that *The Beyond* can be interpreted through a Lacanian theory of the "Real," where "language emerges against the background of an essential abyss of non-meaning" and that through language, "we negate this nothingness" (36). Grant states that such theory can elucidate the non-linear structure of the film, suggesting that it can be seen as more than just an exploitative gorefest.

The next chapter of *The Beyond* takes us to the hospital where Joe's wife (Laura De Marchi) and daughter (Jill played by Maria Pia Marsala) mourn their loss. Beside the still unanimated corpse of Joe is the decrepit corpse of Schweik, discovered earlier by Martha. After some exposition between Emily, the woman with white eyes from earlier (Sarah Keller), and Liza about how the hotel was built on one of the seven gates of Hell, Joe's wife is frightened by something back at the hospital. Next, we see a bottle of acid on the verge of falling from the top of a cabinet. Fulci cuts to a horrified Jill as she sees her father for the first time. Her horror is doubled as she then sees her mother flat on the floor (without explanation), her face being covered by the acid spill from above. Per his style, the revulsion extends far longer than expected, and Jill's mother's face rapidly erodes in a flood of blood and bubbling ooze. The resulting liquid spreads across the floor, and the shell-shocked Jill does all she can to escape contact. In her escape, she stumbles into a room full of upright bodies recently deceased — storage for the morgue in the hospital.

At this point, thirty minutes into the movie, we have seen a grizzly execution, hospitalization (complete with gurgling blood) due to a two-story fall, an attack through a stone wall by two mysterious hands, a decomposed corpse surfacing from the murky water of a bathtub (when Martha finds the remains of Schweik), and a gruesome death via acid spill. Nearly a third of the way through the film we only experience the suggestion of zombies. Clearly, we are not grounded in earthly events like those seen in *Zombie*.

If we discount the initial attack on Joe through the wall — at the time we didn't know who or what was responsible — zombie Joe's encounter with Martha marks the first true zombie appearance in the film. In an illogical frame of displacement, zombie Joe emerges from a murky bathtub (recalling the first encounter with the unanimated Schweik) after Martha unclogs the drain in the bathroom. He slowly rises from the black muck, *sans* eyes but featuring the tell-tale facial gashes of his demise. Unlike the ethereal and messy zombies from *City* that appear with gashes, boils, and blisters without any explanation of how such wounds were received, this figure is recent; there is no additional disfigurement or decline.

The next encounter with zombies is the most perplexing in any of the three films, with the possible exception of the bar room zombie attack in *City*. The other-worldly (but benevolent) Emily is menaced by the film's growing catalog of the dead. However, these zombies appear but do not attack. Emily frantically pleads that she doesn't want to "go back" and that she had done what she had been asked to do. At this point we can surmise that Emily has been sent to collect Liza, but chose to warn her instead. As a result, the dead have come to take Emily back to Hell as punishment for her failure. Schweik and Joe are clearly identifiable in the scene, as are Martha's son Arthur (a small role in the film), Mary-Anne (Joe's wife), and Martin (who earlier died from some nasty tarantula bites, to be discussed later). The condition of the zombies is varied. Schweik and Joe appear as they did before: the former a decomposed corpse and the latter a recent cadaver. However, the three other zombies recall the aesthetic approach taken in *City*, covered with oozing pustules and flesh dripping from faces. Even more curious is how Emily "dies." Instead of the gang feast of so many zombie films, Fulci's small gathering of the undead simply stands guard and prevents Emily's escape. They barely even move to enclose her. Finally, Emily has a moment of clarity and commands her seeing-eye dog to attack. The German shepherd lunges at Schweik and they wrestle on the ground while Emily encourages her companion. After a bit of grappling reminiscent of the underwater zombie/shark episode, all of the undead suddenly disappear. Unfortunately, the danger has not passed for Emily. Just as viewers begin to feel at ease with the chain of events, the guardian/guide dog rips open Emily's throat in an impressive explosion of pumping blood in an act of ultimate betrayal. The dog then decides to remove her ear as an additional insult to her already fatal injury. Since Emily's eyes have already been established as useless (at least in the conventional sense), Fulci attacks the next most significant sense to gauge reality.

It must be mentioned that the dog attack is not the only exploitation of the animal world in the film. As we will see, tarantulas can be equally aggressive. Just as *Zombie* offers the eye splinter, the underwater zombie fight with the shark, and the rising of the conquistador zombie and *City* features the gut vomiting, the drill through the head, and the maggot storm, *The Beyond* also has three especially memorable scenes. The acid bath of Joe's wife discussed earlier thrilled gore-crazed audiences, but no one could have predicted the fate of Liza's architect friend Martin (Michele Mirabella) as he discovers the original blueprints of the hotel in a local bookstore. Up on a ladder to gain access to the book, Martin realizes the supernatural history of the building, and promptly falls off (recalling the painter's death at the beginning of the film). He becomes paralyzed from the fall, and out from under the bookcases, a slew of tarantulas appear. In a flawed but ambitious directorial moment, Fulci mixes real tarantulas with animated rubber models. To Fulci's credit, aside from a few shots where the differences are obvious, he is quite successful through focus between foreground clarity and background blur. The tarantulas soon reach their victim and proceed to stab and tear at Martin's eye, nose, bottom lip, and tongue. Fulci has succeeded in destroying all of the physical senses of his character and gives the audience yet another unforgettable sequence of pleasurable disgust.

The last type of zombie seen in Fulci's "unassailable zombie masterpiece" is encountered in the hospital, the setting for the third image in the sequence (Balun: 39). Liza and McCabe find themselves back in the hospital after the hotel is overrun by the living dead. While trying to get to the lab in an attempt to discover an explanation, corpses throughout the hospital begin to reanimate. As discussed earlier with the cemetery zombies in *City*, these cadavers are reminiscent of *Zombie* (albeit in a sterile environment). While a few of them are in less than stellar condition as a result of fresh autopsies, there are is equal amount that are not damaged at all. However, according to Fulci, they are the worst part of the movie and were only included at the request of the film's international sales department in attempt to lure a German audience that was "the richest client in Europe" and believed to be clamoring for zombies at the time (Curci and Gingold: 65). Another similarity to the first film in the loose trilogy[9] is the fact that these zombies can only be eliminated with a gunshot or blow to the head (in line with Romero's living dead).

As zombies seemingly inundate every wing of the hospital, Liza and McCabe do all they can to escape, recalling the claustrophobic invasion of *Night of the Living Dead*. They eventually stumble across young Jill and attempt to rescue her. Liza approaches first as McCabe fends off the onslaught. The now white-eyed Jill then suddenly attempts to attack Liza, as she has also joined "The Beyond," but Fulci quickly thwarts that with a completely unexpected jolt of gore that trumps the acid bath and tarantula attack. McCabe shoots Jill in the head, thereby exploding nearly half of her cranium. This image is so repulsive, and yet intriguing, that Balun (1997) chose it as the cover to his tribute book. Instead of extending the repulsion as seen in the splinter scene, the drill scene, or the acid bath, Jill's execution is quick and terrible, taking viewers by surprise. Yet, he lingers on the effect in slow motion, thereby transitioning from fright to horror. The gunshot shocks the audience; the image of little Jill missing literally half of her head horrifies them. Somehow, we find pleasure in it all.

Liza and McCabe find their way into the hospital basement, but as they descend, they find themselves inexplicably back in the basement of the hotel. Having nowhere else to turn, they proceed into the basement, which has suddenly become the corpse-riddled wasteland of Schweik's painting. As they "face the sea of darkness and all therein that may be explored," their eyes turn white and "The Beyond" claims them and they disappear.

Despite the over-the-top gore sequences, the vision of Lucio Fulci cannot simply be written off as schlock. His concept and portrayal of the zombie is much more complex than many of his contemporaries. Although these movies "feature close-ups of rotting flesh, maggots, and sunken empty eye sockets, scenes which maximize the disgustingness of the zombie," they are more than easily dismissive exploitation flicks (Gregson, 2005: 11). Fulci strikes at something more visceral — not only the body, but life itself. This visual attack is embodied in his zombie figures. Whether it be the traditional Haitian undead, ethereal zombie apparitions, or the reanimations of the recently deceased, Fulci provides a unique and highly influential imagining of the living dead. Through his combination of gore sequences and aesthetic zombies, Fulci delivers an unrivalled experience of horror to an audience that remains unforgettable — and we enjoy it, even though we know we shouldn't.

NOTES

1. Films such as *The Gore-Gore Girls* (1972), *Blood Feast* (1972), and *The Wizard of Gore* (1970) are outrageous and thoroughly enjoyable, but have an intentional comedic quality.

2. Bishop (2010) argues that Fulci's Zombies symbolize racial clashes, pointing out that only the visitors, doctor and his wife are Caucasian. I believe, however, that those details are incidental to Fulci's aesthetic of disgust and revulsion.

3. Isabel Cristina Pinedo (2004) argues that "Fear and pleasure commingle" in what she terms "recreational terror, a simulation of danger not unlike a rollercoaster ride" (106). I combine this concept with Steven Jay Schneider's assertion that horror is "one's contemplation of, or even fixation on [an object, event, or image's] violative status" (2004: 140) to define pleasurable disgust — when horror and revulsion combine as a result of an image or sequence of images to form a pleasurable response. In part, this includes a necessary reaction of disbelief, as pointed out by Jeffrey Goldstein (1999). Pleasurable disgust also relies upon the level of imagination and uniqueness involved in such outrageous images, as noted by Stephen Prince in "Violence and Psychophysiology in Horror Cinema" (qtd. in Schneider, 2004: 139). Audiences are not merely fascinated by such images; they take pleasure in the revulsion resulting from them.

4. Twitchell defines horror as "more internal and long-lasting" than terror, which he describes as "external and short lived" (1985: 16). Fulci is consistent with this approach — striving for a lasting impact rather than a temporary fright or shock.

5. Amando de Ossorio's films in the series are *Tombs of the Blind Dead* (1971), *Return of the Blind Dead* (1973), *The Ghost Galleon* (aka *Ship of Zombies*) (1974), and *Night of the Seagulls* (1975).

6. By "traditional," I refer to the "limping, shambling, decaying ghoul in search of human flesh" made popular by Romero's *Night of the Living Dead* and John Gilling's *Plague of the Zombies* (Dendle, 2001: 11).

7. According to Pinedo, the postmodern horror consists of films that 1) Fracture the operation of our everyday world through violence; 2) Expose and break boundaries; 3) Confront reason and logic; 4) Abandon closure; 5) Generate a "bounded experience of fear" (90–91). The three films of Fulci discussed in this essay would certainly qualify as "postmodern" under Pinedo's definition.

8. *The Beyond* is typically referenced as Fulci's most successful and influential film. Director Quentin Tarantino resurrected the film in his midnight movies circuit, and the film was celebrated by a new generation of fans. Tarantino often cites the film as an influence on his own movies (Anderson, 1998).

9. Thrower (1999) and Russell (2006) both identify Fulci's zombie trilogy as *City of the Living Dead*, *The Beyond*, and *House by the Cemetery* (1981), I contend that the sequence should start with *Zombie* and not include *House*, as the latter is less about a reanimated corpse, but instead a figure that never dies. Continually decomposing, Dr. Freudstein attacks anyone who enters his basement.

The Mutated Spirit
The Hollywood Zombie as Psychopomp

Keira McKenzie

Psychopomp—A conductor of souls to the place of the dead
(*The Shorter Oxford English Dictionary*, 3rd edition, 1973)

When we were all creatures of the forest, life was very different: our food was lively, our gods were lively too, and closer. So were our deaths — very close, frequent, inexplicable and terrible. Life was, as they say, nasty, brutish and short, but then our souls were eased into the twilit shades of the underworld by psychopomps, animal spirits or shamans guiding our souls to the land of the dead. For a long time things remained that way, but now the forests themselves are mostly gone, shamans as good as disappeared, and scientific thinking replaces faith, yet death still remains "the undiscovered country from whose bourn no traveler returns" (Shakespeare, *Hamlet*, Act iii, Sc 1) — except for zombies.

In this essay, I intend to examine the relationship of the Hollywood zombie, from its first appearance in George A Romero's *Night of the Living Dead* (1968) through to one of its current incarnations in the *28* films (2002 and 2007), with the original Haitian zombie, a creature whose existence is barely acknowledged and exists only in the shadows of a vibrant culture. By examining the similarities with and the differences between the Haitian zombie, and the Hollywood zombie, I hope to reveal how the living dead horror of the modern Hollywood zombie films can be read as a psychopomp to Western civilization.

In broad terms, a psychopomp is an ancient function that allows for communication between this world and the spirit world. At its most basic, a psychopomp is a spiritual guide that conducts souls to the land of the dead. It is a means to cross the barriers that separate the spheres of the living and the dead. Mircea Eliade discusses shamans serving as psychopomps, including some societies whose shamans have to "see the souls of the dead which means that they *become* spirits, that they are dead" (1989: 86). These shamans have been to that other world, therefore they know the way. Similarly, because of that familiarity with the other world, some societies employ their ancestral spirits to serve as psychopomps, spiritual guides through the passage to that other world. The Hollywood zombie, the living dead that have stalked the lands of an entire genre of Hollywood horror films since 1968, fulfills a central function of the psychopomp: having died and returned, the Hollywood zombie knows the way to the land of the dead. But this creature also reveals a breach, a breakdown in the barrier between the spirit world and the world of the everyday. Unlike the Haitian zombie, Hollywood zombies don't spring from the spiritual, but are constructs of secular concerns. They are impersonal and unbiased — everyone is the same to the Hollywood zombie — but unlike psychopomps throughout humanity's history, the Hollywood zombie is not an individual guide; it is here to conduct entire societies to the land of the dead.

Spiritual beings that guide us in spiritual matters are not foreign to the Christianized West; folkloric beliefs in psychopomps are maintained in many regions, the form varying from region to region. Eliade mentions that almost all animals from the beginning of human history have been considered as psychopomps; animals retain their connections with the spirit world which humans lost in the mythical "fall," that time when they lost their peaceful relationship with all animals (1989: 99). Of these, birds are obviously favored as they fly, coming physically closer to the spirit world, the sky, where the Beyond is often situated (1989: 93–94), while horses and dogs are also familiar as close companions to humans, either in war, hunting or the domestic sphere; horses can carry the soul to the land of the dead, and dogs are frequent participants in funerary rites (consider Anubis, or Cerebus, the three headed canine guardian of the underworld). All of these — birds, dogs, horses — are represented in the films I intend to consider; in four of the films, these animals are involved in this ancient role, but in all the films, the overwhelmingly dominant form the psychopomp wears is that of the zombie.

Not until the appearance of the Hollywood zombie of George Romero did the possibility of the zombie as a psychopomp seem possible. The first shots of the zombie in the original *Night of the Living Dead* — the dead man appearing in a cemetery, shambling from a background shot into the foreground, attacking with unprovoked, unexpected aggression — reveal the nature of the psychopomp: liminal and monstrous, transgressing the most obvious of boundaries of life and death. Unlike in earlier films such as *Plan 9 from Outer Space* (1959), or *The Plague of the Zombies* (1966), in Romero's film there was no external agency inducing the abrupt attack. These new zombies attacked seemingly of their own accord. This horror looked like a normal, everyday person — except it was dead, and there was more than just the one. There were many of these dead people, resulting in and from, as a newsman in *Night* says, an epidemic of mass murder. Enter the psychopomp, the first appearance of the thing that would wipe the face of the earth clean of the living in so many films, in a perversion of Ishtar's threat from *The Epic of Gilgamesh*: "I shall bring up the dead to eat food like the living; and the hosts of dead will outnumber the living" (Sanders, 1960: 89).

The goddess's powerful threat illuminates the need for separating the spheres of existence — living and dead. Even so, while She intimated that the dead would eat the living out of a home, she didn't say anything about the dead eating the living, but from Romero's first film, that's what happens. "When there's no more room in Hell, the dead will walk the earth," says Peter in Romero's *Dawn of the Dead* (1978), and from here and ever after the barriers between living and dead are dissolved. Through actions as deliberate as those of maggots breaking down the flesh of the dead, these living dead similarly process the flesh of the living. It's a very nasty addition to the psychopomp *ouvre* of spirit guides and guardian animals. Robin Wood theorizes that the horror films of the 1970's differed from the classical horror film in that the monster is not defeated at the end, and that during this decade, films acknowledged within themselves that the monster is indestructible (2003: 78). By the end of Romero's second film, *Dawn of the Dead*, the zombies have overwhelmed society and are, en masse, an indestructible force devouring all before it.

Of all the manifestations of undead, amongst the legions of ghosts and vampires, the Hollywood zombie is the most repulsive and revolting — and the most apocalyptic. After Romero's first zombie film, once zombies appear on the scene, there is little hope for society, or indeed Western civilization. Just as imagination mutated the zombie into this exponentially increasing mass of monsters implacably pursuing the living, so this mutated zombie warps the concept of the psychopomp into a malevolent interactive entity that seeks not only your death, but the transformation of the Earth itself into the land of the dead.

In examining the evolution of the Hollywood zombie as psychopomp from its Haitian genesis to its current depiction, I will concentrate predominately on film, which seems to be the most popular media for the Hollywood zombie. The work of Max Brooks alone attests to the popularity of text-based zombies, but *World War Z* is slated for film release in 2012; likewise, Robert Kirkman's *Walking Dead* series made a hugely successful transition from graphic novel to television. These liminal creatures are, I would argue, best suited to an audio-visual experience with their moans and screams and the almost unlimited avenues for special effects and prosthetics. Of the many films available, four distinct series or franchises present the major phases or "mutations" of the Hollywood zombie: George A. Romero's seminal *Dead* series (1968, 1978, 1985, 2005, 2007, and 2009); the *Return of the Living Dead* series spawned by John Russo, from which the zombie penchant for brains originates; the *Resident Evil* franchise (2002, 2004, 2007, 2010) based on the successful video game franchise of the same name; and Danny Boyle's *28 Days Later* (2002) and *28 Weeks Later* (2007), from which the "fast zombie" is born. These three groups of films illustrate the mutations of the zombie after its not so humble beginnings in the mysterious and vibrant belief system of Haiti's Vodou.

Vodou and zombies were made accessible to the Western imagination by William Seabrook's travel tale, *The Magic Island*, in 1929. His curiosity about magic and the darker mystery of "Voodoo," is the beginning of the zombie of our story. A decade later, Zora Hurston's *Voodoo Gods* (1938), touched on the mystery without dispelling it.[1] Even after Wade Davis' highly controversial and contested works — *Serpent and the Rainbow* (1985) and his more scholarly *Passage of Darkness* (1988) — the mystery remains, despite further investigations by physicians, clinicians and philosophers (see Chalmers; Dennett, 1995; Littlewood and Douyon, 1997).[2] The word *zombi* itself is of confusing origin, but the closest meaning seems to be from the Kongo: *nzambi*, meaning "the spirit of a dead person" (Davis, 1988: 57). But the Haitian zombie has little do with some horror risen from the grave really, really hungry. In the Voodoo religion each person has two souls, the *ti bon ange* which gives character and purpose and the *gros bon ange* which is the physical soul. It may or may not be truly dead, but the zombie has certainly lost its *ti bon ange*. Such binary realizations of the spiritual self are not found within Western metaphysical spheres, and while some would say even the soul is in doubt, the mind is not and the Hollywood zombie possesses no mind, no personal character. It is just plain dead.

The lack of authoritative knowledge concerning Haitian zombies makes of them a scaffold for many stories of both mystery and horror, but the zombie was not *in itself* regarded as evil in early films anymore than in real-life Haiti. Robin Wood makes the same point: "In the zombies there is no evil" (2003: 102) Similarly, Davis observed that no-one fears zombies in Haiti, but there is great fear of *becoming* one (1988: 9). Yet, post–Romero, it is the zombie itself that has become a creature to be feared, becoming one is almost incidental.[3] Since Romero's films, the Hollywood zombie has come to represent the disintegration of the fabric that holds individuals together within society, contrasting with the Haitian zombie which seems to be a mute and somber reminder of what keeps society coherent and functioning; the two types of zombies not only represent differing world views but also present very different outcomes.

"Living dead" is a good description of a zombie's physical appearance and engagement with the world. In most films up until the advent of Romero's *Night*, there is no hint of the zombie as psychopomp because the poor creatures have no power, neither physically nor spiritually. Many of the very earliest zombie films, such as Victor Halperin's *White Zombie* (1932), or Val Lewton's *I Walked with a Zombie* (1941), retained both the magic and mystery inherent in the Haitian zombie tradition, though these early filmic representations of zombies were not strictly accurate. Gary Don Rhodes observed during his commentary on the Roan Group's 1999 DVD restoration of *White Zombie* that this first of the zombie films was a "pastiche of William Seabrook's 1929 *The Magic Island*." *I Walked with a Zombie*, for its part, is loosely based on *Jane Eyre*. Horror film buffs are aware that most horror films have a long literary tradition behind them (the most obvious exam-ple being Bram Stoker's *Dracula* and the many films it has inspired), but these earliest zombie films glossed over the realities because, quite simply, they weren't known. Instead, colored by gothic overtones, made exotic by incomprehensible magic, these films concerned themselves with separation and isolation, and were generally set in equally exotic tropical locations.

While presenting a westernized interpretation of the magic involved, these earlier films had at their heart a mystery that reinforced that of zombies themselves as well as the fascination with alien cultures. The zombies are a horrific visual undertone, providing an eerie, dare I say lifeless, pivot to the evolving story. There is great dread of them evinced by the characters within the story because of the power that made them and because they represent a soulless existence condemned to drudgery, something every self-respecting, well-off Westerner abhors. In *Voodoo Gods*, Zora Hurston noted that it was also a horrific possibility for the upper-class Haitian, "to contemplate the probability of his resurrected body [...] set to toiling ceaselessly in the banana fields, working like a beast, unclothed like a beast..." (1938: 172).[4] There is nothing about the zombies of earlier films to inspire any thought of a psychopomp.

Then in 1968, Romero's *Night of the Living Dead* hit the screens. Even this film had a literary reference as Romero had "mutated" the vampires of Richard Matheson's *I Am Legend* (Matheson, 1954) into flesh-eating ghouls. Most importantly, Romero's zombies were dead. Not just dead to the world. They were really dead. Decomposing dead. A *gros cadavre* indeed! There is no magic inherent in the existence of the Hollywood zombie, no spirituality at all. In this and following zombie films, "[t]he unknown and terrifying world of death assumes form" and "the inhabitants of the world of death becomes visible" (Eliade, 1989: 510–511).

Romero had devised a creature both infectious (like the vampires of Matheson's novel) and more repulsive with discolored, rotting flesh (the original film was black and white, but imagination works wonders) and limbs hanging by tendons, utterly divorced from the magical by their very physicality and their horrific effect on the characters within the film. From the "mysterious radiation" mentioned in the original film, thought to have caused the initial outbreaks, comes these flesh-hungry plague monsters that now populate an entire film genre. It has become such a powerful concept that the word itself has entered the both the academic and the common lexicon.

Hollywood zombies parody as well as contrast with the Haitian zombie in many respects. Seabrook (1929), Hurston (1938), and Davis (1988) report that the making of a Haitian zombie include the ritual use of human remains, a ritual parodied by the Hollywood zombie in using living humans to sustain itself while engendering more zombies. Perhaps the most striking contrast is the generality of the zombie infestation. What starts in an iso-lated farmhouse has, by the second film in Romero's series, become a global phenomenon. This pattern is repeated in all four franchises: what begins in isolation then crosses all boundaries, affecting, indeed infecting, the entire world. Another major contrast is the autonomy of the Hollywood zombie. Pre-Romero, zombies were always bound to the will of another, acting only on their masters' commands. But after Romero's zombie films, the creatures, while mindless, are monsters under their own aegis, not held by the will of an evil magician or extraterrestrials.

The Hollywood zombie has become a transforming symbol; in contrast with the Haitian zombie which is incapable of interaction with its world unless guided by the *bokor*, the Holly-wood zombie is compelled to interact with living humanity. The interaction is inarticulate and violent, but the grunts, moans, and screams symbolize the end of civilization, and in con-suming the living, by changing them also into more living dead, the Hollywood zombie trans-forms not merely societies, but the face of the entire planet into humanity's land of the dead. A psychopomp extraordinaire, bridging the worlds of life and death most explicitly.

This becomes apparent in *Night of the Living Dead*. Audiences — like characters within the story — were bewildered, appalled, and horrified. Maybe the most haunting aspect of the film was that ordinary, everyday people had become the horror — families and farm-houses. Robin Wood notes that Romero's zombie films exploded the gothic tradition of the classic horror film; instead of the monstrous being external to the society, threatening normality by its existence, in these films, "the monstrousness [was] returned to normality where it belongs" (2003: 101). But that monstrousness, both the zombies on the outside and the disintegration of the family structure on the inside, was negated at the end of the film as the sheriff's posse cleaned up bodies, zombies and mistakes alike (2003: 103). *Dawn of the Dead* concludes with something grimmer. Normality is represented by the shopping mall and the paired off characters, but the conclusion leads towards the devastated civi-lization of *Day of the Dead* where there is no longer even the veneer of normal relationships or society. *Dawn of the Dead* does present honesty as well as despair, and this helps keep hope afloat: the last actions of the two survivors are filled with a quiet courage and dignity in the face of the seemingly impossible.

In Romero's first two zombie films, the zombies are avoided by the human characters as much as possible, but in *Day of the Dead*, scientists actively study them, researching ways of either controlling or eliminating the effects of the virus. The cruelty displayed towards the zombies, despite them displaying signs of limited intelligence, underlines the cruelty of the humans towards one another. The antagonism between two groups of survivors (soldiers on one side, and scientists on the other) as well as gender-related antipathy causes the breakdown of security and the zombies are let into the safe area by a victim of both zombie bite and prejudice. Three people escape to live out their remaining days on an isolated island somewhere in the sun. There is no hint that there are any survivors anywhere on the earth, but in *Land of the Dead*, chronologically the last of Romero's zombie films, it is obvious that pockets of humanity have managed to prosper. Survivors are well organized and again living in a city. This film is set well after the events of the previous films and, building on the indications of residual memory and possible intelligence the zombies displayed in *Day of the Dead*, the zombies have begun to organize. Survivors plunder the remains of their old civilization to maintain their fortified and defended city, but their oasis cracks beneath the pressure of corruption, greed, and in-fighting. In the leveled playing field that ensues after the zombies invade, a balance between living and *living dead* is intimated as one group of survivors head off towards freer lands, and the zombies take over the city.

All Romero's films build on the concept of the living dead multiplying, reproducing through means of death, a complete inversion of the normal means of reproduction and a perversion of the command to be fruitful and multiply. It's a slow dissolve of civilization through the four films. Through the interactions of the people trapped in the farmhouse, the zombies begin to effect a breakdown of the social narrative. Throughout the rest of the series, while the zombies remain slow and shambling, their destructive reach annihilates western culture. They themselves, however, remain a mystery. The origin of what caused the dead to rise is never known for certain. A "mysterious radiation" is mentioned in the first film, while Peter in *Dawn* seems to imply there is some "voodoo" at play, but the mystery remains just that, a mystery.

Romero's films are peculiarly anthropocentric. There is only one shot in the entire series, in *Night*, where a living dead consumes a grasshopper on a tree, otherwise, the zombies in Romero's films are concerned only with humanity. From humanity they come, and unto humanity they will return with only one thing on their mostly destroyed minds: devouring human flesh. The pockets of humanity that survive in each film remain isolated from the rest of life on the planet. The *Dead* films posit a new earth, one where the living must share their space with the dead, and the Hollywood zombie has been successfully installed as an interactive, though un-invested transforming influence. "They are us," says Peter in *Dawn*. The perverted form of Ishtar's curse has come true.

The monster, generally regarded as "other," has become a reflection of the society it came from; humanity will be its own guide to the land of the dead. "The rhetoric of monstrosity is part of a political system of fantasy that is intended to *discipline*, in the word's conjoined meanings of teach and punish" (Ingebretsen, 2001: 37). Ingebretsen is speaking more of the gothic tradition which, as Robin Wood says, Romero's films broke from (2003: 108), but the monstrous Hollywood zombie is still framed within the broad spectrum of the fantastic. They are neither hybrids nor defeated, both expectations of the gothic, but they do come to teach and punish. As psychopomps, they perform the ultimate sanction without prejudice or favor.

However, while Romero's films are the start of the march of the apocalyptic Hollywood zombie, they do leave a glimmer of hope. Humanity is decimated, and the living dead have become psychopomps for civilization on a global scale, but the (chronologically) last film is open ended, inviting "the possibility of moving beyond the apocalypse," as Wood (2003: 107) said of the ending of *Dawn*, though it is true for *Land* even more so. The *Resident Evil* films (and to some degree, the *Return of the Living Dead* films) present a different psychopomp: human-engendered, they therefore cannot be laid at the feet of some mysterious external agency. However, the possibility of surviving the "zombie apocalypse" is also true; despite the utter devastation they depict, the films also posit the means and the direction for life to begin anew. It's not as blatant a hope as in the fourth of the Romero films with survivors well-equipped enough to know that they will be sharing the earth with the living dead, but it is there, couched in the same fantasy/science fiction tropes as the films: a savior in the form of the major characters of the franchise, Alice, who, like the zombies, is mutated to exist outside of humanity. Not until the *28* films, with its zombie psychopomps also created by human actions, do we understand what the psychopomp in its guise as Hollywood zombie can accomplish — a world devoid of humanity.

In the Romero films, humanity exists alongside the Hollywood zombies who remain perhaps as a warning against complacency. In the *Resident Evil* films, it has gone too far for humanity to effect its own rescue. The *Resident Evil* series follows the same pattern as Romero's *Dead* series in that it begins with an isolated outbreak that over the films spreads to encompass the entire world. The first *Resident Evil* details the results of T-virus contamination in the Hive, a secret underground research facility beneath a large city, owned by the Umbrella Corporation, a powerful corporate entity involved in everything from health care to military weapons, specifically bio-weapons and viral weapons. A chain of events both human and computer-generated leads to the release of the zombies, infected by the T-virus. A team sent to investigate must confront and fight their way to safety through hordes of zombies, both human and canine. This is the first indication that the virus affects more than humans. Through curiosity and greed, the virus is released from containment in the Hive to the city above and the sequel, *Resident Evil: Apocalypse*, details the banding together of a few survivors who will carry over into the following film.

Resident Evil: Apocalypse deserves its name as it is filled with revelations. The first is that the T-virus was created by a scientist to improve the life of his daughter, the antidote created because he knew how dangerous it was; the Umbrella Corporation took the T-virus to research its effects as a viral weapon. The second revelation is that Alice has also been injected by the T-virus. This film concentrates more on the growing powers of Alice and the other revelations, but the zombies have also grown in power. They are more active in searching out human victims, and when encountered are more terrifying. Alice successfully battles both human and non-human zombies, emerging as a powerful force to single-handedly counter the might of the Umbrella Corporation. She is the antithesis of the zombies, mutated by the same virus, but their opposite, as liminal though she straddles the boundaries between human and *super*human.

The third film, *Resident Evil: Extinction*, reveals that the virus is inimical to all life, even water. Unlike Romero's series, these films engage with the global environment and while the films focus on humanity, the psychopomps that the dead become transform everything. It is not just civilization that has been destroyed, the entire face of the earth is decimated. Survivors scavenge a civilization reduced to scant ruins, peopled by the desperate, the depraved or deadly zombified creatures, human and otherwise. In this film, the earth really has become the land of the dead. Even the film's palette (shades of yellows and ochres, desert colors), is reminiscent of Sheol. Massive flocks of zombified crows, birds long considered portents of death, are now aggressive and deadly, a return to more common forms of psychopomp, except no spiritual guide tore out the soul to send it on its way to the land of the dead with such savagery. The visual reference to Hitchcock's *The Birds* (1963) is almost lost in the added horror of the birds being dead and therefore capable of infecting whoever they scratch or stab. The zombified dogs that lurk in the hidden darkness guard the land of the dead with equal savagery. However, these just accentuate the power of the ultimate psychopomp — the Hollywood zombies lying in wait in hidden places. Despite this slide to annihilation, as in Romero's films, the *Resident Evil* films offer hope: though Alice is not completely human, for humanity she is a beacon of continuity. She is not only the counterpoint to the zombies, but to the monstrous Umbrella Corporation, thereby offering the possibility, even if far off in the future, that the earth will be made whole again.

The earth itself seems to reject humanity in these films. As *Resident Evil: Extinction* is yellows and ochres of searing sunlight scorching all in sight, *Resident Evil: Apocalypse* is blues and greys. The entire film is shadow-touched, as though everything remains within the confines of the cathedral where Alice first appears in the fullness of her physical powers, destroying terrifying mutations that desecrate the site of the remnant of the sacred — a church.

The *28* films revisit the bleak ending of Romero's *Night of the Living Dead*, but on the entire population of mainland Britain. What remains is not the harsh emptiness of *Resident Evil: Extinction*, nor the dark uncertainty of Romero's *Land of the Dead*, away from the burning cities, England is paradisiacal, filled with flowers, green fields, and the warm, bright, summer light. The Rage virus which transforms people into mindless, frenzied zombies, doesn't jump species, but only transforms the human population. The zombie psychopomps in these two films arise from the complex web of humanity's relationship with the environment — not consumerism, not corporations.

As in the *Resident Evil* films, this latest version of the Hollywood zombie also results from a manufactured virus. But unlike the previous films, the dead don't rise. In the space of 30 seconds, a victim goes from being a normal, reasoning individual to a raging monster. Stephen Asma writes: "Rage is a powerful force that, along with the other socially deleterious impulses, lives like a frustrated virus in the dark cellars of the Id" (2009: 209). And someone — a pharmaceutical company or the British government, has let it loose! These monsters, more than in the preceding films, arise from within ourselves — not just from society, but from our own psyches.

The *28* films are concerned with the death of self. Once infected, there is nothing else. Despite all the debate, the "infected" can be read as zombies because they are no longer humans, but inchoate rage personified. *Cogito ergo sum* no longer applies. As with the preceding films, the zombies spread the infection, through a bite, blood, or saliva. Even if the monsters don't kill outright, the victim is infected and can no longer be considered human. Not decomposing dead as Romero's creations, or those from the *Resident Evil* films, but personality and sense of self are gone. They are psychological zombies, though dangerously physical. Humanity reduced to ferocity and mindlessness. That the virus arises from within the individual is reiterated visually several times during both films. "You couldn't tell which faces were infected and which ones weren't," says Mark in *28 Days Later* (2002). During the film's climatic scenes, Jim, the main character, battles the soldiers to save Selena and the teenaged Hannah. In his rage, he resembles an "infected" to the extent that Selena, who saved his life at the beginning to the film, almost kills him. In *28 Weeks Later*, it is impossible to tell panic-stricken civilians from the raging "infected" amongst them. One can almost hear the echoes of Peter in *Dawn of the Dead*: "they are us."

If the previous films were content that humanity was reduced to the level where it had to start again, in the *28* films the transformation is as hyped up as the zombies themselves are. There is no dissolve to chaos and apocalypse, the 28-styled Hollywood zombies have mutated into hyperactive psychopomps, screaming frenzied hordes that race across the landscape in a terrifying parody of the Wild Hunt.

The Rage virus of the *28* films is released in the first film through a misguided act born of ethical concerns, and both films observe the consequences of acts, of moral ambiguity complicating human relationships in the face of catastrophe. All four series of films are scientific horror: horror born of science whether through earthbound experimentation or of extraterrestrial origin — but only in the *28* films is there a sense of the Orwellian concerns that were such a feature of horror films in the 1950's with the intimation that the virus was created for behavioral modification of populations.

28 Days Later references *Day of the Triffids* (1962), but instead of encountering feral plants, the characters encounter feral zombies; the sequel, *28 Weeks Later*, could be read as a commentary on the American invasion of Iraq,[5] but also on the futility and the morally suspect desire of governments and the military to exercise complete control over populations. As in the Romero films, the *28* films also have at their heart the family bonds that underlie and sustain society, placing the monster firmly in the normal, the everyday. Every one of the "infected" is someone's neighbor, relative, or friend. It is not farmhouses, it is suburbs and the living rooms of a parents' home. More akin to Matheson's terrible undead and living vampiric mutations than Romero's slow, relentless menace, the *28* zombies appear to actually require human flesh for sustenance. It is not mere habit, it is real need: humanity feeding on itself to survive.

The films stress a Darwinian response: only the quickest, the fastest-witted, and the most strongly willed will survive, and accordingly, even the uninfected lose their humanity. The actions of the soldiers in *28 Days Later* lack empathy and compassion and are focused on the self. "He's telling me that he's futureless," the psychopathic leaders says, watching an "infected" rage at the end of the chain. But it is society itself that is futureless, devoured from within by rage, and by carelessness of the environment, itself demonstrated by the film's opening in an animal testing laboratory where the virus is being evaluated.

The sequel, *28 Weeks Later* has a terrible human frailty and poignancy about it soon swallowed by the savagery of the "infected." Zombies do not encourage or even allow what Ingretsen calls the "sentimentalities of horror" (2001: 36). The central character is so morally ambiguous that he is both a warm-hearted, flawed human and the vector for renewed infection. Well-meaning actions enable the virus to escape to Europe at the end of the film, setting the scene for a contamination as global as both Romero's and the *Resident Evil* films.

In the *28* films, as in all the others, the psychopomp, while utterly inimical, remains completely focused on humanity. Other species are seen going about their normal lives, insects engage in the routine of cleaning up the carrion humanity leaves behind, intimating the normal cycle of life continues, regardless of humanity. When the "infected" die, which they do of starvation as they eat the land clean of humanity, they do return their dead body to the earth, but it replenishes a land without humans. Though referencing Matheson's plague-ridden vampires, in his novel, the living victims had devised ways of surviving and reestablishing society so that the one remaining human became the monster; in the *28* films, there is no living with the infection.[6] There is no "new normal" for humanity. The psychopomp has achieved its objective and removed humanity to the land of the dead. What remains is an otherworldly serenity.

The Hollywood zombie, so separate from its Haitian origins, is the eternal return in one moment. Unlike other monsters, the Hollywood zombie is an existential threat, transforming time's lineal progression into the "eternal now," the extended moment, the moment between life and death. The Hollywood zombie's body is purely corporeal, it doesn't shift or change, doesn't depend on natural cycles of time such as the vampire or the werewolf, nor does it continue the cycle of life in the living as does the Alien in Ridley Scott's *Alien* films. The Hollywood zombie is stasis. And this is its horror.

In Vodou, the *gros cadavre*, the body, should be returned to the earth at death, to replenish the earth's life force. But the Hollywood zombie multiplies throughout the living population, overwhelming them, and the life energy of the entire planet is reduced. Hollywood zombies hoard the life force of all, or in the *28*, any replenishment is to the benefit of everything excepting humanity. The land of the dead is not about growth, and neither are Hollywood zombies. They are the psychopomps to our own devolution to nothingness. In Vodou, death is not that removed from life, as "...death, like life, stretches far beyond the temporal limits of the body." (Davis, 1985: 186). This is illustrated by the Hollywood zombie, except that the temporality of the body has ceased to have any relevance at all. Death stretches into infinity, blocking the natural cycle of cycle.

Once the Hollywood zombies arrive, time ceases to have any relevance. Unlike the quiet presence of the Haitian entity behind daily life, the Hollywood zombie shambles or screams into daily life and negates it. You cannot have life without death, but Hollywood zombies do not allow for the circle of life to be closed. It is an open-ended shapeless thing that has lost its geometry and all that is sacred falls out. "The centre cannot hold," wrote Yeats, "[m]ere anarchy is loosed upon the world." And one does have to wonder, in the aftermath of the zombie apocalypse, "what rough beast slouches towards Bethlehem to be born." (Yeats, 1920: 923).

NOTES

1. See also Moreman and Rushton, forthcoming, especially essays 2 and 3.

2. See also Inglis, forthcoming.

3. While this is true of the characters in *Night of the Living Dead*, that fear does generate character studies in the sequels, most notably in the first *Resident Evil* film, becoming a subverted plot line in the sequels. Generally though, the fear in the modern films is fear of the hands — or teeth — of the zombies rather than becoming one, though at least one character in every film will face just that with varying degrees of courage.

4. While this theme also appears in *White Zombie*, Tourneur's *I Walked with a Zombie* picks up on an alternative theme as the zombie of the wife of a white plantation owner was created by her mother-in-law, a white female doctor, as a social sanction for disrupting the family and infidelity.

5. See Graham, forthcoming.

6. The more recent film adaptations of Matheson's novel, *The Omega Man* and *I am Legend* (2007) completely rewrite the ending in that it is uninfected human survivors who maintain society, unlike the 1964 film, *The Last Man on Earth,* where indeed, the last human had become the monster to the new society who lived with the infection, a normal society that didn't prey on humanity to survive.

Dharma of the Living Dead
A Buddhist Meditation on the Zombie

CHRISTOPHER M. MOREMAN

We are in the midst of a zombie-craze. Zombies have reached never-before-seen heights of popularity, appearing widely not only in film but also comic books, graphic novels, literature, video games — major cities across North America have become home to organized zombie walks where sometimes hundreds of people dress as the risen dead and wander *en masse* creating gruesome flash-mobs.[1] Zombies first came to a wide public attention in the early 20th-century, especially with Victor Halperin's *White Zombie* (1932), which introduced the zombie to the monstrous roster of the 1930s' horror-movie-cycle. Alongside bigger, stronger, smarter, and more sympathetic creatures like King Kong, Mr. Hyde, Dracula, The Mummy, and Frankenstein's monster, the mindless, servile zombie paled by comparison. Still, zombies have remained a feature of cinema for over seventy years. Over this span, zombies have evolved considerably, going through their most radical transformation with George A. Romero's classic *Night of the Living Dead* in 1968. This particular film and its five sequels have shaped the modern zombie and created their own sub-genre within horror fiction and cinema.

This essay aims to explain the zombie in light of its origins in Haitian Vodou, via African spirituality, and how this product of a particular culture has been adapted to modern times. In its original context, the zombie will be seen to have embodied a fear of slavery whether economic, political, or spiritual. In African traditions, creatures akin to zombies are often described in relation to forced servitude, an image further accentuated in the Haitian context (see Ackermann and Gauthier, 1991; Blier, 1995; Corzani, 1994; Geschiere, 1997; Niehaus, 2005). Through distinctly Christian symbolism, the zombie can be seen to represent a subversive rejection of an enforced Catholicism — Vodou's "antagonistic mentor," in Jack Cosentino's words (1995: 26). The transformation from a Haitian mindless slave to the flesh-eating ghouls of the modern cinema is a radical shift. That these new creatures are recognized as zombies, however, illustrates the importance of the earliest associations for a modern understanding of the creature itself. That the modern zombie grows out of the 1960s counter-cultural revolution will be seen as critical to the modern zombie's retaining both the elements of slavery and anti-authoritarianism (and so, anti-

Christian-ism). The associations with Haitian zombies have been supplemented by anxieties growing from the anomie resulting from a monolithic authority structure weakened by secularism, pluralism, and cultural relativity. Zombies, thus, have become slaves without masters, subject to their basest desires and without hope of divine salvation. An attempt will be made, then, to illustrate how these modern zombies can be viewed through a Buddhist lens which allows for a kind of salvation from death that does not require a supernatural theodicy. Relating Buddhist notions of life and death to the philosophy of Martin Heidegger, this essay will demonstrate how the modern zombie acts as teacher pointing the intelligent viewer towards an authentic awareness of one's self in order to live with the reality of death as a reasonable member of society.

When Deleuze and Guattari (2005) refer to the zombie as the only modern myth, they come at it from a clearly Freudian-Marxist view, in which capitalism is the root of the so-called death drive. Though considering the zombie-myth shortly after the release of *Night of the Living Dead*, their ideas retain scholarly interest thirty years later (see Adkins, 2007). As people become de-humanized by commodification, they can increasingly look forward only to death. The zombie, then, comes to represent the de-humanized person oppressed by anonymous corporate overlords. Certainly, many modern zombie depictions, and especially Romero's, lend themselves well to a Marxist interpretation. But this is not all there is to the zombie. For one thing, other movie monsters can often be equally seen as representations of oppression by the anonymous corporation.[2] Further, not all zombie images lend themselves immediately to such a reduction.[3] This is but one interpretation of the *role* of the zombie in specific films. This notion of the zombie as slave does, however, have roots in its Haitian origins, and it is to these origins that we must first turn to get an adequate grasp of the creature's meaning.

Stories of the dead returning to the realm of the living, either as spirits or walking corpses, exist cross-culturally throughout recorded history. The zombie specifically, however, derives from the historical context of Haiti and the African diaspora.[4] Hispaniola, the island of which Haiti constitutes the western third (the eastern two-thirds being today the Dominican Republic), was originally a Spanish colony discovered by Christopher Columbus. From the early 16th century, the island received African slaves to aid in the colonization process. San Domingue, as Haiti was then named, was given to France in the Treaty of Ryswick in 1697. Spanish interest in the island waned, and San Domingue outstripped the Spanish Santo-Domingo (present-day Dominican Republic), its larger neighbor, in both wealth and population, soon after becoming the richest and most populous European colony in the Caribbean. Over the next century, the French imported unprecedented numbers of slaves to the island. By the time of the French Revolution, San Domingue was home to an estimated 500,000 slaves, who outnumbered their French masters by a ratio of 10 to 1. The spark of revolution first flickered in Haiti in 1791 and took thirteen years to fully ignite, bringing independence from France in 1804. Haiti thereby became only the second independent nation in the New World, after the United States of America, and its first independent Black state. This massive, and successful, slave revolt struck fear into slave-owners throughout the New World, and in the United States in particular, affecting American attitudes towards Haiti to this day.

The slave population of Haiti, as large as it was, was composed of a wide array of

African cultures. In the face of forced dispossession, the diverse groupings found common ground in their shared African identity. This shared identity was further cemented in a response to the forceful attempts at conversion made by the Catholic Church, legislated by the so-called *Code Noir* (see Breathett, 1988). Terry Rey and Karen Richman point out that a large proportion of the Haitian slave population had already developed a syncretised religious *habitus* merging Catholicism with traditional Kongolese spirituality (Rey and Richman, 2010). While the roots of syncretism can thus be traced to Africa, rather than finding its origins in the New World, the conditions under which this syncretism was imported can be seen to further alter the currents of its development. The Haitian slave population adopted Catholicism nominally and symbolically while at the same time maintaining traditions carried with them from Africa. The syncretism of beliefs created what is known as Vodou (the preferred spelling over the more popularly used Voodoo), in which traditional African beliefs exist under the veneer of Catholic symbols. With the revolution and independence, the Catholic Church pulled its priests out of the island nation and waged a war of words against the perceived heathenism of its people.

The Catholic anti–Haitian/anti–Vodou propaganda incited and encouraged the fears latent in American slave-holders. Stories of Haitian savagery spread throughout the United States, replete with tales of magic, child sacrifice, and cannibalism. James Hastings' *Encyclopaedia of Religion and Ethics*, published in the early twentieth century, reflects a repugnant colonial ignorance with long-lasting consequences. What ought to be a reliable academic source negatively describes the Haitian religion, stating: "Voodoo is devil-worship and fetishism brought from the Gold Coast of Africa by negro captives to the United States and West Indies. Its chief sacrifice is a girl child, referred to by the initiates as 'the goat without horns'... There is a regular priesthood to intimidate and rob the devotees..." (Owen, 1908–1922: 640). Depictions of Haiti as a Caribbean version of the "Dark Continent" heightened cultural anxieties towards the former slave colony, and eventually facilitated an American takeover of Haiti in 1915. The invasion was ostensibly carried out in order to protect Haiti from the Germans, but it did nothing to ingratiate Haiti in the American mind. Neo-colonial rhetoric referring to the lack of civility among inhabitants and their inability to rule themselves was used to justify the continued occupation of Haiti. A 1920 issue of *National Geographic* commented on the U.S. occupation in an article titled, "Haiti and Its Regeneration by the United States." "Here," the magazine says of Haiti, "in the elemental wilderness, the natives rapidly forgot their thin veneer of Christian civilization and reverted to utter, unthinking animalism, swayed only by fear of local bandit chiefs and the black magic of voodoo witch doctors" (Rhodes, 2001: 73). Haitians did not take kindly to a re-imposed foreign rule, and civil unrest forced the Americans to withdraw earlier than had been originally planned. Haiti returned to self-rule in 1934, two years ahead of schedule. Shortly before this withdrawal, "Voodoo" made its big screen debut with Bela Lugosi's performance in *White Zombie* (1932).

Before discussing its appearance in film, we must discuss the Haitian view of the zombie in the context outlined above. In African folklore, the zombie is a creature born of evil magic. A sorcerer, called a *bokor* (not to be confused with Vodou priests and priestesses, respectively termed *houngans* and *manbo*), is believed to have the power to create a zombie. The *bokor* can revive a recently dead person and turn him or her into a mindless slave by removing a crucial spiritual component of his or her being. Haitians believe humans to have two spirits, one higher (*gros bon ange*) and constituting the conscious self, or soul, and a lesser spirit (*ti bon ange*), which is responsible for basic bodily functions.[5] Upon death, the *gros bon ange* leaves the body, though it may remain nearby for several days. If left unguarded, the body might fall into the hands of a *bokor* who can use his magic to trap the *gros bon ange* in a jar, tying the *ti bon ange* to the body, and thus allowing the body to be animated, but without the self within it. The animated corpse is thus a slave to the evil sorcerer for as long as it is needed. These sorcerers are thought to use their magical slaves to work for them, or to otherwise make their own lives easier. Often enough, when the sorcerers are finished with a given zombie, they might sell it to another slave-master or simply sell the animated corpse to a butcher for meat.

Reports of real zombies are relatively common in Haiti. Medical professionals in Haiti are accustomed to the appearance of zombies, believed to have somehow gained freedom from their captors. Louis Mars estimates that as many as a thousand new cases of zombification appear every year (Littlewood and Douyon, 1997). These real zombies appear to display various symptoms of mental deficiency or illness (Littlewood and Douyon, 1997), though physiological causes have also been determined, such as the potential use of a numbing poison that can induce a death-like state (Davis, 1988). Wade Davis, who discovered a poison that is said to be used to make zombies, also suggests that zombification plays a social role (Davis, 1988: 213–240). Davis argues that before a person can be subject to zombification, he or she must first be found to have broken some specific social norms, such as stealing the wife of another man, and thus it exerts a positive social control. The folklore of the zombie is intertwined with the social functioning of Haiti to the extent that actual zombies appear and laws have been put in place to govern them and their creation.[6]

The zombie-as-slave, while found in African tradition, takes on a more poignant significance given Haiti's role in the history of the slave-trade. Zombies are not feared in Haiti, but are rather the object of pity. Those believed to be zombies are taken in by relatives, sometimes adopted and cared for. Rather than the zombie itself, what is truly feared is the possibility of being returned to slavery, cast in the folklore as occurring through the powers of a sorcerer. As Deleuze and Guattari observed, the zombie/slave is de-humanized and so loses its self-hood. Having struggled mightily to gain freedom and so recognition as independent people in their own right, the prospect of losing self-determination again remains an ever-present fear; the American occupation of Haiti is a reminder of the possibility. The idea of becoming a slave can be equated with the fear of death in that both might represent a loss of freedom and ultimately of the self, and so the zombie is a person who has both died and become enslaved (cf. Hegel's master-slave dialectic: Hegel, 1977: 111–138).

Given the Catholic history in Haiti, it is not surprising that some aspects of Christian symbolism would appear even in such a uniquely Haitian creature. Jack Corzani explains how this should come as no surprise, "since the West Indians generally associated the terrors of African witchcraft and the horrors of their American slavery with the demons of Christianity" (Corzani, 1994: 134). In comparing death with slavery, the zombie/slave is literally a resurrected body. The slave-masters of Haiti were not solely economic or political but religious as well. The Church in Haiti was yet another arm of European oppression. The notion of a Christian resurrection foisted upon the slave population represents the possibility, if the Christian doctrine of a final resurrection is correct, for a return to eternal subjugation. I am not trying to suggest here that all Haitians will have read the symbolism in this way, but rather only pointing out that given the circumstances, such a reading could have been made. Certainly, from the perspective of the Christian, the zombie blatantly smacks of blasphemy as a perversion of the resurrection. It is well worth noting that the traditional African zombie does not necessarily appear as a risen corpse, but more often is an enslaved spirit, called a *zombie astral*, much like a genii in a bottle (Ackermann and Gauthier, 1991). That the latter has all but disappeared in the post–Haitian zombie folklore is significant. Along similar lines, it is interesting to note that the idea that a *bokor* might sell a zombie for food is disturbing not so much for the fate of the corpse, but for the belief that eating the flesh of a zombie might prove fatal, or will at least make one seriously ill. Again, Christian symbols are recognized and rejected here. Communion is the central feature of Christian ritual practice, wherein the body and blood of Christ are eaten. In Catholicism, with the doctrine of transubstantiation, the eating of flesh and blood is taken literally. For Christians, this is a communion with Jesus Christ, the savior who died and was raised for the sins of humankind. In another perspective, this is the flesh and blood of a man who died and came back to life. It is no matter that the folklore provides an evil wizard as the source of zombification, as the symbols used to depict the zombie are patently Christian. Further, the repulsion caused by the idea of eating the flesh of a zombie suggests a surreptitious rejection of the core ritual of those self-same oppressors. For Haitians, then, the zombie can represent the monster of the loss of self through slavery and subjugation both physical and spiritual.

Through to the 1960s, zombies lurched across screens at the whim of many masters, sometimes the result of Vodou, but just as often the slave-masters were invaders from outer space, mad scientists, or even Nazis. What is especially important to note, however, is that throughout this period zombies remained enslaved by some master. With *Night of the Living Dead*, this element was eliminated, freeing the zombies unto their own recognizance and unleashing the horror of the modern zombie that has swept all other monsters aside in terms of sheer popularity. Romero introduced several new details to the lore of zombies, and essentially re-created the monster, thereby establishing a new sub-genre of zombie-horror. Though my sense is that my reading of zombies can be applied across the zombie-genre generally, for the specific purposes of this essay I will focus attention on the post–Romero zombie, especially those most closely adhering to his "rules."[7]

R. H. W. Dillard (Dillard, 1973; Dillard, 1987) wrote what has been described as one of the earliest, and still among the most convincing, interpretations of Romero's classic (Waller, 1987). Dillard, among others, sought to come to some understanding of the underlying meaning behind *Night* and its popularity. Though Dillard makes some useful points, he ultimately misses the point of the significance of the monster itself. He acknowledges the importance of the fear of death, but glosses over this in favor of the fear of the dead themselves as more important to the film. Certainly, in Romero's vision, the risen dead are threats. They have returned to life without a master, save for their insatiable appetite for living flesh. Dillard begins with some discussion of the fear of the dead as a cross-culturally occurring human experience, which is certainly true. He points out that the risen dead unleash this "ancient fear" upon both the characters and audience members. He dismisses this fear as the central fear, however, pointing out that the characters quickly discover that the walking corpses have no real power and can be kept at bay with a torch and thwarted with a swift blow to the head.

Dillard criticizes some claims made by other critics at the time of the film's release who suggested that *Night* was an anti–Vietnam-war piece (Dillard, 1973; Dillard, 1987). Just as earlier critics had linked *White Zombie* and other horror films to the angst of the time (particularly the Great Depression), so too critics read Romero's film as a reflection of the uncertainties of its time. Certainly, there is something to be said for such an argument, but as Dillard points out, this tells us little about the unique-ness of Romero's zombies, such an analysis applying just as readily to other contemporary films. Similar kinds of explanations have been made of other of Romero's films. His first sequel, *Dawn of the Dead* (1978), takes place in a mall, allowing for a scathing criticism of capitalism and consumerist society as the living *and* the zombies become mindless consumers wandering the mall's corridors. Steven Shaviro sees "the life-in-death of the zombie [as] a nearly perfect allegory for the inner logic of capitalism, whether this be taken in the sense of the exploitation of living labor by dead labor, the deathlike regimentation of factories and other social spaces, or the artificial, externally driven stimulation of consumers" (Shaviro, 1993: 83). Such an interpretation gains credibility from the Haitian context as the rich are called *gros manjeurs* and the poor described as being eaten (Sheller, 2003: 146). Wood offers an excellent analysis of Romero's films ranging over racial and gender issues, as well as a psycho-analytic approach to family and sexuality (Wood, 2003: 101–119 & 287–294). The zombie as slave can be seen as symbolizing the slavery of the masses to masters corporate, political, or militaristic, and so on. Francis Gooding describes the range of meanings available when zombies are actors, referring here specifically to the original *Dawn of the Dead*:

> Completely overdetermined in its meanings, it also contains an allegory of the emptiness of consumer culture; a picture of the doomed fantasy that the privileged can maintain their control of the world's wealth; a commentary on class and race distinctions; a morality tale about cruelty; manifestations of a lingering fear of communism, and so on [Gooding, 2007: 27].

Certainly, such interpretations work, but they relate to the zombie only insofar as they focus on one aspect of its being.

Romero's zombies differ greatly from the established folklore of Haiti, or even of previous zombie movies. In fact, Romero did not originally use the term to describe his monsters, referring to them instead as ghouls, or the walking dead. That viewers and critics labeled the creatures as zombies is important in its own right, illustrating a desire to attach Haitian notions of the zombie to the flesh-eating corpses devised by Romero. That viewers and readers now recognize the zombie, not only in Romero's monster but in all manner of revenants, is evidence that the aspect of the walking dead that points specifically to the zombie is crucial today.[8] The actual inspiration for Romero's creatures is the vampires of Richard Matheson's *I Am Legend* (Matheson, 1954).[9]

Matheson's novel tells the story of the last living survivor of a plague that has turned the rest of humanity into vampires. Matheson's protagonist (Neville) secures his home during the day, when the vampires must hide from the sun, by placing garlic, mirrors, and crosses on the outside of his house. Further, Neville makes daily forays into the vampires' homes to drive stakes through their hearts. Nightly, monstrous, animalistic vampires surround his house calling out to him to surrender himself to them. The shock of the novel comes with the realization that in addition to these monstrous vampires who harass Neville, there is also a new breed of intelligent vampire who have adapted to life with the plague. For these intelligent vampires, Neville is seen as the monster as he indiscriminately destroys vampires in their sleep regardless of whether they are monstrous or intelligent. Gregory Waller points out: "As the vampire hunter, Neville is no more an embodiment of Good than the undead are an embodiment of Evil" (Waller, 1986: 258). More than simply a reversal of dichotomies, *I Am Legend*'s greatest feat is in casting the protagonist who hides behind the traditional Christian defenses against vampires not as the hero but as a mere protagonist unaware of his own status as villain. Though following the argument further would take the present discussion far off course, it is also worth noting that Matheson is influenced by Theosophy and admits to finding ways to embed this metaphysical philosophy into his fiction (Matheson, 1993: 11; for more on this see Moreman, 2012). For now, the most significant implication of Matheson's impact on zombie lore comes from his revolutionary view of the Christian dominant order being overturned.

Romero transformed Matheson's creatures from vampires to what have come to be known as zombies. Instead of craving human blood, these new creatures desire human flesh. Romero's ghouls have none of the weaknesses of vampires. They are able to walk in broad daylight, immune to garlic, and do not respond to any holy symbols. In removing the supernatural elements from the creature, Romero introduced a monster that was entirely human, and in so doing exploded the normal dichotomy of us versus them. Now, Them were Us. In a recent article, Francis Gooding places the zombie in the context of normalized states of life and death, and argues that the zombie in Romero represents a complete breakdown in society as the result of the disintegration of roles for the dead and the living. In the West, "The dead must always die, and so must the living live; confusion is not tolerable" (Gooding, 2007: 29). In this way, Romero incorporates Matheson's exploding of black-and-white definitions of life and death and good and evil. Robin Wood believes that this effect of Romero's films "represents the most progressive potentialities of the horror film, the possibility of breaking the impasse of the monster/normality relationship..." (Wood, 2003: 108).

Conrad Ostwalt recognizes the increasing popularity of apocalyptic films which focus on a secular end of the world, though his analysis of these ignores the zombie apocalypse (Ostwalt, 1995; Oswalt, 2000). Ostwalt argues that the secular apocalypse is one that can be held off by human ingenuity and science, and so ignores the unavoidable end predicted in Jewish and Christian eschatology. Others, like Charles Mitchell, consider the zombie apocalypse to be within the realm of end-of-the-world cinema and, thus, unavoidable (Mitchell, 2001). The zombie apocalypse is one that allows for the success of no human ingenuity.[10]

In terms of *apocalypsis*, I contend that the zombie-craze represents the recognition of revealed truth in the zombie, however secular such a truth may be. The zombie apocalyptic offers a wide array of examples of human attempts to overcome the onslaught of the dead, but to no avail. Some have suggested that Romero puts forth a nihilistic, or at least extremely cynical, view of the world; it matters not what anyone does because ultimately we all die and become zombies. Furthermore, the human characters tend to come into conflict with one another in the face of impossible odds, often resulting in the facilitation of their own downfall. Dillard concludes that rather than a fear of death or the dead, what the viewer is to take away from zombie films is "the fear of life itself," and ends his paper stating that in the face of life, "there is nothing we can do that will make any difference at all" (Dillard 1987: 22 & 28). Kim Paffenroth recognizes in this futility a criticism of selfishness rather than a fear of the world around us:

> ... zombie movies appreciate and mock that uniquely modern and particularly American predilection, fierce individualism, as something that can sometimes temporarily save us in a crisis, but which can also doom us in the long run. [...] as the crisis continued, unless our individualism could give way to feelings of trust, sharing, and community, we would be doomed as our individual supplies of ammunition and food gave out and we fell to fighting ourselves ... [Paffenroth, 2006: 21].

Paffenroth's argument has support. Some have argued that the fear of the dead is one of the earliest, if not the earliest, universal human fear. Akop Nazaretyan, for instance, recently argued that the fear of the dead actually played an evolutionary role in the development of society, suggesting that those early humans who feared the dead made more efforts to keep their own people alive and to foster a community, the alternative being a dog-eat-dog world where the living indiscriminately killed their own (Nazaretyan, 2005). In this light, the walking dead do represent a form of social control aimed at limiting selfishness and promoting community. As a Christian theologian, Paffenroth goes on to suggest that the moral of the zombie apocalypse is that "the only way for people to be really happy is by loving God in community with other human beings, and not by selfishly loving and accumulating material possessions on their own" (Paffenroth, 2006: 22). Though he can be found to have some sociological and anthropological support for his general contention, Paffenroth seeks to demonstrate how such films can be applied to a (particular) Christian way of thinking. Though Paffenroth correctly notes the observation that the zombie embodies a lesson against individualism and selfishness, his desire to add God to the equation stems more from an ideology he brings to the material than it does from an analysis of the zombie itself. By way of example, when discussing *Night of the Living Dead* Paffenroth comes to the conclusion that, while the characters all end badly, the supremacy of faith in God is still established. Despite the fact that religious faith and scientific reason both fail to save the lives of the protagonists, faith does not promise to save the *physical* self and so, in the end, remains unscathed (Paffenroth, 2006: 41–43). However, both the Haitian Vodou origins of the zombie and the influences of the 1960s counter-culture would suggest a limited applicability of elements *supportive* of a Christian interpretation.

As was shown above, the zombie can be seen to represent a subversive rejection of Christianity and the idea of a final resurrection. In recognising the implications of Haitian history on the zombie-as-slave, the associations with Christianity are unavoidable. Many of these same associations — a sense of the majority's oppression and a rejection of all forms of authority — appeared clearly in the 1960s. Unlike previous zombies, however, the modern zombie is raised under the control of no master at all in a completely God-less resurrection. Those who are raised remain the self-less, soul-less, corrupt bodies that they were at death (and perhaps were also in life). When Romero stripped Matheson's vampires of their weaknesses, he also stripped the power of God to stop them. Paffenroth responds paradoxically to the state of godlessness in Romero's works (and the remake of *Dawn of the Dead* [2004]) as a "sobering" reminder of what the world would be like without faith and hope. Though love and charity may appear in the films, "Without faith and hope, even love fails, because God, the only real and eternal object of all love, is not there to draw it upwards and complete it" (Paffenroth, 2006: 113). While Paffenroth does make some useful observations in terms of lessons against selfishness and hyper-individualism, his Christian reading ignores important details. For one thing, many characters in these movies *do* have faith and resort to prayer and holy symbols to no avail. This is not a world without faith that is being depicted, but a world where faith makes absolutely no difference. As Wood asserts, "the social order (regarded as in all Romero's films as obsolete and discredited) *can't* be restored" (Wood, 2003: 105 — original emphasis).[11]

In fact, I would agree that the films at face value appeal to a faithless world-view. *Night of the Living Dead* came out in the midst of the counter-cultural revolution during a period in which all forms of authority were being overturned. Many critics have recognized the racial, feminist, anti-capitalist, anti-war, and generally anti-authoritarian stances in Romero's films. Few, if any, have paid much heed to the religious implications, however. When religion appears in these films, it is generally shown to be ineffective. *Night* opens with a zombie attacking a girl praying in a cemetery. *Day of the Dead* (1985) includes a character who sacrifices himself to zombies while clutching his crucifix as he is devoured. *Dawn* includes a one-legged Catholic priest who laments the power shift from recognized authority to zombie, as well as both a zombie-nun and zombie–Hari Krishna. The remake of *Dawn* (2004) includes an atheistic church organist, as well as a television evangelist who preaches God's wrath as the meaning behind the zombie apocalypse. And *28 Days Later* (2002) introduces the zombies infesting a church led by their priest in attacking the protagonist. In a post-modern culture, there is no reverence for religion.

Peter Berger (1967) describes a "sacred canopy" that covers society and provides meaning to all those who dwell under it. In the context of the West, a predominantly Christian theodicy lay at the foundation of social authority structures. The Enlightenment wore away at the authority held by religion, leading to an increasing tendency towards secularization. The legitimacy of not only religious authority but an increasingly secular public life came to a breaking point during the 1960s with negative public reactions to racial segregation, gender equality, and the war in Vietnam, among other things. Berger uses the term "nomos" to define society's norms. He explains that, composed by a constantly changing collective of individuals, the nomos is subject to change. A complete lack of stability, however, would result in chaos and anomie, and so religion bestows a sacred order upon the nomos (thereby forming the sacred canopy), thus legitimating it despite the tendency towards change. The 1960s represented a turning point as the prevailing nomos finally lost its legitimacy as a critical mass of society moved against it. The weight of public sentiment created a revolutionary spirit that fought against the mainstream, Christian-founded authority structures. Competing beliefs had progressively moved onto the stage, punching holes in the sacred canopy. With a lack of confidence in the old theodicy, people turned to new ideas to bring meaning to life. Many adopted some form of humanism, while others turned to alternative spiritualities, some of which had been imported as American interests in Asia grew. Asian religion had been attracting interest in North America since the late 19th-century, though involvement in World War II and Vietnam and the exile of the Dalai Lama from Tibet raised awareness of Buddhism especially. A panoply of new religions formed in the wake of the canopy's rending. Many of these have been influenced by Eastern religions; others focus on innate human potential; some reject Christianity outright in favor of pre–Christian-inspired beliefs; while still others redefine Christianity itself. The common thread is a rejection of traditional forms of authority. Just as the Haitian zombie can be seen to represent the perversion of a rejected authority's resurrection, so too does the modern zombie indicate the rejection of the dominant authority and the resurrection that comes with it.

What this godless resurrection also illustrates, however, is an utter fear in the face of death. The zombie is the dead. Becoming a zombie occurs at death. The mystery of death had, under Berger's sacred canopy, been effectively explained by the doctrine of resurrection and the judgment of the good and the evil. With the authority of that message disabled, the mystery of death, and with it the problem of evil, returns to the fore as a problem that requires solving. Ernest Becker (1973) described Western culture as "death denying," but zombies do just the opposite — they force death upon the viewer relentlessly. The horror of the zombie lies, to large extent, in the realization that each of us will die regardless of what we might do to forestall it, and that as a culture, we have now rejected our traditional source of solace.

Martin Heidegger, "one of the most original and influential philosophers of the twentieth century" (Reich, 1995), describes death, which itself is one's own and cannot be shared, as the culmination of all one's possibilities as a human being (1962: especially Part II, Section I, p. 279–311),[12] who "reaches its wholeness in death" (281). He described the individual self (called *Dasein*) as, in a sense, moving towards its end as the fulfillment of its possibilities. One is often inclined to imagine the future as filled with innumerable possibilities, but focusing on the end reveals that death remains the one certainty — Heidegger stresses that far from mere possibility, "[d]eath is something that stands before us — something impending" (294). As we move closer to that end, whenever it may be, possibilities will have fallen into place as certainties in the past throughout a life. In death, there are no future possibilities for Dasein, and one can also recognize that, in fact, all one's possibilities have been effectively coalesced into a static reality of "having been." Retrospectively, one might say, the truth of the individual becomes clear, but as Heidegger describes it, from the perspective of the living, the possibilities which lie before Dasein may be unknowable before they gel, but they *are* Dasein. "Dasein *is* already its 'not-yet,' and is its 'not-yet' constantly as long as it is" (Heidegger: 289 — original emphasis).

Dasein is individuated by the confrontation with death, which in being one's own alone and as the fulfillment of one's potentialities, separates one from every other Dasein (see Heidegger: 294). Individuation serves to delineate the boundaries of the self and thus define an individual. The individual *Dasein* finds meaning, as per Berger, only in relation to society and others, but it also finds form only through recognition of its own self, defined as it is through death. Death is not something easily apprehended; the experience of death and the rational acceptance of its inevitability are commonplace only insofar as it happens to others. Death, then, is something that happens to other people. "In such a way of talking," explains Heidegger again, "death is understood as an indefinite something which, above all, must duly arrive from somewhere or other, but which is proximally *not yet present-at-hand* for oneself, and is therefore no threat. The expression 'one dies' spreads abroad the opinion that what gets reached, as it were, by death, is the 'they'" (297 — original emphasis). A temptation to focus on the limitless possibilities of Society rather than the impending reality of one's own end leads one into an inauthentic manner of being.

Heidegger describes the authentic self as that which acknowledges its own finitude and incorporates it; the inauthentic self is one that denies death and flees it (Heidegger: 304–305). Society, as a mass that survives the death of any one individual, safely ignores death as an immediate threat — ultimately, the death of one individual has no practical effect on society. The inauthentic self lives according to societal expectations, and so does not live as a properly individuated self. The authentic self is one that lives as both self *and* member of society. Becker's denial of death points to the inauthentic *Dasein*. More subtly, however, a belief in eternal life also flees from the acceptance of finitude and so prevents the individuation of selves. Paffenroth complains of a hyper-individualism in Western culture, but this is not what Heidegger intends by the individuated *Dasein*. For one thing, "care" is described as fundamental to the nature of human Being, and though Heidegger is not interested in practical applications of his ideas, some have found his work insightful for the development of an ethic of care useful in health care and other fields (see Bishop and Scudder, 1991; Reich, 1995; Stack, 1969). "Care" is that aspect of Dasein that can motivate one towards authenticity instead of caving to the anxiety that drives one into the arms of society. The hyper-individual is similarly inauthentic in being unable to conceive of its own demise. It is this hyper-individual, or inauthentic *Dasein*, that finds horror in death and the godless resurrection of zombies. As the zombie is recognized as Us, so "[w]ith death, Dasein stands before itself..." (Heidegger: 294). Essentially, the inauthentic *Dasein* flees from death and runs into the arms of society, thus failing to be individuated. How, then, can one come to accept one's finitude authentically and avoid a self-less state of slavery to the fear of our own mortality and the societal denial of death?

A number of connections between Eastern philosophies (particularly Buddhism and Taoism) and Heideggerian thought have been observed (May, 1996; Parkes, 1987). In describing the paradoxical problem of coming to terms with one's own mortality, Heidegger describes death as, "the possibility of the impossibility of any existence at all..." (307), and accepting one's end as standing "*face to face* with the 'nothing' of the possible impossibility of [one's] existence" (310). Nirvana, as the realization of one's own being as "not-self," sounds remarkably similar.

The core of Buddhism rests in the Four Noble Truths, central to which are the notions of attachment, impermanence, and suffering. The Buddha came to the realization that all things come to an end, and that all that we see as real is in fact impermanent and ever-changing. That reality is at all static is an illusion, and this impermanence applies to all things, including the self. The most important realization that one must make is that the self is impermanent and ever-changing. In Buddhism, there is no eternal soul, but only a constantly changing state of flux, a collection of aggregates that form and reform at every moment. I have the sense of having been the self-same person I was yesterday and last week. I may recognize some changes in my self over time, but there remains a sense of coherence through these changes that gives a sense of permanence. From the Buddha's perspective, however, the self that I am now is not the same self as was a moment ago, or the one that will be tomorrow. Subtle changes occur over time which make one moment's self different, if even slightly, from the next's. The self that I was even a moment ago has already changed and so is gone forever. Essentially, we move through a series of little deaths throughout life. Our final death is but another change like any other.

Of course, stemming from an Indian background, Buddhism accepts a belief in rebirth. At death, I will likely be reborn. The new birth that I will have will be a significantly different self from the one I am now, but the self that I am now is significantly different from the one that I had upon my birth into this present life. In any event, birth, death, and rebirth represent an ongoing cycle (*samsara*) in which the self fluctuates, dying and being reborn in every moment.

That we are attached to permanency, especially of our selves, results in much suffering since we cannot grasp anything for more than a moment before it is gone and has been replaced by something new. When I accept the illusion of my own permanence, I am unable to accept its eventual end and so reject death. In the Buddhist worldview, my attachment to life will be enough to have me reborn. If I do not want to end, then I will be reborn upon death. Unlike a theory of resurrection that teaches that the resurrected self will be the exact same one that lived, Buddhist rebirth is simply a continuing process of changing selves moving through *samsara*. Though centuries of debate over the nature of resurrection have yet to reach a unanimous conclusion, the importance of the eternity of the *individual* remains central.[13] Some, like Hans Küng, make the case that in losing one's self in the presence of God one in fact gains the fulfillment of the self. According to Küng, "[b]y *entering into the infinite, the finite person* loses his limits, so that the present contrast of personal and impersonal is transcended and transformed into the *transpersonal*" (Küng, 1984: 112 — italics in original). On the other hand, what remains important for the average Christian is that the self that one recognizes in the present life remains so in the next. As the former Archdeacon of Durham, Michael Perry, puts it: "Unless John Jones knows that he has survived and that he is still John Jones despite the traumatic experience [death] through which he has gone, no meaning can be given to the word 'survival'" (Perry, 1975: 9). Regardless of doctrines suggesting some perfection of the self through resurrection, the importance of the individual remains paramount. From a Buddhist perspective, however, all suffering is caused by attachments and in order to get over my attachment to things I must literally get over my self. In the Buddhist context, the self must be completely overcome. In Heidegger's terms, *Dasein* must accept its finitude and in so doing move towards individuation. A self without end is not a self at all. The end provides the defining limit of the self. In such an individuation, the self can be experienced with its end and so life lived accordingly as an authentic, albeit temporary, Being.

The zombie resurrection illustrates the rebirth of the self that fears death. The protagonists struggle tooth and nail to avoid becoming one of the dead, but all of their efforts ultimately fail. Attachment to life forces them to fight, but fighting for life does nothing to avoid rebirth. In this case, the rebirth as zombie emphasizes the suffering inherent in the attachment to *samsara*, birth and death. The zombie seeks only the fulfillment of its craving for flesh, an insatiable and fruitless hunger. A scene in *Day of the Dead* drives home the pointlessness of the zombie appetite as one captured zombie continues to try to eat despite the fact that its internal organs have been removed and so the "food" simply drops to the floor upon being swallowed. Just as the living fight for their lives, so too do the zombies strive for nourishment, both to no avail. So, the pointlessness of craving and attachment are plainly illustrated. The zombie presents a mirror to the self and the attachment thereto. So long as we remain attached to this life, we have only further suffering to look forward to in the next.

There exist varying Buddhist practices of meditation focused upon death or the dead body.[14] The goal in these efforts is to drive home the reality of personal impermanence through an association of self and other, and in so doing expose the pointlessness of attachment to any kind of permanent self. The Buddha himself became enlightened upon his encounter with the finitude of death; after meeting first an old man, then a sick man, and a finally a corpse, Gautama realized the impermanence of life and the suffering of being attached to it. Therefore, the meditation on death can provide an effective means to the cessation of attachment. One form of the meditation on death simply has the individual sit alone in private to contemplate the fact of his or her eventual death. The effort is to remind one's self that death will come to everyone, including oneself. Another form, which corresponds closely to the act of watching a zombie film, is the meditation on the foulness of the corpse.[15] Here the meditator is instructed to sit next to a corpse, perhaps one awaiting cremation, and meditate over its state. The gory details of the body's corruption are central to the meditation. Alan Klima quotes the description of one Buddhist nun: "This body opens up for you to see. You see bodily ooze. Clear oozelike in the brain; thick, filmy ooze and clear ooze. The body splits open into intestines, intestines the size of your wrist, *na*. Liver, kidneys, intestines, the stomach, you can see it all" (Klima, 2001: 554; see also Klima, 2002). Certainly, such imagery is ever-present in zombie cinema. The Pali canon (Buddhist scriptures) teaches the meditator to consider the dead body, and to think: "As this [my body] is, so that is; as that is, so this is," and further, "Indeed this [my] body is of this [foul] nature, will become like this, and cannot escape this" (Bond, 1980: 247).[16] Through observing the corpse and realizing the connection to oneself, the meditator can realize both the impermanence of things as well as the suffering inherent in attachment to the body. The foulness of the body is meant to powerfully bring home the fact that the body is in a state of perpetual dying, even throughout what we consider life. As Klima notes, "the corpse in its gory, abject, and repulsive state is the most desirable aesthetic" (Klima, 2001: 562). Such meditations force the mindful to become aware of their own being-towards-death, and by accepting it realize the truth about life. Effectively, the finitude and impermanence of the self suggests that the death that one fears is in reality occurring every moment. Death is a reality not only in some unforeseen future, but is happening as we live in this very moment. I am dying, I will continue dying, and I have been dying since I was born. The more I want life, the more prolonged my dying will be. By accepting the absence of a permanent self from one moment to the next, one can overcome the fear of death and so actually live free of dying.

It is worth noting that stories of animated corpses exist in a Buddhist context as well. For instance, Tibetan Buddhism includes the possibility that a corpse may be revived as what is called a *ro-langs* (Walter, 2004; Wylie, 1964). This can happen either through the conjuration of a shaman or from possession by an evil spirit. Tibetan Buddhism incorporates a complex series of rituals surrounding the death of a person in order to facilitate that person's transition from this life into the next world, leading to probable rebirth, but potentially leading instead to *nirvana* if the individual is able to overcome attachments. The possessing spirit represents a kind of rebirth that remains filled with cravings and so needs to incarnate by stealing a body that has recently become free, so to speak. The horror of these creatures is two-fold: on one hand, there is the fear of the invading spirit, recognized as being filled with craving, and so is much like the zombie of Romero; on the other hand, there is also the fear for the safety of the deceased as one's spirit might be threatened by this turn of events and so may not have a successful rebirth. Here, as we have seen in other cases, there is both the fear of the zombie's master (in this case, the invading spirit), but also the fear of becoming a zombie (in this case directed towards a loved one for fear that they may suffer further by not being able to move effectively towards nirvana, or at least a better life).

Two Chinese stories are also worthy of note, from the 18th-century Chan Buddhist writer Yuan Mei. The first, "Two Scholars of Nanchang" (Francis, 2002: 138–139),[17] tells of two friends who studied together. The elder of the two died, leaving his younger friend in mourning. During the night, the elder scholar visited his friend while he was in bed. At first afraid, the younger scholar was convinced that the ghost's intentions were benevolent. He came to console his still living friend but also to ask that he repay some unpaid debts for him. The elder scholar having delivered his message intended to leave, only to have the younger scholar ask for just a little more time since they would likely not see each other again, the one being dead and the other alive. At this request, the elder scholar's face began to change, become ugly and decayed. The younger scholar once again became frightened and demanded that his friend leave him. Instead the corpse stood staring, and then chased the younger as he stood and ran. The corpse chased him until the younger man escaped over a wall. While he lay at the bottom of the wall, the corpse simply looked at him from the top, drool dripping on him from its dead mouth. In the morning, the young man was found lying in the street, and the corpse of his friend was found on the other side of the wall.

A second story from Yuan Mei, "An Artisan Paints a Zombie (*jiangshi*)" (Francis, 2002: 141–142),[18] tells of a son who hires an artist to do a portrait of his recently deceased father. The painter agrees and once he begins his painting the father's corpse sits up in his bed. The painter determines to keep painting, and the corpse begins to imitate his actions, moving his hand in the air as if the corpse were painting as well. Rather than running as the young man in the previous tale did, the painter freezes and waits for help to arrive, in response to which the corpse simply sits frozen in the same position as the painter. The corpse is returned to a dead state once again when some passersby bring brooms with which to sweep away the evil influence.

Both of these stories reflect both traditional Chinese belief and Buddhism. Traditionally, the Chinese have believed in multiple spirits. The *hun* is the seat of consciousness and the *po* the animating principle, which can be loosely compared to the Haitian conception of *gros* and *ti bon anges*. Without the *hun*, an animated corpse has no self. More interestingly for our present purposes, however, is the *raison d'être* for each of these zombies. In the first story, the elder scholar appears out of compassion to his younger friend and also out of duty for he asks his friend to take care of some unpaid debts for him, both of which are common tropes in ghost stories. The elder friend transforms into a walking corpse once the younger friend asks him to stay longer. Here, the elder scholar can be seen exercising the Buddhist virtue of compassion (for his friend) and perhaps a Confucian sense of duty (the repayment of debts), but things go wrong when the younger scholar is compelled to ask for more time due to his attachments to his friend's earthly existence. The lesson to avoid attachment is here taught by the dead friend's transforming into a rotting corpse and pursuing the young man through the night. Just as modern Hollywood zombies thrust themselves at a death-denying audience, so to the corpse here forces its message on the young man. In the second story, again the problem stems from attachment to the dead. The son here wishes to immortalize his father in a portrait. The beginning of said portrait causes the corpse to rise. It is attachment to the deceased that results in its re-animation. Reinforcing the relationship between the living and the dead, the body then mimics the painter as if it is his reflection. The painter and the corpse are not unlike each other, just as the one meditating on a corpse will come to realize: "as that is, so this is." When corpses rise of their own accord in a Buddhist context, the cause can clearly be seen to be attachment, the root of all suffering. The fear of the re-animated corpse stems from a refusal to accept the connection, an attachment to the comfort of ignorance.

The modern zombie-craze, then, can be seen as growing out of a 1960s countercultural depiction of life in the face of impending death without the sacred canopy of a formerly Christian authority. In its place, the risen corpses force the living to recognize their own mortality and in so doing recognize the impermanence of the self. The modern zombie as zombie illustrates an enslavement to attachments and cravings. Just as the Haitian zombie signifies a loss of the self in slavery to a foreign master, the modern zombie signifies a loss of self in the very pursuit of its existence. The self does not exist in a permanent state, and so does not exist in the way that we typically wish. By attachment to this dream of immortality, we force ourselves to be reborn in a perpetual state of zombified craving. Whether this takes the form of capitalist consumerism or some other fetishization, the root remains the attachment to the empty non-existent self. By confronting the zombie, and so confronting our own mortality, we can come to accept finitude and thus become authentically individuated Beings unconcerned with selfish but impossible yearnings. Heidegger notes that the individual's "uttermost possibility lies in giving itself up, and thus [shattering] all one's tenaciousness to whatever existence one has reached" (308). As selfless Beings, society can thus function effectively, and its individuals need not suffer for, literally, naught.

NOTES

1. One discussion list for such events can be found online at: http://www.zombiewalk.com/. Cited Nov. 18, 2008.

2. Aliens are commonly employed in this regard, as in John Carpenter's *They Live!* (1988). Annalee Newitz (2006) includes robots, cyborgs, and serial killers alongside zombies as monstrous embodiments of a capitalist society.

3. Even Romero's *Day of the Dead* does not specifically lend its zombies to a corporate or capitalist cri-

tique, but levels its attack on militarism and scientism, or perhaps Western society on the whole. But even an attack on Western society generally, though Western society is, among other things, capitalist, does not equate with an attack on capitalism itself.

4. Bellegarde-Smith (2006) remains a valuable resource on the history and culture of Haiti.

5. The terms are sometimes reversed, depending upon the source (Ackermann and Gauthier, 1991).

6. Interestingly, since the 1960s similar reports of zombies have been reported in West Africa. Though originally at the root of much of traditional Haitian belief, the zombie is a new form coming back to the source from Haitian Vodou (Geschiere and Nyamnjoh, 1998).

7. I have targeted my interpretation even more precisely elsewhere in a close reading of Romero's *Night of the Living Dead* itself (Moreman, 2008a).

8. For instance, that repository of all things pop-culture, *Wikipedia*, includes a reference to the Epic of Gilgamesh as containing the earliest reference to a zombie. Reading "zombie" into such occurrences of walking corpses simply illustrates the importance of zombieness. See "Zombie," *Wikipedia*, online: http://en.wikipedia.org/wiki/Zombie. Accessed Dec. 23, 2010.

9. In addition to inspiring Romero, Matheson's novel has now also been made into three movies: *The Last Man on Earth* (1964), *The Omega Man*, and *I Am Legend* (2007). For a review of the latest, see (Moreman, 2008b).

10. Those zombie films that do provide succor to the living are typically comedies, such as Edgar Wright's *Shaun of the Dead* (2004) and Andrew Currie's *Fido* (2006).

11. Though Wood is here specifically talking about *Dawn of the Dead* (1978), his observation applies more broadly.

12. Although Heidegger's main interest in *Being and Time* is not death, per se, his musings on death are relevant to understanding the zombie as cipher. The following section on Heidegger has been revised from the original paper in order to more clearly express Heidegger's thought, and the manner in which I wish to apply them. I thank Robert Farrow for his helpful observations.

13. Badham (1976) offers a highly digestible overview of a wide range of modern theological opinions on the subject.

14. For a good overview of such forms of meditation in the Theravadin Buddhist tradition, see Bond (1980). See also Conze (2003, especially p. 86–106).

15. Buddhaghossa outlines what are termed the Ten Foul Objects of meditation, which include the various forms of decaying corpse found in zombie cinema (*Visuddhimagga* 110–111).

16. Bond here cites first the *Smyutta-Nikaya* (203) and secondly both the *Digha-Nikaya* (2.295) and the *Angutta-Nikaya* (3.324).

17. Francis here cites *Yuan Mei quan ji*, vol. 4, p. 3.

18. Francis here cites *Yuan Mei quan ji*, vol. 4, p. 93–94. It is worth noting that the term "*jiangshi*" is sometimes also translated as "vampire," though the creature behaves like neither zombie nor vampire as conceived of in the West.

PART III

Zombies into the Future

Digital Dead

Translating the Visceral and Satirical Elements of George A. Romero's Dawn of the Dead *to Videogames*

GARETH SCHOTT

NUMP, NUMP, NUMP, NUMP. Wave after wave they bear down on a lone defender futilely
attempting to preserve a way of life.
NUMP, NUMP, NUMP, NUMP, goes the lumbering repetitive tone of a plodding yet
methodical advancement that implies the inevitable demise of the human race.
NUMP, NUMP, NUMP, NUMP. Movement from left to right, in and out of cover, becomes
more frantic and skittish the closer they get.
NUMP, NUMP, NUMP, NUMP. There is no winning state.
NUMP, NUMP, NUMP, NUMP. How long can the inevitable be deferred?[1]

In 1978, long before the digital games remediated the zombie, Toshihiro Nishikado's
Space Invaders was captivating players' attention, sparking the infestation of videogame
cabinets into the public domain as games occupied spaces in restaurants, supermarkets, movie
theatres (Sellers, 2001) and of course shopping malls. Players engaged in pay-for-play trans-
actions deposited coin after coin (resulting in a shortage of 100 yen coins in Japan) to pit
themselves against an unthinking, relentless and infinite threat. Much like the zombie genre,
this game and the industry it went on to inspire, captured the imagination of many despite
its simplicity. Following the theme of *Space Invaders*, the game medium itself was quickly
considered a menace, something that needed to be wiped out. While more pronounced today,
the first crusade against the dangers of videogames was mounted against *Space Invaders* in
Mesquite, Texas (De Maria and Wilson, 2002). As an interactive text, it was considered an
"excellent metaphor for the frustration of the individual in our society," addressing the forces
that array against the individual that threaten to suffocate them (Crawford, 2003: 20).

In the same year that videogame cabinets began to line the walls of shopping malls
(e.g. *Air, Atari Destroyer, Super Bug, Canyon Destroyer*), George A. Romero's influential
refashioning of the zombie continued with the release of *Dawn of the Dead* (1978). Regularly
interpreted as a scathing commentary on American consumer culture, the shopping mall
was effectively employed by Romero as a symbol of the numbing effects of materialism

and vacuity of consumer culture. His script describes the department stores that bookend the mall setting in Monoroeville, Pittsburgh as "great symbols of a consumer society" (Romero, cited in Jones, 1982). Romero's employment of the hedonistic icons of North American culture manifests a sentiment that Kenneth Jackson later expressed thus: "The Egyptians have pyramids, the Chinese have the great wall, the British have immaculate lawns, the Germans have castles, the Dutch have canals, the Italians have grand churches. And the Americans have shopping centers" (1996: 1111).

While the idea of flesh-eating undead has long been a feature of world mythology, Romero succeeded in transforming the mystical Haitian *zombi* of W.B. Seabrook's 1929 novel *The Magic Island* into an apocalyptic nightmare and metaphor for government ineptitude, societal decay, greed and exploitation. Yet, contained within Romero's translation, the zombie retains its connection to slavery and oppression. Aligned with the zombie genre's status as a "maligned cinematic underclass" (Harper, 2002), the walking dead in *Dawn of the Dead* possess an instinct to return to the mall (a site of consumption) that portrays them (and us) as "slaves" to consumption and therefore little more than "cultural dupes" (Fiske, 1989).

As the demographic most popularly associated with videogame culture, adolescents too are increasingly and exclusively framed as consumers, adopters and appropriators of little understood and allegedly dangerous technologies. There now exist market constructions further delineating adolescent markets into *tweens* (ages 8 upwards) and *tweenagers* (ages 10–12). Furthermore, Gen Z or iGeneration, is used to describe how those born after 1992 are distinguished by a lifelong relationship with media and communication technologies. Game players who take pleasure from, show commitment to, and place investment in game play are often portrayed as wasting time — "time that could be spent engaging in more constructive activities" (Griffiths, 1997: 233). Instead of perceiving game players as possessing active, critical and productive relationships with popular texts, they are more popularly demeaned as simply avid, loyal consumers of the mass-produced commodities of popular culture. Goss' comments (1993: 32) that the "terror of time and space evaporates for millions of Americans at the mall," is often considered equally true of the immersive second lives of game players. Similarly to the mall, games are described as a "free activity standing quite consciously outside 'ordinary' life as being 'not serious' but at the same time absorbing the player intensely and utterly[...]. It proceeds within its own [...] boundaries of time and space," as found in Huizinga's (1955: 13) classic study.

Zombies and Spatial Storytelling

Jamie Russell (2006) acknowledges the zombie lacks a strong literary heritage in comparison to other coveted Hollywood ghouls and monsters, such as Stoker's Dracula, Shelly's Frankenstein monster or Stevenson's Dr. Jekyll and Mr. Hyde. While the zombie film is clearly a narrative form, closer to games, the nameless army of living dead present the uninfected with a range of complications, surprises and obstacles. As with games, *Dawn of the Dead* revels in "second act" hurdles, setbacks and conflicts of the three-act film structure. In doing so, *Dawn of the Dead* possesses what Bittanti (2001) has termed a techno-ludic quality more commonly attributed to film/videogame translations (e.g. *The Matrix* or *Run Lola Run*).

Many associations can be drawn between the setting of Romero's *Dawn of the Dead* and the structure and nature of videogame texts, all of which converge so successfully in the game *Dead Rising* (Capcom). Muzzio and Muzzio-Rentas (2006: 141) argue that the mall setting of *Dawn of the Dead* corresponds to Foucault's (1986: 24) concept of "heterotopia," as "all real sites that can be found within the culture are simultaneously represented, contested and inverted" within it. It is less well understood, but game designers too function as "symbol creators" (Hesmondhalgh, 2002) constructing texts by creating new assemblages from existing cultural symbols. One such example would be the work of Rockstar Games, the developers of *Grand Theft Auto*, who have produced an ode to urban life, presenting the player with not just a game but also a city. Thompson (2008) argues that Rockstar are "utterly in love with the idea of the American city: the riot of decay and grandeur, the garish commercialism, the violence and beauty, the architectural delights hidden in every corner." He goes on to state that: "Each street corner is a piece of randomly generated theater: Primly dressed art students wander around with portfolio cases, homeless crack addicts mutter to themselves as they brush past hipster dudes toting Starbuckian sleeves of coffee." Much like the designed experience of the game, mall developers employ environmental and architectural analyses in planning the form and experience of shopping. The ultimate goal for mall designers is the "Gruen transfer"— the process of transferring a "destination buyer" into an impulse shopper. Indeed, one of the many techniques for achieving this has been to theme malls thus presenting the consumer with the "myths of elsewhere." Spaces are created that aim to make us feel like we are on vacation, appealing to what Martha Wolfenstein (1951) terms "fun morality," a mindset that is less attentive to the nature of our spending. Maitland (1985: 9–10) unintentionally summarizes the relationship between the mall and game design, when he describes the mall as "a channel for the manipulation of pedestrian flows."

Don Carson who has worked as a Senior Show Designer for Walt Disney Imagineering, the theme park design arm of the Walt Disney Company, knowingly creates a clear link between malls, theme parks and game design when he discusses the capacity of spatial design to draw upon and utilize environmental storytelling. That is, telling a story through the experience of traveling through a real, or imagined physical space. He argues that the "story element is infused into the physical space a guest walks or rides through. It is the physical space that does much of the work of conveying the story the designers are trying to tell" (Carson, 2000). The setting for Romero's zombie apocalypse provides a space that communicates more about what the destruction of the present order entails, possibly more so than the zombies themselves. The uninfected are captivated by the ideology of the deserted mall despite the reality of their presence there, as Stephen comments to Fran, "you should see the great stuff we got, Frannie, all kinds of stuff. This place is terrific…. It's perfect … we've got it made here." Whereas Fran shows greater awareness stating that: "You're hypnotized by this place, all of you. It's so bright and neatly wrapped you don't see. It's a prison too." The mall provides a staged area where the collapse of social order that began with the visceral horror of *Night of the Living Dead* (1968), can be replayed over again. It is the continued delusions and foolish antics of the living that ultimately put their survival in jeopardy, this reaffirming Fran's insight that "it's not the dead that are the problem, but the living."

The design of traffic flow within malls is said to work effectively by luring patrons deeper inside to disorient them in a bid to keep them contained as long as possible (e.g. hexagonal floor plans; Rushkoff, 2000). Games too employ a maze-like quality presenting the players with a myriad of equivalent-looking rooms and corridors, some of which contain beneficial items for advancement while others contain dangerous adversaries. The game environment represents "a constrictive topology of nodes and connections" designed to interfere with "unhindered movement" (Aarseth, 1997: 7). In addition, the zombies of *Dawn of the Dead* represent a force, comparable to the natural opponent facing the would-be survivors of both the 1972 and 2006 *Poseidon* films, who are relentlessly pursued, pushed forward by the penetration of seawater further into the ship. Trailed, the characters are unable to pause or retrace their steps, but are instead compelled to make rash decisions as they confound the need for immediate refuge with finding an escape route. In such instances the uninfected too, like the game player are pitted against the environment (Atkins, 2003) as much as their antagonists. Survival becomes firmly connected to spatial mastery. As Aarseth (1997) has pointed out with reference to the game *Myth*, "when the chaos of battle erupts, efficient control is no longer possible" (11). Much then, depends on how well the player has taken note of formation, landscape variation, and knowledge of enemy positions.

In selecting the mall, Romero effectively chose a site imbued with narrative significance. Game spaces similarly permit the player to arrive at their own conclusions about a previous event or suggest impending danger just ahead. Typical examples found in game design include, doors that have been broken open, traces of a recent explosion, a crashed vehicle, or the charred remains of a fire. When traversing a gamescape, the environment and the location provide signifiers that tell the story. Thus, by transferring environments from the spreading chaos of the zombie outbreak to the deceptive safety of the mall in *Dawn of the Dead*, Romero was able to highlight the absurdity of protecting modern values. Just as consumerism is a process whereby objects are transformed by acts of dissociation and association, the uninfected also attempt to dissociate themselves from their social and material contexts in inhabiting the mall. Faced with the apocalypse, the uninfected turn to the essential function of consumption — its capacity for making "meaning." As Douglas and Isherwood (1978) argue, "consumption is a ritual process whose primary function is to make sense of the inchoate flux of events" (65). Yet, as "a nonverbal medium for the human creative faculty" (62), it is short lived.

Gen Z and the Enduring Relevance of the Zombie

Like the modern First Person Shooter (FPS) genre, the recurrent exhortation of *Dawn of the Dead* is "shoot them in the head!" The much-revered head-shot in any FPS is also commonly understood as the only way to stop zombies. Yet, it also symbolizes the irrationality of a chaotic and "headless world" (Russell, 2006) — a world in which videogames are habitually blamed for the "debauched innocence of our young" (Buckingham and Bragg, 2004). As Romero (cited in Jones, 1982: 36–37), referring to his film commented, "it carries things to such an absurd degree that we know it is absurd. Nothing I do will have a causative effect. No one is going to come out of [Dawn of the Dead] and eat anyone."

Yet, in 2006 the Romero homage, *Dead Rising* (discussed below), was refused a rating in Germany by the Federal Verification Office for Youth Endangering Media, making selling the game a criminal offense. Indeed, nothing has been able to abate the volume of "effect" research that critiques videogames for their amplification of negative psychological, moral and behavioral states. State-driven legislation, news media, and advocacy groups selectively utilize experimental research to express concern for what they believe to be an uncritical and non-resistant market of young people who, once exposed to videogame violence, develop aggressive thoughts, feelings and behaviors (Anderson and Bushman, 2001; Anderson and Dill, 2000; Gentile, *et al.*, 2004). Young people actively engaging with these texts inevitably become stigmatized by the stereotypes implicit in such research and codified within "protective" legislation as either anti-social, unintelligent, or non-creative (Morris, 2004).

Many contend that the horror genre is actually progressive in its nihilism. Additionally, digital games have been hailed as catalysts of cultural change, due to their interactive and transformative qualities. Games-as-learning advocate, Gee (2003) argues that digital games create projective identities which may be an inversion of that which is normally adopted, allowing for new perspectives and therefore a reflection on that which is experienced. Likewise, Frasca (2003) has also argued that the experimental *what if* of interactive games permits players to reflect on complex issues producing an understanding not normally found in non-interactive mediums. That is not to say that film, as a linear medium, has abandoned the use of the zombie to make similar arguments. In Edgar Wright's 2004 UK–based comedy and Romero-homage *Shaun of the Dead,* explicit parallels are drawn between the infected and the pre-outbreak dead-eyed commuters who journey to work each day, detached from and unacquainted with those that share the same daily routines. Wright suggests that there is something to be contemplated as we watch the unanimity with which a line of commuters waiting at a bus stop check their mobile phones, the checkout staff at supermarkets process trolley after trolley of groceries, or nodding pedestrians navigate the city to the soundtracks on their iPods. Indeed, when questioned in interviews as to who the zombies are, Romero typically adopts the character Peter's assertion from *Dawn of the Dead*, that "they're us!"

Understanding Violence in an Increasingly Resistant Climate

Young people, representative of a generation for whom digital and electronic games constitute the most familiar and preferred medium, were researched more generally by the author in exploration of the enjoyment and appeal of "violent" interactive texts (Schott, 2009). For young people that opt to engage with texts containing "game violence," there have been few opportunities to articulate their appeal, function and pleasures. An exchange of ideas amongst game players was thus achieved via weekly game clubs that provided both regular-access to participants and permitted exploration of a range of game texts. The game clubs also functioned to permit direct and pseudo-longitudinal observations of game play and also effortlessly allowed the initiation of discussions around issues such as preference, motivation, and reception. More structured focus group discussions and individual interviews were also conducted throughout the process. Five schools throughout the

Waikato and Bay of Plenty regions of Te Ika-a-Māui (New Zealand's North Island) granted the project access to their students. In total, 61 students (53 male and 8 female) participated in the research, which ran for the duration of a full school year.

Players were given the opportunity to nominate the games they wished to play during game clubs. In doing so, they selected *Dead Rising*, an interactive impression of the concept underpinning Romero's *Dawn of the Dead*. The experience offered by *Dead Rising* centers around Willamette Parkview Mall, which spreads the terror of a zombie infiltration across the mall's multiple floors, themed areas, roller coaster, supermarket, movie theatres, park, and an underground maintenance tunnel system. The mall area itself contains six sections simulating the variety of shops all containing a wealth of interactive objects that can be used as weapons or improve the player's health.

Much like the narrative driving Romero's *Diary of the Dead* (2008), players of *Dead Rising* engage in a kind of reporting, becoming Frank West, a photojournalist who captures and then investigates the zombie outbreak in Willamette, Colorado. The game begins with Frank hanging out of the back of a helicopter witnessing and recording the chaos on the streets below through a player controlled camera. Beyond the obvious imitation of the employment of a helicopter, each photograph taken by the player is scored and assigned a genre (horror, erotica, drama, etc.). In employing game's conventional use of the first person perspective, the audience of *Dawn of the Dead* were effectively sutured into the horror; *Dawn of the Dead* contains countless gory headshots that are viewed directly through the lens of a rifle. As a game, *Dead Rising* uses the still camera to distance the player from being in the action. Detached voyeuristic spectatorship allows the player to observe what Kingsepp (2003), applying Bahktin's work, calls "carnivalesque death." That is, death that highlights "the bloody, the gory and the grotesque" (Kingsepp: 2–3). Playing as Frank, the camera is used in pursuit of the "Perfect Photo," the iconic image that captures the scale and horror of zombie outbreak. At one point during the opening helicopter flight a person is observed on a building rooftop surrounded by zombies. Eerily similar to the iconic 9/11 image, "The Falling Man," it is possible to capture the person as they choose to fall to their death rather than become a zombie. Throughout the game the player has to manage the desire to get close enough to capture the experience with staying alive.

The game experience, however, truly begins when Frank is dropped off on the roof of the mall. The pilot is instructed to return in 72 hours. The chief aim of the game is therefore to explore as much as possible, find out what you can, whilst staying alive and returning to the helipad within the designated timeframe. A complex sub-plot exists beneath the zombie infestation that may either be followed or ignored by the player, depending on how completely the role of journalist is assumed. Fragments of the sub-plot are revealed by encounters with survivors that also need Frank's assistance as well as other people driven to madness by the zombie infestation, known as "psychopaths." Irrespective of whether the player closely follows the underlying narrative or not, should they succeed in getting Frank back to the helipad they find that a zombie attacks the helicopter pilot causing him to crash the helicopter into the mall's park. The game seemingly ends with Frank on his knees in defeat, failing to react to the impending danger from the small group of zombies approaching him from behind. Beyond the main body of the game is an epilogue termed "overtime mode," that leads to a further mode, "infinite mode," upon its completion. In the infinite mode the goal is to survive as long as possible in the mall. There is no levelling up and Frank can now die of hunger. The longest survivals are proudly posted online at an Xbox Live ranking board.

Despite no awareness of Romero's body of work amongst the young people who played *Dead Rising* during the study, his stylizing of the zombie has so successfully pervaded popular culture that it possessed the same charm and interest for the study's participants as those that have thrilled film audiences for decades. Indeed, the motivations behind players' selection of *Dead Rising* echoed the many pleasures that Romero, his production crew, and, most crucially, his zombie extras have themselves articulated concerning the filmmaking process. For example, in Perry Martin's documentary, *The Dead Will Walk* (2004), countless numbers of contributors to *Dawn of the Dead* express the sentiment that working and living in the mall during shooting created a sense of being a "kid in a candy store." For the game players too, the virtual freedom to loot anything from the mall was a major draw and thrill of *Dead Rising*.

The act of videogame playing is rife with examples of the need for virtual consumption. As Molesworth and Denigri-Knott (2005:1) argue: "Videogames now enable players to spend virtual fortunes on exotic virtual goods and even create and sell virtual artifacts." In all these contexts (the making of the film, the film itself, and the game) the imaginary is allowed to collide with real in a way that extends the limit of material consumer desire, which Shields (2003) labels the "actually possible" (the transformational promise of consumption). In the case of *Dead Rising* the digital space invites the player to "own" anything (subjective ideal), but makes it real when performed through play (idealized reality is actualized). More mundane examples of the actualization of fantasy beyond what the material market can offer, are provided by Molesworth and Denigri-Knott who highlight the playful, consumption-like activities of 60 percent of online shoppers who fill their virtual baskets before abandoning them at the checkout. While games typically offer a simulated or alternative version of material wealth to control the degree of consumption, *Dead Rising* inverts the process of material consumption by creating an aperture for unconstrained acquisition of material objects. Thus, while the notion of mall-as-utopia is a flawed one for the characters in *Dawn of the Dead*, it works effectively for the player of *Dead Rising* engaging in consumption as play.

Inventiveness of Death

Additionally, player motivation to engage with the game conformed to the variety and forms of zombie deaths that Romero's special effects artist Tom Savini describes having so much fun inventing and constructing. Zombie film deaths are commonly described as "gags," which invokes the harmless facsimiles of disgusting objects (e.g. fake vomit or excrement) or terrifying states (e.g. arrow through head) available for practical jokers to purchase from magic/joke shops. Indeed, the tools employed by Savini (latex, fake blood, etc.) are often put to use in comedic scenarios. For example, *Dawn* features a zombie attack on a Hell's Angel biker sitting at a blood pressure reading device. Only his dismembered arm is left attached to the machine, thus sending the reading off the scale. Russell (2006:

95) argues that the "comedy exaggerates the horror by making us even more aware of just how ridiculously vulnerable the flesh is."

Game scholar Jesper Juul (2003: 43) was quick to point out that "games contain a built-in contradiction," referring to the way we take the interactivity of videogames to mean "free-form" play devoid of constraints. Yet, in playing videogames we "choose to limit our options by playing [...] with fixed rules." Players themselves were quick to articulate how virtual deaths offer players a sense of presence, creativity and agency within the game system. As one participant noted:

> A story, especially a good one, usually creates a situation of conflict then resolves it.... They tend to be a mixture of puzzle solving and conflict resolution, with violence often being the means of resolution.... A game conversation, though, at the moment, is pretty much "pick the right option," and is thus not only boring, but highly linear. A violent situation is much more easily modeled in such a way that it is highly nonlinear, and so that a huge variety of novel tactics can be employed to arrive at the desired goal.

Dead Rising is noteworthy for the sheer variety of ways in which zombies can be creatively and often humorously halted. Utilizing the contents of the mall, zombie deaths can be inflicted with almost any item. Players were observed using chainsaws, golf clubs, cash registers, children's toys, guitars, and shower-heads (sending a cascade of blood over the infected when inserted in the tops of heads). Soccer balls may not kill zombies but they too were used effectively to pummel a crowd of the undead and clear pathways for Frank. The notion of merchandising is fittingly inserted amongst the malls artifacts made available to players, allowing the developers to slot in intertextual references to other games (e.g. battle axe from Blizzard's *World of Warcraft*) and films (a lawnmower allows the player to replay the infamous scene from Peter Jackson's 1992 film, *Braindead*). Indeed there are many claims posted online as to the number of intertextual references contained within the game. Most prominent throughout the game are the many items and references that pertain to Capcom's other titles, such as *Mega Man* and *Ghost 'n' Goblins*. Frank is able to unlock *Ghost 'n' Goblin* boxers, don a servbot helmet, Mega Man X armor, and use a Mega Man toy-blaster (that fires tennis balls). Beyond these there are claims of numerous references to the *Resident Evil* videogame series. For example, the mall shop "Jill's Sandwiches" is considered a reference to a line in *Resident Evil 1*: "You were almost a Jill sandwich."

Writerly Texts and Textual Poaching

While its inhabitants are possessed by the "alienating imperative to consume" (Modleski, 1986: 156), the mall also possesses dramatic potential as a site of resistance against the forces that regulate consumerism (Harper, 2002). Morris (1995) argues that the commanding presence of mall's massive structural stability often contrasts with the constantly shifting composition of its population that includes the often-unwanted presence of the teenager. In a recent organized event, "zombie shoppers" were employed to draw attention to "Buy Nothing Day." Malls, like game spaces, constitute a social space for "hanging out," a place for friends to meet and digest an "inexhaustible bank of images to be turned into personal style and statement" (Muzzio and Muzzio-Rentas, 2006: 143).

Films like Kevin Smith's *Mallrats* (1995) serve to emphasize how the mall is "consistently at risk of being turned into the disorder of those who use them" (Fiske, 1989: 43). The teenage protagonists in *Mallrats*, T. S. and Brodie, pit themselves against the mall's managers and security staff turning the space into a center for rebellion. Likewise, games and the broader digitization of media have spawned digital cultures that reflect an attitude shift in respect to long-established norms of ownership, authorship and consumer rights (played out in the distribution of copyrighted products), as well as social norms (the neglect of customary privacy conditions on social networking sites). Media savvy and literate teenagers are frequently portrayed as "menacing," as they threaten or undermine social norms (through playing violent videogames, for example), parental/institutional authority (through their neglect or rejection of traditional rights), or for their celebrations of media-grounded bad taste (from *South Park* to *Jackass*).

When discussing *Dead Rising*, players variously acknowledged the constant vying that occurs between different *traces* of the "representational" as it is subsumed within, and evoked by orientational and presentational truths of the text (Kress and van Leeuwen, 1996). More prominent than the suggestion of objective truth, the orientational function of the text serves to address the player, situating them within its particular dramatic modality. The exhortation from the game, to "be" or "become," highlights the imperative mood of games requiring the player to assent to the demands of the game and its game world. The concept of presentational truth allows us to understand how the text is true to its genre as distinct from its represented world. Thus as players activate the game text, they employ a schematic reasoning appropriate to their particular orientation in a territory of scripts and rules, exploiting the system and conforming to the expectation established by the genre. Despite their reputation, games are not unrestrained spaces for players to act out whatever fantasies and desires they possess.

Player understanding of the "act of playing" produced views that loosely conform to Giod Berro Rovira's (2001) definition of "violence" as "obeying the purpose of maintaining, changing or destroying a given order of things, situations or values" rather than some premeditated desire to murder. Common with other game genres that heavily utilize conflict, *Dead Rising* engages players in a struggle for survival; in this case, against the lumbering crowd of undead that collectively overwhelms the player rather than the more common superior or advanced enemy. Perceived as morally defensible actions within a powerful and meaningful text, the players believed they embody a form of heroism, with their avatar (Frank) credited as possessing a high moral stature and envied for being indefatigable in the face of overwhelming odds. Irrespective of the "prior" of the narrative that conveys Frank's initial desire for notoriety as a photojournalist, his pursuit of the truth and attempts to avoid a pandemic under control of the player leads to the eventual exposure of the cause of the zombie infestation (post game). The player's role in realizing the story helps these factors became more notable and illustrative of what the game experience entails.

Beyond the motivations to play and their expected pleasures (as outlined in previous sections), players also commonly experienced unanticipated enjoyment and reflection from their engagement with *Dead Rising*. Confounding anticipation associated with acting upon a game environment and its possibilities for the player, the game would often impose itself upon the players. Thus, while players were drawn to factors such as consumerism as play and creative disposing of zombies, they were also able to reflect on the inherent satire that the game reproduces. Indeed it is difficult to avoid when non-interactive cut-scenes disrupt the process of play to illustrate the game's underlying message. An example of this included the owner of a supermarket, who laments the death of consumerism over and above his own demise. As he faces death on the shop floor he asks: "Who will run it when I'm gone?" before crying out "my food, my sales ... my customers." The shop manager's outburst places greater emphasis on the preservation of the culture of consumption over the individual, suggestive that the manager has long since lost his soul.

Conclusion

The game *Dead Rising* offers players of the iGeneration an enhanced encounter with Romero's zombie-mediated critique of society's value-structures. Unusually, little is lost in its translation from film to game. Instead, much is gained, as players are drawn into and reflect upon the way the experience of "consumerism as play" also leads to an equivalent of post-purchase dissonance; recognizing too, the absurdity of limitless and inventive digital carnage. For players stigmatized by opinion makers for their investment in game texts, the extreme nature of the game only served to further illustrate what they perceive as the preposterous nature of claims made by moral entrepreneurs who unimaginatively and conveniently scapegoat interactive games in response to violent crime. Furthermore, in an age where malls, as self-promoted public spaces, have become anything but that, as evidenced by not only their design, but also the banning of teens that sport hooded sweatshirts from shopping malls in countries like the UK, *Dead Rising* offers players an opportunity to resist the forces that control social spaces. Like the hard boundaries that confine and limit the players' movements in games and life, the collective force of the zombie transforms them from soft boundaries to something more dense and impassable, something that requires resistance in order to unlock space and release themselves. At the same time, more commonly found cinematic appreciation of the zombie, as a celebrated disruptive force was also evident irrespective of their threat to player progress and advancement.

NOTES

1. This essay is an outcome of the project "Videogame Violence: Understanding its seductions and pleasures for young people in New Zealand," funded by the Royal Society of New Zealand: Marsden Fund (06-UOW-042).

How the Zombie Changed Videogames

Matthew J. Weise

The zombie, as a mythological figure, easily meets the different needs and wants of a wide range of audiences. It is what Tony Bennett and Janet Woollacott (1987) call a *mobile signifier*, a cultural symbol that shifts meaning over time and in different contexts. At their most provocative, zombies have been used as a vehicle to comment on our times (in films like *Dawn of the Dead* or novels like *World War Z*) and deal with topics like family, capitalism, and politics. At their least provocative (in films ike *Return of the Living Dead* or on stickers, television commercials, and endless Halloween attire) zombies tend to be clownish *grand guignol* figures, throw-away cultural icons that allow for cheap, guiltless destruction of the human body.

It is this latter image that probably springs to mind when one thinks of zombies in videogames, of how the figure has been appropriated and used in interactive digital entertainment. Largely identified (at least in the mainstream) with vicarious thrills and shameless power fantasies, videogames might not seem like the ideal medium to house the great diversity of thought and purpose the figure has enjoyed in other media. There is, however, more to videogames' treatment of the zombie than can be gleaned from browsing the local game store, where titles like *OneChanbara: Bikini Zombie Slayers* (2008) sit alongside endless military games, beat'em-ups, and shooters. Zombie games have a deeper, more varied, more interesting history than such a cursory glance would suggest.

In the eyes of some cultural commentators zombie videogames were instrumental in revitalizing the figure in the late 90s. Jamie Russell (2006: 171) has no qualms about calling this popularity boom "The *Resident Evil* Effect" in reference to the popular Playstation game. For Russell it was not film but videogames — and particularly this game — that resurrected the figure for a new generation. Others like actor/writer Simon Pegg, who played a *Resident Evil*–obsessed gamer on his late 90s TV show *Spaced*, instinc-tively echo this view. Pegg, along with *Spaced* director Edgar Wright, cites *Resident Evil* as a major influence on their decision to make *Shaun of the Dead* (Pegg, 2008). *Resident Evil* had a huge impact on game design and gamer culture when it was released in 1996. It coined a new term, *survival horror*, to describe what would quickly come to be considered a new game genre.[1] *Resident Evil*'s comparatively unglamorous, methodical scenarios which pitted average humans of average ability and limited resources against mindless hordes of classic, George Romero-style zombies influenced countless games that followed, and gave the figure a mass-media foothold it hadn't enjoyed since the 70s.

Zombie films have often been talked about as markers of their time, and zombie games are no different. *Resident Evil 1* (1996) says something about the 90s the way *Resident Evil 4* (2005) says something about the post–9/11 era. The fact that this is often not recognized, I feel, says more about gaming discourse than it does about games themselves. Videogames are a young medium, and therefore a technologically and formally unstable one, so how such instability complicates interpreting certain design choices as representational of popular anxieties (and not, say, as responses to certain technological or formal problems) can be confusing. One might argue the awkward vulnerability felt when playing *Resident Evil* wasn't a response to anything cultural, but to the limitations of the Sony Playstation hardware. Such arguments ignore the agency gamemakers have in how they choose to approach such problems. The evolving conventions of zombie videogames are, of course, responses to techno-formal challenges, but the way gamemakers chose to address those challenges also have ideological implications. This is why one can see a certain *ideological drift* in zombie videogames, in spite of the youth of the medium.

The Birth of the Modern Zombie

The sort of zombie *Resident Evil* popularized and has since come to dominate videogames is what one might call the *modern zombie* or *Romero zombie*, notable for its first appearance in George Romero's 1968 film *Night of the Living Dead*. Romero's revenants were different from traditional zombies in several ways. They were first of all autonomous, needing no sorcerer to animate or control them. They ate flesh, being driven by an endless desire for victims. Lastly they were infectious, meaning they could turn the living into zombies by biting them. These three elements were not synonymous with the figure as it appeared in *White Zombie* (1932), *I Walked with a Zombie* (1943), *Plague of the Zombies* (1966), and other pre–Romero efforts. The zombies of those films were derived from the figure as it appeared in Haitian folklore and the Vodou practices of the Caribbean, and basically constituted a form of undead slavery, with corpses resurrected to do the bidding of a sorcerer or sorceress. (Russell, 2006) The only feature Romero's self-motivated infectious predators retained from their Vodou cousins was a certain trance-like quality, a mindless slow movement that resembled sleep-walking.

Romero's reconfiguration of the figure was really an amalgamation of several things, including Richard Matheson's epic vampire novel *I Am Legend*, which Romero (2008) cites as inspiration for the viral and apocalyptic aspects of his film. This child of the Vodou slave and autonomous vampire became the de facto "zombie" for many horror films from the early 70s onward including *Children Shouldn't Play with Dead Things* (1972), *The Living Dead at the Manchester Morgue* (1974), *Zombi 2* (1979), the *Night of the Living Dead* remake (1990), *Braindead* (1992), *Shaun of the Dead* (2004) and Romero's entire series. These films and others — with some notable variation — helped solidify the shambling, rotting, hungry, viral menace we associate with the figure today.

The modern zombie's film-centric origin may have something to do with how *visual* the figure remains in popular culture, how synonymous it is with spectacular displays of gore and viscera. The cinematic zombies that pre-date Romero had a different (though arguably as sensationalist) visual appeal. The uncanny shock of seeing an animated corpse, with it sunken eyes and emaciated form, was no doubt part of the voyeuristic thrill of early zombie films, though a bigger draw was likely watching the often female, often loosely dressed protagonists (in such films as *White Zombie* and *I Walked with a Zombie*) puppeteered by a mysterious dark magic. Post-Romero, and with the collapse of film censorship in the late 60s, the main carnal thrills of zombie films were built increasingly on gore effects. The fact that Romero's zombies violently consumed human flesh made them an ideal exploitation-cinema icon, always ready to show the audience a good disemboweling. Limited film budgets also arguably shaped the narrative conventions surrounding the figure. Stories typically involved a small band of survivors defending themselves against the ever growing zombie hordes in a remote location, with the clear implication that society at large (unseen for obvious budgetary reasons) is crumbling just beyond the horizon.

It is of course impossible to say precisely which media borrow which elements from each other, though it is probably safe to claim that modern zombie films very much set the tone — the set of iconic traits — for later zombie fiction in other media. Other media practitioners have, in some instances, used the freedom provided by their chosen form to explore aspects of the figure that would be difficult in film, mostly for budgetary reasons. Robert Kirkman, for example, states clearly in the intro to volume 1 of *The Walking Dead* (2004) that his serial comic is designed to be "the zombie movie that never ends," an opportunity to follow a survivor protagonist for his whole life, to unshackle him from the 90-minute prison of commercial cinema. The cheapness of paper and the imagination of the reader is also arguably what makes possible epic novels like Max Brook's *World War Z* (2006), which directly depicts large scale combat with zombies on a global level. Although scope and focus seem to change according to the media form and the desires of the author, it is significant that neither the core rules of zombies nor the tendency towards apocalyptic narratives seems to change much across media. When these things do change the genesis still seems rooted in film, as in the case of the "fast zombies" that appeared in Zack Snyder's *Dawn of the Dead* remake (2004), which themselves were arguably inspired by the sprinting hordes of Danny Boyle's *28 Days Later* (2002), a film that's status as a zombie film is debatable (the hordes are infected, not dead) yet had an undeniable influence on the genre, and which later appeared in the *Left 4 Dead* games (2007; 2009).

The modern zombie is still a figure in flux, but it is striking what a hold the Romeran zombie has on the imaginations of contemporary filmmakers, comic book writers, novelists, and, of course, videogame designers. The relatively recent wave of "serious" zombie stories across a variety of media might even be seen as an attempt to reclaim the figure from its more comical incarnations, notably those that stem from *Return of the Living Dead*, the film which can be directly credited with inventing "funny" zombies that co-exist in pop-culture right alongside the "serious" Romero variety.[2] Max Brooks specifically cites *Return* as cheapening the figure, and positions his own novel as a kind of rebuke to its campy legacy (Brooks, cited in Jim, 2006). This obsession with reclaiming the "serious" zombie, of bringing back the glory days when the figure was deeply scary, was also the guiding principle of Shinji Mikami, director of the original *Resident Evil*, and may (if Russell's assessment of *Resident Evil*'s impact is to be believed) have paved the way for the later reclamations cited above. It may not be a coincidence that the hardcover edition of *The Walking Dead* advertises itself as "a continuing story of survival horror." *Resident Evil* and the "survivor horror" genre it coined gave audiences weaned on Romero the opportunity to do more than imagine how they'd act if faced with a zombie apocalypse. It gave them a chance to actually find out, an advent the current culture has not yet forgotten.

A Pre-History of Digital Zombies

If we can take Romero's *Night of the Living Dead* as the zombie ur-text of cinema, the text that appears to define the figure for most following texts, then we can easily take *Resident Evil* as the zombie ur-text of videogames. The impact it had on games was significant because it represents a cross-over point when cinema really began to inform game *rules*, not just game visuals. I've argued elsewhere (Weise, 2009) that *Resident Evil* is a prime example of *procedural adaptation*, the practice of interpreting other media forms in terms of *process*, in terms of *rules*, and modeling them in game systems. Another way to say this would be that games like *Resident Evil* attempt to *simulate* conditions of a particular story genre (in this case the zombie survival story) thus allowing players to role-play and experiment within that genre. How gamemakers choose to model zombie fiction systemically — in response to cultural norms, technical limitations, or commercial pressures, or mere personal preference — constitute a form of authorship, a stance on how zombies and zombie fiction "should work," and this can be examined quite clearly in the case of *Resident Evil* and other zombie games.

Similar to *Night of the Living Dead*, *Resident Evil* was not the first work of its medium to feature zombies. Examples of digital zombies exist as far back as the early 80s, and not all of them from horror games. Early fantasy role-playing games like *Wizardry* (1981) and classic action/arcade games like *Castlevania* (1986) featured zombies. In such games, zombies were often distinguished by their necrotic appearance alone, with behaviors that generally didn't stray far beyond the conventions of their respective genres. Flesh eating, infection, shambling movement, and weakness to brain trauma rarely appeared in any functional capacity, meaning these zombies mostly required no special strategy to survive or defeat. If anything these zombies felt closer to Haitian zombies than Romero zombies, as they were often rooted in occult magic.

Other games, such as the point-and-click adventure *Uninvited* (1986), featured zombies "right out of a Living Dead film," to borrow a phrase from the game. Textual descriptions such as this were a staple of the adventure genre, and *Uninvited* used them to illustrate its flesh-eating hordes in gory detail. Functionally speaking however, *Uninvited*'s zombies were not entirely Romero-inspired. Defeating them required not a bullet to the head but a "holy pendant" that could instantly kill them. On the other hand, *Uninvited* very clearly described the player being eaten alive and reborn as a zombie should they do something stupid, like trying to interact with a zombie.[3] While it might be difficult to see such limited choices — in which players are fatally punished by making one wrong decision — as a simulation of the complex challenges faced by zombie film protagonists, it is worth considering that the survival logic of zombie films is comparatively binary. In modern zombie films a single bite — a single mistake — is as fatal as it is in *Uninvited*, which makes it possible to read the game's rules as reflecting a cursory sort of zombie logic.

One game that took zombie logic much further was *Zombi* (1986), an unapologetic (and unauthorized) attempt to model Romero's *Dawn of the Dead*. Aside from adopting the mall setting of the film, it contained zombies that followed Romero's rule set in several important ways. The only way to kill zombies was a gunshot to the head, which was achieved by carefully aiming with the mouse cursor. No number of shots to other areas of the body would kill the creatures, and their shambolic slowness made it easy to try. Such brutal adherence to Romero's rules was typical of the game, with the possible exception of infection. *Zombi* employed a traditional health meter, meaning that the player could sustain several wounds before dying. The gamemakers sidestepped having to deal with infection, however, by having zombies attack with their hands, not with their teeth. Zombification greeted players only upon death, implying that infection, while not something that could "spread" according to the game's rules, was still the ultimate lose state.

Another important game in the evolution of digital zombies was *Alone in the Dark* (1992). Though more inspired by H.P. Lovecraft than George Romero, the way it portrayed zombies was instrumental to how the figure would come to be represented later. One of the first horror games to utilize 3D graphics, *Alone in the Dark* featured a dark mansion full of (among other things) shambolic, mindless terrors. Players were given a gun with only a few bullets and left to fend for themselves against these marauding corpses. None of the Romero rules applied beyond slowness, though this behavior alone — combined with the then-novel 3D movement — gave *Alone in the Dark* an unmistakable Romero-like tension. *Alone in the Dark* was one of the first games to feature cinematic camera angles, as opposed to the flat map-like spaces of 2D games. The camera in *Alone in the Dark* was immobile, and instead would "cut" to different angles depending on where the player moved. This allowed the gamemakers to exploit the frame the way a filmmaker would, by using it to hide zombies. A player might be forced into a particular camera angle, only to see a zombie slowly creeping up on their avatar from off screen. Such suspense came at a cost, however, by necessitating "tank" controls that functioned independent of the game's ever-changing camera. Pressing "left" would always rotate the character left regardless of viewing angle, "right" would rotate it right, etc. Consequently players could not simply flee their undead assailants at the press of a button. They had to back up, turn, and run: each separate actions that required thought and timing. This made *Alone in the Dark* the first game to model the real-time logistics of close-quarters zombie combat, a stride that would serve as the entire basis for later games, most notably *Resident Evil* and its immediate successors.

Resident Evil—*The Ur-Text*

Resident Evil (1996) at first glance is uncannily similar to *Alone in the Dark*, so much so that it feels almost like a streamlined version of Infogrames's little horror experiment — complete with oblique camera angles, tank controls, and even the mansion setting — but with all elements removed save those that relate directly to zombie combat. By focusing the game in such a way, Shinji Mikami created a "zombie game" in the same sense one would speak of a "zombie film:" a media artifact built solely around the figure.

Unlike most previous games featuring zombies, *Resident Evil* explicitly presented itself as a zombie survival narrative. The players assumed the roles of rescue workers sent to investigate a remote mansion near an American small town. Once inside, they become trapped by hordes of walking dead and must discover a way to escape. Mikami was quite clear on the sources of his inspiration, citing not only Romero's films but their Italian cousins, specifically Fulci's *Zombie 2* (Mikami, 1996). This may partially explain *Resident Evil*'s surreal quality (which includes, among other things, a zombie shark), although it arguably has as much to do with the game's lingering connection with *Sweet Home*, a haunted house game released by Capcom in 1990. *Resident Evil* began production as a remake of *Sweet Home*, with the original plan involving ghosts, but shifted towards zombie survival because of Mikami himself (1996). The mansion setting was a hold-over from *Sweet Home*, but when combined with the tank controls, oblique camera angles, and roaming zombies, the overwhelming similarity to *Alone in the Dark* is hard to ignore. The slow, methodical zombie combat is virtually identical, save for the fact that the "missing" zombie behaviors — specifically flesh-eating and destruction of the brain — have been added. The only thing missing was infection, which *Resident Evil* omitted from its gameplay system but reinforced through its backstory about a viral outbreak stemming from bio-weapons research. The impression left by *Resident Evil* at every turn was that it *was* a modern zombie movie, and *you* were the protagonist.

Zombies in *Resident Evil* are much what one would expect from any Romero film. They are slow, flesh-eating ghouls that are extremely difficult to kill except by destruction of the brain. The game consists almost entirely of dealing with these creatures in a strategic fashion, of discovering ways to get past or destroy them in order to successfully escape the mansion. It was unusual, especially at the time, to fill a game with primarily one enemy type, and this is partially why *Resident Evil* leaves such a strong impression of being a "zombie game" and not just a "horror game." Though a few other types of creatures do appear (such as mutant dogs, snakes, and other escaped bio-weapons) they were always secondary to zombies, which appeared in virtually every room. The player got to spend a lot of quality time with them, to get to know them in all their variations as a discrete strategic problem.

Dealing with *Resident Evil*'s zombies effectively demanded a clear understanding of the subtle threat they posed. Because of their slowness and stupidity (zombies would sometimes walk into walls, rather than attack the player) they were only dangerous if badly planned for. Players had ample time to assess the layout of a room or hallway before deciding how to spend their precious bullets. One of *Resident Evil*'s most famous design concepts was to make ammunition scarce, thus forcing players to manage resources and assess evolving situations in terms of risk. This risk usually involved how likely it was that a zombie would be able to bite the player in the confines of a small hallway or room, which would in turn suggest whether removing the undead obstacle was necessary. Players could not, however, rely on their marksmanship skills to pick off zombies. Aiming for the head was impossible in *Resident Evil* due to the static camera inherited from *Alone in the Dark*. It could not move into a first-person position for aiming, leaving players to simply point their guns in the general direction of a threat and hope for the best. Mikami and his team got around this limitation by hard-coding the ability to hit zombies in the head to certain weapons as well as some context-dependant actions. Using a magnum (as opposed to a pistol) would shatter a zombie's skull every time, as would a shotgun at close-range or kicking a zombie when grabbed from below. In each case the destruction of the head was reinforced as the most efficient way to kill a zombie, even if it wasn't the only way. Pistol bullets would down zombies in five to seven rounds, which often put them too close for comfort by the time they finally fell. The value of guaranteed headshots was obvious, making them key to any successful survival strategy.

The zombies in *Resident Evil* behaved very much like Romero zombies, and this means they *did not* behave like typical video game enemies. Slow moving enemies (not to mention a game filled with them) were quite unusual. Gamemakers both then and now generally strive to craft opponents who are spry and intelligent, not lethargic and mindless. As a strategic challenge, slow opponents put players in an entirely different mindspace than fast ones. *Resident Evil* was, ultimately, not a game about reflexes but about preparation and planning. Though there was a small skill-based component (in that an especially nimble player might be able to dodge a zombie or two on occasion) the stiff tank controls were just not responsive enough to ensure survival. Rather players were forced to ration ammo and survey the mansion's zombie-ridden corridors with the eye of a desperate strategist. Five bullets here, three bullets there, a shotgun shell here, a mad dash there; and all this just for the sake of getting to the next room. This was in stark contrast to the power fantasies many games offered, which seem to be about giving players the thrill of killing weaker, less-skilled opponents.[4] Mikami's appropriation of Romero's slow-motion terrors made players feel vulnerable in ways videogames rarely did. This was helped by the strong "everyman" vibe of the game's protagonists. Although *Resident Evil*, like most Japanese games, had strong ties to the aesthetics of anime and manga, and therefore nominally presented its cast of survivors as "cool" members of an elite rescue squad, they were *functionally* quite mundane.[5] They didn't have super powers, uncommon human dexterity, or fantastical weapons. Game story shelves are choked with games that feature such comforting affordances, and *Resident Evil*'s complete lack of them was striking. It was even possible to use up all one's ammo too early, rendering the game impossible to complete — a daring move that challenged commercial wisdom. Should all games strive for some generalized notion of player gratification, or can some gratify based on particular aesthetic goals? If Mikami was indeed trying to make players feel like the main characters of zombie films, rewarding prudence with survival and punishing recklessness with death certainly fits. All successful *Resident Evil* players are those who behave like the cool-headed protagonists of Romero's films.

For all his ambitions to emulate zombie cinema, Mikami balked at the idea of modeling infection, opting instead for a traditional health meter. Players can sustain countless bite wounds (as long they are healed with first-aid items) without ever becoming infected or turning into a zombie. Such a system is one of the oldest conventions in video games, and its value — allowing players the flexibility to bounce back from a series of mistakes — is self-evident. Yet the price it comes at in *Resident Evil* is to omit one of the figure's core traits. Not only did this soften the "everyman" vibe of the game system (it was, in fact, possible to survive wounds that should in all logic be fatal) it created some ambiguity as to whether or not infection even existed as part *Resident Evil*'s narrative universe. Infection is never shown in cut-scenes and there is no direct evidence in the story that infection is spread by biting. The journals and diaries found around the mansion (another element that feels cribbed from *Alone in the Dark*) speak of a "virus" but never say how it's transmitted. Although it is easy enough for players to fill in the blanks, it's important to recognize that *Resident Evil* remained somewhat cagey about the diegetic status of infection. It points to a tension — one that exists in all zombie games — of how far gamemakers are willing to go in privileging the logics of zombie cinema over the logics of traditional game design, as well as how those decisions are rationalized — or not — by the game's narrative.

If we look at *Resident Evil* in retrospect we can see a struggle to reconcile modern zombie behaviors with certain video game conventions. Mikami and his team chose which game conventions would be superseded by zombie conventions and vice versa. Staggered movement, flesh-eating, and head trauma superseded conventional notions of empowerment and difficulty balance. Conventional notions of player damage superseded zombie infection. One can assume that Mikami, like any commercial videogame maker, was looking for a marketable balance, not wanting consequences to be too dire but also not too forgiving. The result was some zombie rules applied and not others, a process one might call *selective abstraction.*[6] This sort of process is common enough in game adaptations, since no game system can model literally *all* aspects of a text and must therefore involve some sort of abstraction of its source. This is how *Resident Evil* can model only some zombie rules but still register as a "complete" piece of zombie fiction, making it more than the sum of its Romero-inspired parts. Its biggest contribution to gaming aesthetics was difficulty design, making players feel vulnerable by making zombies dangerous in ways they were in films and hadn't traditionally been in videogames. In this sense it recreated certain emotional and thematic dynamics found in Romero's films and the films he inspired, most notably the way they portray the value of forethought versus panic in apocalyptic circumstances.

Zombies After Resident Evil

Resident Evil did not spawn, as one might imagine, a genre of "zombie games" even though it in many ways was one. Videogame genres tend to align more around behaviors or functions than theme or setting (though the two are often related). This is why *Resident Evil*'s most direct progeny was the "survival horror" genre, a functional genre built around a behavior — survival — and its many possible applications within the broad thematic universe of horror. Many of the games credited with being inspired by *Resident Evil*— most notably *Silent Hill* (1999), *Fatal Frame* (2001), *Siren* (2003), and *Clock Tower 3* (2002) games — do not involve zombies. They do, however, follow the philosophy of difficulty design, strategic thinking, and vulnerability pioneered by *Resident Evil*, and achieve it by adopting many of the same conventions of controls, combat, etc. In a sense, *Resident Evil* could be said to have spawned an "everyman" genre, with concepts applicable to a wide variety of themes, but which originated in the logics of Romero/Fulci as adapted by Mikami.

There were, of course, many games after *Resident Evil* that included zombies, and the increased popularity of the figure was arguably due to *Resident Evil*. However, not all of them were survival horror games, and included games like *House of the Dead* (1996) (a light-gun game) and *Stubbs the Zombie* (2005) (an open-world real-time strategy game). Most of the ones that were survival horror were sequels to or spin-offs of *Resident Evil*, which quickly grew into a massive franchise that to date boasts over 20 titles. Zombie behavior evolved greatly as the *Resident Evil* series expanded, which is why "*Resident Evil*" cannot, as a franchise, be considered as a single text. Mikimi did not stay on to helm every single game, but rather was only directly involved in two more *Resident Evil* games: a remake of his original *Resident Evil* and *Resident Evil 4*. *Resident Evil 2* (1998), 3 (1999), 5 (2009), and several other spin-off titles were made by other Capcom staff, many of whom took different approaches to the zombie figure. These various experimental offshoots of *Resident Evil*, along with a few other notable zombie games released since the late 90s, constitute what we might call the "contemporary" digital zombie as it exists today.

The evolution of the contemporary digital zombie is to some extent an on-going attempt to model a more "complete" set of zombie behaviors, while at the same time staying within the evolving boundaries of commercial game design, which were gradually skewing away from horror and towards action. This evolution can be charted by examining how various games dealt with each cardinal zombie rule — flesh-eating, destruction of the brain, slow movement, and infection — and how these approaches changed over time.

Let us begin with destruction of the brain. Given the prevalence of shooting in videogames, letting players shoot zombies in the head seems like it should have been easy, but in fact it took quite a while to catch on. A decade and a half ago there were very few games that allowed players to line up a headshot on a zombie. *House of the Dead* — released the same year as *Resident Evil* — was one example. Challenge existed exclusively in terms of holding the light-gun as if it were a real weapon and blasting zombies as they appeared on-screen. A skilled marksman could kill zombies in one hit by aiming for the head, whereas a less skill marksman would need to shoot a zombie several times to blow their body to pieces. *House of the Dead*'s incorporation of the headshot rule was more literal and less abstract than *Resident Evil*'s, but this was arguably a byproduct of its genre more than a conscious desire to model zombie survival mechanics. Light-gun games are basically shooting galleries, and typically don't even allow the player to control their own movement, instead moving them as if on-rails through environments as they blast away at whatever pops on screen. *House of the Dead* was therefore not much of a zombie survival simulation, but a carnivalesque (if gory) game about the thrill and fun of shooting.

The *Resident Evil* series avoided giving players direct ability to aim for as long as possible, while still managing to reinforce brain destruction as an element of suspense. *Resident Evil: Director's Cut* (1997), a special modified version of the first game, added a probability-based element to the pistol in which each shot had a small chance of being a fatal headshot. This had a subtle effect on the game in which it now seemed as if the character was always *attempting* to shoot zombies in the head, with only occasional success. Such probability-based mechanics are normally considered mathematical abstractions of character skill, as they are in pen and paper role-playing games like *Dungeons and Dragons*. Rather than allowing the player to exercise their own skill, *Director's Cut* (and later *Resident Evil* games such as the remake and *Zero* [2002]) represented marksmanship as part of the abstraction of the character, how good the *character* was at firing the weapon, not the player ... and the character was never very good.

It wasn't until *Resident Evil: Dead Aim* (2003) that players were given the opportunity to use their real life aiming skills to kill zombies. *Dead Aim* used a special light gun that also functioned as a standard controller, which meant players could both shoot *and* move a character around a 3D environment. This made possible types of complex gameplay not normally found in light gun games. *Dead Aim*'s innovation consisted of combining *Resident Evil*'s traditional exploration and resource hunting with the intensity of real marksmanship. As for the problem of allowing exceptionally good marksmen to breeze through the game, *Dead Aim* countered with a hardcore dose of Romero. Zombies in *Dead Aim* could only be killed if the player hits them in the brain and the brain alone ... that is, the part of their head above their nose and between their eyes. Anything less was a glancing blow and therefore not fatal. Since marksmanship quality generally decreases as fear increases, the game required either a great deal of emotional control or the prudence to retreat when one's aim became unreliable.

It took *Resident Evil* seven years and eleven games to fit skill-based aiming into its survival horror formula. Other, non-survival horror games in that time were freer to experiment with the headshot rule, most notably *Time Splitters 2* (2002). *Time Splitters* was not a horror series but a colorful, comical first-person shooter series that exploited time travel as a story device to justify a plethora of different settings and themes, one of which involved zombies. Even though it was just a minor aspect of the game, the makers of *Time Splitters* clearly put some thought into zombie behavior, creating some nerve-wracking encounters with the undead. In a genre where simply unloading on opponents usually did the trick, it was a shock to meet a zombie and suddenly realize you *had* to aim for the head or they would just keep coming. The aiming in *Time Splitters* was rather precise, and the uneven shamble of the zombies difficult to follow, making it surprisingly hard to land a hit. This is likely why *Time Splitters 2* appears in *Shaun of the Dead*, being played by characters early on in the film, and then referenced later when one of them attempts to shoot a zombie in the head for the first time, finding it unexpectedly difficult. As any *Time Splitters* player can tell you it *is* difficult ... a lot more difficult than it looks in the movies.

All these games retained the shambling movement of classic Romero zombies, even the ones that allowed aiming. *Time Splitters* and *Dead Aim* featured zombies that were as slow as those in *Resident Evil* and *Resident Evil: Director's Cut*. The only difference was that the zombies in *Time Splitters* and *Dead Aim* were more spastic, more unpredictable in their lumbering movements. They were not fast, but as they stumbled along their heads would roll about their necks like a ragdoll's. This was an elegant way of preventing skill-based aiming from making a zombie game "too easy," but it was more or less ignored by games that followed, most of which featured skill-based aiming but paired it with the "fast zombies" popularized by *28 Days Later* and the *Dawn of the Dead* remake. In a way this makes sense, since the quicker enemy movement off-sets (in theory at least) the advantage skill-based shooting affords, making it possible to preserve the tension of survival horror by stepping up the abilities of both zombies and players. In practice, however, it eroded the power politics of early survival horror and pushed the genre toward the "normal" gratification patterns of action gaming.

Resident Evil 4 is often credited (some might say "blamed") for instigating this shift. It not only featured fast zombies and let people pop heads to their hearts' content. It also bestowed upon players all sorts of superhero-like moves, including roundhouse kicks and suplexes. These moves could be performed on zombies that got too close, making *Resident Evil 4* a bizarre combination of zombie survival, martial arts, and wrestling. It's interesting that Mikami, returning to the series after years in absence, attempted to "revitalize" it partially by adding such badass moves. *Dead Aim* proved that simply adding skill-based shooting to *Resident Evil*'s existing combat dynamics could work, and Mikami could have applied a lot of the same principles without adding so many "action hero" elements. This is especially ironic considering that, just a few years earlier, Mikami's own remake of *Resident Evil 1* took the series closer to a Romeran "everyman" aesthetic than ever before. The remake not only retained the original's slow zombies, it added a new rule taken directly from *Night of the Living Dead*—destroying zombies by burning—which hasn't been featured in the series before or since. Players were given a lighter and a limited supply of kerosene, which they had to ration (just like ammo) in order to ensure a downed zombie would not rise again later. This not only heightened the original's aesthetic of strategic thinking, it was arguably a statement about returning to the "roots" of survival horror by returning to Romero.[7] The game even began by visually quoting *Dawn of the Dead*: in a pre-title image of a zombie slowly sitting upright from a hospital bed, as if to announce its purist intentions to the player.

Such explicit Romeran references are largely absent from *Resident Evil 4*. Instead, the game seems to be based on a range of influences from John Carpenter's *The Thing* (1982) (in its switching the infection from a virus to a body-altering parasite) to *The Texas Chainsaw Massacre* (1974) (in its portrayal of weapon-wielding, homicidal country folk) to *28 Days Later* (in its portrayal of living, infected hordes). Like the Boyle film, it is a bit of a misnomer to even call *Resident Evil 4* a zombie game, since its infected technically aren't zombies but parasite-infected people capable of speech, complex group behavior, and tool use. It remains, however, a "sequel" in the sense that it is clearly built off of the same rules and systems established in early *Resident Evil*. It was thus seen as a legitimate revision of the genre the original *Resident Evil* invented eight years before, ushering in a new era of action-centric horror games.[8]

Fast-moving parasitic baddies appeared again in *Resident Evil 5* (2009) and virus infected maniacs appeared in the first-person shooter series *Left 4 Dead* (2007 and 2009). *Left 4 Dead*'s sprinting hordes are in some ways closer to the actually undead athletes of Zack Snyder's *Dawn of the Dead* remake. Though technically not, they look much more "dead" than *Resident Evil 4*'s dazed yokels, showing actual signs of bodily decay. This doesn't stop them from moving like cheetahs, bounding over buildings, and climbing on walls. On one hand this makes sense since fast movement and marksmanship is an essential component of the first person shooter genre. On the other hand, both *Left 4 Dead 1* and *2* go out of their way to portray their core protagonists as average people, dressing them in everyday clothes and in general emphasizing their "normalness" as much as possible. This is a core selling point of the games, part of an attempt to position the games in relation to real world anxieties and events like Hurricane Katrina, which is referenced quite heavily in the New Orleans setting of *Left 4 Dead 2*.

Left 4 Dead appears to defy the fast zombie/super protagonist behavioral pairing popularized by *Resident Evil*, however it is worth noting that the established conventions of the first-person shooter genre embody certain super-human aspects that have become invisible through wide use. The speed at which players can move, switch weapons, climb ladders, jump over obstacles — and all while still being able to accurately aim and shoot — extends well beyond what anyone in reality would be capable of ... and especially what the "average" protagonists of *Left 4 Dead* would be capable of. Simply by virtue of being a first-person shooter, *Left 4 Dead* remains a high-action, high-adrenaline experience, a game that — on a purely behavioral level — is more or less indistinguishable from other fast-paced first person shooter games. This is arguably why headshots hardly seem to matter in *Left 4 Dead*, since zombies move so quickly the only useful strategy ever is to simply spray them with bullets until they fall, a tactic which could potentially kill anything.

Post *Resident Evil 4* there are not many commercial videogames that feature slow zombies. *Dead Rising* (2007) is one, featuring both classical Romeran zombies and skill-based aiming. *Dead Rising* is easily the most transparent attempt to adapt Romero since Ubisoft's *Zombi* (1986). It takes place in a giant 3D mall and features literally thousands upon thousands of zombies, all of which are pathetically slow and uncoordinated. This gives players ample opportunity to try and outsmart them, with often comical results. Blows or bullets to the head will kill zombies every time, but the problem, of course, is that there are just too many to kill. Three or four is easy, but there are 400 right behind them ... or behind you. Successful *Dead Rising* players are able to recognize when a situation has grown out of their control, which is not as easy as it sounds. The slowness of zombies ensures that hordes coalesce and enclose around players gradually — like watching a clock — which forces them to maintain their cool or else get eaten alive.

Getting eaten alive is naturally the fail state of all these games (save *Resident Evil 4* and *5*, where you typically get bludgeoned or chainsawed to death). How each game presents this fail state says much about how they generate tension. On one hand it might be easy to consider flesh eating a mere aesthetic trait. Whether or not digital zombies "eat flesh" depends on whether or not a game's graphics depict damage from zombies in this way. While it's true that "damage" is functionally the same across most zombie games, the loss of agency that sometimes accompanies it constitutes an important experiential difference. Zombies in the original *Resident Evil* embraced, and therefore paralyzed, characters when biting them, whereas zombies in *House of the Dead* did not. Both games graphically depicted zombies attacking players with their mouths, but only *Resident Evil* made this feel like an intimate violation, the warding off of which (via frantic button tapping) feels almost like a defense against sexual violence. Suffering a loss of agency in accordance with being eaten reinforces a sense of being an object, a literal "piece of meat," and heightens the sense of being the prey in a world of predatory monsters driven by sub-logical desire. This may be why zombie games that follow Romero closely tend to emphasize loss of agency in the eating process. *Dead Rising* turns being eaten into a full-blown mini-game, complete with special controller actions, in which players try desperately to wrestle their way out of a zombie mob. The *Resident Evil* remake featured "defense moves" that let players slip out of a zombie's imminent embrace, and these were later revised into *Resident Evil 4*'s kung-fu kicks that served a similar function. (This is a good example, incidentally, of how *Resident Evil 4* builds off the logic of its predecessors while undercutting their Romeran vibe.) *Left 4 Dead*, by contrast, softens its sense of violation by having zombies paw at you but clearly not manhandle you. While this pawing results in some loss of agency (your movement slows down and you become trapped if enough zombies surround you) the player is not "embraced," which weakens the predatory connotation. Also, although there is some loss of agency, it is what one might call a "soft" loss of agency since player control does not technically "shut off" but merely becomes slowed.[9]

One thing all these games have in common is that even if the player character is bitten to death they never, ever reanimate. *Resident Evil*'s iconic game-over scene showed the player character overpowered and ripped to pieces by the zombies they failed to kill, splattering blood (literally) all over the screen. The screen then faded out to the sound of zombies munching away, but there was never a further moment where players saw themselves "reborn" as a zombie. The same goes for most other *Resident Evil* games as well as *Dead Rising*, and both *Left 4 Dead* and *Time Splitters* include not even the implication that zombies eat, let alone infect, their victims. Infection indeed seems to be one of the least portrayed zombie rules, both as a fail state and as a genuine component of a game's rule system.

One exception was *Resident Evil: Outbreak* (2004). It was the first game in the series to attempt online play, and real-time infection was one of its many experimental features. Players each had an "infection meter" which showed how saturated their bloodstream was with the zombie virus. The meter reaching 100 percent meant instant death followed by rebirth as a zombie, which served the handy function of giving eliminated players something to do while their friends kept on playing. This convention is common in online shooters, where killed players are able to float around as ghosts while they wait to play again. Such a system only works if play sessions are short and numerous, hence *Outbreak*'s strategy of dividing itself up into several smaller scenarios of zombie survival, each taking a few hours to complete. *Outbreak*'s infection mechanic functions like a time limit, forcing players to finish each scenario before succumbing to its effects. Consequently, *Outbreak*'s infection model does not much resemble zombie films. While being bitten does make a player's infection level spike, so do other sorts of contact with zombies, including being hit by them or in some cases even just bumping into them. A player's infection level will sometimes go up without coming into contact with zombies at all, making biting feel even less consequential to the process. No narrative explanations are given for these gameplay rules, though lingering implications that the virus might be airborne suggest some. Yet even this would not explain why characters who successfully survive the scenarios do not turn into zombies in the cut-scene epilogues. Infection in *Outbreak* thus remains a curious contradiction of diegetic and non-diegetic logic, though obviously less so than in games which fail to model it at all.

The cause/effect logic of infectious biting, as it is portrayed in most zombie films, is not difficult to understand. Its simplicity is what gives it such terrifying power. This power has proven too much for conventional game design to handle in many cases, since it would mean players could not make a single mistake the entire game. This may be why some zombie games, rather than deal with infection's unforgiving logic head-on, go out of their way to construct alternate mythologies that exclude it. *Left 4 Dead* explains its lack of infection mechanics by implying that the four main protagonists are immune to the disease. This easily gets it off the hook for allowing players to be wounded endlessly and never turn. A cheekier example would be *Dead Rising*, which milks confusion about its own zombie rules for humor. At one point the player comes across a bitten girl who is convinced she is turning into a zombie, insisting she has "seen movies." The player character tells her she's mistaken, that "this isn't a movie" (which is, after all, true — it's a videogame). Both examples show the easy way out in dealing with infection, though they obviously allow greater coherence in terms of reconciling gameplay and fiction.

One game that manages to remain coherent without omitting infection is *Stubbs the Zombie* (2005), though it does so only by changing infection from a punishment to a reward. In *Stubbs,* players take the role of a zombie trying to infect people, with those infected becoming foot soldiers in one's own shambling undead army. This mechanic resembles those of real-time strategy games, in which a goal is to create or recruit as many soldiers as possible. *Stubbs* offers evidence that it's not the mechanics of infection itself but its negative consequence that is difficult for developers to stomach. While there might be nothing fun about slowly turning into a zombie, it's worth noting that the threat of this horrible fate is how zombie cinema generates much of its apocalyptic and existential anxiety, making infection one of the biggest and commercially risky under-explored aspects of digital zombies.

Ideological Drift

Zombie games have definitely changed in the last 14 years. From their modern inception in *Resident Evil* they have evolved and expanded in a variety of directions. The gradual incorporation of aiming and shooting as a skill-based game mechanic has had a major impact on the figure, causing it to "respond" by becoming quicker and more agile. The loss of agency that comes with being eaten alive remains more closely associated with the slow zombies than with the fast ones, and infection is such a difficult concept to reconcile with conventional videogame punishment/reward schemes that it has barely been tried, remaining part of digital zombie lore but diegetically omitted from most gameplay systems.

In recent years, there has definitely been a spike in "fast zombie" representations in videogames, *Left 4 Dead* probably being the most popular example. *Resident Evil 4* played an important part in this process, redefining the survival horror genre (which was not an exclusively zombie-themed genre but was shaped by zombie cinema) towards a more action-based aesthetic and giving legitimacy to this shift through its powerful name-brand. Since then action-oriented zombie survival games, built around shooting as the primary skill-based activity, have eclipsed strategic zombie survival games, built on selective agency and resource management.

What can one conclude, if anything, about this evolution? If the zombie is indeed a mobile signifier that expresses popular anxieties of the times, what are these games — in their various mutations — expressing? Examining each one of them in detail would require a much longer discussion, but there are a few conclusions we can draw just from the patterns identified above.

It is clear that there has been a general drift away from the anxiety of disempowerment towards the thrill of empowerment, a change which has some pretty obvious ideological implications for zombie games. These implications can most easily be seen in the *Resident Evil* series, in how the recent sequels adopt more empowering political narratives to match their more empowered player affordances. It is not coincidental that the superhuman abilities and fast-paced action of *Resident Evil 4* and *5* are paired with Hollywood-like, xenophobic, military "hero" narratives that resonate strongly in a post–9/11 world. *Resident Evil 4* pits a notably badass yank protagonist against anti–American religious extremists in rural Spain, while *Resident Evil 5* (somewhat more disturbingly) shifts the location to Africa and features a massive, body-building white American battling hordes of infected poverty-stricken black people. These framing narratives are a far cry from those of *Resident Evil 1–3*, which all took place in an American small town, starred relatively normal people, and dealt with classic anti-establishment themes of corporate and government corruption. The villain in *Resident Evil 1–3* is a pharmaceutical corporation, Umbrella Inc., which has shady government ties and a stranglehold on the local economy of Raccoon City, the game's setting. The plots of these games primarily concern Umbrella trying to cover up the zombie outbreak it has caused, with the protagonists trying to expose this corruption. This culminates in the government dropping an atomic bomb on Raccoon City in *Resident Evil 3*, not only to contain the outbreak but to erase all evidence of the bio-weapons they paid Umbrella to make.

It is difficult, in the case of *Resident Evil* at least, to take this ideological shift entirely at face value. *Resident Evil* is of course a Japanese game series, filled with anime/manga archetypes, silly and/or distorted representations of America and American people, and various other details that code it as "Japanese" to Western audiences. On the other hand, its makers have full knowledge of the franchise's global popularity, and aim it, to a certain degree, at a Western market. The sincerity behind *Resident Evil*'s apparently "American" post–9/11 reactionary politics remains therefore debatable (especially in the case of *Resident Evil 4*'s trademark goofiness, which at times can be read as camp). Sincere or not, it doesn't change the fact that its Rambo politics go hand-in-hand with a Rambo game design, or that this approach has proven more popular in our terrorism-obsessed age.

I consider *Left 4 Dead* part of the same basic ideological drift, though softened considerably by its deliberately "realistic" atmosphere. *Left 4 Dead* is American made, which makes it easier to read in terms of American and/or Western anxieties. Since it is basically a first-person shooter, without many unique mechanics inspired by zombie fiction, most of its apocalyptic expression is bound up in the disturbing familiarity of its various destroyed locales. The second game in particular begs the question of what being able to play out a zombie survival narrative in an uncanny, digital recreation of post–Katrina New Orleans offers contemporary audiences. Though fast, kinetic, and requiring no special strategy to deal with zombies, both *Left 4 Dead* games manage to model the basic survival narrative of being a refugee facing a disaster, with the goal of each location being to reach a helicopter, boat, or some such ticket to government-sponsored asylum. The military definitely represents safety in the world of *Left 4 Dead*, with the army showing up to save the protagonists at the end of each game.

Left 4 Dead probably says something about how (particularly American) players fantasize surviving a Katrina-like disaster: by being well-armed and kicking a lot of butt. The concessions it makes to the first-person shooter genre however, as well as the fact that its "zombies" look the part more than behave the part, make *Left 4 Dead* feel lightweight as an allegorical use of the figure. Its positive view of the military, and the corresponding suggestion that society isn't completely collapsed, also seems to speak to the post–9/11 timidity mainstream American culture has towards fatalistic anti-establishment narratives.

Dead Rising, by contrast, seems to be one of the few post–9/11 zombie games to embrace counter-cultural thinking, giving us a sharp satirical view of America in the tradition of classic zombie cinema. Its producer, Keiji Inafune, had just finished *Lost Planet* (2006),[10] a game which he himself described as a commentary on the Iraq War (Wollenschlaeger, 2007). *Dead Rising* extends this tendency for social criticism much farther, sporting an extremely cynical (and darkly humorous) view of government, capitalism, and human nature in general. In true Romeran fashion, the real danger in *Dead Rising* is *other people*, citizens whose latent amorality has erupted in the absence of civilization. Crazy priests, corrupt cops, a gun-crazy father who tells his adolescent children that it is their "American right" to kill — these psychopaths will attack the players on sight, forcing them to either respond or retreat into the comparative "safety" of the indifferent zombie horde. These increasingly disturbing encounters culminate with the arrival of the military, who are of course there to kill survivors as well as zombies, in order to cover up the fact that the outbreak was itself the result of a U.S. sponsored experiments in South America. In the final battle — which takes place on top of a tank amid a swarming ocean of zombies — the player faces off with the military commander, a fascist who expresses no remorse for killing civilians in the interest of national security. Even if successful, it is unclear whether the protagonist makes it out alive to expose the corruption. The final cut-scene shows him surrounded by zombies with no help in sight.

Conclusion

I've tried to show how the zombie figure has transformed in its journey through the digital medium — from its early days, through its watershed moment in *Resident Evil*, through its popularity explosion and diversification thereafter — as well as offer some examples of how this transformation can be read ideologically or allegorically ... as we are so want to do with the figure. The particular design constraints of the original *Resident Evil*, as well as how later games either expounded on or ignored those constraints, played a major role in the figure's subsequent evolution. Mikami's original design can be read as "Romeran" in certain ways that, at the time, flew in the face of commercial game design. As the figure has become more popular it has drifted farther away from this initial conception, so that today, with a few notable exceptions, it has become almost completely indistinguishable from "normal" videogame enemies, conveniently morphing to the conventions of whatever genre gamemakers wish, rather than forcing players to confront the apocalyptic logics that are unique to zombie fiction.

It is unclear whether zombie games in the future will experience a revival of more Romeran procedural adaptation, or whether they will continue down their Hollywood path into instant gratification and power fantasy. It was, after all, partially a fortuitous accident that *Resident Evil* offered such limited agency. In the mid and late 90s, commercial videogames were going through the crisis of transitioning from 2D graphics to 3D graphics, as well as learning to utilize the explosion in storage space brought on by the CD. In that short temporal window it was common for even big budget games to experiment with new ideas. Because *Resident Evil* emerged at that historical moment it was able to experiment in ways similarly commercial games just a few years later could not. This freshness catapulted the zombie to mainstream popularity, transforming it into a "blockbuster" videogame figure that functioned comfortably within dominant ideologies in spite of its lingering association with counter-cultural cinema.

Perhaps the zombie simply needs independent games to come to its rescue, like independent cinema did in the 1960s and 70s. Several indie gamemakers have already experimented with zombie mechanics large companies shy away from, most notably *Urban Dead* (2005), a web-based multiplayer game which actually models infection. It's surprising, however, how even these games tend to soften the brutal logic of traditional zombie fiction. *Urban Dead* allows players to get bitten and turn into zombies, but it also allows them to turn back, effectively turning zombiism into a lifestyle (or playstyle) choice rather than a horrific confrontation with one's own mortality.

Allowing zombie logics to dictate game design still seems a dangerous prospect for many gamemakers, perhaps because facing mortality is the farthest thing one might imagine from being fun. "Fun" though is itself a sort of ideological trap, a universal excuse to cater to gamers' basest desires in the name of market viability. If zombies gain their power from being a "perversion of the normative order" (Kryzwinska, 2008: 168), it follows that they become powerful when they *pervert the normative order of conventional game design*. That is the real normative order that gamers value, the one that makes them feel safe and in control. When zombie games challenge this order, they provoke the sense of the shocking uncanny found in the best zombie fiction, shattering our sense of expected reality and forcing us to redefine our perception or perish. When they don't they simply contribute to the figure's endless, increasingly ironic remediation ... and there's already enough of that to last us until the next apocalypse.

NOTES

1. Some people, including Russell, claim the phrase "survival horror" was coined by critics and players. It was, in fact, unambiguously coined by *Resident Evil*'s creators, appearing both in-game and on the original Japanese box art.

2. "Funny" zombies in a way also evolved from Romero's co-writer on *Night of the Living Dead*, John Russo. Russo favored a more campy approach than Romero, and created *Return of the Living Dead* (first as a novel and then as a film) as his own alternate sequel to the original, hence the title similarity.

3. "The zombie grabs your arm with its boney hands. Quickly, it takes a voracious bite out of you. Your blood drains rapidly from your body, providing a nice salty beverage for your boney friend. The miserable dead now welcome your company."

4. Examples of this are so numerous and pervasive that bothering to mention them seems almost silly, but a few would be *Call of Duty* (2003), *Duke Nukem* (1991), *God of War* (2005), *Halo* (2001), and *Castlevania* (1986). Almost any game series that features combat as a central component affords players the opportunity to slay literally hundreds of opponents single-handedly.

5. The two main characters — the strapping, square-jawed Chris Redfield and the sexy, clever Jill Valen-

tine — very clearly resemble American action-movie archetypes, albeit filtered through a pop–Japanese sensibility. The resulting impression, to Western audiences at least, is of Japanese cartoon versions of Hollywood stars having wandered into a George Romero movie by mistake.

6. Jesper Juul claims that all videogames involve "a certain level of abstraction" in how they create fictional worlds and relate them to game rules (2007). Not all elements implied by a game's visuals or story are modeled in the rules of the game itself. All players, in understanding a game, must understand what its level of abstraction is, i.e. which rules implied by the game's fictional context are part of the game system and which are not.

7. This rule was not really picked up on after *Night of the Living Dead* as being a major component of modern zombie lore, which is one of the reasons why Mikami's modeling of it feels like such an obvious reference. His game and Romero's film might be alone in depicting burning as the preferred method of zombie disposal.

8. Examples include *Dead Space* (2008), *Silent Hill: Homecoming* (2008), *Dimentium: The Ward* (2007), and the 2008 action reboot of *Alone in the Dark*. All these games are noticeably more combat-oriented than previous survival horror games and came out after *Resident Evil 4*.

9. A "hard" loss of agency occurs when a fantastical monster grabs you with tentacles, but this creature isn't a "zombie" in any recognizable sense, feeling more like a random alien from any given sci-fi first person shooter. The fact that *Left 4 Dead* calls it a "zombie" says much about the game's rather cavalier attitude towards the figure.

10. *Lost Planet* is a sci-fi military shooter set on a distant, icy world. The main storyline involves the planet's indigenous life forms being killed so humans can harvest their internal biological heat source, a natural resource upon which our space-faring civilization depends.

Undead Is the New Green
Zombies and Political Ecology

GREG POLLOCK

In *World War Z* (2006) Max Brooks imagines the emergence, climax, and containment of a global zombie menace. The zombies' speculated origins are uncannily familiar — perhaps spawned by reckless biotech engineers or the black market trade in human organs, allowed to grow by governments more likely to deny than solve their problems — as is the world that takes shape in their wake. Though the trauma of the zombie war marks society indelibly, the social institutions are recognizably our own. The unthinkable horror is, in the long run, almost anti-climactic.

The strangest thing, for the reader and the survivors, is the givenness of zombies for the generations born after the war. "The pups born after the crisis came out of the womb literally smelling the dead. It was in the air, not enough for us to detect, but just a few molecules, an introduction on a subconscious level" (Brooks, 2006: 283). As a result, these litters don't react to zombies with paralyzing terror but with practical threat avoidance. Similarly, human children learn to stay away from zombie-prone places in the same way that earlier generations learned not to take candy from strangers. Post-zombie generations of all species are able to experience and communicate about zombies in a way not possible for those who saw "the living dead contradict[ing] every other law of nature" (239). After the trauma of the undead event has been absorbed into the texture of the everyday, a difference still exists, recorded in those "few molecules" in ecological circulation and from there translated into the psychology and sensoria of future generations.

The conclusion of *World War Z* can be turned on its head to help us understand the environmental politics of today. Whereas atmospheric circulation of zombie particles reshapes the dogs and people of World War Z, today we face the possibility of catastrophic reshaping of the ecological circulatory systems on which human life depends. At issue is not necessarily the apocalyptic "either/or" of extinction/survival but, as in *World War Z*, the interdependence between the form of human life and the context in which it takes form. As Donna Haraway (1991) points out, science fiction and social reality are two side of the same coin. Following Bruno Latour (2004), I contend that what connects these two visions — zombie apocalypse flip-flopping into nagging environmentalism and vice versa —

is a shared conception of "nature" as extra-political. By "extra-political" I mean something outside of the operations we use for collective decisions, as opposed to "non-political," meaning something not at issue in those operations. Zombies and ecologies are extra-political in that they refuse to engage in talks, circumscribe territories, be satisfied by a dialectic of enfranchisement, or in any other way participate in collective decision-making (and they still haven't registered to vote!). If the silence of the non-political is the quagmire of environmental politics, zombies can offer one way in which to map the connections between our political capacities and the requisites of meaningful environmental politics.

Part of the problem is that environmentalist discourse tends to rely on a realist epistemology that appears out-dated and flawed to many critics. For example, Gary Snyder's essay "Is Nature Real?" answers its titular question with a resounding "yes," hoping to "take these doubting professors out for a walk, show them a bit of the passing ecosystem, and maybe get them to help clean up a creek" (2000: 354). Environmental justice activists likewise point to the harms done to people by pollution as obviously real (Johnston, 1994). Who would deny that the tree right in front of you is real, or that poisoned water is harmful?

Yet the point of critics like William Cronon (1996) and Ramachandra Guha (1989), who have called into question the wilderness ideal, is not that forests and pollutants do not exist, but that their appearance is only possible under certain cultural conditions and that often those conditions favor some cultural interests over others. Even the image of the Earth from space, a powerful trope for galvanizing the environmental movement, was only made possible by a space program that also allowed First World leaders to more effectively view Third and Fourth World nations as nuclear test sites and chemical dumping grounds (Kato, 1993). The "environment," seemingly a self-evident fact, thus becomes an object that appears differently from different perspectives. (In fact, the word "wilderness" derives from Germanic roots and only exists in English and German; other Romance languages use cognates of "desert." The "wilderness" of the Bible is likewise a translation that might better be rendered as "desert.") Add to this rich matrix the chain of technical instruments, analytic techniques, and personnel who produce ecological facts, not to mention the more obviously "cultural" elements through which those facts are received, and "the environment" ramifies into further complexity. While we might readily be convinced that this tree right here exists, politically meaningful claims — humans are causing global warming by burning fossil fuels, for example, or that this tree right here should not be used for toilet paper — are always a composite of multiple partial perspectives.

One could think of "the environment" like a three-dimensional figure rendered on a flat page. The whole can't be seen all at once, so we choose angles that show the parts we find most important, resulting in different, even unrecognizably disparate, pictures. Thus the realism/social constructivism debate is a false dilemma; rather, the real existence of "the environment" has the same structure as social constructions, even though it is not reducible to a human production or projection (Latour, 1993). Because of this situation, Ursula Heise argues that risk theory can best articulate the probabilistic balancing act needed to represent environmental problems. "Many of the hyperboles and the simulations that have typically been interpreted as examples of postmodern inauthenticity become, from this perspective, manifestations of daily encounters with risks whose reality cannot be assessed with certainty" (2002: 757). To recognize the world of our "real" concerns we require such "hyperboles and simulations" as the airborne toxic event in Don DeLillo's *White Noise* (1985).

The probabilistic and perspectival problems in talking about the environment extend all the way to the core value of "life" driving environmental politics. While we are probably sure of the difference in most cases—Abraham Lincoln is dead right now and you are not—the concepts of "live" and "dead" cannot rigorously and consistently be defined in general. "Life," too, is a matter of perspective. Alan Rayner (1998: 72–4) observes that if we look at a river the same way evolutionary biologists look at organisms we discover how marvelously the river adapts to and shapes its environment to better sustain itself—just like other living things! Conversely, Rayner goes on to show how fluid dynamic models can predict the behavior patterns of ants, wildebeests, and other herd animals (81–5). If we try to find the essential kernel of "life" by breaking down large things like populations and individuals into their microscopic components, like cells and DNA, we again encounter difficulties. Bacteria and other micro-organisms (especially those of interest to biotechnology researchers) play havoc with the task of defining criteria for vitality (Helmreich, 2009; Shostak, 1998).

Microscopic "life" might be defined locally once we have decided on the boundaries of our context, but does not exist "in itself" apart from any context. Richard Doyle nicely captures the double movement where "life" explodes to re-emerge in inorganic matter: artificial life "emerges out of a context in which quite literally, life disappears, as the 'life effect' becomes representable through the flicker of networks rather than articulable and definable locales" (Doyle, 2003: 24). Context, for Doyle as for Rayner, is key to how and where we draw boundaries between living versus nonliving, self versus nonself, determinate versus indeterminate, and so on. The contextual frame of environmental politics, I hope to show, will re-draw the boundary of "life" in such a way as to suddenly bring the dead back to life, rendering an image of zombies that can help us reflexively understand what "environmental politics" means today.

If this is the case, we have much to learn from taking zombies seriously. I don't mean that we should imitate zombies, but that the imaginative worlds opened up by zombie stories might give us new and better ways for re-drawing boundaries in environmental politics, particularly concerning what kind of "life" we want to, and are able to, foster. This essay develops such an understanding of zombies by examining how the crises in "life" described by Rayner and others react with recent work on biopolitics, and how *Dawn of the Dead* and *World War Z* imagine different forms of political organization in virtue of their undead subject matter.

This essay's view of zombies builds on but departs from the critical tradition of reading zombies allegorically. Depending on the film under consideration and one's particular critical affiliations, zombies can persuasively be read as symbols of virtually all social anxieties, a cultural "barometer" as Peter Dendle (2007) calls it. For Haitian Vodou, zombies are "consistently associated with economy and labour" as well as racial and national oppression (46). In the Depression era, "the zombie arguably served as a cinematic mechanism for raising awareness of gender issues" (48). During the Cold War, zombies are seen to represent the erasure of individuality threatened by communism. After that, they do a symbolic about-face to represent, as they had earlier, the dehumanization of workers and the loss

of individuality to the demands of capital. And with the successful globalization of capitalism in the 1970s, Steve Beard (1993) sees in the zombies of *Dawn of the Dead* the dis-
satisfactions of unemployment in the post-industrial world. Thus zombies are seen
sympathetically — as in *Land of the Dead* (2005) or *Fido* (2006) — or antagonistically — as
in *Zombieland* (2009) — depending on where one's allegiances lie. While an account like
Dendle's is useful to understand the significance of zombies to culture and to chart the
changing concerns of 20th-century America, we ultimately come to an impasse concerning
whether zombies are good or bad. To move beyond the allegorical impasse, this essay does
not try to argue that zombies "represent" environmental politics, but that environmental
politics and zombies present similar problematics with similar impasses.

Biopolitics Without Life

The work of Michel Foucault (1990) led to the theorization of modern governance
as the shift from a sovereign's power to kill subjects to the sovereign's ability to control the
life of subjects by shaping the way in which they are recognized and the possibilities
available to them. More recently, Giorgio Agamben has built on Foucault's insights to
argue that the essential structure of biopolitics is not a uniquely modern invention but the
structure of political organization itself. For both, the way in which power defines a living
being — as primarily something that can be killed, or primarily something trying to survive
and grow — is crucial to understanding political formations (Bull, 2007). The shift that
Foucault sees between these modes of power points to the historical variability of "life"
and its capacity to be redefined with changes in human social structures. Agamben, on
the other hand, emphasizes that human "political life" has been understood in the European
tradition in relation to "bare life" from its inception. Yet if Foucault is correct that "life"
and "politics" remain available to historical change, and the Western idea of politics hinges
on a split with Nature, a truly ecological politics would require, if not produce, a subject
that is defined as "living" in some new way.

A crucial moment in Agamben's conception of the relation between political life and
life in general ("bare life") is his reading of Aristotle's dictum that "man is by nature a
political animal." In Agamben's reading, the human capacity for politics hinges on the
way in which the "political animal" simultaneously leaves behind and conserves the human's
animal nature. As I will argue, however, the conceptions of human and animal beings with
which Aristotle and Agamben are working are rendered moot by zombies in a way that
parallels the political capacity's inability to deal with environmental problems.

The link between bare life and politics is the same link that the metaphysical definition
of man as "the living being who has language" seeks in the relation between phonē and
logos.... The question "In what way does the living being have language?" corresponds
exactly to the question "In what way does bare life dwell in the polis?" The living being
has logos by taking away and conserving its own voice in it, even as it dwells in the polis
by letting its own bare life be excluded, as an exception, within it (Agamben, 1998: 7–8).

The difference between the sounds animals make and truly human language parallels
and models the difference between the meager animal existence of bare life and a truly

human life of political engagement through reasoned speech. Agamben highlights what happens between the "before" and "after" of these moments as a relation of "inclusive exclusion." Human language and social life replace their baser original forms, but, Agamben argues, those original forms are then reserved as powers of the sovereign. Thus humans can live uniquely rich lives, but at the expense of living under (some kind of) sovereign power that always retains the power to debase them — to hear in their language only animal sounds, or see them as barely, in the most automatic way possible, alive (which sounds pretty much like a zombie).

This raises an additional problem, which necessarily goes unspoken even in a critique of sovereignty like Agamben's: what about things which cannot be excluded or included. The transformation from zoë to bios gives the impression that there is no remainder — that anything excluded will already have been captured through the dynamic of the inclusive exclusion. But if the animal life of zoë is subject to exclusive inclusion, what about the even more basic "life" of the organism conceived through fluid dynamics models that can also describe the wider environment? The supposition that there is no remainder is bound up with certain other beliefs about living beings that no longer have the self-evidence they did for Aristotle. The ontological division between human and animal language is constantly being eroded and, as discussed by Rayner and Doyle above, life has become a fluid construct. So too, the kind of questions posed by environmental politics simply cannot fit within the frame of political life envisioned by Aristotle. It does not make sense to speak of the environment as either excluded or included — it is everywhere and nowhere, totally global and always local — and so the kind of "political life" that will come to grips with environmental questions will not be that recognized in the older model. And yet, despite the insufficiencies of the Aristotelian model, defining or redefining life remains at the center of imagining collective purposive existence.

The remainder of the biopolitical inclusive exclusion, what we call the environment, needs to be conceptualized through a different logic than that used to define the human as political animal. Jean Baudrillard's (1995) formulation of the remainder is useful to imagine the thing that is neither included nor excluded. Baudrillard defines the remainder as what is left when we subtract all from all; rather than nothing, according to Baudrillard, there is the remainder. Baudrillard concludes that what negates this remainder is not some further subtraction (for what more could we subtract?), but the ceaseless movement of everything he finds characteristic of postmodernism. Constant motion thus makes the concept of addition, and so also subtraction, meaningless. Within this ecology/eschatology, speeding up our response brings us further into the orbit of a political without remainder. Assaying the social problem of ecological degradation directly and furiously — as its urgency and importance, not to mention endless commercials for eco-efficient washing machines and hybrid vehicles, tell us we must — reproduces not only the economic system creating those problems, but the structure of the biopolitical as being without remainder.

The temporal paradox of environmental politics thus appears as an ontological condition of political being, confounding the possibility of meaningful resistance. It is precisely this problem Derrida confronts in the apocalyptic fantasy of nuclear discourse. The first technique of nuclear discourse, he observes, is to install itself as "the end of time." By positing this horizon as its baseline, nuclear discourse is itself "nuclearized": it deploys the absolute weapon against temporality, effectively cutting off any potential for change. This absolutization of temporal finitude quickly arrives at a world without remainder: "the limit case in which the limit itself is suspended, in which therefore the krinein, crisis, decision itself, and choice are being subtracted from us, are abandoning us like the remainder of that subtraction" (Derrida, 1983: 22–3).

Derrida, however, resists the horizon of resolved contradiction with which Baudrillard closes his discussion of the remainder. Instead of nihilism, Derrida opts to invoke two contradictory temporal modes as a performance against nuclearism: "I wanted to begin as quickly as possible with a warning in the form of a dissuasion: watch out, don't go too fast. [...] But this dissuasion and deceleration I am urging carry their own risks" (21). If we indulge too long in "the critical zeal that leads us to recognize precedents, continuities, and repetitions at every turn" we run the risk of allowing by omission the coming of the unthinkable event.

Derrida imagines the critical community caught in its complacency as "suicidal sleepwalkers, blind and deaf alongside the unheard-of" (21). The image evokes victims of nuclear deployment: stunned, like the sleepwalker uncertain of his status, blinded and deafened by light and noise. But the event does not produce the critic-as-sleepwalker in its wake as a separation from the previously wakeful critic, as it separates the victim from health and wholeness. Rather, it shows that they will have been somnambulists. Going forward, they will no longer be somnambulists; the bomb will have cured them. This event is not guaranteed, however, and so we cannot preemptively respond to or correct for our sleepwalking. Only by this unheard-of event do they retroactively become sleepwalkers. The undecidability of whether we will have been "sleepwalkers" prevents us an easy escape into apathy: we don't know, and so cannot resign ourselves to one fate or the other.

In this way Derrida counters claims to authority (whether issuing from government, industry, or military) that would place the speaker as the gatekeeper of temporality. Everyone is in the position of the potential sleepwalker, just as everyone in a zombie movie is potentially a zombie. Baudrillard's critique of authority is similar in its conclusion: the logic of nuclearism is all or nothing, and the "nothing" of nihilism is absolute. But while both are equally distant from the masters of war, where Baudrillard concludes on a null value Derrida redoubles the terms of power. Derrida's text performs the space of the subject as simultaneous contradictory temporalities — both brake and gas pedal, so to speak, an impossible combination that is nonetheless our situation.

Derrida's critique of nuclearism is worth repeating as the twin hegemonic uses of the environment borrow heavily from its techniques for foreclosing the future. Indeed, one of the seminal texts in the American environmental movement, Rachel Carson's *Silent Spring* (2002), borrowed some of its force by evoking extant nuclear anxieties (Lutts, 1985). The end is near, the prophets of nuclear or environmental apocalypse warn us, and the possibilities of the future are few. Capital asserts that the future will be the same — that it simply does not exist as "future," but as variation within a set of calculations. Hegemonic environmentalism, on the other hand, leverages a vision of collapse to assert a vision of an "alternative" future just as rigidly determined.

Environmental apocalypticism departs from nuclearism in that it does not posit an event at the close of history. The nuclear fear promises a definitive sign — a massive explosion and iconic mushroom cloud. In the environmental dystopia, the temporal indeterminacy of the nuclear sleepwalker is relocated from the divine descent of the bomb from above to the ground, water, and air as they pass through us in banal ecological metabolism ("metabolism" comes from the Greek "ballein," to throw, the root of "ballistics"). The apocalypse is no longer an event subject to confirmation, and so the environmental dystopian fantasy does away with the vestige of temporal determinacy retained in nuclearism. Environmentalism in this regard is more nuclear than nuclearism, and Derrida's critique all the more appropriate.

This difference also affects how we imagine the world brought into being by this apocalypse. Because of the divergences between the nuclear and environmental apocalyptic fantasies, each imagines a different kind of survivor after-life. The nuclear event releases the uncertainty of the event yet to come. The survivors know that they have passed through a nuclear event, and in a sense it is a clean start; the nuclear powers have destroyed each other, and the world is a young "state of nature" again. The survivors of the environmental apocalypse, on the other hand, do not have such a clear marker of "before" and "after." Thus, like zombies, they "survive" in the sense of living on or beyond, but do not enter the temporal cycle where they would get to start over from scratch. They merely continue.

The temporality of these dystopian fantasies returns us to the problem of the remainder in the passage from bare life to political life. Whereas the nuclear event moves from one form of life to another, and yet retains its fear of the nuclear past in the form of the state of nature, the environmental dystopia evokes Baudrillard's constant shuffling that undoes any ontologically superior form of life and any sense of a sovereign power. Rather than a break and rebirth, a passage from one kind of life to another, environmental catastrophe is the loosening of the very distinctions between those forms of life. In fact, as with Derrida's "fast and slow," the beings in an environmental post-apocalypse would be simultaneously both of those types, doubled beings constituted around the ongoing apocalyptic fold.

If apocalypse is imagined as environmental degradation rather than nuclear event, a different enemy responsible for the apocalypse must be imagined, too. The localized threat of the bomb came from the localized threat of national powers, such as the U.S. and USSR during the Cold War. In the environmental paradigm, however, the threat is fully integrated into the world, such that even the ego is part of it. A figure for environmental crisis cannot be like a human Other, someone or thing different we stand against. Rather, this figure would instead constitute itself as a series of reversibilities within the subject, so that what appears at one moment as victim appears at another as monster (but, like the three-dimensional object in a two-dimensional plane, is really both all the time). And it would posit an apocalypse that put an end to time but would actually redouble temporality, folding it back on itself from death to a parodic form of life.

Zombies and New Boundaries of Reversibility

I have hopefully deferred (but speedily!) the arrival of zombies long enough as to allow them to appear as neither victim nor executioner, but as an image of environmental politics. In the zombie menace we have something corresponding to the threat of ecological collapse, but more importantly a monster built on temporal disjunction: where time for the subject ceases in death, the zombie turns that moment into a fold. As K. Silem Mohammad (2006) notes, the zombie horrifies with an uncanny temporality that cuts across the concepts of "life" and "death" and reveals them to be heuristic or contextual. Zombies threaten us, not as symbols of a taboo difference made flesh, but as the non-difference between life and death in a general economy of motion (like fluid dynamics). Mohammad uses Deleuze's reading of Spinoza to understand the "ethics" of the zombie. For zombies there are not good or evil actions, just good or bad "encounters," those that contribute to or subtract from the zombie horde. Romero's classic zombies follow Derrida's counsel to move as quickly as possible into measured slowness. These zombies are slow and uncoordinated and yet, as every zombie movie shows, inevitably catch up to their human prey.

The temporal strangeness of the zombie that speaks to Derrida's anti-nuclearism — the fold of death, the dangerous slowness — allows us to return to Agamben's dynamic of inclusive exclusion in the movement from voice to speech and bare life to political life. While individual zombies are uncoordinated, zombies as a whole function as a highly effective collective. Thus they fold back the terms of human bios (political life) as well: by remaining human, yet stripping away the logos (reasoned speech) that would allow them to reach collective decisions, zombies achieve the unity that politics aims for but never achieves. This fold, however, is not a mere negation of the human ability to speak. An epistemological crisis common in zombie movies is the uncertainty attending the border between human and zombie. Confronted with a zombie for the first time, one must struggle to determine whether a zombie is speaking or moaning — to what extent the once-human is still human. Rather than a simple negation of the human, zombies create a constant shuffling of Aristotle's borders of speech political capacity, as Baudrillard says of the remainder. In terms of both life and language, the parallel criteria of the political subject of bios and logos that emerges against zoë (bare life) and phonē (voice), zombies and the environment are remainders that cannot be negated.

The zombie moan creates one such problem: zombies lack language but they do not entirely lack voice. They moan. This moan, however, creates a division within voice: whereas voice is defined by the sounds animals make to signal pain or pleasure, zombies do not moan to signal pain, and the idea that they experience "pleasure" on scenting humans is only an inference based on human experience — and the first thing we know about zombies is that they overturn what we know about ourselves. Like Derrida's "yes yes," the affirmation that precedes an affirmation simply by agreeing to respond, the zombie moan points to what has been made extra-political about the environment in the installation of "voice" (phonē) as the threshold of political sound. Ecologies do not "speak," either to cry in pain or joy, but they do produce sound, and we often ventriloquize on their behalf, translating the amount of rainfall or mercury parts per million into eloquent exordia on their behalf. The "yes" that defines voice as the limit of politicization emerges from an undecidable field of sound waves in which the zombie moan's relation to speech and language is undecidable.

Though zombies and ecologies fall outside of the dynamic of bare life and form of life, they are both emblematic of the practices authorized by its conceptual apparatus. The zombie, like homo sacer, can be killed without punishment (Agamben, 1998: 71–2). The problem, however, is whether the concept of "kill" can be rigorously applied to a zombie, whether a zombie really "dies" in the same way that a person does, since a person only dies once. Here the zombie's double death echoes the two bodies of the sovereign, the king who is both his mortal corporeal person and the immortal body of his station (as in, "the king is dead, long live the king"). But whereas the sovereign marks a singular paradoxical point both inside and outside of the law, zombies are neither singular nor concerned with an economy of law (Agamben, 1998: 15–7).

This problem in speaking about death, and the modeling of double death on the sovereign position of the king, is especially evident when we speak of forests, ice caps, and oceans "dying." While supportive of life and filled with life, they do not die in the same way that humans do. Rather, like zombies, environments suffer what Deborah Bird Rose calls a "double death" (2004: 175). Death is vital to healthy ecological turnover, but "multiple invasions" that both kill and prevent the connection to the dead can kill ecosystems: "The multiplying invasions [of opportunistic species] are equally producing erasures across time, wiping out the life-giving systems that were the signs of the ancestors, and ultimately, we must imagine, wiping out the living presence of the dead" (175). For both zombies and ecosystems, death is two-fold, but in neither case does this status secure the juridical power of the sovereign.

The kinds of things where we might find Rose's concept of double death most useful, like ecosystems, are difficult to perceive within the order of magnitude available to unmediated human senses. Zombies, however, allow the limit cases of life and death — the microbe at one end, the totality of earthly ecology at the other — to appear within the scale of the human. For either the very large or the very small, representational mediations (i.e., photographs of micro- or telescopic images) intervene to reproduce the separation between these forms of existence and our own. The image provides visibility but reassures us that the thing is elsewhere. This gap, as Benjamin (1977) argued in the case of daguerrotypes, has a temporal quality. Daguerrotypes are haunted by the lengthy time of exposure. When looking at scanning electron microscope pictures of viruses, it is the production process that adds the trace of duration to the immediacy of the image. The zombie produces a fold in this temporal economy: on one hand, the degree of make-up and special effects used to make zombies look "real" speaks to a production process; we have likewise never seen an actual zombie, but the humans menaced by the zombies look very much like us. By being forthrightly "unheard-of," as Derrida says, zombies shift the boundaries of what can become visible. While zombies do not make micro- or macro-ecologies visible, they make visible the very impossibility of our seeing such objects directly by their status as impossible, unheard-of. Thus, while zombies do not represent the environment, they create a situation in which we can approach the same problems as we encounter in representing the environment.

The zombies of *Night of the Living Dead* and *Dawn of the Dead* display the characteristics enumerated above for the figuration of environmental politics. The question that remains, however, is how zombies create a bridge between the extra-political position of environmental concerns and the existing world arguably still governed by the conception of human political capacity found in Aristotle and the sovereign as both inside and outside of law.

Dawn of the Dead *and* World War Z

Dawn of the Dead presents a scenario that, like the problematic of sovereignty, is both inside and outside of political conceptualization. It is obviously a commentary on consumerism, racism, and sexism, among sundry other failings of American culture. "American society is cast in the role usually given to an individually hatable character," as Kim Newman puts it, the villain in a diatribe against social vices (1988: 209). Yet the irony of the film is that its premise of zombie apocalypse evaporates the referent of those morals. In *Dawn of the Dead* American society is, for better or worse, no more. Its prejudices are now weighed by a cold functionalism rather than the aspiration from zoë to bios. Sexism, for example, is a hypothesis rather than an abhorrence: "both Peter and C. J. [in the 2004 remake, also discussed by Paffenroth] seem simply convinced by experience that women are to be respected; they are not swayed by emotion or some moral code, but just factually disproved, as it were" (Paffenroth, 2006: 61). The political value viewers sense in *Dawn of the Dead* is more complexly structured than the assertion that consumerism, racism, and sexism are bad. Rather, *Dawn of the Dead* reorganizes the structure of politics in such a way as to allow environmental concerns to surface through zombies.

In this eminently political film, there is no group that reaches the threshold of exercising political capacities. This absence could be read as a "state of nature" which would be a mirror image of a political state. But no sovereign emerges, and what we see is hardly the war of all against all. There is a clear division between the social spaces and practices of the zombies and the survivors, and within those spaces precarious civility prevails. Thus there is neither a strong negation (state of nature) or assertion (inclusive exclusion) of politics, but a redistribution of "political life" caused by the numerical lack of living humans. The mall in which the survivors take up residence becomes more like a very small household (though without the command structure of an oikos) than a polis, and their activities closer to domestic habits — dressing up, going out to eat, watching television, playing cards — than the deliberative speech of logos. The absence of political life within the film does not expose the survivors' bare life to any sovereign power, however. The human survivors, like the zombies whose dull eventless lives mirror their own, begin to live in a social arrangement structured differently than the dynamic of zoë and bios mediated by sovereign power.

The non-political life of the survivors is made meaningful to the viewer by the displacement of political organization onto the numerically plentiful zombies. The viewer does not just recognize herself in the zombie as a satirical reflection; the formal position of the viewer is occupied within the film by zombies, whose eyes and interests stay fixed on the survivors, including a camera shot from the zombie points of view when one of the bikers throws a pie in its face. These zombies fall well below bios, but within the film they are measured by survivalist functionalism. In this paradigm, they are a political success: they don't fight with each other, they all obey the same law (eat humans), they produce or reproduce zombies and zombie society as well as they can, and, because of their unity of purpose, language is superfluous: they are language, not mediated by it. The humans viewing this film never live up to this standard of political excellence, except for the duration of their viewership, in which time they play the part of silent machines for the reproduction of the society of images. The consummation of the political is then displaced from action or activism to viewership in parallel with the intra-diegetic displacement from humans to zombies, and *Dawn of the Dead* becomes legible as a robustly political film. This process is not conscious but the logical substructure which allows one to see politics in a situation that asserts itself as anything but political.

In consummating political life, the zombies of *Dawn* also annihilate it, putting language and identity behind them. The apocalyptic rupture is not in the quantitative destruction of humans but the gap between a politics of debate without end, and the accomplishment of the regulative ideal of reason in the zombie multitude. Zombies are great conservationists, recycling each fallen human to produce a zombie. The net number of humanoids remains roughly the same in this transition. Whereas late capitalism cannot seem to contain all of its toxic effluents, the zombies do quite well. Initially the zombies "live off the detritus of industrial society, and are perhaps an expression of its ecological waste," but once the "waste" has become predominant, humans become the raw material, the detritus of the past (Shaviro, 1993: 85). The polluted environment has become a political agent, freeing itself from the concept of "pollution" by destroying the separation between politics and environment.

The sense of rebirth that some critics have found in *Dawn* may derive from the passage of the political mantle from humans to zombies. Though things do not turn out well for the humans, the zombies get the "really and unambiguously happy ending of the movie" (Paffenroth, 2006: 55). Robin Wood, on the other hand, sees the possibility for a new human form of life emerging from catastrophe: "*Dawn of the Dead* is perhaps the first horror movie to suggest — albeit very tentatively — the possibility of moving beyond apocalypse" (2003: 107). This conclusion should be weighed against the originally planned ending, in which Peter and Fran commit suicide and, as the credits roll, the escape helicopter runs out of gas, implying they were doomed regardless. Whether for humans or zombies, Wood is correct to see *Dawn* moving beyond apocalypse, positing a break in one temporal order as something that happens within time and constitutes a new subject. *Dawn* ends with the geopolitical zombie watching the birth of a new human, pointing to a different arrangement of politics and life.

World War Z takes up the challenge of imagining humanity surviving a zombie apocalypse. Part of *World War Z*'s accomplishment is to give due measure to how the specific character of zombies informs this trauma in a way that other disasters (like a meteor hitting the Earth) would not. The emergence of zombies represents a violent rupture in the understanding of how the universe works, but it does not bring time to an end; the bodiliness of the zombie, as opposed to something like the ghost, holds together the paradox of an apocalypse within time, this world as the next world. *World War Z* succeeds in representing this kind of rupture and aftermath without tilting into the theological time of something like *A Canticle for Leibowitz* (Miller, 2006). *World War Z* thus builds on the temporality of zombie apocalypse introduced by Romero's films. David Pagano argues that "Romero's zombie films are meta-apocalyptic [...] if we acknowledge that the apocalyptic prophet represses time in favor of space, we can say that Romero stages the return of this repression" (2008: 74–75). In *World War Z*, even more than the limited survival prospects of *Dawn of the Dead*, time returns to haunt humans during the zombie apocalypse.

The structural possibilities of written narrative allow Brooks to encompass a greater breadth of content than typical of zombie films. The novel unfolds as a series of vignettes from survivors all over the world, lacking unity of time, place, character, and action. Or rather, as in the displacement of politics in *Dawn of the Dead*, the unity is constructed by its relocation outside of the dialectics of human politics: the place is the world, the "time" that of apocalypse, humanity or life the protagonist, and survival the action. Stephen Greenblatt (2005: 324) observes that in Shakespeare's reworking of the source material for *Hamlet* and other late tragedies, the playwright uses "the excision of motive" to create deep subjective interiority. By the same logic, the environmental political narrative is created by subtracting the epistemological unity of the subject. In this way *World War Z* overcomes the problem of the zombie films preceding it, which sought to give the impression of a collective calamity but devolved into narratives of small groups (as in *Dawn of the Dead*, which begins with a wide-ranging montage of a society in crisis, but must settle for the spatial constriction of survivalism). In *World War Z* the micro- and macro-narratives share a similar superstructure, representing the universal through the particular, as Coleridge would have it, except that the universal remains stubbornly non-transcendental.

This universal experience is zombie war: with the collapse of nations and global class structures, all humans are imperiled and must defend themselves or perish. Carl Schmitt's (2007) version of the political as the collective formed in the confrontation with the foe, a concept from which Agamben borrows, describes the zombie pushback quite handily. In this view, the war against zombies fulfills the dream of political humanism in uniting all humans against a common foe who represents our own desirous unreason. This vision of a universal political body enlivens much environmentalist enthusiasm — the end of a dialectics of difference as we all come together against a common threat — and for this is both celebrated (as alliance politics) and feared (as proto-fascism) (Radcliffe, 2000). There is something of this fantasy in *World War Z* as the U.S. president recalls reading everything "from Henry J. Kaiser to Vo Nguyen Giap" to recreate his father's New Deal–era successes with "methods that were almost Marxist in nature, the kind of collectivization that would make Ayn Rand leap from her grave and join the ranks of the living dead" (Brooks, 2006: 138). With his post-ideological pragmatism the president is able to "fuse a fractured landscape into the modern American war machine" (138). The appropriation of Leninist obedience in the service of an American military juggernaut: what more could capitalism wish for?

Yet this reading of *World War Z* misses the way in which the world is different after zombies, and so negates the essence of zombies; it becomes a book about war with an alien race, not with an existential and ontological condition cross-cutting humanity. Brooks does not evoke the triumphalism of capitalism without end. The world is still broken at the close of *World War Z*, and this damage is made most apparent in attention to and comparison with nonhuman populations.

> You know who lost World War Z? Whales.... Amazing creatures, the California grays, and now they're all gone.... So the next time someone tries to tell you about how the true losses of this war are "our innocence" or "part of our humanity...." [He spits into the water.] Whatever, bro. Tell it to the whales [Brooks, 2006: 341].

An interviewee aboard a space station recalls seeing "the mega swarms over central Asia and the American Great Plains. Those were truly massive, miles across, like the American Buffalo must have once been" (Brooks, 2006: 259). The environmentalist-primitivist celebration of the ecology of pre-contact North America is turned on its head as the buffalo return, not as the success of endangered species protection, but as the spectral referent for exterminatory power in general. "For all our enhanced optics, nothing had quite the same impact as the naked eye. To just look through the view port down on our fragile little biosphere. To see the massive ecological devastation makes one under-estimate how the modern environmental movement began with the American space program" (260).

With the end of the "hot" portion of the zombie war, zombies become fully integrated into an ecology of violence. Global destruction, of and by humans, alters the atmosphere: "That was the first Gray Winter, when the filth in the sky started changing the weather. They say that a part of that filth, I don't know how much, was ash from human remains" (Brooks, 2006: 129). In the arctic, zombies thaw in the spring and return annually: "Spring's like winter used to be, nature letting us know the good life's over for now" (320). Shades of nuclear winter and the Holocaust filter into Brooks's post-apocalyptic world, circulating physical matter and tropes among the bodies of everything remaining. Ultimately, zombies cannot be eradicated, at least not for the foreseeable future, and so they are normalized. Deep sea divers tag zombies on the ocean floor to monitor horde patterns, "trying to find them, track them, and predict their movements so maybe we can have some advance warning" (299). The management of seaborne zombies recalls our society's efforts to avert climate change and deal with the consequences that have become unavoidable through similar means. The normalization of zombies as environmental phenomena hints at a post-vital interpretation of our own very similar efforts.

The appeal to think more carefully and caringly about the ecological blowback of our actions is strong in *World War Z*, but it is important to recognize how it transforms the concepts of ecology and politics. Zombies are not symbols for an environmental "other" that it will be our political task to pacify or patronize. Rather, zombies fundamentally overturn the dialectic of a politics of suffrage, and it is this lesson for political ecology that we stand to learn from them. The environment is not "out there" any more than zombies are: both are fully continuous with the embodied human. Just as the formal qualities of viewership in *Dawn of the Dead* relocate the political away from humanity, the formal qualities of *World War Z* as a narrative without protagonist—the interviewer being its absent center—make it a narrative of humanity as an ecological being that survives the end of the political. *World War Z* arrives at something like political ecology without nature that Latour (2004) advocates. "Nature" dies when the first zombie crawls from its grave, and in the aftermath of that temporal confusion the lines of politics and ecology can and must be redrawn for a plausible narrative of human survival.

The result is less an "elevated consciousness" of the value of nature or other natural beings than a different way of seeing them altogether. In the final chapter the interviewer speaks again with the former U.S. president whose quasi-Marxism has redistributed the concept of "labor" away from the human subject and onto the beingness of beings. In this political ecology any being has standing in the work of the world.

"We're still at war, and until every trace is sponged, and purged, and, if need be, blasted from the surface of the Earth, everybody's still gotta pitch in and do their job...

[We stop by an old oak tree. My companion looks it up and down, taps it lightly with his cane. Then, to the tree...]

You're doin' a good job" [Brooks, 2006: 329].

The "we" first refers to the U.S. and its military, then to humanity, and finally, after his address to the tree, it refers to all life on earth. Yet its sense carries beyond subjects-of-a-life because the zombies, too, are still at war. To articulate one's own position in this war is to speak also the position of the other, and so fold alterity and identity into each other. This rearrangement of the subject-object split around the politicization of life is what makes *World War Z* a novel of political ecology, not its reminder that whales are aesthetically or even ethically interesting for us.

The fold in the logic of enunciating total zombie war is equivalent to the fold in time Derrida uncovers in the discourse of the apocalypse and the end of time. More war and less, faster and slower, the paradoxical counsel of deconstruction finds representation in the interruption of the zombie. The struggle to preserve humanity becomes the struggle to return the dead to the ground, to not preserve humans indefinitely. If zombies have anything more to tell us, it is that this shift is not necessarily accomplished without destruction. *Dawn of the Dead* and *World War Z* may not be the alarum that prevents disaster, just anticipatory approximations of "life" after it. Time will tell.

Plans Are Pointless; Staying Alive Is as Good as It Gets

Zombie Sociology and the Politics of Survival

Sara Sutler-Cohen

Our lives can pass before us when confronted with the immediacy of death. As popular (and varying) renditions of what we think happens when we die shift and grow, countless depictions of cultural conceptions of death and dying come to life on the silver screen. Of all of our beloved monsters, perhaps the Zombie has undergone the most drastic shift in their social roles and identity construction in recent years. Here, at the beginning of the 21st-century, there has been a sharp and steady rise in post-apocalyptic Zombie cinema (Bishop, 2009), mirroring a fascination, paranoia, and socio-politico-cultural moment of war. Horror movies (monster movies in particular) help to make sense of ill-timed spaces of death, but also serve to elude us: we do not have control, only different ways to wrestle with the inevitable. In today's Zombie films, we're confronted with new possibilities as the Walking Dead demand to be social actors in society with rights and responsibilities.

Sometimes, Horror and Sci-Fi filmmakers have a social message to broadcast. In these occasional cautionary tales, we are warned of the perils of the propensity for greed, mindless self-indulgences, and a collectively blatant abuse of the planet. The popular narrative of the economically destitute coming after the affluent (as in *The Hills Have Eyes* [1977] or *Wrong Turn* [2003]) works when marginalized groups continue to be seen as collective political outsiders who have no real cultural citizenship; they have been forgotten about and are therefore available for popular consumption. Horror and Sci-Fi films also play on common fears: nightmares, boogey men and of course, the unknown space of death. But of all of the "monsters" out there, perhaps The Zombie is among the most frightening: *We can become them. At any given moment.* Depending on which Zombie legend you follow (the slow moving, the fast moving, the immediate transforming, the possible immune, etc.) the Walking Dead pose a variety of threats to survival. Scarier still, Zombies multiply. Quickly. No matter whose story or survival guide you might follow.

Or in some cases, we may already *be* the Walking Dead. In *Shaun of the Dead* (2004), the Zombies fool us in the beginning of the film; we cannot immediately tell the difference between those sleepwalking through life, and those who have become the Walking Dead. It is no surprise at the end when Shaun's (Simon Pegg) best friend Ed (Nick Frost) is tethered in the basement glued to video games: has his life really changed all that much? As social commentaries go, Zombie stories weave relative realities into a moral code. When so many of us operate in Zombie-like abandon shopping in malls with controlled air and no clocks, how many of us would notice the change? *Shaun of the Dead* was a unique approach to telling the story of Zombie survival, not the least of which was a surprisingly successful comedic approach to the terror and shadow of death and survival of the threat of post-apocalyptic death in the modern world; a direct confrontation with, and slap in the face to a seemingly collective death anxiety. The film also wrestled with our collective moral compass. Ed becomes a Zombie and Shaun cannot leave his friend; he cannot do his brain in. Instead, he cuddles up in the shed with him, and their way of life continues (perhaps, as mentioned earlier, nothing really changed all that much).

In this article, I explore the shift in Zombie characteristics and the ways in which cinematic Zombies have begun to struggle with a distinct identity that is rooted in political survival going well beyond the confines of flesh and brain consumption. With the advent of Zombie trends in popular culture there are three specific films which project an ideological shift in the identity of the Walking Dead: *Fido* (2006), *American Zombie* (2007), and *Zombies Anonymous* (*Last Rites of the Dead*) (2008). In these films, the Walking Dead have taken on a group consciousness threatening the Living in new and politically-informed ways that offer a corporeal reality encompassing the liminal space between life and death. Where death offers no finality, Zombies must now construct a new reality for themselves in a world where they are violently unwelcome. Here, we bear witness to the politics of redefined civil rights with a postmodern perspective, however ironic that may be. This is a modern-day nightmare; one that includes multiple ways in which movie Zombies defy an unchanging definition.

The subjects of death and dying are definitional struggles in Zombie films, and today's Zombie (the infected, the monsters, the revenants, etc.) fulfill a kernel of truth for would-be horror film fans as discourses on who is and is not a Zombie, how Zombies become Zombies, how you kill a Zombie, how fast or slow a Zombie is ... the potential for late-night arguments is unlimited in scope and degree. What is interesting in this most recent wave of Zombie movies are the Zombies themselves and the strength of character they increasingly possess, including power, quick reflexes, care for community, and even brain activity. We face a cultural shift concerning the celluloid Walking Dead, as Zombies struggle for socialization and freedom to create an identity of self and community.

What some of these recent filmic incarnations of the Zombie remind us is that we must micromanage our lives as the mysterious (or not so) veil of death is lifted, and the stench of rot surrounds us; Zombies must also micromanage their half-lives by betraying their birthright as unthinking flesh eating monsters. Like the Living, Zombies must continue to reconcile their existence by human methodologies for survival.

The Walking Dead have changed. Historically speaking, Zombie movies have been about survival of the living and the *avoidance* of death, but as decades pass and the trend for Zombie paraphernalia comes in the form of things as innocently popular as a Hello

Kitty toy, fans are asked to sympathize with the undead as we also continue to seek to violently avoid becoming one of them. Or, as *Zombies Anonymous* (2008) and *American Zombie* (2007) claim, the time has come for Zombies to not only be the ones to survive, but rally for social justice and social change as they are susceptible to violent hate crimes. It is complicated at best when contemporary settings for Zombie movies confront our age-old sensibilities about what (and who) Zombies are and what they're capable of. Can Zombies become well-meaning citizens and are these new social roles simply revisioning attempts at cultural reinvention, or not? Maybe Zombies are the perfect postmodern monster, ever reminding us that nothing is static; even the fantastical shape of death.

In either case, it is easy to hang on to purity. Even this writer is hard pressed to say that a Zombie movie is a Zombie movie is a Zombie movie. Whether they are hated or embraced (for whatever reason), the legend goes on: the Walking Dead chase the Living and the Living hunt down and slaughter the Walking Dead in order to preserve the sanctity of life, even a post-apocalyptic life. If death is the barometer by which we measure life's worth, one might find oneself wondering what we are left with as we hunt it down to its finality as would-be Zombie killers, seeking to brain the Walking Dead. With the Walking Dead now claiming the streets in Seattle's Zombie Walk, et al., along with cinematic recreations of what it means to be a Zombie, there is a cultural shift afoot and this confronts assumptions of the early Romero films that have Zombies slow, starving and (relatively) easy to kill.

Given these changes, there are questions fans of the celluloid Walking Dead must face and grapple with when investigating the sociological meaningfulness of Zombie "societies" and the political nature of survival, which must also mirror the morphology of the Zombie. As tradition would have it, the early Romero Zombies seemed to roam aimlessly, driven only by a desperate need to feed on the flesh of the living. In later incarnations, it was campiness as Zombies entered a world of slapstick horror and ceased to be terrifying or confrontational. After all, when you name the Zombie "Bub" it's hard to be afraid of him. So we see, time and time again for the audience, the Walking Dead are eventually and explicitly given to hilarity, particularly through the 1980s. However, while that sense of Zombified humor continues to be refined today, the terror of the possibility of a life with the roaming dead has once again morphed and the "joke" is seated comfortably in the possibility that a future with Zombies just might be real. Max Brooks' works (2003, 2006) on surviving the Zombie Apocalypse has cinched this possible Third Wave of Zombie styling, which now includes these two possibilities; first, that Zombies will survive their own apocalypse and work in convenience stores or serve as pets, and second that we now have directions from Brooks on how to live full lives in their world by learning about who they are, their many nuances and survivability. For both of these scenarios, we are at war with Zombies and our choices become political: which side are we on?

Sociologically speaking, particularly when we are referring to the construction of identity, humor tends to be an extension of reality — *Cracked Magazine*, in its online publication, even came out with its own list of possibilities for a Zombie Apocalypse in Sloth and Wong's article, "5 Scientific Reasons a Zombie Apocalypse Could Actually Happen." In it, the authors note the several possibilities which lend themselves to a temptation to believe. Awareness of these "5 Reasons" for the coming apocalypse helps not only to prepare those invested in its possible reality, but it also presents a future of Zombie animus that would extend beyond that early and unidimensional (albeit brilliantly imagined and crafted) Romero-esque drive to tear apart the living. In the article, the authors present the following:

Brain parasites: A bug that normally infects rats, toxiplasmosa gondii, eats away at the cerebral cortex. Bitten by a rat with the gondii bug, scientists have suggested that the condition would spread rapidly.

Neurotoxins: Some poisons work to dramatically slow bodily functions, so much so that people can slip into a state of suspended animation and appear deceased.

A Real Rage Virus: Demonstrated in 28 Days Later and 28 Weeks Later, scientists might work with chimpanzees to test the lethality of Rage Possession. Recent outbreaks of "Mad Cow" disease across the United States and Canada also carry a very real worry that when transferred to humans through a bite or deep cut, victims may display Zombie-like characteristics.

Neurogenesis: With the advent of stem-cell research, scientists working in the field may be able to regenerate brain tissue in cadavers.

Nanorobotics: To combat biological warfare (or really, to be active participants in it), nanotechnicians can create the tiniest microorganism that is also a microrobot — one that moves like an insect and can attach itself to the enemies' brain stems. The result is much like Neurotoxins [Sloth and Wong, 2007].

So, we have the old meeting the new. Zombies and the possible coming apocalypse have gone from moaning, slow-moving, disorganized monsters whose condition was effected by the rare and relatively unbelievable occurrence of comets or space-probe radiation to complex analyses of very real, scientifically-sound Zombification. Add to this the filmic claims of *Fido, Zombies Anonymous,* and *American Zombie* and the further possibility that Zombies can and will be not only a distinct social class with their own culture and identity, but a group whose political survival further threatens the fabric of our lives, the future with The Walking Dead just became even more interesting. All of these possibilities beg many questions. Are our lives redefined in these cities of the Dead? Do the Walking Dead have a survival instinct? How have recent constructions of 21st-century Zombies redefined the genre if they are suddenly rendered not only *mostly* dead, but social outcasts? If the one thing that moves us is the terror of death (Becker, 1973), then it stands to reason that in the case of the Walking Dead, our fears turn our terror back to us, forcing immediate confrontation towards resolution.

One of the foremost critical thinkers of death and dying was Ernest Becker whose work on the social-psychological realm of death dramatically shifted the way death and dying is discussed today. For the most part, it remains an elusive ill-studied area in Sociology, with scant course offerings and even less scholarly consideration. But as minor considerations go, the Sociology of Death is a riveting, dynamic, and important area of study, particularly when coupled with popular culture, as in the case of the Zombie Movie. Becker felt that when living under the constant threat of death, people behaved accordingly, as it is one of the "major psychological problems of man [sic]" (Becker, 1973: 20). This *death anxiety* spills out into our social landscape, painting a vividly imaginative picture of the shape of things to come. It is entirely possible that death anxiety is a root cause for the behavior of the Living in today's Zombie films on a deep psychological, sociological, spiritual, and cultural level. If daily life in the post-apocalyptic world of the Zombie includes living under the constant threat of death, then that social world includes fundamental behavioral changes; in today's Zombie movie, folks are being asked to settle into a life with and in spite of Zombies living side by side with the Living.

The terror of death is the heartbeat (no pun intended) of a good Zombie flick. It is the terror of death, the sheer madness of the hollowed out eyes, and the fear beneath the gore of the corporeality of the Walking Dead that is the pulse of Zombie Movies. Death anxiety grips *all of* the characters and the audience to create a collective sense of their own mortality—and when the mortality you face is a walking ghoul, that collective fear is heightened by yet one more possibility of what happens to you when you die. Of course, what it comes down to for horror fans is that death can be either exciting or terrifying, but either way death is the big Question Mark. Nobody really knows what happens when we pass over so we remain free to explore this notion of the afterlife and do with it what we will. We then have full creative license to imagine the space of death, extending to the liminal space of death in which the Zombie occupies.

Becker also claimed that death anxiety was a primary motivator of human behavior, specifically aggression and violence (1973). We can relate this readily to contemporary Zombie movies, even and especially the arc of the Zombie Movie in that the only way to resolve the Zombie Problem is through violence. It is interesting also that these very recent incarnations of the Zombie (*American Zombie, Zombies Anonymous*, and *Fido*) have created a tamer, more polite Zombie bent on becoming a veritable part of Societies of The Living. In this way, death becomes that social barometer by which we measure social inequities. In these films, themes smack of civil and human rights as they borrow from our own history of violence in laws and policies against the *Other*, which purportedly threatens the good and the will of the people (the Living people).

In *American Zombie* and *Zombies Anonymous*, the Walking Dead desperately attempt to hang on to some form of human dignity. Both films have multiple characters wrestling with their newfound identity; almost as though they are wrestling yet again with young adulthood, while straining to find hope in a world in which they cannot yet fit. In both films, identity construction is based on a newfound social stratification that smacks of Civil Rights–era segregation. From questioning the employment of a Zombie waiter in *Zombies Anonymous* to his later capture, truss, trunk ride and subsequent murder (the waiter is ironically Black) to the varying politically correct nomenclature for Zombies, including "Decedents," "Revenants," or "The Non-Living Community" (*American Zombie*), it is clear that there are socio-political problems in these Zombie societies. It is no wonder that *American Zombie* starts off with an Isaac Asimov quote: "Life is pleasant. Death is peaceful. It's the transition that's troublesome." Troublesome indeed—in *American Zombie*, "human" rights become a strategic political issue when would-be policy makers distinctly express that "Revenants" are neither stricken with a disease, nor are they living with a disability. They are, a "new population and they need our attention" (*American Zombie*, 2007).

In another turn of identity-wrestling for Zombies is the 2007 film by Andrew Currie, *Fido*. In a retro-themed 1950s idyllic setting we find a sleepy suburban town whose present-day life in post-apocalyptic culture brought on by "(s)pace particles (causing) the reanimation of dead bodies" (*Fido*) includes the safety net of a corporation called "ZomCon" whose scientists ensured the safety of the Living with "The Domestication Collar." Following the Zombie Wars, the development of the Collar has allowed the Walking Dead to weave themselves into society as they seek to "live" albeit under the thumb of political, cultural, and social dominance. In a commercial during the film, we hear the pledge, "Thanks to ZomCon, we can all become productive members of society even after we die." Further explanations of the benefits of the Collar include: "The Zombies' desire for human flesh is contained, making the Zombie as gentle as a household pet." Smacking of hegemonic media imperialism, the wool is pulled over the eyes of the community, who are all too willing to remain blinded by an obvious lie. Everyone's behavior, excepting ten-year-old Timmy (K'Sun Ray) and later his mother (Carrie-Anne Moss), is automated as the film goes on; nobody questions their lives among the collared Walking Dead. And so we continue to play with the mythos of Zombies in these films. For example, Fido and Timmy's relationship blossoms, as Fido clearly has emotional and intelligent responses to the dramaturgical events throughout the film, which include bullies and closed-minded adults. Timmy is a misunderstood boy who sees the social problems of the day clearly and distinctly.

It is certainly possible that the Walking Dead exist in a state of immortal terror; dying to feed, driven to complete their journey to the valley of death, even if and when on their merry way, they possess a desire to be sewn into the fabric of their old social worlds which the living occupy (*Zombies Anonymous* and *American Zombie*), or if their relative possibility of mere existence threatens to undo the cinematic legend by outrunning their would-be assassins during the chase (Levin, 2004). As postmodernity would have it, these representations of the multiple possibilities in occupying the space of death stretch the limits of possibility and believability; Zombies, the Walking Dead, Revenants ... similar issues, different stitches in time, variant methods of coping. The most interesting thread of commonality in all of these possibilities of our beloved Walking Dead monstrosities is that of death denial. For, why else would these new personalities bear down on screen and provide so many ways of looking at, facing, or even cheating death but for a taste of immortality (regardless of the rot)?

In *Zombies Anonymous*, a film where any Zombie can learn to cope and be "normal" in a 12-Step Program, how one zombifies is simply not discussed and there is no explanation. "You die, you become one of them. It doesn't matter how" (*Zombies Anonymous*). The film, then, is deliberately part of an unchanging Zombie narrative if only by clearly linking to the Romeroesque legend of becoming a Zombie. Just like the Marlboro man needs no cigarette to be identified in advertisements, neither does a Zombie film need to demonstrate how people become Zombies. All you need is the social landscape of a post–apocalyptic world and a little reanimation. Presentation is everything. So, when people die, it is only a matter of time before the medics come and pronounce them dead, and simply give up and leave the bodies where they have fallen. "Nobody's immune to this," quips an interviewee in the beginning of the film; "Nobody's dying," says another. So this presents an even bigger problem: that of overpopulation — perhaps one of the reasons for Zombie Bashing we see in the film, second only to the wanton discrimination Zombies are forced to endure. In the beginning of the film we hear that "there appears to be a heartbeat every one or two minutes but it is certainly not enough to sustain life" and that "the only people that are affected by this are the recently deceased." Given this "fact," we are left with an interesting discussion about the way in which Zombies are defined on screen. Clearly, there is a wrestling with these definitions of our beloved Zombies, and the culture in which they can live, as well as their social habits. And, in *Zombies Anonymous*, the Zombies are simply woven into the fabric of society, not unlike a caste system; not only that, but there is virtually no explanation for their Walking Dead status. When you die, you Zombify!

It would be unwise at any point of a Zombie article to not mention George A. Romero as the veritable "Godfather" of modern day Zombie cinema. Though he may argue to the contrary, admitting his theft of the core story of Matheson's *I Am Legend* to develop *Night of the Living Dead* (*Zombiemania*, 2009), Romero set the tone for what has become a maniacal obsession with all things Living Dead. From Brooks' breakout bestsellers, *The Zombie Survival Guide* (2003) and *World War Z* (2006) to the churning out of so many Zombie flicks, it has become nigh impossible to keep up, including the newly defined Zombies walking and "living" among us. Romero unwittingly started an onslaught of what has now casually been referred to as "The New Vampire." Zombies are so fashionable and so accessible, that Zombie Walks litter city streets at the level of weekly flash mobs, not bothering to wait until Halloween.

These films wrestle with the question: What constitutes a Zombie? In *28 Days Later*, Zombies are never mentioned; they're "*The Infected*." *[Rec]* (2007) also doesn't call these roaming, flesh-eating beasts Zombies; in fact, they are never identified as anything other than terrifyingly confusing, mystifying even the most seasoned Zombie fans, until in the end of the film we get a hint at the possibility of a Catholic conspiracy to create possession. In *Zombies Anonymous*, well, they're Zombies, but there is no myth, no story, and no explanation. You die, you become a Zombie. There is a place for you in the 12-Step Community: "Choose Life!" cheers on a hanging flower made out of construction paper and mounted on the wall of a closed-in apartment. In Group, you do what "normal" people do at 12-Step meetings. You eat doughnuts and chug coffee — and come to the meeting with your own puke bucket to regurgitate that which you, as a flesh-eater, simply cannot digest. But like in *The Omega Man* (also an adaptation of *I Am Legend*), *Zombies Anonymous* reflects civil rights issues as Zombies are treated with disdain, spat upon, raped, and threatened with indentured servitude. The Zombies in *Zombies Anonymous* are threatened daily by Zombie Bashing (although this is never addressed explicitly as a Hate Crime in the film) — it's the Living against the Walking Dead. Best just to cope. The political problem of what to do with the Walking Dead is raised, noted, and shut down immediately before the film even begins in earnest.

Another film that never explicitly defines how Zombies zombify and presents new and interesting ways that Zombies and the Living exist among one another is *Shaun of the Dead* (2004). This may indeed be part of its charm because one of the key components in *Shaun* was that it parodied several possibilities for zombification in the end of the film, paying homage to the Zombie legend itself, and possibly also ribbing the "seriousness" with which Zombie movies are occasionally considered. As Liz (Kate Ashfield) and Shaun (Simon Pegg) are watching the news following the Zombie Plague, the reports mention several possibilities including a rage virus (from *28 Days Later* and *28 Weeks Later*). These clearly note the glorious history of Zombie Movies, Romero's *Dawn of the Dead* in particular, with numerous references throughout the film (including Foree Electric where Shaun works — paying respects to Romero legend, Ken Foree). The Zombies in *Shaun of the Dead* are otherwise relatively traditional mindless, ghoulish Zombies whose braining-in render them harmless. We do not see, as we do in *Zombies Anonymous, Fido*, and *American Zombie*, the need to belong, the wrestling with identity, or the institutional discrimination of social stratification.

In *Zombies Anonymous*, we are introduced to frantic Angela (Gina Ramsden) cowering in her bathroom while her boyfriend breaks down the door to gun her down (the film has an interesting undercurrent of domestic violence throughout the story, which feeds also into the violent tendencies of poor Angela's boyfriend, who he continues to hunt her down even after she zombifies). The film then immediately cuts to confused newscasters discussing the impending Zombie Plague where people are simply "getting up and walking away" quite soon after death. "Volunteer Euthanasia Facilities" crop up all over town wherein Zombies can electively be brained to a guaranteed finality. As the storyline develops we see other possibilities, which demand a sense of empathy for Zombies in this film. When Angela is fired from her job, possibly for simply leaking all over her desk from a gunshot wound, she pounds the pavement, rotting skin and all. As she grips the handle to an office building door, she turns, nerve-wracked and skeptical, and we follow her gaze across the street to an ad for "Look Alive!" whose caption reads: "Alive or Dead? Only she knows.... Look Alive! It's our little secret...." The product guarantees to smooth out zombified skin to a luster that also permits the dolling up of oneself (in a television commercial for the product, apparently it is extremely painful for the dead to apply makeup). She aces the job interview only to discover that a job is impossible. The interviewer informs her of a new Anti-Zombie policy for which she must submit a blood test. Daunted, she returns to her 12-Step Meeting of Zombies Anonymous to choke on doughnuts with her fellow Walking Dead compatriots.

As the film moves to its conclusion, an undercurrent of discrimination becomes a key point in the plotline and outright "Zombieism" gives way to rape, assault, kidnapping, and murder. Zombies must band together to fight the newfound hate-filled crimes they are faced with. As one Zombie would have it "There comes a time, when you think things can't get any worse. But then they do. This is when we have to stay strong. I tell you, we haven't seen the worst of this. There are dark, dark days ahead. Let me tell you." Things do get dangerous — as war breaks out between the Zombies and the Living (headed up by the self-described Commandant (Christa McNamee), a hardened possible ex-militant with a rage problem), current and very real social problems become themes in the film with respect to race, age, and the domestic violence between Angela and her ex-beau. "Why did you rape a dead White girl?" the Commandant screams at a Black man over and over at gunpoint. The Commandant eventually shoots this Zombie, who denies raping the girl through to his untimely death. The film trudges on, hinting at but not dealing head-on with the issues it raises. As an interesting side note, there are apparently at least two versions of this film, one which does not have the aforementioned scene. Furthermore, this scene is ill-placed and without context, full of bloopers and awkward time sequencing. It has a string of narratives that are never taken on directly, although the issue of miscegenation is front and center in another scene when a couple is videotaped whilst being slain for making out on a park bench — one of the lovers is a Zombie.

That *Zombies Anonymous* does not seriously grapple with the issues it raises is not a big surprise — social messages notwithstanding, racism is a topic still relatively taboo in horror films. People of color might appear in horror films but that hardly means that the films are about race. So, it is impressive that director Marc Fratto attempts a dance with racism in *Zombies Anonymous* and does so in an uncomfortable way, asking the audience to come to terms not only with its reality on screen, but the very real experience of contemporary racism in the United States. Hearkening back decades to a time of public lynching and violence against Blacks is not simply hinted at but exposed head on with purpose. That the film has no resolution toward racism is forgivable. That it is present in the film at all, when contextually it did not have to be is surprising and well done. In the end, Angela stares in her bathroom mirror at her mangled and bloodied body and tosses her jar of "Look Alive!" into the trash, thereby showing a sense of pride in being dead and a political message toward fighting for one's rights to trudge on as a marginalized member of society.

Again, *Shaun of the Dead* offers another perspective on life during and after the Zombie Apocalypse. Shaun has tamed Zombie Ed, offering another possibility for social navigation. After all, in a post-apocalyptic world, how might you best occupy your time than to tame or chase a Zombie? When society has broken down in such a way as to eradicate all ethical and legal boundaries, we are left with a collective consciousness driven purely by survival; which is odd, considering that the war for survival is between the living and the (walking) dead.

In order to fully understand the complexities of possibilities that Zombies occupy, it is important to recognize first and foremost that Zombies *only* live in a post-apocalyptic world. The social commentary Zombie films offer is at the feet of a dystopic world, beset by problems we can no longer manage, all of which are rooted in scientific engineering resulting in human diastrophism (factory farming resulting in mad cow disease to humans in *Zombieland* [2009] or military weaponry development in *28 Days Later* and *28 Weeks Later*). One could argue that *Zombies Anonymous* does not seem post-apocalyptic, but by virtue of survival after a Zombie Plague, I suggest it does indeed occupy that space. That there was survival following a plague suggests a post-apocalyptic world even if society itself operates "normally." These manifestations of social change, then, necessitate the stories of the Walking Dead. The post-apocalyptic world tends to force a separation of the genre from other monster movies, given the cultural currency of violence, war, and terrorism, and so this contemporary end-of-the-world monster may be demonstrative of collective cultural anxieties of the day.

In his article, "Dead Man *Still* Walking: Explaining the Zombie Renaissance," Kyle Bishop suggests that, "Because the aftereffects of war, terrorism, and natural disasters so closely resemble the scenarios of Zombie cinema, such images of death and destruction have all the more power to shock and terrify a population that has become otherwise jaded by more traditional horror films" (2009: 18). His argument that there has been a rise in Zombie films since 9/11 suggests our cultural microscope is focused on today's warzones as the lines of real-life horror stories of violence and mayhem are blurred on screen. Today's

Zombie films suggest an anarchic societal breakdown of postmodern proportions. Settings for Zombie films are sewn into the post-apocalyptic landscape where this idea of society's foundations breaking down in such a way as to provide a world where terror presents itself to us in ways inescapable. Unlike other monsters we are charged with hunting down and killing, the Zombies come and find us, much like the way in which the real terrorist story of 9/11. And isn't that sometimes why we go to see horror films, to seek out new ways of terrifying ourselves because we feel so safe? The connection between the terror of death and Zombie films is something to look at quite closely. Is the backdrop of a post-apocalyptic world really all that far-fetched? As Max Brooks would have it, "When the living dead triumph, the world degenerates into utter chaos. All social order evaporates" (2003: 155). The fact is that Zombies are changing. They are faster, smarter, and have the gumption to stand up for themselves.

Whatever the cause or varying personality traits and quirks, there are some common themes in Zombie cinema that make Zombies, Zombies. The Walking Dead experience a sort of entrapment. Cultural citizenship does not apply to them, and as our death-obsessed culture would have it, the line between the living and the dead is always blurred. Zombies feed on flesh. Zombies are mindless ghouls. Zombies are always hungry. Zombies rarely have any real social organization (although this myth is burst in recent years). Zombies are hopeless. Even in *Zombies Anonymous* where the Walking Dead may make the altruistic choice to feed on bits of uncooked skirt steak instead of your little sister, and talk about their feelings in meetings, they don't fit into society. They can't. They're Zombies.

Humanity as The Living understand it is missing; as Zombies are often infected with something, they are also walking diseases, and as germ panics are certainly part of our social landscape, biological terrorism becomes another possible factor in the Zombie narrative. As postmodernity would have it, reality as represented in popular culture, celluloid in particular, is like a stream of consciousness, and serves as a constant reminder of our infallibility. We are so close to death that we privilege ourselves as living beings and play with death simply as an idea, far removed from the reality of our impending doom. Zombies allow us to flirt with death but not take it seriously. Take it seriously, but do so in a tongue-in-cheek way (does Brooks *really* have a compound in Colorado?). As Sheldon Solomon mentions in the 2003 documentary *Flight From Death: The Quest For Immortality*, "The explicit awareness that you're a breathing piece of defecating meat destined to die, ultimately no more significant than let's say a lizard or a potato, is not especially uplifting." This fact alone pushes us to play with an idea we cannot avoid, but obsess about as a form of eventual reality.

Most incarnations of the Zombie are a metaphor for human complacency, but our re-visioned Zombies who wrestle with a sense of belonging are experiencing a *social death* wherein they explicitly fall outside the lines of cultural citizenry and must socially navigate an increasingly distrustful world. Survivors of the Zombie Apocalypse think and live in a state of animated flux — they think, they plan, and they quickly (very quickly) surrender to the elements of half-lives. No bills, but no going out to dinner. No alarm clocks, but no sleeping in on a Sunday. Oh, and no paper, either. Or television. Or movies. Theater. At the end of the day, however — to be a survivor, relationships are key. As Selene puts it in *28 Days Later*, "Plans are pointless. Staying alive is as good as it gets."

But we're not alone; Zombies are now part of the survivor narrative as the definitions shift and change. Do they become pets, menial workers, or thought-provoking activists? Will 12-Step Programs help them to cope in a future world in which they are no less than second-class citizens? Today's Zombie is faced with all of these possibilities in addition to still being clear representations for human complacency as they have always been vehicles for social commentary. Even and especially with the new shape of things, Zombies continue to represent a post-apocalyptic world because no matter how they might become Zombies or what happens after they do so, our world as we know it changes fundamentally. As the future of Zombie movies are changing, so our relationship with these fabled characters also changes. Whatever the shape future films do take, it is abundantly clear that Zombies won't be contained.

Bibliography

Aarseth, E. (1997). *Cybertext*. Baltimore, MD: John Hopkins Press.

Ackermann, Hans-W., and Jeanine Gauthier. (1991). "The Ways and Nature of the Zombi." *The Journal of American Folklore* 104 (414): 466–494.

Adkins, Brent. (2007). "A Rumor of Zombies: Deleuze and Guattari on Death." *Philosophy Today* 51: 119–124.

Agamben, G. (1998). *Homo Sacer: Sovereign Power and Bare Life*. D. Heller-Roazen, (Trans.). Stanford: Stanford University Press.

Alexie, Sherman. (2008). "Ghost Dance." In John Joseph Adams, (Ed.), *The Living Dead*. San Francisco: Night Shade Books. 68–77.

Alter, Robert. (2000). *Canon and Creativity: Modern Writing and the Authority of Scripture*. New Haven and London: Yale University Press.

Anderson, C. A., and B. J. Bushman. (2001). "Effects of Violent Games on Aggressive Behaviour, Aggressive Cognition, Aggressive Affect, Physiological Arousal and Prosocial Behaviour: A Meta-analytic Review of the Scientific Literature." *Psychological Science* 12: 353–359.

Anderson, C. A., and K. E. Dill. (2000). "Videogames and Aggressive Thoughts, Feelings and Behaviour in the Laboratory and in Life." *Journal of Personality and Social Psychology* 78 (4): 772–790.

Anderson, Jeffery M. (1998). "Bonkers About 'The Beyond.'" *Combustible Celluloid*. Archives. June 12th. Online: <http://www.combustiblecelluloid.com/archive/beyond.shtml>. Accessed Dec. 18, 2010.

Asma, Stephen T. (2009). *On Monsters, An Unnatural History of our Worst Fears*. Oxford: Oxford University Press.

Atkins, B. (2003). *More Than a Game: The Computer Game as Fictional Form*. Manchester: Manchester University Press.

Auerbach, Nina. (1997). *Our Vampires, Ourselves*. Chicago: U. of Chicago Press.

Austen, Jane, and Seth Grahame-Smith. (2009). *Pride and Prejudice and Zombies*. Philadelphia, PA: Quirk Books.

Badham, Paul. (1976). *Christian Beliefs about Life after Death*. London: MacMillan Press.

Bakhtin, Mikhail. (1968). *Rabelais and His World*. Bloomington, IN: Indiana University Press.

Baldini, Chiara. (2010). "Dionysus Returns: Tuscan Trancers and Euripides' *The Bacchae*." In Graham St John, (Ed), *The Local Scenes and Global Culture of Psytrance*. NY: Routledge. 170–186.

Balun, Chas. (1997). *Lucio Fulci. Beyond the Gates*. Key West, FL: Fantasma Books.

Bark, Jasper. (2009). *Way of the Barefoot Zombie*. Oxford: Abaddon Books.

Bataille, Georges. (1988). *The Accursed Share*, Vol. 1. Robert Hurley, (Trans.). NY: Zone.

Baudrillard, J. (1995). *Simulacra and Simulation*. S. F. Glaser, (Trans.). Minneapolis: University of Minnesota Press.

Beal, Timothy K. (2002). *Religion and its Monsters*. NY and London: Routledge.

Beard, S. (1993). "No Particular Place to Go." *Sight and Sound* 3: 30–31.

Becker, Ernest. (1973). *The Denial of Death*. NY: Free Press.

Beisecker, David. (2011). "Nothing but Meat? Philosophical Zombies and their Cinematic Counterparts." In Christopher M. Moreman and Cory James Rushton, (Eds.), *Race, Oppression and the Zombie: Essays on Cross-Cultural Appropriations of the Caribbean Tradition*. Jefferson, NC: McFarland.

Bellegarde-Smith, Patrick. (2006). *Haiti: The Breached Citadel*. Toronto: Canadian Scholars' Press.

Benjamin, W. (1977). "Short History of Photography." P. Patton, (Trans.), *Artforum* 15: 46–51.

Bennett, Tony, and Janet Woollacott. (1987). *Bond and Beyond: The Political Career of a Popular Hero*. NY: Methuen.

Berest, Joseph J. (1970) "Report on a Case of Sadism." *The Journal of Sex Research* 6 (3): 210–219.

Berger, Peter L. (1967). *The Sacred Canopy*. Garden City, NY: Doubleday & Co.

Berro Rovira, Guido. (2001). "Violence as a Medical and Legal Problem." *Iinfancia: Bulletin of the Inter-American Children's Institute* 237 (70). Online: <http://www.iin.oea.org/Revista%20Bibliografica%20237/articulo_guido_berro_ingles. PDF>. Accessed Jan. 24, 2011.

Bertsch, Devon. (2008). "Review: Porn of the Dead." *Digital Retribution*. Online: <http://www.digital-retribution.com/reviews/dvd1/002.php>. Accessed Dec. 23, 2010.

Bishop, Anne H., and John R. Scudder, Jr. (1991). *Nursing: The Practice of Caring*. NY: National League for Nursing Press.

Bishop, Kyle. (2010). *American Zombie Gothic*. Jefferson, NC: McFarland.

_____. (2009). "Dead Man *Still* Walking: Explaining the Zombie Renaissance." *Journal of Popular Film & Television* 37 (1): 16–25.

_____. (2006). "Raising the Dead: Unearthing the Non-Literary Origins of Zombie Culture." *Journal of Popular Film and Television* 33 (4): 196–205.

Bittanti, Matteo. (2001). "The Technoludic Film: Images of Videogames in Movies (1973–2001)." *Master's Theses*. Paper 2206. Online: <http://scholarworks.sjsu.edu/etd_theses/2206>. Accessed Feb. 1, 2011.

Blier, Suzanne Preston. (1995). "Vodun: West African Roots of Vodou." In D. J. Cosentino, (Ed.), *Sacred Arts of Haitian Vodou*. LA: UCLA Fowler Museum of Cultural History. 61–87.

Bodie v. Purdue Pharma Co., 236 F. Appx. 511 (11th Cir. 2007).

Bond, George D. (1980). "Theravada Buddhism's Meditations on Death and the Symbolism of Initiatory Death." *History of Religions* 19 (3): 237–258.

Bondeson, Jan. (2002). *Buried Alive: The Terrifying History of Our Most Primal Fear*. London: W.W. Norton & Co.

Booth, William. (1988). "Voodoo Science." *Science* 240 (4850): 274–277.

Boring, M. Eugene. (2006). *Mark*. New Testament Library. Louisville and London: Westminster John Knox Press.

Bourke, Joanna. (2007). *Rape: A History from 1860 to the Present*. London: Virago.

Braidotti, Rosi. (2004). "Meta(l)morphoses: The Becoming-Machine." In Andrew Blaikie, et al., (Eds.), *The Body: Critical Concepts in Sociology— Volume V: "Alternative" Bodies*. NY: Routledge. 89–141.

Breathett, George. (1988). "Catholicism and the Code Noir in Haiti." *The Journal of Negro History* 73 (1): 1–11.

Briefel, Aviva. (2005). "Monster Pains: Masochism, Menstruation, and Identification in the Horror Film." *Film Quarterly*, 58 (3): 16–27.

Britt, Lory, and David R. Heise. (1992) "Impressions of Self-Directed Action." *Social Psychology Quarterly* 55 (4): 335–350.

Bronfen, Elisabeth. (2000). "The Body and its Discontents." In Avril Horner and Angela Kane, (Eds.), *Body Matters: Feminism, Textuality, Corporeality*. Manchester: Manchester University Press. 109–123.

Brooks, Max, (2006). *World War Z: An Oral History of the Zombie War*. NY: Three Rivers Press.

_____. (2003). *The Zombie Survival Guide*. NY: Three Rivers Press.

Brophy, Philip. (2000). "Horrality—The Textuality of Contemporary Horror Films." In Ken Gelder, (Ed.), *The Horror Reader*. London: Rutledge.

Buckingham, D., and S. Bragg. (2004). *Young People, Sex and the Media: The Facts of Life?* Basingstoke: Palgrave Macmillan.

Bull, M. (2007). "Vectors of the Biopolitical." *New Left Review* 45: 7–25. *Callahan v. Campbell*, 427 F. 3d 897 (11th Cir. 2005).

Campbell, John Gregorson. (2005). *The Gaelic Otherworld*. Ronald Black, (Ed.). Edinburgh: Birlinn.

Canetti, Elias. (1962). *Crowds and Power*. Carol Stewart, (Trans.). NY: Noonday Press.

Canter, David V., and Natalia Wentink. (2004). "An Empirical Test of Holmes and Holmes's Serial Murder Typology." *Criminal Justice and Behavior* 31: 489–515.

Carroll, Noël. (1987). "The Nature of Horror." *The Journal of Aesthetics and Art Criticism* 46 (1): 51–59.

Carson, Don. (2000). "Environmental Storytelling: Creating Immersive 3D Worlds Using Lessons Learned from the Theme Park Industry." *Gamasutra: The Art & Business of Making Games*. Online: <http://www.gamasutra.com/view/feature/3186/environmental_storytelling_.php>.

Carson, R. (2002). *Silent Spring*. NY: Mariner Books.

Castro, Adam-Troy. (2008). "Dead Like Me." In John Joseph Adams, (Ed.), *The Living Dead*. San Francisco: Night Shade Books. 369–76.

Castronovo, Russ. (2000). "Political Necrophilia." *Boundary 2*, 27 (2): 113–148.

Cettl, Robert. (2008). "Review: Porn of the Dead." *Wider Screenings*. Online: <http://www.widerscreenings.com/pornofthedead3.html>. Accessed Dec. 23, 2010.

Chalmers, David J. (1996). *The Conscious Mind: In Search of a Fundamental Theory*. NY and Oxford: Oxford University Press.

Chapman, Ivan. (1972). "The Dyad: Social and Para-Social." *International Journal of Contemporary Sociology* 9 (4): 182–87.

Clark, Simon. (2006). "The Undead Martyr: Sex, Death, and Revolution in George Romero's Zombie Films." In Richard Greene and K. Silem Mohammad, (Eds.), *The Undead and Philosophy: Chicken Soup for the Soulless*. Chicago: Open Court. 197–210.

Clover, Carol J. (1995). "The Eye of Horror." In

Linda Williams (Ed.), *Viewing Positions*. New Brunswick, NJ: Rutgers University Press.

Connolly, John. (2010). "Lazarus." In Christopher Golden, (Ed.), *The New Dead*. NY: St. Martin's Griffin. 1–8.

Conze, Edward. (2003). *Buddhist Meditation*. NY: Dover.

Cooley, Charles H. (1902). *Human Nature and the Social Order*. NY: C. Scribner's Sons.

Corsaro, William. (1985). *Friendship and Peer Culture in the Early Years*. Norwood, NJ: Ablex Publishing.

Corzani, Jack. (1994). "West Indian Mythology and its Literary Illustrations." *Research in African Literatures* 25 (2): 131–139.

Cosentino, Donald J. (1995). "Imagine Heaven." In D. J. Cosentino, (Ed.), *Sacred Arts of Haitian Vodou*. LA: UCLA Fowler Museum of Cultural History. 25–55.

Crawford, C. (2003). *Chris Crawford on Game Design*. Indianapolis, IN: New Riders.

Creed, Barbara. (1993). *The Monstrous-Feminine: Film, Feminism, Psychoanalysis*. NY: Routledge.

Cronon, W. (1996). "The Trouble with Wilderness; or, Getting Back to the Wrong Nature." In William Cronon, (Ed.), *Uncommon Ground*. New York: W. W. Norton & Co. 69–90.

Crowell v. Knowles, 483 F. Supp. 2d 925 (D. Ariz. 2007).

Curci, Loris, and Michael Gingold. (1995). "One Step Beyond." *Fangoria* 141: 62–68/82.

Curran, Bob. (2009). *Zombies: A Field Guide to the Walking Dead*. Franklin Lakes, NJ: New Page Books.

Currie, Dawn H., and Valerie Raoul. (1992). "The Anatomy of Gender: Dissecting Sexual Difference in the Body of Knowledge." In *The Anatomy of Gender: Women's Struggle for the Body*. Ottawa: Carleton University Press. 1–34.

Dahmer, Lionel. (1994). *A Father's Story*. NY: William Morrow and Company.

Davis, J. C. (1981). *Utopia and the Ideal Society: A Study of English Utopian Writing 1516–1700*. Cambridge: Cambridge University Press.

Davis, Wade. (1988). *Passage of Darkness: The Ethnobiology of the Haitian Zombie*. Chapel Hill, NC: The University of North Carolina Press.

_____. (1985). *The Serpent and the Rainbow: A Harvard Scientist's Astonishing Journey into the Secret Societies of Haitian Voodoo, Zombis, and Magic*. NY: Simon & Schuster.

Davis, Wayne A. (1987). "The Varieties of Fear." *Philosophical Studies* 51 (3): 287–310.

De Lauretis, Teresa. (1987). *Technologies of Gender: Essays on Theory, Film and Fiction*. Basingstoke, Eng.: Macmillan.

Deleuze, Gilles, and Felix Guattari. (1972/2005). *Anti-Oedipus: Capitalism and Schizophrenia*. Robert Hurley, Mark Seem, and Helen R. Lane, (Trans.). Minneapolis, MN: U. of Minnesota Press.

DeLillo, Don. (1985). *White Noise*. NY: Viking.

De Maria, R., and J. L. Wilson. (2002). *High Score! The Illustrated History of Electronic Games*. NY: Hill Osborne Media.

Dendle, Peter. (2007). "The Zombie as Barometer of Cultural Anxiety." In N. Scott (Ed.), *Monsters and the Monstrous*. NY: Rodopi Press. 45–58.

_____. (2001). *The Zombie Movie Encyclopedia*. Jefferson, NC: McFarland.

Dennett, Daniel C. (1995). "The Unimagined Preposterousness of Zombies: Commentary on Moody, Flanagan and Polger." *Journal of Consciousness Studies*, 2: 322–6.

Dickstein, Morris. (1984). "The Aesthetics of Fright." In Barry Keith Grant (Ed.), *Planks of Reason: Essays on the Horror Film*. Metuchen, NJ: Scarecrow Press. 50–62.

Dillard, R. H. W. (1987). "Night of the Living Dead: It's Not Just Like a Wind That's Passing Through." In Gregory A. Waller, (Ed.), *American Horrors: Essays on the Modern American Horror Film*. Urbana and Chicago: University of Illinois Press. 14–29.

_____. (1973). "Drawing the Circle: A Devolution of Values in Three Horror Films." *Film Journal* 2 (2): 6–35.

Douglas, Mary. (1966). *Purity and Danger: An Analysis of Concepts of Pollution and Taboo*. London: Routledge.

_____, and Baron Isherwood. (1978). *The World of Goods: Toward an Anthropology of Consumption*. NY: W.W. Norton.

Downing, Lisa. (2003). "Death and the Maidens: A Century of Necrophilia in Female-Authored Textual Production." *French Cultural Studies* 14 (2): 157–168.

Doyle, Richard. (2003). *Wetwares: Experiments in Postvital Living*. Minneapolis: University of Minnesota Press.

Dudley, Scott. (1999). "Conferring with the Dead: Necrophilia and Nostalgia in the Seventeenth Century." *ELH* 66 (2): 277–294.

Dujovne, Beatriz E. (2004). "Disavowal and the Culture of Deadening." *Psychoanalytic Psychology* 21 (4): 633–37.

DVD World. (2006). "DVD Review: *Porn of the Dead*." *DVD World* 40: 83.

Eberle v. City of Newton, 289 F. Supp. 2d 1269 (D. Kan. 2003).

Eder, Donna, Catherine Colleen Evans, and Stephen Parker. (1995). *School Talk: Gender and Adolescent Culture*. Rutgers, NJ: Rutgers University Press.

Ehrenreich, Barbara. (2006). *Dancing in the Streets: A History of Collective Joy*. NY: Metropolitan Books.

Eliade, Mircea. (1968). *The Sacred and the Profane: The Nature of Religion*. Translated by Willard Trask.

_____. (1989). *Shamanism, Archaic Techniques of Ecstasy*. London: Arkana. Boston, MA: Harcourt.

Eshun, Kodwo. (1998). *More Brilliant than the Sun: Adventures in Sonic Fiction*. London: Quartet.

Evans, Craig A. (2003). *Jesus and the Ossuaries: What Jewish Burial Practices Reveal about the Beginning of Christianity*. Waco, TX: Baylor University Press.

Feit, Josh, and Dan Savage. (2006). "Raving Mad: Teen Dances Aren't the Problem; They're the Solution." *The Stranger*, Mar 30—Apr 5: Online: <http://www.thestranger.com/seattle/raving-mad/Content?oid=31362>. Accessed Oct. 20, 2010.

Ferguson, Everett. (1993). *Backgrounds of Early Christianity*. 2nd ed. Grand Rapids: Eerdmans.

Fiske, J. (1989). *Reading the Popular*. London: Routledge.

Forisha, Barbara. (1979). "The Outside and the Inside: Compartmentalization or Integration?" In Anees Sheikh and John Shaffer, (Eds.), *The Potential of Fantasy and Imagination*. NY: Brandon House. 124–147.

Foucault, Michel. (1990). *History of Sexuality. Vol. I*. R. Hurley, (Trans.). NY: Vintage Books.

_____. (1986). "Of Other Spaces." *Diacritics* 16 (1): 22–27.

Francis, Sing-chen Lydia. (2002). "'What Confucius Wouldn't Talk About': The Grotesque Body and Literati Identities in Yuan Mei's *Zi buyu*." *Chinese Literature: Essays, Articles, Reviews (CLEAR)* 24: 129–160.

Freud, Sigmund. (1957). *The Standard Edition of the Complete Psychological Works*, Volume VII. James Strachey, (Trans.). London: The Hogarth Press and the Institute of Psycho-Analysis.

_____. (1919/2003). "The Uncanny." Hugh Haughton, (Trans.). Harmondsworth, Eng.: Penguin.

Frye, Northrop. (1981). *The Great Code: The Bible and Literature*. Toronto: Academic Press.

Gagne, Paul R. (1987). *The Zombies That Ate Pittsburgh: The Films of George A. Romero*. NY: Dodd, Mead & Company.

Gelder, Ken, (Ed.). (2000). *The Horror Reader*. London: Routledge.

Gentile, D. A., P. J. Lynch, J. R. Linder, and D. A. Walsh. (2004). "The Effects of Violent Video Game Habits on Adolescent Aggressive Attitudes and Behaviours." *Journal of Adolescence* 27: 5–22.

Geschiere, Peter. (1997). *The Modernity of Witchcraft: Politics and the Occult in Postcolonial Africa*. Charlottesville, VA: University Press of Virginia.

_____, and Francis Nyamnjoh. (1998). "Witchcraft as an Issue in the 'Politics of Belonging': Democratization and the Urban Migrant's Involvement with the Home Village." *African Studies Review* 41 (3): 69–91.

Gilbert, Jeremy. (1997). "Soundtrack to an Uncivil Society: Rave Culture, The Criminal Justice Act and the Politics of Modernity." *New Formations* 31: 5–24.

_____, and Ewan Pearson. (1999). *Discographies: Dance Music, Culture and the Politics of Sound*. London: Routledge.

Goffman, Erving. (1963). *Stigma: Notes on the Management of Spoiled Identity*. NY: Simon and Schuster.

Goldstein, Jeffrey. (1999). "The Attractions of Violent Entertainment." *Media Psychology* 1 (3): 271.

Gooding, Francis. (2007). "They Still Believe There's Respect in Dying: Wittgenstein, Tercier, Romero." *Film Quarterly* 49: 3: 13–30.

Gordon, Robert M. (1980). "Fear." *The Philosophical Review* 89 (4): 560–578.

Goss, J. (1993). "The Magic of the Mall: An Analysis of Form, Function, and Meaning in the Contemporary Retail Built Environment." *Annals of the Association of American Geographers* 1: 18–47.

Graham, Becki A. (2011). "Post-9/11 Zombies: Unpredictability and Complacency in the Age of New Terrorism." In Christopher M. Moreman and Cory James Rushton, (Eds.), *Race, Oppression and the Zombie: Essays on Cross-Cultural Appropriations of the Caribbean Tradition*. Jefferson, NC: McFarland.

Grant, Barry Keith. (1996). "Taking Back the Night of the Living Dead: George Romero, Feminism, and the Horror Film." In Barry Keith Grant, (Ed.), *The Dread of Difference*. Austin: University of Texas Press. 200–12.

Grant, Michael. (2004). "Fulci's Waste Land: Cinema, Horror and the Abominations of Hell." *Film Studies* 5: 30–38.

Green, O.H. (1982). "Fear of Death." *Philosophy and Phenomenological Research* 43 (1): 99–105.

Gregson, Kimberly. (2005). "Understanding the Appeal of Zombie Films: A Disposition Theory Approach." Paper presented at the International Communication Association conference, New York.

Griffiths, M. (1997). "Computer Game Playing in Early Adolescence." *Youth and Society* 29 (2): 233–237.

Grosz, Elizabeth. (1995). "Animal Sex: Libido as Desire and Death." In Elizabeth Grosz and Elpeth Probyn, (Eds.), *Sexy Bodies: The Strange Carnalities of Feminism*. London: Routledge. 278–299.

_____. (1994). *Volatile Bodies: Towards a Corporeal Feminism*. Bloomington, IN: Indiana University Press.

Guha, Ramachandra. (1989). "Radical American Environmentalism and Wilderness Preservation: A Third World Critique." *Environmental Ethics* 11: 71–83.

Gutierrez, Roberto, and Roger Giner-Sorolla. (2007). "Anger, Disgust, and Presumption of Harm as Reactions Behaviors." *Emotion*, 7 (4): 853–68.

Hamilton, Laurell K. (2008). "Those Who Seek Forgiveness." In John Joseph Adams, (Ed.), *The Living Dead*. San Francisco: Night Shade Books. 202–10.

Haraway, Donna. (1991). *Simians, Cyborgs, and Women*. London: Routledge.

Hare, R. D. (1993). *Without Conscience: The Disturbing World of the Psychopaths Among Us*. NY: Pocket Books.

Harper, S. (2002). "Zombies, Malls, and the Consumerism Debate: George Romero's *Dawn of the Dead*." *Americana: The Journal of American Popular Culture (1900-present)* 1 (2): Online: <http://www.americanpopularculture.com/journal/articles/fall_2002/harper.htm>. Accessed Oct. 20, 2010.

Hautala, Rick. (2010). "Ghost Trap." In Christopher Golden, (Ed.), *The New Dead: A Zombie Anthology*. NY: St. Martin's Griffin. 263–79.

Hegel, G. W. F. (1977). *Phenomenology of Spirit*. A. V. Miller (trans.). Oxford: Clarendon Press.

Heidegger, Martin. (1962). *Being and Time*. John Macquarrie and Edward Robinson, (Trans.). London: SCM Press.

Heil, John. (2003). *From an Ontological Point of View*. Oxford: Oxford University Press.

Heise, Ursula. (2002). "Toxins, Drugs, and Global Systems: Risk and Narrative in the Contemporary Novel." *American Literature* 74: 747–778.

Hemment, David. (1996). "E is for Ekstasis." *New Formations* 31: 23–38.

Hesmondhalgh, D. (2002). *The Cultural Industries*. London: Sage Publications.

Hicks, Faith Erin. (2007). *Zombies Calling*. San Jose: SLG.

Hill, Andrew. (2003). "Acid House and Thatcherism: Contesting Spaces in late 1980s Britain." *Space and Polity* 7 (3): 219–32.

_____. (2002). "Acid House and Thatcherism: Noise, the Mob and the English Countryside." *The British Journal of Sociology* 53 (1): 89–105.

Hirschi, Travis. (1969). *Causes of Delinquency*. Berkeley: University of California Press.

Holland v. Apfel. 188 F. 3d 513 (9th Cir. 1999).

Horner, Avril, and Angela Keane, (Eds.). (2000). *Body Matters: Feminism, Textuality, Corporeality*. Manchester: Manchester University Press.

Huizinga, J. (1955). *Homo Ludens*. Boston, MA: Beacon Press.

Humphreys, Laud. (1970). *The Tea Room Trade*. NY: Aldine de Gruyter.

Hunt, Leon. (2000). "A (Sadistic) Night at the Opera." In Ken Gelder (Ed.), *The Horror Reader*. London: Rutledge. 324–335.

Hurston, Zora Neale. (1938). *Voodoo Gods*. London: J.M. Dent & Sons.

Hutcheon, Linda. (2006). *A Theory of Adaptation*. NY and London: Routledge.

Iberoamerican Electronics, S.R.L. v. Moore Business Forms, Inc., 679 So. 2d 295 (Fla. Dist. Ct. App. 3d Dist.1996).

In re Chicago Truck Center, Inc., 398 B.R. 266 (Bkrtcy.N.D.Ill. 2008).

In re Conservatorship of Groves, 109 S.W. 3d 317 (Tenn.Ct.App. 2003).

In re Hedged-Investments Associates, Inc., 84 F.3d 1281 (10th Cir. 1996).

In re Merck & Co., Inc., 2009 WL 331426 (D.N.J. Feb. 10 2009).

Ingebretsen, Edward J. (2001). *At Stake: Monsters and the Rhetoric of Fear*. Chicago: University of Chicago Press.

Inglis, David. (2011). "Putting the Dead to Work: Wade Davis, Haitian Vodou, and the Social Uses of the Zombie." In Christopher M. Moreman and Cory James Rushton, (Eds.), *Race, Oppression and the Zombie: Essays on Cross-Cultural Appropriations of the Caribbean Tradition*. Jefferson, NC: McFarland.

Jackson, Kenneth. (1996). "All the World's a Mall: Reflections on the Social and Economic Consequences of the American Shopping Center." *American Historical Review* 101: 1111–21.

Jentsch, Ernst. (1906/1995). "The Psychology of the Uncanny." Roy Sellars, (Trans.). *Angelaki* 2 (1): 7–16.

Jim. (2006). "Exclusive Interview: Max Brooks on World War Z." *Eatmybrains.com*. Oct. 20th. Online: <http://www.eatmybrains.com/showfeature.php?id=55>. Accessed Feb. 1, 2011.

Johnston, B. R., (Ed.). (1994). *Who Pays the Price? The Sociocultural Context of Environmental Crisis*. Washington, D.C.: Island Press.

Jones, A. (1982). "George Romero Interview." *Starburst* 4 (12): 36–37.

Jones, Stephen. (2010). "Introduction: Shoot 'em in the Brain." In Stephen Jones, (Ed.), *The Dead that Walk: Zombie Stories*. Berkeley, CA: Ulysses Press. 1–4.

Juul, Jesper. (2007). "A Certain Level of Abstraction." In Akira Baba, (Ed.), *Situated Play: DiGRA 2007 Conference Proceedings*. Tokyo: DiGRA Japan. 510–515. Online: <http://www.jesperjuul.net/text/acertainlevel/>. Accessed Oct. 20, 2010.

_____. (2003). "The Game, The Player, The World: Looking for a Heart of Gameness." In M. Copier and J. Raessens, (Eds.), *Level Up: Digital Game Research Conference 2003*. Utrecht: U. of Utrecht Press. 30–45.

Kato, M. (1993). "Nuclear Globalism: Traversing Rockets, Satellites, and Nuclear War via the Strategic Gaze." *Alternatives* 18: 339–360.

Katz, Jack. (1988). *Seductions of Crime: Moral and Sensual Attractions in Doing Evil*. NY: Basic Books.

Keppel, Robert. (1997). *Signature Killers: Interpreting the Calling Cards of the Serial Murderer*. NY: Pocket Books.

King, Stephen. (2006). *Cell.* NY: Scribner.

_____. (1983). *Pet Sematary.* NY: Doubleday.

Kingsepp, E. (2003). "Apocalypse the Spielberg Way: Representations of Death and Ethics in *Saving Private Ryan, Band of Brothers* and the Videogame *Medal of Honor: Frontline.*" In M. Copier and J. Raessens, (Eds.), *Level Up: Digital Game Research Conference.* Utrecht: University of Utrecht Press.

Kirk, Robert. (2005). *Zombies and Consciousness.* Oxford: Oxford University Press.

Kirkman, Robert. (2009). *Fear the Hunters. The Walking Dead* 11. Berkeley: Image Comics.

_____. (2010). *Too Far Gone. The Walking Dead* 13. Berkeley: Image Comics.

_____. (2004–2010). *The Walking Dead, Volumes 1– 11.* Berkeley: Image Comics.

Klepak v. State, 622 So.2d 19 (Fla.Dist. Ct. App. 4th Dist. 1993).

Klima, Alan. (2002). *The Funeral Casino: Meditation, Massacre, and Exchange with the Dead in Thailand.* Princeton, NJ: Princeton University Press.

_____. (2001). "The Telegraphic Abject: Buddhist Meditation and the Redemption of Mechanical Reproduction." *Comparative Studies in Society and History* 43 (3): 552–582.

Knowles, Murray, and Rosamund Moon. (2005). *Introducing Metaphor.* London: Routledge.

Kraut, Robert. (1986). "Feelings in Context." *The Journal of Philosophy* 83 (11): 642–652.

Kress, G., and T. van Leeuwen. (1996). *Reading Images: The Grammar of Visual Design.* London: Routledge.

Kryzwinska, Tanya. (2008). "Zombies in Gamespace." In Shawn McIntosh and Marc Leverette, (Eds.), *Zombie Culture: Autopsies of the Living Dead.* Lanham, MD: Scarecrow Press. 153–168.

Küng, Hans. (1984). *Eternal Life?* Edward Quinn, (Trans.). NY: Doubleday.

Landau, James. (2004). "The Flesh of Raving: Merleau-Ponty and the 'Experience' of Ecstasy." In Graham St John, (Ed.), *Rave Culture and Religion.* London: Routledge. 107–124.

Langer v. Presbyterian Medical Centre of Philadelphia, 1995 WL 395937 (E.D. Pa. July 3 1995).

Langley v. Barnhart, 373 F. 3d 1116 (10th Cir. 2004).

Latham, Robert. (2002). *Consuming Youth: Vampires, Cyborgs, and the Culture of Consumption.* Chicago: U. of Chicago Press.

Latour, B. (1993). *The Pasteurization of France.* A. Sheridan and J. Law, (Trans.). Cambridge, MA: Harvard University Press.

_____. (2004). *The Politics of Nature.* C. Porter, (Trans.). Cambridge, MA: Harvard University Press.

Lauro, Sarah Juliet, and Karen Embry. (2008). "A Zombie Manifesto: The Nonhuman Condition in the Era of Advanced Capitalism." *Boundary 2* 35 (1): 85–108.

Leland, John. (2004). *Hip: The History.* NY: Ecco Press.

Leverette, Marc. (2008). "The Funk of Forty Thousand Years; or, How the (Un)dead Get Their Groove On." In Shawn McIntosh and Marc Leverette, (Eds.), *Zombie Culture: Autopsies of the Living Dead.* Lanham, MD: Scarecrow Press. 185– 212.

Levin, Josh. (2004). "Dead Run: How Did Movie Zombies Get So Fast?" *Slate.com.* March 24. Online: <http://www.slate.com/id/2097751/>. Accessed Feb. 1, 2011.

Levy, Ariel. (2005). *Female Chauvinist Pigs: Women and the Rise of Raunch Culture.* NY: Free Press.

Levy, Donald. (1980). "Perversion and the Unnatural as Moral Categories." *Ethics,* 90 (2): 191–202.

Lindenmeyer, Antje. (1999). "Postmodern Concepts of the Body in Jeanette Winterson's 'Written on the Body.'" *Feminist Review* 63: Negotiations and Resistances. 48–63.

Littlewood, Roland, and Chavannes Douyon. (1997). "The Clinical Findings in Three Cases of Zombification." *The Lancet* 350 (9084): 1094 – 1096.

Locke, Don. (1976). "Zombies, Schizophrenics, and Purely Physical Objects." *Mind* 85 (337): 97–99.

Locke, John. (1694). "Of Identity and Diversity." In *Essay Concerning Human Understanding.* Reprinted in John Perry, (1975), *Personal Identity.* Berkeley: U. of California Press. 33–52.

Lutts, R. H. (1985). "Chemical Fallout: Rachel Carson's Silent Spring, Radioactive Fallout, and the Environmental Movement." *Environmental Review* 9: 210–225.

MacCormack, Patricia. (2008). *Cinesexuality.* Aldershot, Eng.: Ashgate.

MacKinnon, Neil. (1994). *Symbolic Interactionism as Affect Control.* Albany, NY: SUNY Press.

Maitland, B. (1985). *Shopping Malls: Planning and Design.* NY: Nichols.

Marsella, Anthony J. (2008). *Ethnocultural Perspectives on Disaster and Trauma.* NY: Springer.

Martin, Raymond, and John Barresi. (2003). "Personal Identity & What Matters in Survival: A Historical Overview." In Raymond Martin and John Barresi, (Eds.), *Personal Identity.* Malden, MA: Wiley-Blackwell. 1–26, 37–48, & 54–75.

Masters, Brian. (1986). *Killing for Company: Case of Dennis Nilsen.* London: Hodder and Stroughton.

_____. (1993). *The Shrine of Jeffrey Dahmer.* London: Hodder and Stroughton.

Matheson, Richard. (1954). *I Am Legend.* Greenwich, CT: Fawcett.

_____. (1993). *The Path: A New Look at Reality.* NY: Tor Books.

Matthen, Mohan. (1998). "Biological Universals and the Nature of Fear." *The Journal of Philosophy* 95 (3): 105–132.

May, Reinhard. (1996). *Heidegger's Hidden Sources:*

East Asian Influences on His Work. Graham Parkes (Trans.). London: Routledge.

McCall, George J., and Jerry L. Simmons. (1966). *Identities and Interaction.* NY: Free Press.

McClellend, John. S. (1989). *The Crowd and the Mob: From Plato to Canetti.* London: Unwin.

McDonald v. Ritchie, 2006 WL 435999 (D.Kan. 2006).

McIntosh, Shawn. (2008). "The Evolution of the Zombie: The Monster That Keeps Coming Back." In Shawn McIntosh and Marc Leverette, (Eds.). *Zombie Culture: Autopsies of the Living Dead.* Lanham, MD: Scarecrow Press. 1–18.

McKay, George. (1996). *Senseless Acts of Beauty: Cultures of Resistance Since the Sixties.* London: Verso.

McKenna, Terence. (1993). *True Hallucinations: Being an Account of the Author's Extraordinary Adventures in the Devil's Paradise.* San Francisco: Harper.

Mead, G. H. (1934). *Mind, Self, and Society from the Standpoint of a Social Behaviorist.* Chicago: University of Chicago Press.

Meadan, Bryan. (2001). *TRANCENational ALIENation. Trance Music Culture, Moral Panics and Transnational Identity in Israel.* Raleigh, NC: Lulu Publishing.

Melechi, Antonio. (1993). "The Ecstasy of Disappearance." In Steve Redhead, (Ed.), *Rave Off: Politics and Deviance in Contemporary Youth Culture.* Aldershot, Eng.: Avebury. 29–40.

Metevier, Bobbie. (2008). "The Loneliest Man in the World." In Kim Paffenroth, (Ed.), *The World is Dead.* [United States]: Permuted Press. 164–173.

Mikami, Shinji. (1996). "Shinji Mikami Interview." *GamePro Magazine* 91, April: 32–33. Online: <http://img69.imageshack.us/img69/8454/gamepro091apr19960033.png>. Accessed Jan. 25, 2011.

Miller, W. M. (2006). *A Canticle for Leibowitz.* NY: Eos Books.

Millikan, Ruth. (1989). "In Defense of Proper Functions." *Philosophy of Science* 56 (2): 288–302.

Mitchell, Charles P. (2001). *A Guide to Apocalyptic Cinema.* London: Greenwood Press.

Modleski, T. (1986). *Studies in Entertainment.* Indianapolis, IN: Indiana University Press.

Mohammad, S. K. (2006). "Zombies, Rest and Motion: Spinoza and the Speed of Undeath." In R. Greene and S. K. Mohammad (Eds.), *Philosophy and the Undead.* Chicago: Open Court Press. 91–102.

Molesworth, Mike, and Janice Denegri-Knott. (2005). "The Pleasures and Practices of Virtualized Consumption in Digital Spaces." In S. de Castell and J. Jenson, (Eds.), *Changing Views: Worlds of Play: Proceedings of DiGRA 2005 Conference.* Burnaby, BC: Simon Fraser University Press. Online: <http://www.digra.org/dl/db/06276.33335.pdf>. Accessed Feb. 1, 2011.

Moore, Sarah. (2009). "Zombie Ants Walk the Earth in Texas." *McClatchy — Tribune Business News* 21 May.

Moorat, A. E. (2009). *Queen Victoria: Demon Hunter.* London: Hodder & Stoughton.

Moreman, Christopher M. (2012) "Let This Hell Be Our Heaven: Richard Matheson's Spirituality and Its Hollywood Distortions." *Journal of Religion and Popular Culture.* 24(1): Online <http://utpjournals.metapress.com/Content12221337>.

_____. (2010). "Dharma of the Living Dead: A Meditation on the Meaning of the Hollywood Zombie." *Studies in Religion/Sciences Religieuses* 39 (2): 263–281.

_____. (2008a). "A Modern Meditation on Death: Identifying Buddhist Teachings in George A. Romero's *Night of the Living Dead.*" *Contemporary Buddhism* 9 (2): 151–165.

_____. (2008b). "Review of *I Am Legend.*" *Journal of Religion and Film* 12 (1): Online: <http://www.unomaha.edu/jrf/vol12no1/reviews/ILegen.htm>. Accessed Oct. 20, 2010.

_____, and Cory James Rushton, (Eds.). (2011). *Race, Oppression and the Zombie: Essays on Cross-Cultural Appropriations of the Caribbean Tradition.* Jefferson, NC: McFarland.

Mori, Masahiro. (1970). "Bukimi No Tani," ("The Uncanny Valley"). *Energy* 7 (4): 33–35. Karl F. MacDorman and Takashi Minato, (Trans.). Online: <http://www.androidscience.com/theuncannyvalley/proceedings2005/uncannyvalley.html>. Accessed Dec. 18, 2010.

Morris, S. (2004). "Shoot First, Ask Questions Later: Ethnographic Research in an Online Computer Gaming Community." *Media International Australia: The Game Issue* 110: 31–41.

Muzzio, Douglas, and Jessica Muzzio-Rentas. (2006). "A Kind of Instinct: The Cinematic Mall as Heterotopia." In M. Dalaene and C. De Cauter, (Eds.), *Heterotopia and the City: Public Space in Post Civil Society.* London: Routledge. 137–149.

Myerhoff, Barbara. (1980). *Number Our Days.* NY: Touchstone.

Nazaretyan, Akop P. (2005). "Fear of the Dead as a Factor in Social Self-Organization." *Journal of the Theory of Social Behavior* 35 (2): 155–169.

Newitz, Annalee. (2006). *Pretend We're Dead: Capitalist Monsters in American Pop Culture.* Durham, NC: Duke University Press.

Newman, Kim. (1988). *Nightmare Movies: A Critical History of the Horror Film, 1968–88.* London: Bloomsbury Publishing.

Niehaus, Isak. (2005). "Witches and Zombies of the South African Lowveld: Discourse, Accusations and Subjective Reality." *Journal of the Royal Anthropological Institute* 11 (2): 191–211.

Nunez v. State, 2006 WL 3026326 (14th Dist. 2006).

Oates, Whitney J., (Ed.). (1957). *The Stoic and Epicurean Philosophers*. NY: The Modern Library. 30–33.

Ostwalt, Conrad. (2000). "Armageddon at the Millennial Dawn." *The Journal of Religion and Film* 4 (1): Online: <http://www.unomaha.edu/jrf/armagedd.htm>. Accessed Oct. 20, 2010.

_____. (1995). "Hollywood and Armageddon: Apocalyptic Themes in Recent Cinematic Presentation." In Joel W. Martin and Conrad E. Ostwalt, (Eds.), *Screening the Sacred: Religion, Myth, and Ideology in Popular American Film*. Boulder, CO: Westview. 55–63.

Owen, Mary A. (1908–1922). "Voodoo." In James Hastings, (Ed.), *Encyclopaedia of Religion and Ethics*. New York: Charles Scribner's Sons. 640–641.

Owens, Timothy J., and Suzanne Goodney. (2000). "Self, Identity, and the Moral Emotions across the Life Course." *Advances in Life Course Research. Self and Identity through the Life Course in Cross-Cultural Perspective*, 5: 33–53.

Paffenroth, Kim. (2006). *Gospel of the Living Dead*. Waco, TX: Baylor University Press.

Pagano, David. (2008). "The Space of Apocalypse in Zombie Cinema." In S. McIntosh and M. Leverette, (Eds.), *Zombie Culture: Autopsies of the Living Dead*. Lanham, MD: Scarecrow Press. 71–86.

Palwick, Susan. (2008). "Beautiful Stuff." In John Joseph Adams, (Ed.), *The Living Dead*. San Francisco: Night Shade Books. 137–47.

Parfit, Derek. (1971). "Personal Identity." *Philosophical Review* 80 (1): 3–27.

Parkes, Graham, (Ed.). (1987). *Heidegger and Asian Thought*. Honolulu, HI: University of Hawaii Press.

Parsons, Zach. (2006). "The Horrors of Pornography: Porn of the Dead." *Something Awful*. Online: <http://www.somethingawful.com/d/horrors-of-porn/porn-dead.php>. Accessed Dec. 23, 2010.

People v. Long, 2004 WL 887202 (Cal.App. 2d Dist. 2004).

People v. Marsh, 8 Cal. App. 4th Supp. 1 (Cal.Super. 1992).

Perry, Michael. (1975). *The Resurrection of Man*. Oxford: Mowbrays London and Oxford.

Pegg, Simon. (2008). "The Dead and the Quick." *The Guardian*, Tues., Nov. 4. Online: <http://www.guardian.co.uk/media/2008/nov/04/television-simon-pegg-dead-set>. Accessed Jan. 25, 2011.

Penner, Jonathan, Steven Jay Schneider, and Paul Duncan, (Eds.). (2008). *Horror Cinema*. Köln: Taschen.

Perry, John. (1978). *A Dialogue on Personal Identity and Immortality*. Indianapolis: Hackett.

Pierce, David. (2007). "Forgotten Faces: Why Some of our Cinema Heritage Is Part of the Public Domain." *Film History: An International Journal* 19 (2): 125–143.

Pinedo, Isabel Cristina. (2004). "Postmodern Elements of the Contemporary Horror Film." In Stephen Prince, (Ed.), *The Horror Film*. New Brunswick, NJ: Rutgers University Press. 85–117.

Poovey, Mary. (1990). "Speaking of the Body: Mid-Victorian Constructions of Female Desire." In Mary Jacobs, et al, (Eds.), *Body/Politics: Women and the Discourses of Science*. London: Routledge. 29–45.

Poynor, Rick. (2006). *Designing Pornotopia: Travels in Visual Culture*. London: Laurence King.

Presdee, Mike. (2000). *Cultural Criminology and the Carnival of Crime*. London: Routledge.

Prince, Stephen. (2004). "Dread, Taboo and *The Thing*: Toward a Social Theory of the Horror Film." In Stephen Prince, (Ed.), *The Horror Film*. New Brunswick, NJ: Rutgers University Press. 118–130.

Prudhomme, Alex, and Mary Cronin. (1991). "Milwaukee Murders: Did They All Have to Die?" *Time Magazine*, May 12. Online: <http://www.time.com/time/magazine/article/0,9171,973592,00.html>. Accessed Dec. 18, 2010.

Radcliffe, J. (2000). *Green Politics: Dictatorship or Democracy?*. NY: St. Martin's Press.

Raoul, Valerie. (1992). "Habeas Corpus: Anatomy/Autonomy in Relation to Narcissism." In *The Anatomy of Gender: Women's Struggle for the Body*. Ottawa: Carleton University Press.

Rayner, A. D. M. (1998). *Degrees of Freedom*. London: Imperial College Press.

Reich, Warren T. (1995). "History of the Notion of Care." In his *Encyclopedia of Bioethics*, 2nd ed. NY: Simon & Shuster. 319–331. Online: <http://care.georgetown.edu/Classic%20Article.html>. Accessed Feb. 1, 2011.

Ressler, Robert. (1997). *I Have Lived in the Monster*. NY: Simon and Schuster.

Rey, Terry, and Karen Richman. (2010). "The Somatics of Syncretism: Tying Body and Soul in Haitian Religion." *Studies in Religion / Études Religieuses* 39 (3): 379–403.

Reynolds, Simon. (1997). "Rave Culture: Living Dream or Living Death?" In Steve Redhead, (with Derek Wynne and Justin O'Connor), (Ed.), *The Clubcultures Reader: Readings in Popular Cultural Studies*. Oxford: Blackwell. 102–11.

Rezec v. Sony Pictures Entertainment, Inc., 116 Cal. App. 4th 135 (Cal. App. 2d Dist. 2004).

Rietveld, Hillegonda. (1993). "Living the Dream." In Steve Redhead, (Ed.), *Rave Off: Politics and Deviance in Contemporary Youth Culture*. Aldershot, Eng.: Avebury. 41–78.

Ritchey v. Continental Ins. Co., 2007 WL 460975 (Cal. App. 6th Dist. 2007).

Rhodes, Gary D. (2001). *White Zombie: Anatomy of a Horror Film*. Jefferson, NC: McFarland.

Roberts, Thomas B., (Ed.) (2001). *Psychoactive Sacramentals: Essays on Entheogens and Religion*. San Francisco: Council on Spiritual Practices.

Robinson v. California, 370 U.S. 660 (U.S. Cal. 1962).

Rogers, Nicholas. (2003). *Halloween: From Pagan Ritual to Party Night*. Oxford: Oxford University Press.

Romero, George (2008). "George Romero Relives His Zombies Through DIARY OF THE DEAD." *FEARS Magazine*, Feb. Online: <http://fear mag.com/08/index.php/ON-THE-COUCH-WITH-J.B.-MACABRE/George-Romero-Rel-ives-His-Zombies-Through-DIARY-OF-THE-DEAD.html>. Accessed Sept. 25, 2010.

Rose, D. B. (2004). *Reports from a Wild Country*. Sydney: U. of New South Wales.

Rushkoff, Douglas. (2000). *Coercion: Why We Listen to What "They" Say*. London: Little Brown.

_____. (2004). "Foreword." In Graham St John, (Ed.), *Rave Culture and Religion*. NY: Routledge.

Rushton, Cory James. (2011) "Eating Ireland: Zombies, Snakes and Missionaries in *Boy Eats Girl*." In Christopher M. Moreman and Cory James Rushton, (Eds.), *Race, Oppression and the Zombie: Essays on Cross-Cultural Appropriations of the Caribbean Tradition*. Jefferson, NC: McFarland.

Russell, Jamie (2006). *Book of the Dead; The Complete History of Zombie Cinema*. Godalming, England: FAB.

Sagiv, Assaf. (2000). "Dionysus in Zion." *Azure* 9 (Spring). Online: <http://www.azure.org.il/arti cle.php?id=289>. Accessed Dec. 20, 2010.

St John, Graham. (2012). *Global Tribe: Technology, Spirituality and Psytrance*. London: Equinox.

_____. (2011). "The Vibe of the Exiles: Aliens, Afropsychedelia and Psytrance." In Tobias van Veen, (Ed.), *Afrofuturism: Interstellar Transmissions From Remix Culture*. Detroit, MI: Wayne State University Press.

_____. (Ed.). (2010a). *The Local Scenes and Global Culture of Psytrance*. NY: Routledge.

_____. (2010b). "Liminal Culture and Global Movement: The Transitional World of Psytrance." In Graham St. John, (Ed.), *The Local Scenes and Global Culture of Psytrance*. NY: Routledge. 220–246.

_____. (2009a). *Technomad: Global Raving Countercultures*. London: Equinox.

_____. (2009b). "Neotrance and the Psychedelic Festival." *Dancecult: Journal of Electronic Dance Music Culture* 1 (1): 35–64.

Saldanha, Arun. (2007). *Psychedelic White: Goa Trance and the Viscosity of Race*. Minneapolis: University of Minnesota Press.

Sanders, N. K., (Trans.). (1960). *The Epic of Gilgamesh*. NY: Penguin Classics.

Sanjek, David. (2000). "Fans Notes: The Horror Film Magazine." In Ken Gelder, (Ed.), *The Horror Reader*. London: Rutledge.

Sceats, Sarah. (2001). "Oral Sex: Vampiric Transgression and the Writing of Angela Carter." *Tulsa Studies in Women's Literature* 20 (1): 107–21.

Schiebinger, Londa. (2000). "Introduction," and "Skeletons in the Closet: The First Illustrations of the Female Skeleton in Eighteenth-Century Anatomy." In Lorda Schiebinger, (Ed.), *Feminism and the Body*. Oxford: Oxford University Press. 1–57.

Schmitt, C. (2007). *The Concept of the Political*. G. Schwab, (Trans.). Chicago: University of Chicago Press.

Schneemelcher, Wilhelm, (Ed.). (1991). *New Testament Apocrypha*. Rev. ed., volume one. Trans. R. McL. Wilson. Cambridge and Louisville: James Clarke & Co. and Westminster/John Knox Press.

Schneider, Steven Jay. (2004). "Toward an Aesthetics of Horror." In Stephen Prince, (Ed.), *The Horror Film*. New Brunswick, NJ: Rutgers University Press.

Scholes v. Lehmann, 56 F.3d. 750 (Ill. 1995).

Schott, G. (2009). "'I Like the Idea of Killing But Not the Idea of Cruelty': How New Zealand Youth Negotiate the Pleasures of Simulated Violence." In T. Kryzwinska, B. Atkins & H. Kennedy, (Eds.). *Breaking New Ground: Innovation in Games, Play and Theory, Proceedings of DiGRA 2009*. Online: <www.digra.org/dl/db/09287.36489.pdf>. Accessed January 21, 2011.

Seabrook, William. (1928). *The Magic Island*. NY: George C. Harrap.

Sellers, J. (2001). *Arcade Fever: The Fan's Guide to the Golden Age of Videogames*. London: Running Press.

Shapiro, Harry. (1999). "Dances with Drugs: Pop Music, Drugs and Youth Culture." In Nigel South, (Ed.), *Drugs: Cultures, Controls and Everyday Life*. London: Sage. 17–35.

Shapiro, Peter. (2005). *Turn the Beat Around: The Secret History of Disco*. NY: Faber and Faber.

Shaviro, Steven. (1993). *The Cinematic Body*. Minneapolis: University of Minnesota Press.

Sheller, Mimi. (2003). *Consuming the Caribbean: From Arawaks to Zombies*. NY: Routledge.

Shelley, Mary. (1818). *Frankenstein; or The Modern Prometheus*. London: Harding, Mavor & Jones.

Shields, R. (2003). *The Virtual*. London: Routledge.

Shildrick, Margrit. (2002). *Embodying the Monster: Encounters with the Vulnerable Self*. London: Sage.

The Shorter Oxford English Dictionary (1973). 3rd Edition. Edited by C. T. Onions. Oxford: Clarendon Press.

Shostak, S. (1998). *Death of Life: Legacy of Molecular Biology*. NY: Palgrave Macmillan.

Sibley, David. (1997). "Endangering the Sacred: Nomads, Youth Cultures and the English Countryside." In Paul Cloke and Jo Little, (Eds.), *Contested Countryside Cultures: Otherness, Marginalisation and Rurality*. London: Routledge. 218–31.

Silcott, Muriel. (1999). *Rave America: New School Dancescapes*. Quebec: ECW Press.

Simmel, Georg. (1950). *The Sociology of Georg Sim-*

mel. Compiled and translated by Kurt Wolff. Glencoe, IL: Free Press.

Simmons, Dan. (2008). "This Year's Class Picture." In John Joseph Adams, (Ed.), *The Living Dead.* San Francisco: Night Shade. 4–21.

Sloth, T. E., and David Wong. (2007). "5 Scientific Reasons A Zombie Apocalypse Could Actually Happen." *Cracked.com.* Cracked Entertainment, Inc. Oct. 29th. Online: <http://www.cracked.com/article_15643_5-scientific-reasons-zombie-apocalypse-could-actually-happen.html>. Accessed Dec. 18, 2010.

Snyder, Gary. (2000). "Is Nature Real?" In Michael P. Nelson and J. Baird Callicott, (Eds.), *The Wilderness Debate Rages On.* Athens, GA: University of Georgia Press. 351–354.

Solomon, Robert C. (1974). "Sexual Paradigms." *Journal of Philosophy* 71 (11): 336–411.

Stack, George J. (1969). "Concern in Kierkegaard and Heidegger." *Philosophy Today* 13: 26–35.

Stallybrass, Peter, and Allon White. (1986). *The Politics and Poetics of Transgression.* London: Methuen.

State of Wisconsin. (1991). *State of Wisconsin v. Jeffrey L. Dahmer.* Circuit Court Criminal Division File M-2472. Milwaukee County. Case #F912542.

Stewart Title Guaranty Company v Sterling, 822 S.W. 2d 1 (Texas, 1991)

Stryker, Sheldon. (1968). "Identity Salience and Role Performance." *Journal of Marriage and the Family* 30: 558–564.

Sullivan, Robert. (1999). *Star Waka.* Auckland: Auckland University Press.

Sutherland, Edwin, and Donald Cressey. (1974). "Differential Association." In *Criminology* (8th edition). NY: J.B. Lippincott.

Sutherland, Meghan. (2007). "Rigor/Mortis: The Industrial Life of Style in American Zombie Cinema." *Framework* 48 (1): 64–78.

Sydie, Rosalind. (1987). *Natural Women, Cultured Men: A Feminist Perspective on Sociological Theory.* Toronto: Metheuen.

Sykes, G. M., and D. Matza. (1957). "Techniques of Neutralization: A Theory of Delinquency." *American Sociological Review* 22: 664–70.

Tebb, William, Edward Perry Vollum, and Walter R. Howden. (1905). *Premature Burial and How It Might Be Prevented.* London: Swan Sonnenschein & Co.

The Bible Speaks v. Dovydenas, 81 B.R. 750 (D.Mass. 1988).

Thomas, Lisa, and David R. Heise. (1995). "Mining Error Variance and Hitting Pay-Dirt: Discovering Systematic Variation in Social Sentiments." *Social Psychology Quarterly* 36: 425–439.

Thompson, Clive. (2008). "*Grand Theft Auto IV* Delivers Deft Satire of Street Life." *Wired.* Online: <http://www.wired.com/gaming/gamingreviews/commentary/games/2008/05/gamesfrontiers_0502>. Accessed Feb. 1, 2011.

Thornton, Sarah. (1996). *Club Cultures: Music, Media and Subcultural Capital.* Middletown, CT: Wesleyan University Press.

Thrower, Stephen. (1999). *Beyond Terror: The Films of Lucio Fulci.* Surrey, England: FAB.

Tilly, Charles. (1995). *Popular Contention in Great Britain 1758–1834.* London: Harvard University Press.

Turner, Victor. (1973). "The Center out There: Pilgrim's Goal." *History of Religions* 12 (1): 191–230.

_____. (1967). *The Forest of Symbols: Aspects of Ndembu Ritual.* Ithaca: Cornell University Press.

_____. (1969). *The Ritual Process: Structure and Anti-Structure.* Chicago: Aldine.

Twitchell, James B. (1985). *Dreadful Pleasures: An Anatomy of Modern Horror.* NY: Oxford University Press.

U.S. v. Farley, 976 F. 2d 734 (Ohio 1992).

U.S. v. Kramer, 168 F. 3d 1196 (N.M. 1999).

U.S. ex rel Harris v. Wilson, 1997 WL 260284 (N.D.Ill. 1997).

Ussher, Jane M. (1989). *The Psychology of the Female Body.* NY: Routledge.

Wagner, Ann. (1997). *Adversaries of Dance: From Puritans to the Present.* Urbana and Chicago: U. of Illinois Press.

Waller, Gregory A. (1987). *American Horrors: Essays on the Modern American Horror Film.* Urbana and Chicago: U. of Illinois Press.

_____. (1986). *The Living and the Undead: From Stoker's Dracula to Romero's Dawn of the Dead.* Urbana and Chicago: U. of Illinois Press.

Walter, Michael. (2004). "Of Corpses and Gold: Materials for the Study of the Vetala and the Rolangs." *The Tibet Journal* 29 (2): 13–46.

Walton, Kendall. (1978). "Fearing Fictions." *The Journal of Philosophy* 75 (1): 5–27.

Warner, Marina. (2002). *Fantastic Metamorphoses, Other Worlds: Ways of Telling the Self.* Oxford: Oxford University Press.

Watkins v. U.S., 589 F. 2d 214 (5th Cir. 1979).

Watson, G., (Ed.). (1982). *Free Will.* Oxford: Oxford University Press.

Webb, Jen, and Sam Byrnand. (2008). "Some Kind of Virus: The Zombie as Body and as Trope." *Body & Society* 14 (2): 83–98.

Weinberg, Martin, Colin Williams, and Douglas Pryor. (1994). *Dual Attraction: Understanding Bisexuals.* NY: Oxford University Press.

Weisberg, Richard. (1992). *Poethics and Other Strategies of Law and Literature.* NY: Columbia University Press.

Weise, Matthew. (2009). "The Rules of Horror: Procedural Adaptation in Clock Tower, Resident Evil, and Dead Rising." In Bernard Perron (Ed.), *Horror Video Games: Essays On the Fusion of Fear and Play.* Jefferson, NC: McFarland. 238–266.

Wellington, David. (2006). *Monster Island: A Zombie Novel*. NY: Thunder's Mouth Press.

Willemen, Paul. (1992). "Letter to John." In *The Sexual Subject: A Screen Reader in Sexuality*. London: Routledge.

Williams, Bernard. (1970). "The Self and the Future." *The Philosophical Review* 79 (2): 161–180.

Williams, Linda. (1989). *Hard Core: Power, Pleasure, and the "Frenzy of the Visible."* Berkeley: University of California Press.

Wolfenstein, Martha. (1951). "The Emergence of Fun Morality." *Journal of Social Issues* 7 (4): 15–25.

Wollenschlaeger, Alex. (2007). "Keiji Inafune Talks Lost Planet, Iraq." *VideoGamesDaily.com* January: Online: <http://archive.videogamesdaily.com/news/200701/044.asp>. Accessed Oct. 20, 2010.

Wood, Robin. (2003). *Hollywood from Vietnam to Reagan...And Beyond*. NY: Columbia University Press.

Worthington, Andy, (Ed.). (2005). *The Battle of the Beanfield*. Dorset: Enabler.

Wylie, Turrell. (1964). "Ro-langs: The Tibetan Zombie." *History of Religions* 4 (1): 69–80.

Yeats, W. B. (1920). "The Second Coming." In Alexander Allison, Herbert Barrows, et al. (Eds), *Norton Anthology of Poetry* (1975). NY: W.W. Norton & Co.

Filmography

28 Days Later. Dir. Danny Boyle. Perf. Cillian Murphy and Naomie Harris. British Film Council, 2002.

28 Weeks Later. Dir. Juan Carlos Fresnadillo. Perf. Robert Carlyle. Fox Atomic, 2007.

Alien. Dir. Ridley Scott. Perf. Tom Skerritt, Sigourney Weaver, and Yaphet Kotto. Twentieth Century–Fox, 1979.

Aliens. Dir. James Cameron. Perf. Sigourney Weaver, Paul Reiser, and Bill Paxton. Twentieth Century–Fox, 1986.

American Zombie. Dir. Grace Lee. Perf. Austin Basis and Kasie Brown. Cinema Libre Studio, 2007.

Apocalypse Now. Dir. Francis Ford Coppola. Perf. Martin Sheen, Marlon Brando, and Robert Duvall. Zoetrope, 1979.

At Twilight Come the Flesh Eaters. Dir. Vidkid Timo. Perf. Vidkid Timo and John Buck. 1998.

Beatrice Cenci. Dir. Lucio Fulci. Perf. Tomas Milian and Adrienne Larussa. Filmena, 1969.

The Beyond. Dir. Lucio Fulci. Perf. Catriona MacColl and David Warbeck. Fulvia Film, 1981.

The Birds. Dir. Alfred Hitchcock. Perf. Tippi Hedren, Suzanne Pleshette, and Jessica Tandy. Universal Pictures, 1963.

Black Sunday (AKA *The Mask of the Demon; La maschera del demonio*). Dir. Mario Bava. Perf. Barbara Steel and John Richardson. Alta Vista Productions, 1960.

Blood Feast. Dir. Emilio Miraglia. Perf. Barbara Bouchet and Ugo Pagliai. Phoenix Cinematografica, 1972.z

Blue Sunshine. Dir. Jeff Lieberman. Perf. Zalman King, Deborah Winters, and Robert Walden. Ellanby Films, 1976.

Braindead (AKA *Dead Alive*). Dir. Peter Jackson. Perf. Timothy Balme and Diana Peñalver. WingNut Films, 1992.

Bride of Frankenstein. Dir. James Whale. Perf. Boris Karloff. Universal Pictures, 1935.

The Brides of Dr. Jekyll (AKA *The Mistresses of Dr. Jekyll; El secreto del Dr. Orloff*). Dir. Jesús Franco. Perf. Hugo Blanco and Agnès Spaak. Eurocineac, 1964.

Candyman. Dir. Bernard Rose. Perfs. Tony Todd, Virginia Madsen, and Xander Berkeley. TriStar Pictures, 1992.

Cemetery Man (AKA *Dellamorte Dellamore*). Dir. Michele Soavi. Perf. Rupert Everett and Anna Falchi. Urania Film, 1994.

Children Shouldn't Play With Dead Things. Dir. Bob Clark. Perf. Alan Ormsby and Valerie Mamches. Geneni Film Distributors, 1973.

C.H.U.D. 2 — Bud the Chud. Dir. David Irving. Perf. Brian Robbins and Robert Vaughn. Vestron Pictures, 1989.

City of the Living Dead (AKA *The Gates of Hell*). Dir. Lucio Fulci. Perf. Christopher George and Catriona MacColl. Dania Film, 1980.

Dawn of the Dead. Dir. George A. Romero. Perf. Ken Foree and Gaylen Ross. Laurel Group, 1978.

Dawn of the Dead. Dir. Zack Snyder. Perf. Sarah Polley and Ving Rhames. Strike Entertainment, 2004.

Day of the Dead. Dir. George Romero. Perf. Lori Cardille. Dead Films Inc., 1985.

Day of the Dead. Dir. Steve Miner. Perf. Mena Suvari and Ving Rhames. Millennium Films, 2008.

The Day of the Triffids. Dir. Steve Sekely. Perf. Howard Keel and Nicole Maurey. Security Pictures, 1962.

Dead and Deader. Dir. Patrick Dinhut. Perf. John Billingsley and Dean Cain. Mindfire Entertainment, 2006.

Dead Snow. Dir. Tommy Wirkola. Perf. Vegar Hoel. Euforia film, 2009.

The Dead Will Walk. Dir. Perry Martin. Perf. Dario Argento and Ken Foree. Anchor Bay Entertainment, 2004.

Demonia. Dir. Lucio Fulci. Perf. Brett Halsey and Meg Register. Eden Video, 1990.

Dialogues With Madwomen. Dir. Allie Light. Irving Saraf, 1994.

Diary of the Dead. Dir. George A. Romero. Perf. Michelle Morgan, Shawn Roberts, and Josh Close. Artfire Films, 2007.

Don't Torture a Duckling (AKA *Non si sevizia un paperino*). Dir. Lucio Fulci. Perf. Florinda Bolkan and Barbara Bouchet. Medusa Produzione, 1972.

Dracula. Dir. Tod Browning. Perf. Bela Lugosi. Universal Pictures, 1931.

Erotic Nights of the Living Dead (AKA *Sexy Night of the Living Dead*; *La notti erotiche dei morti viventi*). Dir. Joe D'Amato. Perf. Laura Gemser and George Eastman. Stefano Film, 1980.

Erotic Orgasm (AKA *Orgasmo esotico*). Dirs. Joe D'Amato and Mario Siciliano. Perf. Marina Hedman and Sonia Bennett. Metheus Film, 1982.

The Exorcist III. William Peter Blatty. Perf. George C. Scott and Samuel L. Jackson. Morgan Creek Productions, 1990.

The Fearless Vampire Killers. Dir. Roman Polanski. Perf. Jack MacGowran and Sharon Tate. Cadre Films, 1967.

Fido. Dir. Andrew Currie. Perf. Carrie-Anne Moss, Billy Connolly, and Dylan Baker. Lionsgate, 2007.

The Fifth Element. Dir. Luc Besson. Perf. Bruce Willis and Milla Jovovich. Gaumont, 1997.

Flesh Eating Mothers. Dir. James Aviles Martin. Perf. Robert Lee Oliver and Donatella Hecht. Academy Entertainment, 1988.

Flight from Death: The Quest for Immortality. Dir. Patrick Shen. Perfs. Gabriel Byrne and Perrin Sprecace. Transcendental Media, 2003.

Flight of the Living Dead. Dir. Scott Thomas. Perf. David Chisum and Kristen Kerr. Imageworks, 2007.

Frankenstein. Dir. James Whale. Perf. Boris Karloff. Universal Pictures, 1931.

The Ghost Galleon (AKA *Ship of Zombies*; *El buque maldito*). Dir. Amando de Ossorio. Perf. Maria Perschy and Jack Taylor. Ancla Century Films, 1974.

The Gore-Gore Girls (AKA *Blood Orgy*). Dir. Herschell Gordon Lewis. Perf. Frank Kress and Amy Farrell. Lewis Motion Pictures Enterprises, 1972.

Gore Whore. Dir. Hugh Gallagher. Perf. Audrey Street and Brady Debussey. Ill-Tex, 1994.

Harry Potter and the Half-Blood Prince. Dir. David Yates. Perf. Daniel Radcliffe, Emily Watson, and Michael Gambon. Warner Bros., 2009.

The Hills Have Eyes. Dir. Wes Craven. Perf. Susan Lanier and Robert Houston. Blood Relations, 1977.

La Horde. Dir. Yannick Dahan and Benjamin Rocher. Perf. Claude Perron, Jean-Pierre Martins, and Eriq Ebouaney. Capture Films, 2009.

Hostel II. Dir. Eli Roth. Perf. Lauren German and Roger Bart. Lionsgate, 2007.

The House by the Cemetery (AKA *Quella villa accanto al cimitero*). Dir. Lucio Fulci. Perf. Catriona Mac-Coll and Paolo Malco. Fulvia, 1981.

House of 1000 Corpses. Dir. Rob Zombie. Perf. Chad Bannon and Karen Black. Spectacle Entertainment Group, 2003.

I Am Legend. Dir. Francis Lawrence. Perf. Will Smith and Alica Braga. Warner Bros., 2007.

I Walked with a Zombie. Dir. Jacques Tourneur. Perf. James Ellison, Frances Dee, and Tom Conway. RKO Radio Pictures, 1943.

I Was a Teenage Zombie. Dir. John Elias Michalakis. Perf. Michael Rubin. Periclean, 1987.

In the Mouth of Madness. Dir. John Carpenter. Perf. Sam Neill and Julie Carmen. New Line Cinema, 1995.

Invasion of the Body Snatchers. Dir. Don Siegel. Perf. Kevin McCarthy and Dana Wynter. Allied Artists, 1956.

King of the Zombies. Dir. Jean Yarbrough. Perf. Dick Purcell and Joan Woodbury. Monogram Pictures Corporation, 1941.

Land of the Dead. Dir. George Romero. Perf. Simon Baker, John Leguizamo, and Dennis Hopper. Universal, 2005.

The Last Man on Earth. Dir. Ubaldo Ragona. Perf. Vincent Price. Associated Producers, 1964.

Last of the Living. Dir. Logan McMillan. Perf. Morgan Williams and Robert Faith. Gorilla Pictures, 2009.

The Living Dead at the Manchester Morgue (AKA *Don't Open the Window*; *Non si deve profanare il sonno dei morti*). Dir. Jorge Grau. Perf. Cristina Galbó and Ray Lovelock. Star Films, 1974.

Mallrats. Dir. Kevin Smith. Perf. Shannon Doherty, Ben Affleck, and Jason Lee. Gramercy Pictures, 1995.

The Matrix. Dir. Andy and Lana Wachowski. Perf. Keanu Reeves, Laurence Fishburne, and Carrie-Anne Moss. Warner Bros., 1999.

The Mummy. Dir. Karl Freund. Perf. Boris Karloff. Universal Pictures, 1932.

Near Dark. Dir. Kathryn Bigelow. Perf. Adrian Pasdar, Lance Henrickson, and Bill Paxton. F/M, 1987.

The Necro Files. Dir. Matt Jaissle. Perf. Isaac Cooper and Steve Sheppard. Threat Theatre International, 1997.

The Necro Files 2: Behind the Screams. Dir. Ron Carlo. Perf. Todd Tjersland and Isaac Cooper. Astaroth Entertainment, 2003.

Night of the Living Babes. Dir. Jon Valentine. Perf. Michelle Bauer and Connie Woods. Magnum Video, 1987.

Night of the Living Dead. Dir. George Romero. Perf. Duane Jones, Judith O'Dea, and Karl Hardman. Image Ten, et al., 1968.

Night of the Living Dead. Dir. Tom Savini. Perf. Patricia Tallman and Tony Todd. Columbia Pictures, 1990.

Night of the Living Dorks. Dir. Mathias Dinter. Perf. Tino Mewes and Manuel Cortez. Constantin Film Produktion, 2004.

Night of the Seagulls (AKA *La noche de las* gaviotas). Dir. Amando de Ossorio. Perf. Victor Petit and Maria Kosty. Ancla Century Films, 1975.

The Omega Man. Boris Sagel. Perfs. Charlton Heston and Anthony Zerbe. Warner Brothers Pictures, 1971.

One Flew Over the Cuckoo's Nest. Dir. Milos Forman. Perf. Jack Nicholson and Danny deVito. Fantasy Films, 1975.

Otto; or, Up with Dead People. Dir. Bruce LaBruce. Perf. Jey Crisfar and Marcel Schlutt. New Real Films, 2008.

Pet Sematary. Dir. Mary Lambert. Perf. Dale Midkiff and Denise Crosby. Paramount Pictures, 1989.

Plan 9 from Outer Space. Dir. Ed Wood. Perf. Bela Lugosi, Tor Johnson, and Vampira. Reynolds Pictures, 1959.

Planet Terror. Dir. Robert Rodriguez. Perf. Rose McGowan, Bruce Willis, and Josh Brolin. Dimension Films, 2007.

The Plague of the Zombies. Dir. John Gilling. Perf. André Morell and Diane Clare. Hammer Film Productions, 1966.

Porn of the Dead. Dir. Rob Rotten. Perf. Buster Good and Dirty Harry. Punk Productions, 2006.

Porno Holocaust. Dir. Joe D'Amato. Perf. George Eastman and Dirce Funari. Kristal Film, 1981.

Poseidon. Dir. Wolfgang Petersen. Perf. Kurt Russell, Richard Dreyfuss, and Josh Lucas. Warner Bros., 2006.

The Poseidon Adventure. Dir. Ronald Neame. Perf. Gene Hackman, Ernest Borgnine, Roddy McDowall, and Shelley Winters. Twentieth Century–Fox Film Corp., 1972.

Re-Penetrator. Dir. Doug Sakmann. Perf. Joanna Angel and Tommy Pistol. BurningAngel.com, 2004.

[Rec]. Dirs. Jaume Balagueró and Paco Plaza. Perfs. Ferran Terraza, Manuela Velasco, and Carlos Vicente. Sony Pictures, 2007.

Resident Evil. Dir. Paul W. S. Anderson. Perf. Milla Jovovich and Eric Mabius. Constantin Film Produktion, 2002.

Resident Evil: Apocalypse. Dir. Alexander Witt. Perf. Milla Jovovich and Sienna Guillroy. Constantin Film Produktion, 2004.

Resident Evil: Extinction. Dir. Russell Mulcahy. Perf. Milla Jovovich. Constantin Film Produktion, 2007.

Return of the Evil Dead (AKA *Mark of the Devil 5: Return of the Blind Dead*; *El ataque de los muertos sin ojos*). Dir. Amando de Ossorio. Perf. Tony Kendall. Ancla Century Films, 1973.

The Return of the Living Dead. Dir. Dan O'Bannon. Perf. Clu Gulager and James Karen. Hemdale Film, 1985.

Return of the Living Dead Part II. Dir. Ken Wiederhorn. Perf. Michael Kenworthy and James Karen. Greenfox, 1988.

Return of the Living Dead III. Dir. Brian Yuzna. Perf. Melinda Clarke and J. Trevor Edmond. Ozla Productions, 1993.

Return of the Living Dead: Necropolis. Dir. Ellory

Elkayem. Aimee-Lynn Chadwick and Cory Hardrict. Aurora Entertainment, 2005.

Return of the Living Dead: Rave to the Grave. Dir. Ellory Elkayem. Perf. Aimee-Lynn Chadwick and Cory Hardrict. Aurora Entertainment, 2005.

The Revenge of the Living Dead Girls. Dir. Pierre B. Reinhard. Perf. Véronique Catanzaro and Kathryn Charly. Samouraï Films, 1987.

Revolt of the Zombies. Dir. Victor Halperin. Perf. Dorothy Stone and Roy D'Arcy. Halperin Productions Academy, 1936.

Run Lola Run. Dir. Tom Tykwer. Perf. Franka Potente and Moritz Bleibtreu. X-Filme Creative Pool, 1998.

Le Scaphandre et le Papillon (AKA *The Diving Bell and the Butterfly*). Dir. Julian Schnabel. Perf. Mathieu Amalric and Emmanuelle Seigner. France 3 Cinéma, 2007.

Scooby-Doo on Zombie Island. Dirs. Hiroshi Aoyama and Kazumi Fukushima. Perf. Scott Innes, Billy West, and Mark Hamill. Hanna-Barbera Productions, 1998.

The Scotland Yard Mystery (AKA *The Living Dead*). Dir. Thomas Bentley. Perf. Gerald du Maurier and George Curzon. British International Pictures, 1934.

Scream. Dir. Wes Craven. Perf. Drew Barrymore, Neve Campbell, and David Arquette. Dimension Films, 1996.

The Serpent and the Rainbow. Dir. Wes Craven. Perf. Bill Pullman. Universal Pictures, 1988.

Shatter Dead. Dir. Scooter McCrae. Perf. Stark Raven, Flora Fauna, and Daniel Johnson. Tempe Video, 1994.

Shaun of the Dead. Dir. Edgar Wright. Perf. Simon Pegg, Kate Ashfield, and Nick Frost. Alliance Atlantis, 2004.

Star Wars: Episode IV. Dir. George Lucas. Perf. Mark Hamill, Harrison Ford, and Carrie Fisher. Lucasfilm, 1977.

Star Wars: Episode V. Dir. George Lucas. Perf. Mark Hamill, Harrison Ford, and Carrie Fisher. Lucasfilm, 1980.

Star Wars: Episode VI. Dir. George Lucas. Perf. Mark Hamill, Harrison Ford, and Carrie Fisher. Lucasfilm, 1983.

The Stink of Flesh. Dir. Scott Phillips. Perf. Kurly Tlapoyawa and Ross Kelly. Screen Entertainment, 2005.

Survival of the Dead. Dir. George A. Romero. Perf. Alan Van Sprang, Kenneth Walsh, and Kathleen Munroe. Blank of the Dead Productions, 2009.

Suspiria. Dir. Dario Argento. Perf. Jessica Harper, Stefania Casini, and Flavio Bucci. Seda Spettacoli, 1977.

Terror at the Opera (AKA *Opera*). Dir. Dario Argento. Perf. Cristina Marsillach and Ian Charleson. ADC Films, 1987.

The Texas Chainsaw Massacre. Dir. Tobe Hooper. Perf. Marilyn Burns and Allen Danziger. Vortex, 1974.

They Live! Dir. John Carpenter. Perf. Roddy Piper. Alive Films, 1988.

The Thing. Dir. John Carpenter. Perf. Kurt Russell and Wilford Brimley. Universal Pictures, 1982.

Tokyo Zombie. Dir. Sakichi Sato. Perf. Tadanobu Asano and Sho Aikawa. Tokyo Zonbi Seisaku Iinkai, 2005.

Tombs of the Blind Dead (AKA *Mark of the Devil, Part 4*; *La noche del terror ciego*). Dir. Amando de Ossorio. Perf. Lone Fleming and Maria Elena Arpón. Interfilme, 1971.

Undead or Alive. Dir. Glasgow Phillips. Perf. Lew Alexander and Todd Anderson. Odd Lot Entertainment, 2007.

White Zombie. Dir. Victor Halperin. Perf. Bela Lugosi, Madge Bellamy, and Joseph Cawthorn. RKO-Pathe Studios, 1932.

Wild Zero. Dir. Tetsuro Takeuchi. Perf. Guitar Wolf and Masashi Endô. Dragon Pictures, 2000.

The Wizard of Gore. Dir. Herschell Gordon Lewis. Perf. Ray Sager and Judy Cler. Mayflower Pictures, 1970.

Wrong Turn. Dir. Rob Schmidt. Perf. Eliza Dushku and Jeremy Sisto. Twentieth Century–Fox, 2003.

Zombi 3. Dir. Lucio Fulci. Perf. Deran Sarafian and Beatrice Ring. Flora Film, 1988.

Zombie (AKA *Zombi 2*; *Zombie Flesh Eaters*). Dir. Lucio Fulci. Perf. Tisa Farrow and Ian McCulloch. Variety Film Production, 1979.

Zombie Creeping Flesh (AKA *Night of the Zombies*; *Virus*). Dir. Bruno Mattei. Perf. Margit Evelyn Newton and Franco Garofalo. Films Dara, 1980.

Zombie Holocaust (AKA *Zombie 3*). Dir. Marino Girolami. Perf. Ian McCulloch and Alexandra Delli Colli. Flora Film, 1980.

Zombie Ninja Gangbangers. Dir. Jeff Cantauri. Perf. Stephanie Beaton and Jeff Centauri. Plutonium Productions, 1997.

Zombie Strippers. Dir. Jay Lee. Perf. Jenna Jameson and Robert Englund. Stage 6 Films, 2008.

Zombieland. Dir. Ruben Fleischer. Perf. Woody Harrelson, Emma Stone, Jesse Eisenberg, and Bill Murray. Columbia Pictures, 2009.

Zombiemania. Dir. Donna Davies. Perf. George A. Romero, Tom Savini, and Max Brooks. Sorcery Films, 2008.

Zombies Anonymous (AKA *Last Rites of the Dead*). Dir. Mark Fratto. Perf. Joshua Nelson and Gina Ramsden. Well Go USA, 2008.

Zombies of Mora Tau. Dir. Edward L. Cahn. Perf. Gregg Palmer and Allison Hayes. Clover Productions, 1957.

Video Games and Discography

Video Games

Alone in the Dark. (1992). Infograms.
Call of Duty. (2003). Activision.
Castlevania. (1986). Konami.
Counter-Strike. (2000). Vivendi.
Dead Space. (2008). Electronic Arts.
Dimentium: The Ward. (2007). Gamecock Media Group.
Duke Nukem. (1991). Apogee Software.
Fatal Frame. (2001). Tecmo.
God of War. (2005). Sony Computer Entertainment.
Halo: Combat Evolved. (2001). Microsoft Game Studios.
House of the Dead. (1996). SEGA.
Left 4 Dead. (2007). Valve.
Left 4 Dead 2. (2009). Valve.
Lost Planet: Extreme Condition (2006). Capcom.
OneChanbara. (2008). Tamsoft.
Resident Evil. (1996). Capcom.
Resident Evil: Dead Aim. (2003). Capcom.
Resident Evil: Director's Cut. (1997). Capcom.
Resident Evil: Outbreak. (2004). Capcom.
Resident Evil 2. (1998). Capcom.
Resident Evil 3. (1999). Capcom.
Resident Evil 4. (2005). Capcom.
Resident Evil 5. (2009). Capcom.
Silent Hill. (1999). Konami.
Silent Hill: Homecoming. (2008). Konami Digital Entertainment.
Siren. (2003). Sony computer Entertainment.
Stubbs the Zombie. (2005). Wideload Games.
Time Splitters 2. (2002). Free Radical Design.
Uninvited. (1986). ICOM Simulations.
Urban Dead. (2005). Kevan Davis.

Wizardry. (1981). Sir-Tech.
Zombi. (1986). Ubisoft.

Discography

Ananda Shake. 2005. *Emotion In Motion*, Utopia Records.
Attack of the Living Trance Zombies, 2008. Compiled by DJ Pantiestheclown, PsyberTribe Records.
Brazilian V.A.Mpires 2008. (Compilation) Bloodsuck Records.
Chi-A.D. 1999. *Neighbourhood*, MIDIJUM Records.
Contagion Vol. 1, 2008. Dead Tree Productions.
Dark Emotion, 2009. GOAgemein.de.
Don't Forget About it to Remember, 2009. Dark Terror Records.
Double Trouble, 2008. No Comment Records.
Exaile. 2004. *Hit The Machine*, Chemical Crew.
Further Ambivalent Tendencies, 2005. Ambivalent Records.
Juno Reactor. 1994. *Luciana*, Inter-Modo.
Kitab Al Azif: The Necronomicon, 2008. Triplag.
Ministry of Chaos, 2008. Compiled by Mindcore, Yabai.
Multiple Personalities, 2005. Manic Dragon Records.
Multiple Personalities 3, 2008. Manic Dragon Records.
Scatterbrain. 2003. *Infernal Angel*, Digital Psionics.
Snowlightz, 2008. Plusquam Records.
X-Dream. 1998. *Radio*, Blue Room.
Xenomorph. 1998. *Cassandra's Nightmare*. Koyote.
Xenomorph. 2003. *Qlippoth*, Gnostic Records.

About the Contributors

Craig **Derksen** has a degrees in philosophy from the University of Manitoba and the University of Maryland, College Park. He has taught at both of those schools as well as California State University, East Bay, Camosun College, and the University of Victoria. Much of his work involves questions about the nature of evidence.

Michael J. **Gilmour** teaches New Testament and English literature at Providence University College (Manitoba, Canada). When not tracking revenants through the pages of the Bible, he enjoys exploring the intersections of religion and song. He is the author of *Gods and Guitars: Seeking the Sacred in Post-1960s Popular Music* (2009) and *The Gospel According to Bob Dylan: The Old, Old Story for Modern Times* (2011).

Darren Hudson **Hick** is an assisstant professor of philosophy at Susquehanna University, where he specializes in philosophical questions about the nature of art and intellectual property. His work is published in a variety of philosophy journals, legal journals, and edited volumes. He has collaborated on several projects with Craig Derksen and is the author of *Introducing Aesthetics and the Philosophy of Art* (2012, Continuum). More about his work is available at www.typetoken.com

Steve **Jones** is a lecturer in media at Northumbria University, UK. His primary research interests are the horror genre and the topics of gender and selfhood, particularly centering on representations of sex and violence. His recent research has been focused on the "torture porn" phenomenon, online shock imagery, contemporary Japanese horror, and visual tropes that characterize cinematic murder sequences.

Suzanne Goodney **Lea** is a fellow and educational coordinator with the Interactivity Foundation, which promotes democratic citizen discussion and student-centered university classrooms. Her research explores identity formation among violent offenders, examines the anthropomorphizing of intimacy in the late modern age, and evaluates the effectiveness of deliberative, group-based discourse in the university classroom and in public discussions of policy approaches.

Keira **McKenzie** is a Ph.D. candidate at Edith Cowan University in Western Australia, concentrating on monsters and the work of H. P. Lovecraft. She has published short stories, academic articles, and artwork for fantasy and science fiction magazines. Previously, she taught English as a secondary language and worked in SF&F bookshops. This is her first exploration of the zombie manifestation.

Christopher M. **Moreman** teaches courses in comparative religion in the department of philosophy at California State University, East Bay. He is the author of *Beyond the Threshold: Afterlife Beliefs and Experiences in World Religions* (2008; 2010) and editor of *Teaching Death and Dying* (2008); he is also coeditor with Cory James Rushton of *Race, Oppression and the Zombie* (McFarland, 2011), a companion volume of essays to the present work.

Greg **Pollock** is completing an M.A. in literature at the University of California, Santa Cruz. His research concerns the codification of ocean life as "living resources" in twentieth century international law, an event he traces through the use of "depth" in confessional apparatuses. More broadly, his work concerns biopolitics, technology, undeath and environmental issues. He is a game writer and designer in San Jose, California.

James **Reitter** earned his Ph.D. in folklore, film, and literature from the University of Louisiana, Lafayette (2006), and an M.F.A. in poetry from the City University of New York, Brooklyn (1997). He has taught classes on horror in literature and film, and has a particular affinity for creature features and the undead.

Cory James **Rushton** is an associate professor of English at St. Francis Xavier University in Antigonish, Nova Scotia, Canada. He is coeditor with Raluca Radulescu of *A Companion to Middle English Romance* (2009), with Amanda Hopkins of *The Erotic in the Literature of Medieval Britain* (2007), and with Christopher M. Moreman of *Race, Oppression and the Zombie* (McFarland, 2011). He is the editor of *Disability and Medieval Law: History, Literature, Society* (forthcoming).

Graham **St John** is a research associate at the University of Queensland's Centre for Critical and Cultural Studies. As an anthropologist of electronic dance music cultures, festivals, and movements, his latest book is *Technomad: Global Raving Countercultures* (2009). His *Global Tribe: Technology, Spirituality and Psytrance* is forthcoming. He is executive editor of *Dancecult: Journal of Electronic Dance Music Culture* (www.dj.dancecult.net).

Gareth **Schott** is a senior lecturer at the School of Arts, University of Waikato, New Zealand. He has published extensively in the emerging field of game studies, contributing research on the topics of female gaming, game fandom and participatory cultures, the application of multi-modality theory to analyzing game texts, the metrics of violence, and players, player cultures and the player experience. He is one of the authors of *Computer Games: Text, Narrative and Play* (2006).

Sharon **Sutherland** is assistant professor at the University of British Columbia Faculty of Law where she teaches a mediation practicum and a judicial externship program. Her research includes work in child protection mediation, improvisational theatre, and law and popular culture. Her publications include articles on vampires and the law, *Angel*, and cult television.

Sara **Sutler-Cohen** received her Ph.D. in sociology from the University of California–Santa Cruz and she teaches sociology at Bellevue College. She is currently embroiled in research surrounding death and dying in the U.S. and is writing a memoir of her years in the punk and metal scene in the SF/East Bay Area in the 1980s. She plays roller derby for Tilted Thunder Rail Birds, Seattle's only banked track league.

Sarah **Swan** is a J.S.D. candidate at Columbia University. Her research explores the intersections of gender, torts, and law and culture. She has written on a variety of topics related to law and popular culture, including representations of evil, the portrayal of female attorneys on television, issues of morality in post-9/11 works, and dystopic elements in popular texts.

Matthew J. **Weise** studied film production at the University of Wisconsin, Milwaukee, and videogames in the Comparative Media Studies program at MIT, where he became lead game designer for the Singapore–MIT GAMBIT Game Lab. His writings have appeared in various online and book publications and tend to explore practices of film-to-game adaptation. His writing is posted at outsideyourheaven.blogspot.com and games he has collaborated on are available at gambit.mit.edu.

Index

African traditions 16, 34, 88, 102, 123, 124–26
African zombies 125, 126, 127, 138*n*7
Agamben, Giorgio 172–73, 176
agency/autonomy of zombies: vs. base desires 124, 137; vs. determinism 22*n*9; and evolution of zombies in film 37, 45–48, 113, 116, 127, 184–85; vs. God's agency 131; and memory retention 19; and political engagement 37–38, 46, 178, 185; rational agency 14–15, 22*n*8; and sexuality 40, 42, 45–52, 56, 63, 64; and speech 176; and the uncanny 15–16; vs. zombie masters' agency 22*n*11, 64, 116, 125–26, 127, 130, 137, 152; *see also* communal identity of zombies
Agren, Janet 106
AIDS 37, 51, 96
Alien (film series) 121
Aliens (film) 32
Alone in the Dark (video games) 155–56, 168*n*8
American Indian ties to zombies 88, 98*n*4
American Zombie (film) 184, 185, 186, 187, 188
Ananda Shake 34
animals: as "family" 99*n*16; fear in 22*n*6; fear of 13, 21–22; fire ants, as zombie-like 100; as infection carriers 88, 186; innate behaviors in 14; and language 172–73; mad cow disease 186, 191; as psychopomps 113; puffer fish toxin 79; shark as zombie 156; shark vs. zombie 98*n*6, 102, 103, 109, 110; in *World War Z* 169, 180–81; zombification of 2, 99*n*13, 118, 119
Anthony, Piers 22*n*11
Antiochus IV Epiphanes 95–96
apocalypse: *Cracked Magazine* article on 185–86; and environmental disasters 96, 169, 174–75, 181, 191; and feminism 42;

and Garden of Eden 96–97; across genres 6; as God's wrath 131; Judgment Day 98*n*7; across media 153; and nuclear discourse 173–75, 176, 182; and political values in *Dawn of the Dead* 178–79; as renewing or revelatory 4–5, 118, 179; secular vs. spiritual 129–30; trance, and post-apocalyptic ecstasy 29, 35–38; universal vs. local 3–4, 117, 180; zombie as most apocalyptic monster 114, 191–92; in zombie comedies 36, 138*n*11, 184, 191
Apocalypse Now (film) 96
Argento, Dario 34, 103
Aristotle 44, 172, 173, 177
Ashfield, Kate 189
Asimov, Isaac 187
At Twilight Come the Flesh Eaters (film) 48
atomic technology *see* nuclear technology
Austen, Jane 1
automatons 16, 20, 30, 60*n*7, 80; *see also* robots

Bakhtin, Mikhail 146
Baudrillard, Jean 173, 174, 175
Bava, Mario 103
Beatrice Cenci (film) 107
Becker, Ernest 186, 187
The Beyond (film) 100, 104, 107–11, 111*n*8
Bible 87–99; and apocalypse 4, 98*n*7; and bodily consumption in zombie narratives 89, 90, 91; on brevity of life 98*n*5, 99*n*15; Garden of Eden in 96–97; ghosts in 87, 98*n*2; gore and bodily decay in 94–96; on handling corpses 92, 98*n*8; resurrection of Jesus in 87, 93, 94, 95, 98; resurrection of Lazarus in 93, 95, 99*n*10; Western art as influenced by 97; "wilderness" vs. "desert" in 170
biological warfare 88, 118, 156, 165, 192

The Birds (film) 119
Black Sunday (film) 32, 103
Blind Dead (film series) 47, 55, 103, 111*n*4
Blood Feast (film) 111*n*1
Blue Sunshine (film) 30
Bodie v. Purdue Pharma Co. 79
bokors see zombie masters
Boyle, Danny 96, 114, 153, 161; *see also 28 Days Later* (film)
Bradshaw v. Baylor University 82
Braindead (film) 36, 47, 88, 100, 148, 152
Bride of Frankenstein (film) 46
The Brides of Dr. Jekyll (film) 37
Brooks, Max: and biblical imagery 89; and global environmental change 169, 181; on social disintegration 192; and text-based zombies 114, 153, 180; and third wave of zombies 185; *The Zombie Survival Guide* 189; *see also World War Z* (Brooks)
Buddhism 124, 132, 133–37, 138*n*16
Bush, George W. 38

Call of Duty (video game) 167*n*4
Callahan v. Campbell 79
cannibalism: brain eating 14, 16, 33, 39*n*3, 114, 184; of Jeffrey Dahmer 64, 67, 69, 71, 73; as erotic 57–58; and the Eucharist 89, 90, 91, 127; and Lucio Fulci's films 100, 104; in Haiti, alleged 125; pointlessness of zombie appetite 135; and psychopomp tradition 113–14; as Romeran zombie trait 3, 14, 128, 129, 152, 185; and survival 120; and vagina dentata 39*n*3, 50; in video games 156, 159, 162–63, 164; zombies as abstaining from 104, 192
A Canticle for Leibowitz (Miller) 179
capitalism: anti-corporate themes in video games 165; apocalypse as post-capitalist 37; labor exploitation 33, 64, 124, 128; and